不可不知的日韩文化（高级篇）

主编 孙银银 张元婧

中国水利水电出版社
www.waterpub.com.cn

内容提要

每个国家和民族都有自己独特的文化符号，读懂一种文化，它能为你打开一个全新的世界，助你收获一种全新的人生体验。从日本的动漫到韩国的石锅拌饭，翻开本书开始一次精彩异常的日韩文化之旅，你将看到更广阔的世界！

书中涵盖了日本印象、文化韩国、潮流风尚、悠游日韩、爱上韩味、节庆趣谈等，内容以英文材料为主，辅以中文导读。通过本书，你能了解到韩国人如何庆祝生日，日本人是什么性格，还有无处不在的日式咖喱……书中的海外文化专场让你通过地道英文进行更深层次的学习，用英文的思维重新审视日韩文化。

图书在版编目（CIP）数据

不可不知的日韩文化. 高级篇：英文 / 孙银银，张元婧主编. -- 北京：中国水利水电出版社，2015.5
ISBN 978-7-5170-3147-5

Ⅰ. ①不… Ⅱ. ①孙… ②张… Ⅲ. ①英语－语言读物②文化史－日本③文化史－韩国 Ⅳ. ①H319.4：K

中国版本图书馆CIP数据核字（2015）第092920号

策划编辑：杨庆川　责任编辑：邓建梅　加工编辑：于丽娜　封面设计：潘国文

书　　名	不可不知的日韩文化（高级篇）
作　　者	主编　孙银银　张元婧
出版发行	中国水利水电出版社 （北京市海淀区玉渊潭南路1号D座 100038） 网址：www.waterpub.com.cn E-mail：mchannel@263.net（万水） 　　　　sales@waterpub.com.cn 电话：（010）68367658（发行部）、82562819（万水）
经　　售	北京科水图书销售中心（零售） 电话：（010）88383994、63202643、68545874 全国各地新华书店和相关出版物销售网点
排　　版	北京万水电子信息有限公司
印　　刷	北京正合鼎业印刷技术有限公司
规　　格	170mm×240mm　16开本　14.75印张　354千字
版　　次	2015年5月第1版　2015年5月第1次印刷
印　　数	0001—5000册
定　　价	35.00元

凡购买我社图书，如有缺页、倒页、脱页的，本社发行部负责调换

版权所有·侵权必究

前　言

　　从美国的迪士尼到英国的哈利·波特，从日本的动漫到韩国的石锅拌饭，每个国家和民族都有自己独特的文化符号，正是这些文化为我们的世界绘制了一幅绚烂夺目的文明画卷。读懂一种文化，它能为你打开一个全新的世界，助你收获一种全新的人生体验。《不可不知的欧美文化》和《不可不知的日韩文化》就是带你邂逅最美异国文化的人文读本。

　　本套书从大众的视角出发，选材上既做到了内容的丰富性，也兼顾了材料的趣味性。在难度上，欧美文化和日韩文化各分为基础篇和高级篇。基础篇以中文阅读为主，穿插英文词汇学习，高级篇以英文材料为主，辅以中文导读，方便不同水平读者阅读和学习。每本书都是一次精彩异常的文化之旅，带你看到更广阔的世界。

　　《不可不知的欧美文化（基础篇）》共19章，内容涵盖精英教育、时尚密码、名城小镇、影视天堂、欧洲王室、美国名校、英伦视角、街拍美国等。透过本书，你能了解到美国孩子们的校园生活、《神探夏洛克》的五个真相、英国人的排队强迫症以及又萌又奇葩的英式大学运动……第一文化现场用中文帮助你零时差读懂欧美文化，并在其中穿插重点词语的英文表达，让你在品读文化的同时也能轻松学英文。

　　《不可不知的欧美文化（高级篇）》共16章，包括成长的烦恼、影坛盛宴、文化ICON、节日探寻、名人效应、美国视角、时尚魅族等。在这里，你可以看到美国高中舞会守则、世界各地的圣诞传统，还能了解到英国人的英语最难懂、大英帝国五个奇葩奖学金……书中的中文导读帮助你提前了解欧美文化，地道英文让你进一步加深对文化的理解，用英语的思维学习纯正欧美文化。

　　《不可不知的日韩文化（基础篇）》共17章，内容涉及成长的足迹、时尚驾到、韩潮来袭、美食地图、韩国街拍、日本众生相、日韩趣谈等。这里有流行韩国的"自然育儿法"，有穿韩服的讲究，还有日本的"方便面"文化及韩国的宫廷料理……书中穿插了重点词语的英文表达方式，帮助你一边了解日韩文化，一边学习英文。

　　《不可不知的日韩文化（高级篇）》共13章，涵盖了日本印象、文化韩国、潮流风尚、悠游日韩、爱上韩味、节庆趣谈等。通过本书，你能了解到韩国人如何庆祝生日、日本人是什么性格，还有无处不在的日式咖喱……书中的海外文化专场让你通过地道英文进行更深层次的学习，用英文的思维重新审视日韩文化。

这是一套可以让你边品文化边学英文的阅读精品，有着让你拿起来就放不下的五大理由：

一、内容丰富，选材新颖

本套书所收录的材料均经过了严格的筛选，角度多元，便于扩充知识面，同时也能满足不同读者的阅读兴趣。选材上另一大特色，就是深入挖掘熟悉话题中的新亮点，带给你耳目一新的阅读体验。

二、难度适中，分类清晰

欧美文化和日韩文化各分成基础篇和高级篇，方便读者选择，更能做到有的放矢，阅读起来零负担，循序渐进就能看懂、看透异国文化。

三、注释简洁，学习轻松

对于文章中的疑难词汇、重点单词或文化现象，书中做出了精细的注释说明，帮助扫清阅读障碍，便于理解全文，是你最贴心的私房笔记。

四、开拓视野，陶冶情操

本套书将繁多的文化常识化整为零，让读者足不出户也能领略到不同国家的文化魅力，在阅读中开阔个人视野，提高人文素养，拓宽人生版图。

五、提升阅读，助力考试

用地道英文和有趣的中文为你呈现一场异国文化大餐，帮你轻松提高英语语言能力和阅读水平。书中多彩的文化既能丰富你的知识储备，帮你积累个人谈资，也能在考试中助你一臂之力，是集阅读性、学习性为一体的优质文化读本。

也许你无法马上踏上旅行的道路，但可以让灵魂提前开始一场远行，透过字里行间品读浪漫多姿的人文情怀。本套书特别适合广大青少年读者学习异国文化、提升阅读能力，也是英语爱好者提高英语水平的最佳读本。带上它，没时间也能全球深度游，不出国就能读懂全世界！

编者
2015年春天于北京

参编人员：

成应翠　杨金鑫　蒋佳池　石文　祝万伟　何长领　葛俊　成琳　陈翔　王琴
蒋学晨　张艳萍　杨晓丽　王巧梅　马梦原　理　吴淑严　武少辉　孙帅　李远子
刘林　高爱琴　王亚楠

目录 Contents

前言

Chapter 1　古韵馨香：行走在传统文化的长河

01　The "Way" in Japan ······ 2
　　日本之"道" ······ 2
02　Japanese Tea Ceremony: An Art Back to Nature ······ 3
　　日本茶道：回归自然的艺术 ······ 3
03　Ikebana: Japanese Art of Flower Arrangement ······ 5
　　花道：日本的插花艺术 ······ 5
04　Sumo: Wrestling in Tokyo ······ 7
　　相扑：日式国技 ······ 7
05　The Legend of Sword Makers in Old Japan ······ 9
　　走近日本铸剑师 ······ 9
06　Pansori: Traditional Art of Korea ······ 10
　　潘索里：韩国说唱艺术 ······ 10
07　Ancient Petroglyphs in South Korea ······ 12
　　聚光盘龟台岩刻画 ······ 12
08　Korea-Style Birthday Celebrations ······ 14
　　韩国人如何庆祝生日 ······ 14
09　Jangseung: Korea's Totem Poles ······ 16
　　长丞：韩国图腾柱 ······ 16

Chapter 2　日本印象：难忘东瀛文化的一抹亮彩

01　Occasions for Wearing Kimonos ······ 19
　　舞动和服，因时而变 ······ 19
02　Tatami Mats: Japanese Flooring ······ 21
　　日本地铺：榻榻米垫 ······ 21
03　Geta: A Cultural Symbol of Japanese ······ 22
　　木屐：日本文化符号 ······ 22
04　Sake: Japan's National Wine ······ 24
　　清酒：日本国酒 ······ 24
05　Origami: The Ancient Art of Japanese Paper Folding ······ 25
　　传承千年的日本折纸艺术 ······ 25

	06	The Traditional Inns of Charm ········· 27
		日本传统旅店 ········· 27
	07	Japan's Four Great Gates 日本四大鸟居 ········· 29
	08	Japanese Cruising in Yakatabune ········· 30
		屋形船中的日式巡游 ········· 30
	09	A Kingdom of Cats 日本：猫的王国 ········· 32

Chapter 3 文化韩国：藏在时光里的繁华

	01	Taekwondo: A Martial Art of South Korea ········· 36
		跆拳道：韩国武术 ········· 36
	02	What Is Soju 韩国人的烧酒情结 ········· 37
	03	Arirang: A Traditional Korean Song of Joy and Sorrow ········· 39
		《阿里郎》：最熟悉的韩国旋律 ········· 39
	04	Onggi: Traditional Ceramics in South Korea ········· 41
		韩国传统陶器 ········· 41
	05	Traditional Masks in South Korea ········· 42
		韩国的传统面具 ········· 42
	06	Hangeul: Korean Alphabet ········· 44
		韩国人自己的文字 ········· 44
	07	Hanja: Chinese Characters in South Korea ········· 46
		韩国的汉字文化 ········· 46
	08	Hanji Paper 韩国纸文化 ········· 48
	09	Reasons to Stay at a Hanok ········· 50
		下榻韩屋，欣享自然 ········· 50

Chapter 4 寻味日本：穿越时空的味蕾盛宴

	01	A Travel to Sushi ········· 54
		令人回味的寿司盛宴 ········· 54
	02	Sashimi: Traditional Japanese Cuisine ········· 55
		日本传统菜肴生鱼片 ········· 55
	03	Ramen in Japan 香喷喷的日本拉面 ········· 57
	04	Washoku: An Intangible Cultural Heritage ········· 59
		日本传统和食：世界级的享受 ········· 59
	05	Japanese Curry 无处不在的日式咖喱 ········· 61
	06	Natto: The Bad Tasting Food ········· 62
		日本纳豆：难闻的健康食品 ········· 62
	07	Edamame: Twig Beans in Japan ········· 64
		日本枝豆：喝酒好伴侣 ········· 64
	08	Why the Japanese Are Patriotic about Rice ········· 65
		日本人为何对水稻如此钟爱 ········· 65

Chapter 5 爱上韩味：唯美食与文化不可辜负

	01	Korean Bulgogi Insight ········· 69
		透视韩式烤肉 ········· 69

- 02 Korean Gimjang: The Making of Kimchi ⋯⋯⋯⋯⋯⋯ 70
  泡菜：忘不了的韩国味道 ⋯⋯⋯⋯⋯⋯⋯⋯⋯⋯⋯⋯⋯ 70
- 03 Korean Seaweed Spreads Around the World ⋯⋯⋯⋯ 72
  走向世界的韩国紫菜 ⋯⋯⋯⋯⋯⋯⋯⋯⋯⋯⋯⋯⋯⋯ 72
- 04 Songpyeon: Korean Tastes for Chuseok ⋯⋯⋯⋯⋯⋯ 74
  了解美味的韩国松饼 ⋯⋯⋯⋯⋯⋯⋯⋯⋯⋯⋯⋯⋯⋯ 74
- 05 Samgyetang: Korean Ginseng Chicken Soup ⋯⋯⋯⋯ 76
  参鸡汤：韩国夏日必备 ⋯⋯⋯⋯⋯⋯⋯⋯⋯⋯⋯⋯⋯ 76
- 06 Uijeongbu Budae Jjigae: Soup for Koreans ⋯⋯⋯⋯ 78
  部队汤：没有华丽外衣的韩国美食 ⋯⋯⋯⋯⋯⋯⋯⋯ 78
- 07 Patbingsu: A South Korean National Dessert ⋯⋯⋯⋯ 80
  红豆刨冰：韩国的国民甜点 ⋯⋯⋯⋯⋯⋯⋯⋯⋯⋯⋯ 80
- 08 Characteristics of Hansik Cuisine ⋯⋯⋯⋯⋯⋯⋯⋯⋯ 81
  到了韩国吃什么 ⋯⋯⋯⋯⋯⋯⋯⋯⋯⋯⋯⋯⋯⋯⋯⋯ 81
- 09 Eating Out in South Korea ⋯⋯⋯⋯⋯⋯⋯⋯⋯⋯⋯⋯ 83
  外出就餐去哪里 ⋯⋯⋯⋯⋯⋯⋯⋯⋯⋯⋯⋯⋯⋯⋯⋯ 83

Chapter 6　街拍日本：独具一格岛国风

- 01 Karaoke in Japan: Nothing But for Fun ⋯⋯⋯⋯⋯⋯ 86
  日本卡拉OK：开心去唱 ⋯⋯⋯⋯⋯⋯⋯⋯⋯⋯⋯⋯ 86
- 02 Izakaya: Japanese Style Bar ⋯⋯⋯⋯⋯⋯⋯⋯⋯⋯⋯ 87
  日本酒吧：居酒屋 ⋯⋯⋯⋯⋯⋯⋯⋯⋯⋯⋯⋯⋯⋯⋯ 87
- 03 Capsule Hotels: Japanese Life in the Tube ⋯⋯⋯⋯ 89
  日本胶囊旅馆："管子"里的生活 ⋯⋯⋯⋯⋯⋯⋯⋯⋯ 89
- 04 Mansions in Japan: Apartments for Residence ⋯⋯⋯⋯ 90
  日本的特色公寓 ⋯⋯⋯⋯⋯⋯⋯⋯⋯⋯⋯⋯⋯⋯⋯⋯ 90
- 05 Japanese Furniture ⋯⋯⋯⋯⋯⋯⋯⋯⋯⋯⋯⋯⋯⋯⋯ 92
  日本家庭里的独特家具 ⋯⋯⋯⋯⋯⋯⋯⋯⋯⋯⋯⋯⋯ 92
- 06 Department Stores in Japan ⋯⋯⋯⋯⋯⋯⋯⋯⋯⋯⋯ 93
  日本百货公司 ⋯⋯⋯⋯⋯⋯⋯⋯⋯⋯⋯⋯⋯⋯⋯⋯⋯ 93
- 07 Combini: Convenience Stores in Japan ⋯⋯⋯⋯⋯⋯ 95
  日本便利店成功的秘密 ⋯⋯⋯⋯⋯⋯⋯⋯⋯⋯⋯⋯⋯ 95
- 08 Takkyubin: Efficient Delivery in Japan ⋯⋯⋯⋯⋯⋯ 97
  日本宅急便：高效的快递 ⋯⋯⋯⋯⋯⋯⋯⋯⋯⋯⋯⋯ 97
- 09 Train Culture of Japan ⋯⋯⋯⋯⋯⋯⋯⋯⋯⋯⋯⋯⋯ 99
  日本的列车文化 ⋯⋯⋯⋯⋯⋯⋯⋯⋯⋯⋯⋯⋯⋯⋯⋯ 99
- 10 Bicycles in Japan ⋯⋯⋯⋯⋯⋯⋯⋯⋯⋯⋯⋯⋯⋯⋯⋯ 100
  日本的自行车文化 ⋯⋯⋯⋯⋯⋯⋯⋯⋯⋯⋯⋯⋯⋯⋯ 100

Chapter 7　邂逅韩国：开启韩式真生活

- 01 Traditional Markets: The Lifestyle of the Koreans ⋯⋯⋯ 104
  韩国传统市场：韩国人的生活视窗 ⋯⋯⋯⋯⋯⋯⋯⋯ 104
- 02 South Korea Media 韩国媒体大观 ⋯⋯⋯⋯⋯⋯⋯⋯ 105
- 03 An All-Mobile Life in South Korea ⋯⋯⋯⋯⋯⋯⋯⋯ 107
  韩国人的移动生活 ⋯⋯⋯⋯⋯⋯⋯⋯⋯⋯⋯⋯⋯⋯⋯ 107

- 04 Hiking in South Korea 徒步游韩国 ········ 108
- 05 Skiing in South Korea 一起去韩国滑雪 ········ 110
- 06 Water Sports in South Korea ········ 111
  韩国的激情水上运动 ········ 111
- 07 A Better Understanding of South Korea ········ 113
  多了解一下韩国 ········ 113
- 08 A New Attitude to Divorce ········ 115
  韩国离婚新变化 ········ 115
- 09 Decline in the Old Way of Business Culture ········ 116
  职业女性大翻身 ········ 116

Chapter 8　古老文明：追觅历史的沧桑

- 01 Imperial Palace of South Korean ········ 120
  韩国故宫：魅力昌德宫 ········ 120
- 02 Gyeongju: A Museum Without Walls ········ 121
  韩国庆州市：没有围墙的博物馆 ········ 121
- 03 Suwon Hwaseong Fortress 小城故事：水原华城 ········ 123
- 04 Beauty of Gochang 魅力高敞郡 ········ 125
- 05 The Jongmyo Shrine: A Priceless for the World ········ 127
  韩国宗庙：无价的世界遗产 ········ 127
- 06 Historical Villages in Korea ········ 129
  韩国的历史村落 ········ 129
- 07 Joseon Wangjo Sillok: Memory of the World Register ········ 130
  世界记忆遗产：《朝鲜王朝实录》 ········ 130
- 08 Joseon Dynasty Through Films ········ 132
  在电影中相遇朝鲜时代 ········ 132
- 09 Himeji-jo Castle 日本第一名城：姬路城 ········ 134
- 10 Senso-ji Temple 东京最古老的寺庙 ········ 136
- 11 Buddhist Monuments in the Horyu-ji Area ········ 138
  佛教圣地法隆寺 ········ 138

Chapter 9　悠游日韩：一景一色一芳华

- 01 Mount Fuji: A New World Cultural Heritage ········ 141
  世遗新宠富士山 ········ 141
- 02 Osorezan: Entrance to the Hell in Japan ········ 142
  日本地狱之门：恐山 ········ 142
- 03 Kiyomizu-dera Temple 日本清水寺 ········ 144
- 04 Tokyo Sky Tree 东京晴空塔 ········ 146
- 05 A Mansion and a Brilliant Political Family ········ 147
  鸠山会馆：别样政治家宅邸 ········ 147
- 06 Ameyoko: Candy Alley in Tokyo ········ 149
  东京的商店街 ········ 149
- 07 Tokyo vs. Osaka 从东京到大阪 ········ 150
- 08 Jeju Island with Unique Costal Culture ········ 152
  游览济州岛，领略海岸美景 ········ 152

09	Korean Buddhist Temples: A Journey to Peace	154
	韩国佛寺：一次平静之旅	154
10	Gwangjang Market with History and Culture	156
	传承至今的广藏市场	156
11	Trickeye Museum: Visitors as Heroes	157
	独特的特丽爱美术馆	157
12	Pimatgol: Korean Food Alleys	159
	吃货福音：避马胡同	159

Chapter 10　潮流风尚：做个有格调的文化新鲜人

01	What Is Unique about a Korean Soap Opera	163
	欲罢不能的韩国肥皂剧	163
02	Fashion Trend Leading by Jeon Ji-hyun	164
	全智贤引领时装潮流	164
03	K-Pop Collaboration: A Newest Trend in Pop World	166
	世界流行音乐新趋势：K-POP合作	166
04	PSY, the Man of **Gangnam Style**	**168**
	鸟叔的华丽转身	168
05	Webtoons: Digital Comics in South Korea	170
	韩国的网页漫画	170
06	Is Japanese Animation Only for Fun?	172
	日本动漫不可一笑而过	172
07	Uniforms: The Student Fashion in Japan	174
	日本学生的制服热	174

Chapter 11　异国风情：许你一个别样的日韩

01	A Usual Drama in Japan: Duty vs. Emotion	177
	日本人的义理与人情	177
02	A Sight into Japanese Character	178
	日本人是什么性格	178
03	Origin of a Peace Sign in Japan	180
	日本V字形和平手势的由来	180
04	Flower Symbolism in Japanese Culture	181
	日本花语解析	181
05	Itadakimasu: Respect for Food in Japan	183
	尊重食物的日本人	183
06	Diet of Health in Japan 日本食谱：吃出健康	185
07	Korea's Traditional Tea Culture 在韩国喝茶	186
08	Fun Facts in South Korea 你不知道的韩国趣闻	188
09	Fan Death in South Korea 韩国怪谈：电扇致死论	190

Chapter 12　尚礼之道：非礼莫属生活志

01	Seken No Me: Neighborhood Eyes in Japan	193
	爱面子的日本邻居	193

02 Driving a Car in Japan 在日本，谨慎驾驶 ⋯⋯⋯⋯⋯⋯ 194
03 Never Shake Your Legs in Japan 不要在日本抖腿 ⋯⋯⋯⋯ 196
04 Common Lip Service in Japan ⋯⋯⋯⋯⋯⋯⋯⋯⋯⋯⋯⋯⋯ 197
　　日本人的应酬之辞 ⋯⋯⋯⋯⋯⋯⋯⋯⋯⋯⋯⋯⋯⋯⋯⋯⋯ 197
05 Never Pick a Sakura Petal in Japan 毋摘樱花 ⋯⋯⋯⋯⋯⋯ 199
06 Jishuku: The Way Japanese Mourn ⋯⋯⋯⋯⋯⋯⋯⋯⋯⋯⋯ 200
　　日本人的哀悼方式 ⋯⋯⋯⋯⋯⋯⋯⋯⋯⋯⋯⋯⋯⋯⋯⋯⋯ 200
07 What to Wear with Seasons in South Korea ⋯⋯⋯⋯⋯⋯⋯ 201
　　在韩国，随季而"衣" ⋯⋯⋯⋯⋯⋯⋯⋯⋯⋯⋯⋯⋯⋯⋯⋯ 201
08 The Value of the Korean Family ⋯⋯⋯⋯⋯⋯⋯⋯⋯⋯⋯⋯ 203
　　重视家庭的韩国人 ⋯⋯⋯⋯⋯⋯⋯⋯⋯⋯⋯⋯⋯⋯⋯⋯⋯ 203

Chapter 13 节庆趣谈：恋上缤纷节日没商量

01 Lunar New Year in South Korea 韩国的春节 ⋯⋯⋯⋯⋯⋯ 207
02 Dano: a Festival of Health ⋯⋯⋯⋯⋯⋯⋯⋯⋯⋯⋯⋯⋯⋯ 208
　　韩国端午节：为健康祈福 ⋯⋯⋯⋯⋯⋯⋯⋯⋯⋯⋯⋯⋯⋯ 208
03 Korean Thanksgiving Day ⋯⋯⋯⋯⋯⋯⋯⋯⋯⋯⋯⋯⋯⋯ 210
　　秋夕节：韩国的感恩节 ⋯⋯⋯⋯⋯⋯⋯⋯⋯⋯⋯⋯⋯⋯⋯ 210
04 Korea's Traditional Rituals on Chuseok ⋯⋯⋯⋯⋯⋯⋯⋯⋯ 212
　　秋夕节，韩国人还做什么 ⋯⋯⋯⋯⋯⋯⋯⋯⋯⋯⋯⋯⋯⋯ 212
05 Christmas in Korea 圣诞节在韩国 ⋯⋯⋯⋯⋯⋯⋯⋯⋯⋯ 214
06 Celebrations of the Japanese New Year ⋯⋯⋯⋯⋯⋯⋯⋯⋯ 215
　　日本人过新年 ⋯⋯⋯⋯⋯⋯⋯⋯⋯⋯⋯⋯⋯⋯⋯⋯⋯⋯⋯ 215
07 Hatsumode: First Visit to a Shrine of the Year ⋯⋯⋯⋯⋯⋯ 217
　　新年"初诣"：神社首拜 ⋯⋯⋯⋯⋯⋯⋯⋯⋯⋯⋯⋯⋯⋯ 217
08 Coming-of-Age-Day in Japan 在日本过成人礼 ⋯⋯⋯⋯⋯ 218
09 A New Holiday for Overworked Japanese ⋯⋯⋯⋯⋯⋯⋯⋯ 220
　　日本登山节：放下工作，亲近自然 ⋯⋯⋯⋯⋯⋯⋯⋯⋯⋯ 220
10 Hanami in Japan 日本赏花节 ⋯⋯⋯⋯⋯⋯⋯⋯⋯⋯⋯⋯ 222
11 Sea Day in Japan 日本海洋节 ⋯⋯⋯⋯⋯⋯⋯⋯⋯⋯⋯⋯ 224

Chapter 1
古韵馨香：行走在传统文化的长河

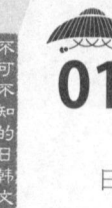

01 The "Way" in Japan
日本之"道"

日本有不少叫做"某道"的传统文化。日本人将这些"道"里最重要的挑出来，合称"日本八道"，包括茶道、艺道、花道、书道、剑道、棋道、柔道和空手道。

日本所谓的"道"文化认为，做事情的过程与结果一样重要，而非西方人看中的是结果。比如，日本的茶道艺术中，与茶水的整个泡制方法、上茶方式以及饮用方法相比，小小的一杯茶便显得微不足道了。这种"道"的思维方式甚至已经渗透到日本人的日常工作当中，比如说，日本员工做起工作来按部就班、十分细致，即便有捷径可循也不会采用。

The Japanese concept of geido (艺道) says that the way you do something is just as important as the result you achieve. It's key to understanding how Japanese people think. As **Ralph Waldo Emerson**, an American poet, said, life is a journey, not a destination. For Japanese, what **matters** to human is right on "the way".

Have you ever noticed how many Japanese martial arts are translated as "the way ..."? For example: kendo (剑道)–way of the sword, aikido (合气道)–way of life energy, judo (柔道)–gentle way. "The way" is also a common term in Japanese traditional arts: sado (茶道) –the way of tea (tea ceremony), kado (花道) –the way of flowers (ikebana flower arrangement), shodo (书道)–way of the brush (Japanese calligraphy).

Western arts are usually defined by their end result. For example, an **impressionist** painting has a particular style– it doesn't matter how the artist went about painting it. But in Japanese arts, the opposite is sometimes the case–the way the art was created is very important. This is called geido (the way of art).

Tea ceremony is often considered the best example of geido. The end result: a cup of tea is **trivial** compared with the process of making, serving and consuming the tea. The

♦ **Ralph Waldo Emerson**
拉尔夫·瓦尔多·爱默生，美国著名的思想家，诗人；他是确立美国文化精神的代表人物，被美国前总统林肯称为"美国的孔子"、"美国文明之父"。

♦ **matter** ['mætə]
vi. 要紧，重要
This does not matter, for, as he often remarked, one is never too old to learn. 这不要紧，因为，正如他一向所说的那样，一个人要活到老学到老。

♦ **impressionist** [ɪmˈpreʃənɪst]
adj. 印象派的，印象主义的
Does the writer belong to the Impressionist school? 这位作家是否属于印象派？

♦ **trivial** ['trɪvɪəl]
adj. 不重要的，微不足道的
A trivial issue was brought to their attention. 一个不重要的问题引起了他们的注意。

♦ **defeat** [dɪˈfiːt]
vt. 击败，挫败，战胜
They were defeated in the battle. 在这场战斗中他们被击败了。

♦ **short cut**
(做某事的) 快捷办法，捷径；近路
I tried to take a short cut and got lost.

process is the art.

Also Japanese martial arts aren't about the result: **defeating** your enemy. They're about the path that gets you there. To put it another way, the Japanese martial artist sees no value in a **short cut**—even when the end result is the same.

Many Japanese people aren't familiar with the term geido. Nevertheless, geido can be seen in the way that Japanese people think. For example, many Japanese workers see no point in short cuts. They believe that the process of work is just as important as the result.

Take the train in Japan and you'll notice that the workers never take short cuts. They have a **detailed** process for everything they do.

Train **attendants** push a cart through the shinkansen selling snacks and beer. Whenever they enter or exit a car they bow facing the passengers. Train **conductors** do the same. Let's say the train was almost empty and everyone was sleeping. Train staff will still bow–even though nobody would notice if they didn't.

Train employees have many processes that involve pointing (with a finger). A platform master will **point at** train doors to ensure they're closed. This seemingly repetitive action is known to help reduce human error. A platform master could easily **skip** this step if she's sure the doors are closed but she never does.

Westerners working for Japanese companies may complain that Japanese workers "like to make things difficult". Japanese coworkers may **refuse** to take shortcuts that "seem obvious" to their Western counterparts. Japanese workers typically like to follow a process. They are open to improving processes but aren't keen to find quick wins.

我本来想抄近路，结果却迷路了。

♦ **detailed** ['di:teɪld]
adj. 详细的，精细的；复杂的
He gave a detailed account of what happened on the fateful night. 他详细描述了那个灾难性夜晚所发生的事。

♦ **attendant** [ə'tendənt]
n. 服务人员，侍者

♦ **conductor** [kən'dʌktə]
n. 列车员，（公共汽车）售票员

♦ **point at** 指向
Take the pointer, point at different things and what they are. 拿着教鞭，指不同的东西，说出他们的名称。

♦ **skip** [skɪp]
vt. 略过，跳过
Let's skip over these details and come to the main point. 让我们略过这些枝节来谈主要问题吧。

♦ **refuse** [rɪ'fju:z]
vi. 拒绝
refuse to do sth. 拒绝做某事
People who refuse to pay tax can be put in prison. 拒绝纳税的人会被送进监狱。

02 Japanese Tea Ceremony: An Art Back to Nature
日本茶道：回归自然的艺术

日本茶道是在日本一种仪式化的、为客人奉茶之事，原称为"茶汤"。日本茶道和其他东亚茶仪式一样，都是一种以品茶为主而发展出来的特殊文化，但内容和形式则有别。现代的茶道，由主人准备茶与点心，还有水果招待客人，而主人与客人都按照固定的规矩与步骤行事。除了饮食之外，茶道的精神还延伸到茶室内外的布置；品鉴茶室的书画布置、庭园的园艺及饮茶的陶器都是茶道的重点。

　　日本的茶道，是一种艺术消遣，更是一种精神自律。在品茶过程中，也会在平静的氛围中欣赏中国传统绘画和其他艺术。花道、陶瓷、书画和禅道等各种元素和谐地融合在严格的仪式和主客之间的轻松交流中。

The Japanese tea ceremony is an artistic pastime unique to Japan that features the serving and drinking of Matcha, a **powdered** Japanese green tea. Though Japanese green-tea had been introduced to Japan from China around the 8th century, Matcha powdered green-tea did not reach Japan until the end of the 12th century. The **practice** of holding social gatherings to drink Matcha spread among the upper class from about the 14th century. Gradually, one of the main purposes of these gatherings, which took place in a Shoin (study room), became the appreciation of Chinese paintings and crafts in a **serene** atmosphere.

Having witnessed or taken part in the Japanese Tea Ceremony only once, one will come to understand that in Japan, serving tea is an art and a spiritual discipline. As an art, the Tea Ceremony is an **occasion** to appreciate the simplicity of the tea room's design, the feel of the Chawan in the hand, the company of friends, and simply a moment of **purity**.

As a discipline, aesthetic **contemplation** of flower arranging, ceramics, **calligraphy**, and the roots of the Tea Ceremony which go **all the way** back to the twelfth century is required. The ritual preparation requires the person hosting a tea party to know how to cook a special meal (Kaiseki), how to arrange the flowers which will be placed in the **alcove** (Tokonoma). When choosing **utensils** and other vessels, the host (Teishu) has to consider the rank and type to make

♦ **powdered** ['paʊdəd]
adj. 粉状的
This looks like the powdered sugar we found in the cab. 这看上去像我们在车上找到的糖粉。

♦ **practice** ['præktɪs]
n. 实践，(通常) 做法
Practice is the only way to learn a language well. 学好一门语言的惟一途径就是实践。

♦ **serene** [sɪ'ri:n]
adj. 平静的，安详的
She has a lovely serene face. 她有一张可爱而安详的脸。

♦ **occasion** [ə'keɪʒən]
n. 机会，时机；场合
It is always an important occasion for setting out government policy. 这历来都是阐明政府政策的重要时机。

♦ **purity** ['pjʊərɪti]
n. 纯洁，纯净
White is the symbol of purity. 白是纯洁的象征。

♦ **contemplation** [ˌkɒntem'pleɪʃən]
n. 意图，沉思
He was lost in the contemplation of the landscape. 他对着眼前的景色沉思起来。

♦ **calligraphy** [kə'lɪgrəfɪ]
n. 书法

♦ **all the way** 一直，完全地
We got there by driving slow all the way. 我们开着车去了那里，一路上开得很慢。

♦ **alcove** ['ælkəʊv]
n. 凹室，壁龛

♦ **utensil** [jʊ(:)'tensl]
n. 器具，器皿

sure that they will **stand out**.

The **objective** of the Japanese tea ceremony is to create a relaxed communication between the host and his guests. It is based **in part** on the etiquette of serving tea (Temae), but is also includes the intimate connections with architecture, landscape gardening, unique tea utensils, paintings, flower arrangement, ceramics, calligraphy, Zen Buddhism, and all the other elements that **coexist** in harmonious relationship with the ceremony. Its ultimate aim is the attainment of deep spiritual satisfaction through the drinking of tea and through silent contemplation. On a different level, the Japanese tea ceremony is simply an entertainment where the guests are invited to drink tea in a pleasant and relaxing room. The **bonds** of friendship between the host and guests are strengthened during the ceremony when the host himself makes and serves the tea.

♦ **stand out** 引人注目，显眼；突出
Red flags stand out brightly, set against the blue sky. 红旗在蓝天的映衬下显得分外鲜艳。
♦ **objective** [əbˈdʒektɪv]
n. 目标，目的
Our objective is a free, open and pluralistic society. 我们的目标是建立一个自由、开放和多元化的社会。
♦ **in part** 在某种程度上，部分地
She was pleased in part that the streets were bright and clean. 街道明亮干净，这使她有几分欣喜。
♦ **coexist** [ˌkəʊɪɡˈzɪst]
vi. 共存，同时存在
At present, the opportunity and difficulty coexist in the development of hydropower. 当前发展水电的机遇与困难并存。
♦ **bond** [bɒnd]
n. （情感的）纽带，契合，亲密关系
A bond of friendship had been forged between them. 他们之间形成了一种友谊的纽带。

03 Ikebana: Japanese Art of Flower Arrangement
花道：日本的插花艺术

花道又称日式插花，是日本传统的插花艺术。日式插花以花材用量少，选材简洁为主流，它或以花的盛开、含苞、待放代表事物过去、现在、将来。日本人强调花与枝叶的自然循环生态美姿是宇宙永恒的缩影。若常以宽宏意境和深邃内涵从事插花艺术的表达，自然能直接体会到园艺家对植物本性认识以至尊重的境界。

日本的插花艺术，并不仅限于女性，男性也可以学习。事实上，在过去，即便最厉害的武士也可以通过插花来消遣时光。如今，插花不仅是艺术，也是男女都可从事的一份职业。其实，严格来讲，插花并不等同于花道，花道更多的讲究对于空间的非对称性应用，使各种材料在空间中表现出相互的和谐之美。

Ikebana is the Japanese art of flower arrangement. It is more than simply putting flowers in a container. It is a disciplined art form in which the arrangement is a living thing where nature and humanity are brought together. It is **steeped** in the philosophy of developing closeness with nature.

As is true of all other arts, ikebana is creative expression within certain rules of construction. Its materials are living branches, leaves, grasses, and blossoms. Its heart is the beauty **resulting from** color combinations, natural shapes, graceful lines, and the meaning **latent** in the total form of the arrangement. Ikebana is, therefore, much more than mere **floral** decoration.

The remarkably high development of floral art in Japan can be **attributed** to the Japanese love of nature. People in all countries appreciate natural beauty, but in Japan, the appreciation amounts almost to a religion. The Japanese have always felt a strong bond of **intimacy** with their natural surroundings, and even in contemporary **concrete-and-asphalt** urban complexes, they display a remarkably strong desire to have a bit of nature near them. Foreign visitors to Tokyo are often surprised to notice that their taxi driver has hung a little vase with a flower or two at the edge of the **windshield**. The Japanese house that does not at all times contain some sort of floral arrangement is rare indeed.

Nature is always changing. Plants grow and put forth leaves, flowers **bloom**, and berries are borne regularly and repeatedly throughout the seasons. Nature has its own rhythm and order. The **awareness** of this is the first step in involving oneself in ikebana.

In principle, ikebana aims not at bringing a **finite** piece of nature into the house, but rather at suggesting the whole of nature, by creating a link between the indoors and the outdoors. This is why arrangers are likely to use several different types of plants in a single arrangement, and to **give prominence to** leaves and flowerless branches as well as blossoms. Even when a single type of flower is used, an attempt is made to bring out its full **implications** as a symbol of nature.

People may doubt whether men are its practitioners. The answer is that both men and women study this art form.

♦ **steeped** [sti:pd]
adj. 充满……的，沉浸在……中的
He said they were unrealistic and steeped in the past. 他说他们脱离现实，总是沉浸在过去。

♦ **result from**
产生于……，由……引起
Many hair problems result from what you eat. 很多头发问题都是由饮食引起的。

♦ **latent** ['leɪtənt]
adj. 潜在的；潜伏的

♦ **floral** ['flɔːrəl]
adj. 花的，以花装饰的

♦ **attribute** [ə'trɪbju(ː)t]
vt. 把……归于
Archaeologists attribute the ruin to a flourishing prehistoric kingdom. 考古学家认为这些废墟属于一个繁荣的史前王国。

♦ **intimacy** ['ɪntɪməsɪ]
n. 亲密，亲近
An intimacy grew up between us. 我们之间的关系亲密起来了。

♦ **concrete-and-asphalt**
adj. 混凝土和沥青下的

♦ **windshield** ['wɪndʃiːld]
n. 挡风玻璃

♦ **bloom** [bluːm]
vi. 开花

♦ **awareness** [ə'weənɪs]
n. 察觉，觉悟，意识
There is a general awareness that smoking is harmful. 人们普遍认识到吸烟有害健康。

♦ **finite** ['faɪnaɪt]
adj. 有限的
The physical universe is finite in space and time. 物质世界在时间和空间上是有限的。

♦ **give prominence to** 突出，重视
Always give prominence to training students' interest. 要始终突出对学生英语兴趣的培养。

Indeed, in the past, ikebana was considered an **appropriate** pastime for even the toughest samurai. Currently, the leading flower arrangers are, for the most part, men. Ikebana is not only an art, but an occupation for men and women alike.

Many practitioners of ikebana feel that the spiritual aspect of ikebana is very important. One becomes quiet when one practices ikebana. It helps you to live "in the moment" and to appreciate things in nature that previously had seemed **insignificant**. One becomes more patient and tolerant of differences, not only in nature, but more generally in other people. Ikebana can inspire you to **identify with** beauty in all art forms–painting, music, etc., and to always expect the best in yourself.

Besides, what distinguishes ikebana from other approaches such as "flower arrangement" is its **asymmetrical** form and the use of empty space as an essential feature of the composition. A sense of harmony among the materials, the container, and the setting is also **crucial**. These are characteristics of aesthetics that ikebana shares with traditional Japanese paintings, gardens, architecture, and design.

♦ **implication** [ˌɪmplɪˈkeɪʃən]
n. 含意，言外之意
♦ **appropriate** [əˈprəʊprɪɪt]
adj. 适当的，恰当的
♦ **insignificant** [ˌɪnsɪɡˈnɪfɪkənt]
adj. 不重要的，毫无意义的；微小的
The levels of chemicals in the river are not insignificant. 河水中的化学物质含量不容忽视。
♦ **identify with** 识别，认同
♦ **asymmetrical** [æsɪˈmetrɪkəl]
adj. 不均匀的，不对称的
Most people's faces are asymmetrical. 多数人的脸并不对称。
♦ **crucial** [ˈkruːʃɪəl]
adj. 至关重要的，关键性的
Talent, hard work and sheer tenacity are all crucial to career success. 才能、勤奋和顽强的意志对事业成功都至关重要。

04 Sumo: Wrestling in Tokyo
相扑：日式国技

相扑来源于日本神道的宗教仪式，被誉为日本的"国技"，在日本有着极高的地位。比赛时，两位相扑手束发梳髻，下身系一条兜带，近乎赤身裸体上台比赛。相扑比赛场中间是直径为4.55米的圆圈，只要让对方除了脚以外的其他部位接触到地面，或者将对方推出圆圈就算获胜。

相扑手为了占据体重优势特意使自己变胖，且异乎寻常的胸围和腰围也会使对方难抓难扯。但是，相扑手因此而引发的糖尿病和痛风等病魔威胁着他们的健康。不过欣慰的是，他们都能娶一位颇具姿色的新娘，日本有很多影视界的美女都把他们当做梦寐以求的郎君人选。

在日本，绝大部分相扑选手都集中在东京地区，游客们可以在东京观看相扑比赛，甚至到他们的训练场所游览一番。

As Japan's national sport, sumo wrestling is a major part of the country's culture. The vast majority of Japan's sumo **wrestlers** live in Tokyo's Ryogoku district, which has served as the sport's **hub** for the past two centuries. With its heavyweight **athletes**, traditional **mawashi**, stiff belt uniforms, and long history, the sport remains a fascinating experience for **spectators**.

Sumo dates back to ancient times and still involves **hints** of the religious **Shinto** rituals it originally involved. Before a tournament begins, the **ring** is **sprinkled** with salt and the wrestlers **stomp** their feet in order to purify the ring and rid it of any evil. Once that's done, the two male competitors face off in an attempt to **knock** the other **over**. The first wrestler to leave the ring or touch the ground with any body part other than their feet loses.

Seeing a sumo match is a quintessential Japanese experience, because while other countries have adopted the sport, Japan is the only one whose athletes compete professionally. Six 15-day **tournaments** are held throughout the year, and visitors can head to the Kokugikan (Sumo Amphitheater) to see a Dohyo-iri (entering the ring) ceremony and catch the action of a **live** match. The Sumo Museum is also a prime spot to see sumo-related **artifacts**, some dating as far back as 1600.

You can also experience sumo culture by visiting the training stables in Tokyo. Very few tourists have the chance to visit a sumo stable and experience the day-to-day life of a wrestler, as the primary (and often only) way to get inside is by tour. Small-group tours take visitors around a training site to see where athletes live year-round, taste the traditional and **hearty** food of sumo wrestlers and maybe even catch one of them preparing for battle.

♦ **wrestler** ['res(ə)lə(r)] n. 摔跤选手
The wrestler tripped up his opponent. 那个摔跤运动员把对手绊倒在地。

♦ **hub** [hʌb] n.（活动的）中心，核心
Egypt was the most populous Arab country, the cultural hub of the area. 埃及是人口最多的阿拉伯国家，是该地区的文化中心。

♦ **athlete** ['æθliːt] n. 运动员
The boy first showed promise as an athlete in grade school. 这个男孩在上小学的时候就初次显示出成为运动员的潜力。

♦ **mawashi** n.（日本相扑选手的）兜裆布

♦ **spectator** [spek'teɪtə] n. 观众
Many spectators watched the baseball game. 许多观众都观看了棒球比赛。

♦ **hint** [hɪnt] n. 迹象，线索
The calm sea gave no hint of the storm that was coming. 平静的海上没有一点迹象显示暴风雨即将来临。

♦ **Shinto** ['ʃɪntəʊ]
n.（日本）神道教，1945年前为日本国教。

♦ **ring** [rɪŋ] n. 相扑场地

♦ **sprinkle** ['sprɪŋkl] vt. 洒，撒
Sprinkle a little salt on the rice. 在米饭上撒点盐。

♦ **stomp** [stɒmp] vt. 跺脚，重踩

♦ **knock sb. over** 把某人摔倒，击败某人

♦ **tournament** ['tʊənəmənt] n. 锦标赛，联赛
The tournament is open to both amateurs and professionals. 这次锦标赛业余选手和职业选手均可参加。

♦ **live** [lɪv] adj. 现场直播的，生动的

♦ **artifact** ['ɑːtɪfækt]
n. 人工制品，手工艺品
The farmer unearthed a valuable artifact while plowing his field. 那个农夫在犁田时挖到了一个很值钱的手工艺品。

♦ **hearty** ['hɑːtɪ] adj. 丰盛的
He prepared a hearty dinner for us. 他为我们准备了一顿丰盛的晚餐。

05 The Legend of Sword Makers in Old Japan
走近日本铸剑师

在古代日本，好的剑是价值连城；而且跟今天的房地产一样，所有的剑都要登记在册，政府会详细记录每把剑的设计和制造过程和来源。

那时候，铸剑是一门兼具科学和哲理的技艺，并不断出现在文学、传说和歌曲之中，顶级的铸剑师绝对是社会名流。其中，最为著名的是十四世纪的两位铸剑大师——Masamune 和 Muramasa。首先，两人的剑质量之高令人匪夷所思。据说，Masamune 的铸剑能够利断铜管而完好无损，Muramasa 的铸剑直令幕府将军震慑。而今天的铸剑业已是另一番景象。

In old Japan, swords were precious **possessions** that could cost as much as a farm. Much like real estate today, swords were **registered**. Government sword registries detailed the maker, history and design of virtually every sword in Japan.

Swordsmanship was both a science and a philosophy. Swords were commonly featured in songs, stories and myth. Top sword makers were essentially celebrities.

The most famous sword craftsman of them all was Masamune (14th century). His swords cost a small **fortune**. They were renowned for their quality and feared for their effectiveness. **Rumors** surrounded his entire life. Masamune's swords were reputed to cut through **copper** pipes without messing the sword's **polish**.

According to one myth, a samurai once cut a man in half with a Masamune sword. At first the man seemed unaffected. No blood was drawn. The cut was so fine that the man walked around for a few hours before falling in two. People became **suspicious** of the quality of Masamune swords. They seemed to **defy** the physics of the metal from which they were forged. Rumors emerged that fresh blood was a key ingredient of Masamune **blades**. Other **whispers** suggested that bodies were regularly found in

♦ **possession** [pə'zeʃən]
n. 财产，所有物
He described the picture as his most cherished possession. 他说那幅画是他最珍爱的财产。

♦ **register** ['redʒɪstə] vt. 登记
They were unwilling to register for the draft. 他们不愿意登记入伍。

♦ **swordsmanship** ['sɔːdzmənʃɪp]
n. 剑术，剑法

♦ **fortune** ['fɔːtʃən]
n. 财富，财产
make a fortune 赚大钱；发财
We must make a fortune by means of industry. 我们必须勤劳致富。

♦ **rumor** ['ruːmə] n. 传闻，谣言
Rumor has it that he is having an affair with his secretary. 谣传他和他的秘书有暧昧关系。

♦ **copper** ['kɒpə] adj. 铜制的

♦ **polish** ['pɒlɪʃ] n. 光泽

♦ **suspicious** [səs'pɪʃəs]
adj. 猜疑的，怀疑的
be suspicious of/about... 对……表示怀疑
I'm very suspicious about his motives. 我很怀疑他的动机。

♦ **defy** [dɪ'faɪ]
vt. 违背，不服从；公然反抗，向……挑战
I wouldn't have dared to defy my teachers. 我可不敢不听老师的话。

the **vicinity** of Masamune's workshop.

Muramasa Sengo was another 14th century sword craftsman who was much feared by his contemporaries. By all accounts he was completely mad and **prone to** violent outbursts. It was said that his madness passed into his swords. According to legend, whoever possessed a Muramasa sword became crazy and dangerous.

Muramasa swords were also known for their astounding quality. Muramasa passed his craft to an **apprentice**. The school of Muramasa sword making continued for over 200 years. In 1603, the Shogun (Tokugawa Ieyasu) banned Muramasa swords. He instructed that they all be melted down. The Shogun had lost several of this relatives to Muramasa swords. He himself was cut by a Muramasa blade but survived the **ordeal**.

Today, Muramasa are difficult to identify because many had their markings changed to avoid the ban. Authentic Muramasa swords are now considered priceless. Many **forgeries** have surfaced over the centuries.

♦ **blade** [bleɪd] n. 剑，刀片
♦ **whisper** [ˈ(h)wɪspə]
n. 私下谈论，谣传
I've heard a whisper that he's going to resign. 我听到了一个传闻说他准备辞职。
♦ **vicinity** [vɪˈsɪnɪti]
n. 附近，附近地区
He told us there was no hotel in the vicinity. 他告诉我们说附近没有旅馆。
♦ **prone to** 倾向于，易于……的
Working without a break makes you more prone to error. 连续工作不停歇使人更容易出错。
♦ **apprentice** [əˈprentɪs]
n. 学徒，徒弟；新手
My son is an apprentice in a furniture maker's workshop. 我的儿子在一家家具厂做学徒。
♦ **ordeal** [ɔːˈdiːl] n. 磨难，折磨
He spoke frankly about the ordeal. 他直率地讲出了苦难的经历。
♦ **forgery** [ˈfɔːdʒərɪ] n. 伪造，伪造物
The painting was a forgery. 这张画是赝品。

06 Pansori: Traditional Art of Korea
潘索里：韩国说唱艺术

潘索里是朝鲜传统的叙事性说唱艺术。发源于朝鲜半岛西南部的全州，大概在17世纪末肃宗王朝时期在百姓间广为流传。

在正主、顺主时期（大约18世纪末19世纪初），潘索里在民间出现了8位名家，各家唱法不一，于是根据名家所居住的地域划分门派。东西便制的区分就以其发祥地的地形为主，譬如山岳对平原等等，西便制是潘索里的一个流派，盛行于朝鲜半岛全罗道的西部，故称为"西便制"，东便制是指东部的唱法。东便制潘索里节奏快也有力，声音雄厚高亢，而西便制则以缓慢的唱法与悲悯的情绪再加上唱腔的多变而著称。在19世纪末潘索里逐渐衰落，直到二战后才又得以复兴。由于潘索里艺术深植于民间，所

♦ **in the interest of**
为了，为了……的利益
Boards need to be overseers of management and act in the interest of shareholders rather than as partners of management. 董事会需要为股东利益服务，成为管理层的监管者，而不是他们的同盟军。
♦ **take place** 发生，举行
Elections take place every four years. 选举四年举行一次。
♦ **schedule** [ˈʃedjuːl]
vt. 排定，安排
The speaker is scheduled to make a speech tomorrow. 演讲者定于明天发

以很艺人都是在街头坊间四处表演。有的终其一生颠沛流离，被人视为下贱的艺人。恰巧潘索里歌唱的故事都很悲，大多反映老百姓生活艰苦的内容，许多潘索里艺人也人如其歌，生活波折。

　　早在1960年代末，潘索里这种民间技艺就已被韩国定为国家非物质文化遗产，到了新千年，甚至成为世界文化遗产，潘索里与艺人的地位都已今非昔比。

　　Pansori is a form of Korean music which has been classified as a National Cultural Intangible Property by the Korean government, **in the interest of** preserving it for future generations. Pansori performances **take place** at Korean cultural festivals, in addition to being **scheduled** as events in their own right, and numerous recordings of such performances are **available** for people who want to listen to or study pansori. The Korean government believes that pansori is a very important part of Korea's national heritage, and there is some **concern** that the art of pansori could die out due to lack of interest.

　　In a pansori performance, there are two performers: the gosu and the kwangdae. The gosu is a drummer, who accompanies the kwangdae, or singer. In more modernized performances, sometimes several singers perform, voicing different characters in the piece to provide more color. The audience is also an **integral** part of the pansori, as they are expected to respond with sounds of encouragement and **applause** at various points in the performance.

　　Pansori performances are classically quite long, with the music being used to tell a traditional Korean folktale. A full madang or story can **take** hours to perform, so modern pansori performances are often offered in sections so that audiences do not get **restless**. During the performance, the audience can hear singing and stylized speech, along with the sounds of the drum and chuimsae, sounds which are made by the gosu as the singer performs. The audience can

表演说。

♦ **available** [əˈveɪləbl]
adj. 能找到的；可获得的
There's no one available at such short notice to take her class. 只提前这么短的时间通知，找不到人替她的课。

♦ **concern** [kənˈsɜːn]
n. 顾虑，担忧
At first this concern appears paradoxical. 这种顾虑起初看来自相矛盾。

♦ **integral** [ˈɪntɪɡrəl]
adj. 基本的，构成整体所必需的
Anxiety is integral to the human condition. 焦虑是人类的基本生存状况之一。

♦ **applause** [əˈplɔːz]
n. 热烈鼓掌；喝彩，欢呼
I kept hearing the sound of applause in the background. 我不断听到隐约的鼓掌声。

♦ **take** [teɪk]
vt. 耗费（时间等）
It took him three years to finish the painting.
他花了三年时间完成这幅画。

♦ **restless** [ˈrestlɪs]
adj. 焦躁不安的，不耐烦的
He felt restless and dissatisfied as he drove home. 在开车回家的途中，他感到烦躁不安，很不高兴。

♦ **epic** [ˈepɪk]
adj. 史诗般的，叙事诗的；宏大的，壮丽的
I read the epic work War and Peace. 我读过长篇巨著《战争与和平》。

♦ **die out**
（指习惯、观念、物种、家族等）绝迹，消失
How did the dinosaurs die out? 恐龙是如何灭绝的？

♦ **grueling** [ˈɡruəlɪŋ]
adj. 紧张的，使极度疲劳的
How would a man in the midst of such grueling competition act so joyously?

also respond with chuimsae of its own.

These **epic** sung folktales have their roots in the 1600s, and they became especially popular in the 1800s. By the 1960s, however, pansori had begun to **die out** in Korea. The training involved is **grueling**, as are the performances themselves, and interest appeared to be **dwindling**. In response, the government attempted to protect and promote this traditional art form, encouraging pansori performers to interact with the public in the hopes of exciting the next generation.

At any given time, several pansori performers typically have a very visible public **profile**, becoming stars in the genre, and an **assortment** of up and coming performers is typically in training. Thanks to the government's measures to protect pansori, pansori performers and trainees often receive generous government assistance, including grants to **sponsor** performances and other events which promote the pansori tradition.

在如此极度紧张的比赛中, 一个人怎么能够显得这样兴高采烈?
♦ **dwindling** ['dwɪndlɪŋ]
adj. 逐渐减少的
It offers an alternative to the dwindling supplies of natural gas. 这为正在减少中的天然气供应提供了另外的来源。
♦ **profile** ['prəʊfaɪl]
n. 形象, 轮廓
We could see the profile of a distant hill if it is very clear. 如果天气晴朗, 我们可看到远山的轮廓。
♦ **assortment** [ə'sɔːtmənt]
n. 搭配
♦ **sponsor** ['spɒnsə]
vt. 赞助
At the beginning, for Olympics, however, no one would like to sponsor the Game at all. 奥运会刚开始举办的时候, 没有谁愿意去赞助它。

07 Ancient Petroglyphs in South Korea
聚光盘龟台岩刻画

韩半岛的东南地区存在着证明从史前时代就已经开始进行狩猎鲸鱼的最早证据。位于蔚山太和江上游的"盘龟台岩刻画", 长10米, 宽3米。在这块垂直的岩石上刻有300多幅动物与人, 以及狩猎鲸鱼的图案。因为岩石整体的形状比较像乌龟壳, 因此这里也被叫做"盘龟台"。

盘龟台岩刻画被发现于1971年。在岩壁上刻制的300多幅图案当中包括鲸鱼、乌龟、鹿、老虎、鸟、野猪等动物, 一个女人, 船、鱼叉、渔网等道具。它也证明, 这些图案刻制于新石器时期到青铜器时期, 历经几个世纪。壁画内容不仅包括狩猎活动和风俗, 还有象征多产的怀有小鲸鱼的母鲸鱼。以现在的分类学角度来看, 各种鲸鱼种类刻制得非常详细。同时, 壁画中也介绍了当时的狩猎鲸鱼技术是利用鱼叉和渔网。

岩刻画的存在被报道之后(这里是能够了解在没有文字的时代的人类的意识和宗教观念的最早资料), 各媒体各领域开始集中聚光这里。2013年, 法国考古学杂志《Archeologie》也介绍该壁画是"像电影和漫画一样, 对移动的对象进行完美表现得非常了不起的艺术作品"。

Numerous ancient rock **engravings** of whales and **whaling** still remain in the southeast area of the Korea Peninsula, attracting **archeologists** from around the world. It has been suggested that they are the first pieces of evidence showing the prehistoric origins of whaling. These **petroglyphs** are found in Bangudae in the **upper reaches** of the Taehwagang River near Ulsan in Gyeongsangbuk-do (North Gyeongsang Province). Nearly 300 figures showing land and sea animals, as well as whale-hunting scenes, are found engraved into the wall over an area spanning 10 meters by 3 meters.

The name Bangudae comes from the Korean ban, the word for a **carapace** or a shell, gu, meaning a **turtle**, and dae, a structure or a site, as in a carving site; the rock formation itself is said to resemble the back of a turtle.

The petroglyphs of Bangudae were discovered in 1971. The figures engraved on the rock wall include humans, various types of animals—whales, turtles, deer, tigers, birds and pigs—and weapons, including a bow and a **spear**. Researchers believe that the engravings were completed over several centuries, from the **Neolithic** to the Bronze Age. Among these are 58 engravings of whales and whaling that have attracted the most attention. The petroglyphs show a diverse range of whales, including one that's bearing a calf. Researchers believe them to symbolize an active hunting culture, prosperity and abundance. Along with the figures, whale hunting skills are shown in the ancient works of art, too.

Until the discovery of Bangudae, it was believed that whaling began in **Norway** in around 4,000 B.C., according to the rock carvings in the Norwegian town of Alta. However, in 2004, the BBC reported that, "Stone Age people may have started hunting whales as early as 6,000 B.C., new evidence from South Korea suggests." This **grabbed** the attention of media and archeologists from across the globe.

Since their discovery, the petroglyphs of Bangudae have

♦ **engraving** [ɪnˈɡreɪvɪŋ]
n. 雕刻（作品）
♦ **whaling** [ˈ(h)weɪlɪŋ]
n. 捕鲸
♦ **archeologist** [ˌɑːkɪˈɒlədʒɪst]
n. 考古学家
♦ **petroglyph** [ˈpetrəɡlɪf]
n. （尤指史前的）岩刻画；岩石雕刻
♦ **upper reach** 上游河段
People could see suspicious ripples at the upper reach.
在那段河道的上游，人们能看到令人生疑的小湍流。
♦ **carapace** [ˈkærəpeɪs]
n. （龟、蟹等的）甲壳，硬壳
♦ **turtle** [ˈtɜːtl]
n. 龟，海龟
♦ **spear** [spɪə]
n. 矛，枪
The spear pierced the lion's heart. 那矛刺穿了狮子的心脏。
♦ **Neolithic** [niːəʊˈlɪθɪk]
adj. 新石器时代的
♦ **Norway** [ˈnɔːweɪ]
n. 挪威（欧洲北部国家）
♦ **grab** [ɡræb]
vt. 吸引，引起……的注意
I jumped on the wall to grab the attention of the crowd. 为了吸引那群人的注意，我纵身跃上墙头。
♦ **peek** [piːk]
n. 一瞥，看一眼
I took a peek at the list.
我偷看了一眼名单。
♦ **oceanographer** [ˌəʊʃɪəˈnɒɡrəfə(r)]
n. 海洋学家
♦ **cartoon** [kɑːˈtuːn]
n. 卡通，动画片；漫画
The cartoon diverted the children. 那部卡通片转移了孩子们的注意力。

been considered an important resource that gives a **peek** into the values, ideas and religions of mankind from a time before recorded history began. **Oceanographer** Daniel Robineau, in his book, "Une Histoire de la chasse a la baleine," or, "A History of Whale Hunting," published in 2007, said that the first whale hunting began in Korea, as shown in the petroglyphs.

French archaeologist and film maker Marc Azéma said the Korean petroglyphs could have possibly been the inspiration for his concept of a movie in his book, "La Prehistoire du cinema," or, "Cinema in Prehistoric Times." In 2013, the rock carvings stepped into the spotlight again when the French journal Archeologie described the art work as a moving object, such as a movie or **cartoon**.

08 Korea-Style Birthday Celebrations
韩国人如何庆祝生日

韩国人过生日要吃海带汤。以至于在为朋友庆祝生日的时候也要问上一句"你吃海带汤了吗？"

以前韩国母亲在生孩子的时候，几乎要吃一个月的海带汤，这一传统传承至今。海带里含有丰富的碘、钙等物质，利于子宫收缩、可增加奶水。而生日时喝海带汤，则是为了纪念母亲怀孕生产时的痛苦，不忘母亲的恩惠。

最近韩国人的庆祝生日方式逐渐变得与西方相似，通常都是送上生日卡片和礼物，在生日蛋糕上插上与年龄相同数目的蜡烛许愿。唯一的一点区别就是，韩国人一般过阴历生日，而西方人则只有阳历生日。当然也有人会与朋友一起过阳历生日，与家人一起过阴历生日的。韩国也是分为阳历（阳历1月1日）和阴历（阴历一月初一）两种生日算法。

在韩国人的生日中，有几个特定的生日是非常重要的，分别是周岁生日、六十大寿和七十大寿。

While birthday cake is fast becoming popular at the office and among circles of friends (typically the ladies), Koreans still **hold fast to** the tradition of eating **miyeokguk**, seaweed soup, on their birthday.

In fact, this tradition is so **deeply-rooted** that it is even common to greet a friend on his/her birthday by asking "Have you eaten miyeokguk?" In the olden days, pregnant women would eat miyeokguk for about a month **prior to** giving birth; this tradition is still prevalent today, but not as **widespread** as it once was. Seaweed is high in **iodine** and

♦ **hold fast to**
紧紧抓住，坚持，坚守（某种思想或原则等）如，Hold fast to this rope, and I will pull you up. 抓紧绳子，我把你拉上来。

♦ **miyeokguk** 海带汤

♦ **deeply-rooted**
adj. 根深蒂固的
Racism is a deeply rooted prejudice which has existed for thousands of years. 种族主义是存在了几千年的根深蒂固的偏见。

calcium, which are thought to be beneficial for **uterine contraction** and milk production. Eating miyeokguk on birthdays is seen as a way to remind children not to forget the pain of childbirth and to appreciate the care given to them by their mother.

In many ways, the birthday culture of Korea has become similar to that of the West. Birthday cards and gifts are common and cakes are prepared with candles corresponding to the person's age. One main difference though is that in many **cases**, people celebrate their birthdays according to the lunar calendar (as opposed to the solar calendar). Consequently, the actual **date** changes every year. Some people celebrate their birthday according to both the solar calendar and the lunar calendar, celebrating their "solar birthday" with friends and their "lunar birthday" with family.

Milestone birthdays like dol (a child's first birthday), hwangap (60th birthday), and chilsun (70th birthday) are usually celebrated with a feast or large party.

Dol is celebrated a year after a child's birth. In the past, when food was scarce and **infant mortality** was high, it was considered a blessing and a true sign of fortune that a child **survived** to its first birthday. In celebration, rice cakes, fruit, and food were prepared and shared with the people of the village in appreciation of the care and blessing of Granny Samsin, the goddess that (according to folk religion) **took care of** a child's birth, life, and health. This custom has been handed down for generations, making doljanchi–literally meaning "**feast** to celebrate the first birthday"–an important event in Korea.

Only a few decades ago, the average Korean **life expectancy** was only around 50 or 60. So when someone turned hwangap, or sixty years of age, a big feast was held in the village in the person's honor.

Recently, more and more people are celebrating their milestone birthdays in **alternative** ways, donating money to those in need or contributing to local scholarship programs.

♦ **prior to** 在……之前
The will was made two days prior to his death. 遗嘱是在他死亡前两天立的。

♦ **widespread** ['waɪdspred]
adj. 分布广的，普遍的
A recent open meeting of College members revealed widespread dissatisfaction. 最近的一次学会成员公开会上，大家普遍流露出不满情绪。

♦ **iodine** ['aɪədiːn] n. 碘

♦ **uterine contraction** 子宫收缩

♦ **case** [keɪs] n. 情况，状况
This is a straightforward case, as these things go. 同其他同类情况相比，这件事还算简单。

♦ **date** [deɪt]
n. 日期，日子
Any entry arriving after the closing date will not be considered. 截止日期之后报名参赛的人将不予考虑。

♦ **milestone** ['maɪlstəʊn]
n. 里程碑
The film proved to be a milestone in the history of cinema. 事实证明这部影片是电影史上的一个里程碑。

♦ **infant mortality** 婴儿死亡率

♦ **survive** [sə'vaɪv]
vi. 幸存，活下来
Companies must be able to survive in the marketplace. 公司必须有能力在市场竞争中生存下去。

♦ **take care of** 照顾
They appointed her to take care of that old man. 他们委派她照顾那位老人。

♦ **feast** [fiːst]
n. 盛会，宴会
This new series promises a feast of special effects and set designs. 这部新的系列剧将会是一场特效和舞美的盛宴。

♦ **life expectancy**
平均寿命，预期寿命

♦ **alternative** [ɔːl'tɜːnətɪv]
adj. 其他的；非传统的，另类的

09 Jangseung: Korea's Totem Poles
长丞：韩国图腾柱

旧时，韩国人在道边、路口、村庄附近立起人像柱子，作为界标、路标和洞里守护神，称作"长丞"，或者叫"长桩"、"长生"、"长承"、"将丞"。长丞分松木制和花岗岩制两种，中部地区多为木制。男性长丞身上一般刻有"天下大将军"，女性长丞身上刻有"地上女将军"字样。

"长丞"作为村庄的"守护神"，除了用来标志村落之间的里程，还跟世界上其他地区的图腾柱一样，用来消灾、避邪。幡杆与"长丞"一起立在村前，是希望的象征，其垂直结构解释为天地人合一的通路，以祈求村庄的安宁、修好以及丰收。"长丞"的起源很早，与古代民族信仰有关。朝鲜时代末期仍很盛行，现只个别地方保留这种风俗。

In the simplest terms, the Korean "angseung" is a kind of **totem** pole." For all intents and purposes, the **functions** are quite similar. The Jangseung serves as a village's spiritual guardian with its fierce **gaze** frightening away evil spirits. The practice of jangseung as representatives of village deities originate from indigenous **animistic** beliefs and rites focused on them culminated in village festivals to pray for health, prosperity, and fertility. The uniqueness of jangseung to their particular **locales** also expresses the identity of their respective villages.

Although commonly known as Jangseung in standard Korean, these "totem poles" also are known as Beoksu (Yeongnam), Harabeoji or Halmeoni (Honam), and Hareubang; variations of the form exist in province to province with no real standard set height, facial features, construction **methodology**, or standard set materials. Wooden **variants** of Jangseung (the one most non-Koreans are familiar with and the ones you can see at the Korean Folk Village in Yongin) were common in the Gyeonggi and Chungcheong regions. Stone Jangseungs were more commonly found in the Honam and Yeongnam regions as well as Jeju Island. Jangseung usually have headgear resembling those of a Confucian scholar-

---

♦ **totem** ['təutəm]
n. 图腾（形象），崇拜物

♦ **function** ['fʌŋkʃən]
n. 功能，作用
The function of the kidneys is to excrete wastes from the body. 肾的功能是排泄人体里的废物。

♦ **gaze** [geiz]
n. 凝视，注视
She felt increasingly uncomfortable under the woman's steady gaze. 那个女人一直盯着她看，让她觉得愈发不自在了。

♦ **animistic** [,ænɪ'mɪstɪk]
adj. 万物有灵论的

♦ **locale** [ləu'kɑ:l]
n.（事件发生的）场所或地点
The director is looking for a suitable locale for his new film. 导演在为新片物色合适的拍摄场地。

♦ **methodology** [meθə'dɒlədʒɪ]
n.（从事某一活动的）一套方法

♦ **variant** ['veərɪənt]
n. 变体，变式，变形
A popular variant of the dominant female is the mother-in-law. 悍妇的一种流行变体是丈母娘。

official and often come in a male-female pair with the male commonly bearing the **inscription** "Cheonha Daejang-gun" (Great General Under Heaven) while the female bears the inscription "Jiha Yeojang-gun" (Female General Under Earth) The facial features typically demonstrate fierceness with eyes **slanting** inwards and exaggerated menacing facial expressions.

Jeju Island's "Dolhareubang" ("stone grandfather") is distinctive although a few jangseung in the Honam region have similar features. Dolhareubangs can be found across the island and are **carved** from the island's volcanic rock. A dolhareubang's particular character can be identified by the placement of its hands; a statue with the right hand above the left on the chest **signifies** a scholar whereas a statue with the left hand above the right signifies a military official.

Until 1945, Jangseung were **commonplace** in the rural landscape of Korea. Modernization has **taken a heavy toll on** the practice of Jangseung creation and worship. Destruction was accelerated at the height of Park Chung-hee's Saemaeul Undong, or "New Village Movement", an ambitious program aimed at the forced modernization of villages and **wholesale** destruction of traditional practice. Ironically, there was a realization that this program of destruction of Korea's traditional past was eerily similar to that of the Japanese colonial government's program. While aspects of Korea's traditional past were systematically destroyed in the Saemaeul Undong, there was at the same time a movement to **document** these practices as well as the Jangseung. In the present day, although there has been some form of a revivalist movement of Jangseung, original Jangseung are highly rare and modern incarnations tend to follow a stylized pattern.

♦ **inscription** [ɪnˈskrɪpʃən]
n. 献词，碑文
The inscription has worn away and can no longer be read. 铭文已磨损，无法辨认了。

♦ **slanting** [ˈslɑːntɪŋ]
adj. 倾斜的，歪斜的
The floodlights were hazy behind the slanting rain. 泛光灯在斜斜的雨丝中显得很蒙眬。

♦ **carve** [kɑːv]
vt. 雕刻，雕塑
Carve the names and gild them. 把姓名刻上去，再镀上金。

♦ **signify** [ˈsɪɡnɪfaɪ]
vt. 象征，意味
Do dark clouds signify rain? 有乌云是否显示要下雨？

♦ **commonplace** [ˈkɒmənpleɪs]
adj. 寻常的，普通的
Computers are now commonplace in primary classrooms. 计算机如今在小学教室里很普遍。

♦ **take a heavy toll on**
造成极大的损害，付出沉重的代价

♦ **wholesale** [ˈhəʊlseɪl]
adj. 大规模的，广泛的

♦ **document** [ˈdɒkjʊmənt]
vt. 记录
Document your experiments as detailed as possible starting with the 1st day. 请从第一天开始就要尽你所能详细地做实验记录。

Chapter 2
日本印象：难忘东瀛文化的一抹亮彩

01 Occasions for Wearing Kimonos
舞动和服，因时而变

日本人季节感极强，穿着随季节变化；在不同的人生阶段，也有相应调整。比如，孩子成长中的标志性阶段会有特殊活动，和服的样式也会随时令和场合变化。

婴儿出生30到100天时，穿着白色内衣和服，随父母兄妹和祖父母去神殿祈福，女婴外穿鲜艳的印花和服，男婴则外穿带有家族徽章的黑色和服。此外，每年11月份的七五三节，父母都会带着五岁的男孩，三岁或七岁的女孩前往当地神殿，感谢神灵保佑孩子健康成当然。这时，孩子们也要身着和服。对于年满20周岁的年轻人，在每年1月份的第二个星期一拜访神殿，举行成人节。此时，女孩穿振袖和服，男孩穿羽织和服，同样饰有家族徽章。

振袖和服只有未婚女子才能穿。从前，在日本，身着振袖和服的女子通过挥舞长袖向男子表达爱意。婚礼上，新娘穿纯白色和服——白无垢，白色象征着新的旅程的开始。一旦成婚，妇女便不能再穿振袖和服，改穿袖子较短的留袖和服，分黑白两款。黑色留袖，绣有家族徽章，仅在亲属婚礼这样的正式场合才穿。其他颜色的和服也有正式场合穿的，但不一定有家族徽章。

场合有不同，季节从不忘。在日本，春天适合穿浅色衣服如淡绿色，而夏天穿淡紫色或深蓝色比较好，秋天的色彩最好与树叶的变化相仿，冬天则穿黑色和红色等浓重色彩的服饰。和服颜色同样如此。如今尽管和服已非日常衣着，日本民众在许多场合仍在穿，人们用和服不同的构造，色彩和传达对四季的热爱。

Japanese people **are keenly aware of** the four seasons, and the clothes they wear are always in keeping with the season. The Japanese are also very **tuned in** to the stages of their lives. Special events are held to mark milestones in children's growth, for instance, and people change their **kimonos** to fit both the season and the occasion.

Between 30 and 100 days after a child is born, the parents, **siblings**, and grandparents visit a shrine together to report the child's birth. The baby is dressed in a white under-kimono. On top of that kimono, the baby wears a brightly colored **yuzen-dyed** kimono if it is a girl, and a black kimono decorated with the family crest if it is a boy.

Another key event in a kid's life is the Shichi-Go-San ("seven-five-three") Festival, which takes place in November. On this day, parents take their five-year-old boys and seven-

♦ **be aware of**
认识到，意识到，察觉到
♦ **tune in** 调整，使协调
♦ **kimono** [kɪˈməʊnəʊ]
n. 和服，日本男女穿的传统民族服饰。
♦ **sibling** [ˈsɪblɪŋ]
n.（常用复数）兄弟姐妹，同胞
There's a friendly sibling rivalry between my sister and me. 我和姐姐之间有一种良性的手足之间的竞争。
♦ **yuzen-dyed** [juːˈzen-daɪd]
adj. 有禅印染的，日本特有的印染技巧，程序繁琐，染布质量极高。
♦ **Coming-of-Age Day**
成人节，日本国家法定的12个节日之一，源于古代的成人仪礼，受中国"冠礼"的影响，目的是为向全国于该年度年满20岁的青年男女表示祝福。

year-old or three-year-old girls to the local shrine to thank the gods for keeping their children healthy and making them grow. The kids are dressed in kimonos for this occasion too.

At the age of 20, young people celebrate their passage into adulthood by visiting a shrine on **Coming-of-Age Day**, the second Monday in January. For this occasion, girls wear **furisode** (kimonos with long flowing sleeves) and boys wear haori (half-coats) and hakama decorated with their family crests.

Furisode kimonos are worn only by unmarried women. Once upon a time, young Japanese women declared their love for a man by **fluttering** the long-flapped sleeves of their furisode kimono.

At weddings, the bride wears a pure white kimono known as a shiromuku. The color white signifies the beginning of a journey.

Once a woman is married, she no longer wears a furisode. Instead, she wears a tomesode, a kimono with shorter flaps on the sleeves. The tomesode can be either black or another color. Black tomesode with the wearer's family crest on them are reserved for formal occasions, such as the weddings of one's relatives. Colored tomesode can also be worn on formal occasions, but they do not always have the family crest on them. A key **distinguishing** feature of tomesode (both black and other colors) is that only the fabric on the bottom half of the kimono is decorated with a pattern.

Whatever the occasion-the first shrine visit of the new year, stopping in to see an older person, or what have you–Japanese people always keep the season in mind when deciding which kimono to wear. Pale colors such as light green are appropriate for spring, while cool colors such as lavender or dark blue are good for summer. Autumn calls for colors that imitate the **hues** of the turning leaves, and winter is the season for strong colors like black and red. It's the same case with colors of kimonos.

Although kimonos are no longer everyday wear in Japan, people still like to wear them at various times throughout the year. And when they do, they use the fabrics, colors, and designs of their kimonos to express their love of the four seasons.

♦ **furisode**
振袖，未婚女子穿的和服。

♦ **flutter** [ˈflʌtə]
vt. 使振动，摆动，拍（翅）
Unknown birds flutter round the skirts of that forest. 叫不出名字的鸟儿在森林四周振翅飞翔。

♦ **distinguishing** [dɪsˈtɪŋgwɪʃɪŋ]
adj. 有区别的，与众不同的
The bird has no distinguishing features. 这只鸟没有明显的特征。

♦ **hue** [hjuː]
n. 色彩，色调，颜色
The cool hue in the picture is distinct from the other ones. 这幅画的冷色调与其他画截然不同。

02 Tatami Mats: Japanese Flooring
日本地铺：榻榻米垫

榻榻米与日本的神道教宗教仪式和茶道都有密切联系，现代许多日本家庭的房屋中仍然至少有一间铺设榻榻米的房间。"Tatami"汉字记做"榻榻米"，也有译作"草垫子"或"草席"的，但都不确切。它比草垫子光亮、平展，也比草席坚厚、硬实。传统的日本房间没有床，也不使用桌椅板凳之类。这"榻榻米"，晚上在上面睡觉，白天把褥收起，在上面吃饭和进行各种活动。客人来了，坐在上面喝茶交谈。

就榻榻米的价值和功效而言，首先是经济。它具有床、地毯、凳椅或沙发等多种功能。同样大小的房间，铺"榻榻米"的费用仅是西式布置的三至四分之一；其次是能有效利用空间。在房间小的情况下，若不摆放床、桌椅之类，可以节省很大空间。这符合日本人国土狭小的实际；再者长期坐"榻榻米"有益于健康。长期坐柔软的沙发，会使腿、臀、腰部肌肉松弛，坐"榻榻米"肌肉处于紧张状态，不会有肌肉松弛的担心。一位教授在报纸上发表研究成果指出，"榻榻米"散发出的草的芳香对人体也有益。

此外，日本人对榻榻米垫的布置方式和数量也极其认真，认为这关系到自己的运气。比如，很少布置成格子的形式，数量上通常是 5.5 块组成。

Tatami **mats** are a traditional form of **flooring** found in Japanese homes and have been deeply rooted in the Japanese culture from the 12th century. During the 12th century, Tatami mats were luxury goods used by emperors, **nobles**, religious leaders and other **high-ranking** officials. It is said that Tatami varied in **thickness** and size, the fabric used on the **edges** were made of different colors and showed the rank of the individual household that owned it. Usage by the upper-class continued until the 17th century, when Tatami found their way into the homes of ordinary people.

Simple straw mats for sleeping **preceded** Tatami. **In a quest for** comfort, these simple grass mats were made gradually thicker and Tatami evolved. In the 15th and 16th centu-

♦ **mat** [mæt]
n. 垫子，席子
Wipe your feet on the mat before you come in, please. 请在垫子上擦擦脚再进来。

♦ **flooring** [ˈflɔːrɪŋ]
n. 地板，铺地板的材料
Stick down any loose bits of flooring, please. 请把松动的地板块都粘好。

♦ **noble** [ˈnəʊbl]
n. (旧时的) 贵族

♦ **high-ranking**
adj. 高级的，职位高的
Several high-ranking diplomats were found to be hand in glove with enemy agents. 有几个高级外交官被发现与敌方人员勾结。

♦ **thickness** [ˈθɪknɪs]
n. 厚度

♦ **edge** [edʒ]
n. 边，边缘
The standard of living today is on the edge of subsistence. 现在的生活水平几乎快要无法维持生计。

♦ **precede** [prɪ(ː)ˈsiːd]
vt. 在……之前发生或出现，先于
Agricultural development simply must precede economic development. 农业的发展必须在整个经济发展中处于领先地位。

♦ **in a quest for** 追求

ries, people began to use them as a form of flooring for the first time, which marked an **evolution** in Japanese people's way of life and giving birth to Japan's unique Tatami culture.

Tatami mats also have health benefits. The tatami's straw inner-core is pressed tight and has lots of air pockets. This makes it very effective at **absorbing** heat. According to studies by Japanese scholars, a Tatami mat can also absorb approximately 500cc of water from the air. When the atmosphere is dry, the water will naturally **evaporate**. Tatami is made of soft reed which according to traditional Chinese medicine calms the spirit. The natural smell relaxes the body and **soothes** the mind.

When laying on the Tatami mats, one has to pay attention to certain rules because the number and layout of tatami mats can bring good or bad fortune. Tatami mats shouldn't be laid in a **grid** pattern, as it will bring bad luck. The only time a grid layout can be used is during mourning. Many shops used to be designed to be the size of "five and half tatami mats," as this will ensure you have good fortune no matter what kind of business you are in.

Man will suffer many disappointments in his quest for truth. 人类在探索真理过程中必然会遭受挫折。
♦ **evolution** [ˌiːvəˈluːʃən]
n. 进化，演变
In the course of evolution, some birds have lost the power of flight. 在进化的过程中，一些鸟丧失了飞行能力。
♦ **absorb** [əbˈsɔːb]
vt. 吸收（光、热等能量）
The material can absorb outward-going radiation from the Earth. 该物质可以吸收地球向外辐射的能量。
♦ **evaporate** [ɪˈvæpəreɪt]
vi.（气体、液体等）发散，蒸发，挥发
While water evaporate, a large amount of heat is absorbed. 水蒸发会大量吸热。
♦ **soothe** [suːθ]
vt. 使平静，安慰
I've managed to soothe him down a bit. 我想方设法使他平静了一点。
♦ **grid** [grɪd]
n. 格子

03 Geta: A Cultural Symbol of Japanese
木屐：日本文化符号

木屐是日本的传统木制凉拖，夏天时跟和服相搭配而穿。在日本，不分老少，都可以穿。在大城市里，木屐则更常见于节日期间，此时，道路上一般禁止行车。

据说，日本的木屐多达50种。其中，口碑最好的当属泡桐木屐，这种木材的轻快、结实，而又不失弹性，穿起来也自然是最舒服的。

传统上，木屐常见于餐馆中。厨师们穿着木屐，可以使脚板离开地板，这样可以在冬天防寒，也可以抵御潮湿的地板。厨师们通常会穿一辈子木屐，就跟他自己用过的道具一样。木屐的绳系穿坏了可以换掉，而一个鞋板可以穿上几十年。

♦ **sandal** [ˈsændl]
n. 草带鞋，凉鞋
♦ **ban** [bɑːn]
vt. 禁止
Top supermarkets are to ban many genetically modified foods. 大品牌超市即将下架许多转基因食品。
♦ **footwear** [ˈfʊtweə(r)]
n.（总称）鞋类
♦ **in accordance to** 依照，根据
In accordance to your request, I am sending you sample pages of the dictionary. 根据你的要求，现寄上词典的样张。

Geta are Japanese wooden **sandals** that are worn with kimonos or yukattas during the summer. Attached to feet with a fabric thong, the sandals are an essential element of traditional Japanese dress.

These wooden shoes are known as geta. They are worn by Japanese people of all ages. In cities like Kyoto, geta are most commonly seen during festivals like the Gion Matsuri. For three evenings, July 14th, 15th and 16th, traffic is **banned** from the city center and turned over to pedestrians. During this period, it is still fashionable for young people to wear summer yukatas and of course the appropriate wooden **footwear**.

Itochu is a retailer in the city center that has been supplying Kyoto's residents with geta for over a century. Craftsmen continue to work at both the back and front of the shop, fitting the fabric thongs to the wooden platform **in accordance to** the size of the customer's feet.

In the past there were said to be as many as 50 different styles of geta. The best geta are normally made from paulownia wood. It is light, strong and has a **flexibility** that means that sandals made of paulownia are comfortable to wear.

Traditionally taka or high geta have been used in restaurants. One reason for their height was to raise the chef's lower body from the kitchen floor to protect against the cold during winter. The height also protects the chef's feet from getting wet because their kitchen floors are normally **damp**.

There is another reason for the design that is perhaps less obvious. **Veteran** chef Kurisu Masahiro explains that the height of the wooden **slats**, known as teeth, that **elevate** the platform of the geta from the ground, is **adjusted** according to the height of each chef.

Similar to a set of knives, geta are tools that a chef will use for much of his working life. As Kurisu explains, the slats in the geta like the fabric thongs can be replaced when they **wear down**, but the platform can last for decades.

♦ **flexibility** [ˌfleksəˈbɪlɪtɪ]
n. 柔韧性，灵活性
The flexibility of a man's muscles will lessen as he becomes old. 人老了肌肉的柔韧性将降低。

♦ **damp** [dæmp]
adj. 微湿的，潮湿的
Things are cooler and more damp as we descend to the cellar. 当我们往下走到地窖时，四周愈见阴冷潮湿。

♦ **veteran** [ˈvetərən]
adj. 资深的，经验丰富的
He is a veteran parliamentarian whose views enjoy widespread respect. 他是个资深议员，其观点受到广泛尊重。

♦ **slat** [slæt]
n. 板条，狭板

♦ **elevate** [ˈelɪveɪt]
vt. 提高，提升
He used a couple of bolsters to elevate his head. 他用两个垫枕垫头。

♦ **adjust** [əˈdʒʌst]
vt. 调整
To attract investors, Panama has adjusted its tax and labour laws. 为吸引投资者，巴拿马调整了税法和劳动法。

♦ **wear down**
磨平，穿坏；磨损，损耗
His heels always wear down on the outside first. 他的鞋跟总是先从外侧磨损。

04 Sake: Japan's National Wine
清酒：日本国酒

当提及日本的饮料时，首先进入人们脑海的一定是清酒。清酒是日本的国酒，也是象征日本的文化符号。在各种典礼以及宗教仪式上都会使用清酒，一般盛在方形木杯中。

清酒源于公元八世纪的奈良时代，十世纪时被牧师用于宗教仪式，之后有记录表明，当时的发酵步骤已经实现标准化，各种原料成分分三步添加。如今，每年的10月1日，是日本的清酒节。

日本的清酒其实也有很多种。由于清酒的味道受到众多因素的影响，比如，不同的水源、大米的品质等，不同地区的清酒风味迥异。日本清酒的酒精度一般在15%以上，比西方大部分葡萄酒的酒精度要高。

Sake is Japan's national drink, and a symbol of Japanese culture. It's used in ceremonies, served in **square** wooden cups, and in religious services. It's the first drink that **comes to mind** when people around the world think of Japan.

Sake is also becoming a favorite **alcoholic beverage** worldwide, right alongside fine wines and classic spirits. It's increasingly common to find sake outside of sushi restaurants, and used as the main ingredient in some cocktails.

Sake is commonly known as "rice wine" but it's actually made more like beer, with **polished rice**, its main ingredient, brewed through a process that turns the starch (rice) into sugar, which is fermented with the addition of koji, a moldy form of fermented rice.

There isn't a **precise** origin for sake in Japanese history, though sake was being brewed by the Nara period in the 8th century. Because sake was used in religious ceremonies, it was brewed by priests attached to shrines and temples by the 10th century. Records of the era show that the fermentation process had been standardized by then, with ingredients being added in three stages. The process is still the same today.

When Japan opened up following two centuries of **isolation** in the mid-1800s, the government **loosened** rules

♦ **square** [skweə]
adj. 方的，正方形的
Click the square icon again to minimize the window. 再次点击正方形图标，把窗口最小化。

♦ **come to mind** 想起，想到
Other means of solving the problem haven't come to his mind. 他还没有想到解决这一问题的其他方法。

♦ **alcoholic beverage** 酒精饮料

♦ **polished rice** 精米，精白米

♦ **precise** [prɪˈsaɪs]
adj. 清晰的，明确的
You appreciate the ability of the human mind to develop clear and precise understanding of nature. 你认为人类必须具有正确、清晰的认识大自然的能力。

♦ **isolation** [ˌaɪsəʊˈleɪʃən]
n. 孤立，孤立状态
We must on no account view problems superficially and in isolation. 我们绝不能表面地、孤立地看问题。

♦ **loosen** [ˈluːsn] vt. 放宽，放松
There is no sign that the Party will loosen its tight grip on the country. 没有迹象显示该党会放松对国家的

on sake breweries and tens of thousands of sake **breweries** were established. Today there are fewer than 2,000 sake breweries. The Japanese government established a research institute for sake in 1904 and has held a sake contest since 1907. The country honors the drink on Sake Day every October 1, to **coincide** with the rice harvest.

As for types of sake, each region of the country has its distinctive sake styles, because so many elements can **affect** the flavor of the finished product, such as the kind of water, the quality of rice harvest, how much each grain of rice is polished before it's used to make sake, and the characteristics of the fermented starter, Koji.

The type of **yeast** in the mix affects the flavor of the resulting sake, which could range from **fruity** to strongly alcoholic. Sakes in general have a higher alcoholic content, at 15% or more, than most Western grape wines. Many people still think of sake as an alcoholic drink that's good for cooking or served with Japanese food heated in ceramic bottles.

严密控制。

♦ **brewery** [ˈbruːərɪ]
n. 酿造厂，酿酒厂
The beer is brewed in the time-honoured way at the Castle Eden Brewery. 伊登堡酿酒厂以传统酿制方式酿造啤酒。

♦ **coincide** [ˌkəʊɪnˈsaɪd]
vi. 巧合，同时发生；与……一致
He happened to coincide with you on this point. 在这一问题上，他与你不谋而合。

♦ **affect** [əˈfekt] vt. 影响
The contract will affect our national prestige in the world. 这一合同将会影响我国的国际声望。

♦ **yeast** [jiːst]
n. 酵母（粉、饼、片）

♦ **fruity** [ˈfruːtɪ]
adj. 有果味的，果香的
This red wine is soft and fruity. 这种红葡萄酒不含酒精而且果味浓。

05 Origami: The Ancient Art of Japanese Paper Folding
传承千年的日本折纸艺术

折纸一般都认为是源自于中国。但真正把折纸艺术发扬光大的却是日本人。最初，折纸在日本是用于祭祀方面。及至造纸普及化后才盛行于民间。而大约于十九世纪初，日本才正式出现了第一本有文字记载及以图示方式教导的折纸书籍。日本人一向把折纸视为他们的国粹之一。而折纸更是全国小学的必修科目。他们认为除了可保存固有的文化外，通过折纸可启发儿童的创造力和逻辑思维，更可促进手脑的协调。

与一般纸类艺术不同，日本折纸艺术并不需要教材、粘贴等步骤，仅仅通过折叠便能做出各种精巧的艺术品。如今，折纸已经走向世界，演化成富有创意的消遣活动。不仅如此，折纸还越来越受到数学家、工程师、科学家等等的关注，折纸艺术正在焕发出无限的光彩。

♦ **puzzle** [ˈpʌzl]
n. 智力玩具，智力测验
Here is a very simple puzzle about money. 这里有一道很简单的关于算钱的智力测验题。

♦ **marvel at**
对……惊奇，惊叹
In retrospect I cannot but marvel at the extent of my naivety and ignorance then. 回首过去，我无法不对自己当时表现出的幼稚和无知程度感到惊讶。

♦ **ingenious** [ɪnˈdʒiːnjəs]
adj. 精巧的，灵巧的，巧妙的
The director used ingenious devices to keep the audience in suspense. 导演用

Origami is the ancient art of Japanese paper folding, an art form spanning over 1,000 years. A folk art, a creative art, a mathematical **puzzle**, a game–all of these terms describe origami. Some people are attracted to origami for its simplicity while others **marvel at** the minds of people who can devise the patterns for such **ingenious** creations. Some look to origami as a way to entertain, while others find it has a calming, relaxing effect.

Origami is unique among paper crafts in that it requires no materials **other than** the paper itself. Cutting, gluing, or drawing on the paper is avoided, using only paper folding to create the desired result. No special skills or **artistic** talent are needed for origami, although a good amount of patience and **perseverance** are very helpful. Models can be folded by following instructions exactly. Experimenting with different folds may lead to a totally new, original paper-fold.

The word "origami" comes from the Japanese language. "Ori" means folded and "kami" means paper. Paper-folding as a traditional folding art **pervaded** the Japanese culture more strongly than any other. But traditional paper-folding did not exist in Japan alone.

Papermaking was developed in China two thousand years ago but the Chinese did not readily share this knowledge. It **eventually** traveled to Korea and then Japan by the seventh century. This "trade secret" then spread in the direction of the **Arab** world, reaching Spain by the twelfth century.

Origami was first practiced in the Japanese **imperial** Court, where it was considered an amusing and elegant way of passing the time. Over the centuries the skill has been passed down to ordinary people, who took it up with enthusiasm and made it into the folk art that it is today.

Today in Japan the art of paper-folding is as widely practiced by children, parents and grandparents as it was centuries ago. And for a number of years now origami has been **immensely** popular here in the western world.

巧妙手法引起观众的悬念。

♦ **other than** 除了
You can't get there other than by boat. 你只能坐船去那里。

♦ **artistic** [ɑːˈtɪstɪk]
adj. 艺术的，（尤指）有美术才能的
The picture on this screen is a good artistic work. 这屏风上的画是件很好的艺术品。

♦ **perseverance** [ˌpɜːsɪˈvɪərəns]
n. 毅力，坚持不懈，坚定不移
They showed great perseverance in the face of difficulty. 他们面对困难时表现出了顽强的意志。

♦ **pervade** [pə(ː)ˈveɪd]
vt. 遍及，弥漫，充满
Science and technology have come to pervade every aspect of our lives. 科学和技术已经渗透到我们生活的每一个方面。

♦ **eventually** [ɪˈventjʊəlɪ]
adv. 最终，终于
Eventually, you'll learn to cry that on the inside. 终有一天，你会学会让泪往心里流。

♦ **Arab** [ˈærəb]
adj. 阿拉伯的
An old Arab proverb says, "The enemy of my enemy is my friend". 一句古老的阿拉伯谚语说，"敌人的敌人是朋友。"

♦ **imperial** [ɪmˈpɪərɪəl]
adj. 皇家的，皇帝的
It used to be a private garden of the imperial family. 它曾是皇家的私人花园。

♦ **immensely** [ɪˈmenslɪ]
adv. 非常，很；极大地
From the back room he brought an immensely old young man. 他从里屋领出一个非常老成的年轻人。

♦ **manipulate** [məˈnɪpjʊleɪt]
vt. 操作，处理；巧妙地控制
The technology uses a pen to manipu-

During this journey, did simple paper-folding spread with the knowledge of papermaking? Or did each country independently discover that paper could not only be written and drawn on, but **manipulated** into forms? Despite the fact that some traditional models from different paper-folding traditions are similar, most people believe that each tradition developed its own paper-folding ideas.

Today, origami is an international creative pastime. Building upon the basics of the traditional designs, many folders follow the creative path of leaders such as Master Akira Yoshizawa and philosopher Miguel de Unanmuno, devising their own new designs. The **repertoire** of a couple hundred traditional folds in the beginning of the twentieth century has grown to over tens of thousands now with endless number yet to be discovered.

Originally considered a child's activity origami now attracts the interest of mathematicians, engineers, scientists, computer programmers, college professors and professional artists. It is an art form than can be practiced by **preschoolers** to senior citizens, those who are **hospitalized**, **handicapped**, or blind, those who wish to share a craft with a group of friends, and those who wish to explore the infinite possibilities of paper-folding.

late a computer. 这项技术使用一支笔来操作电脑。

♦ **repertoire** ['repətwɑ:]
n. 全部技能（或才能）

♦ **preschooler** [ˌpri:'sku:lə]
n. 学龄前儿童

♦ **hospitalize** ['hɒspɪtəlaɪz]
vt. 送……住院（治疗），使留医
We must also move, evacuate, and hospitalize personnel. 我们还必须对人员进行运送、撤离和治疗。

♦ **handicapped** ['hændɪkæpt]
adj. 残疾的，有生理缺陷的

06 The Traditional Inns of Charm
日本传统旅店

Ryokan 作为日本传统的旅店，从江户时代开始至今，建筑风格、房间布置、温泉和花园等一切配置原封不动的保存和传承下来。日本 Ryokan 种类繁多，价格各异，遍布全国，从偏远的小村落到东京这样的繁华大都市，主要集中在各种度假村。

Ryokan 一般都提供各种服务，性价比也很高。比如，旅店会指定专门的随侍人员招待客人，帮忙登记入住，点餐上茶等，解决各种问题。Ryokan 还有让你舒服到家的温泉服务，饮食和娱乐具备，昼夜不歇，令人留恋。

Ryokan are traditional Japanese **inns** that haven't changed much since the Edo-era. Everything is traditional at

♦ **inn** [ɪn]
n. 小旅馆，客栈
Darkness of evening was crowding in when we arrived at the inn. 我们到达小旅馆时天色正在暗下来。

♦ **onsen**
n. 温泉（词源源于日本语）

♦ **charm** [tʃɑ:m]
n. 魔力，魅力
This old town has a charm you couldn't find in a big city. 这个古镇有大城市找不到的魅力。

♦ **shogun** ['ʃəʊˌgu:n]
n. （日本幕府的）将军
Tokugawa shogun 德川幕府

a Ryokan including the building, garden, rooms, bedding, **onsen**, food and clothing. It's like traveling in time to experience the **charm** of old Japan.

In 1603, a warlord named Tokugawa Ieyasu became **shogun** of Japan after winning a series of battles. This began the long reign of a line of Tokugawa shogun that we know now as the Edo-era (1603–1868). Prior to 1603, Japan had been at civil war for centuries (off and on). The Edo-era was the first long period of **domestic** peace in Japan. It made domestic travel safe for the first time in Japanese history. Japanese people began to travel and discover their country. The Ryokan was born.

There are a great variety of ryokan. Some are small family-run establishments while others are massive resorts. Ryokan also vary by price. Ryokan can be **amongst** the most expensive hotels in the world. Others attract budget travelers with low rates. Ryokan prices are always per-person per-night. Prices (usually) include an elaborate breakfast and dinner. Rooms can (normally) **accommodate** 4 people. Prices are cheaper when 4 people share a room (as opposed to 2). Most Ryokan don't accept a single **occupancy** booking.

Ryokan are found anywhere in Japan, from **tiny** remote villages to Tokyo. The vast majority of ryokan are located in resort areas such as Hakone. Even small, remote Japanese villages often have a Ryokan. Such Ryokan may **double as** the owner's family home.

Ryokan generally offer a level of service you couldn't expect at a comparably priced hotel. Good Ryokan assign a single attendant to you. Your attendant will be there to greet you, **check you in**, show you your room, bring your tea, help you with problems, bring your meals, etc. Ryokan (sometimes) serve your meals in your room. Breakfast is Japanese style and dinner is an elaborate **kaiseki** feast. In many cases, the dinner alone is worth the cost of your stay. Meals are scheduled for a particular time (the Ryokan will **confirm** times with you). If you're running late you should inform the Ryokan.

♦ **domestic** [dəˈmestɪk]
adj. 国内的；家庭的
Their new car is a domestic make. 他们的新车是国产的。

♦ **amongst** [əˈmʌŋst]
prep.（表示范围）在……之内；（表示位置）处在……中
He was sitting amongst a group of children, telling them a story. 他正坐在一群孩子中间讲故事。

♦ **accommodate** [əˈkɒmədeɪt]
vt. 容纳，向……提供住处
I guess this hall to accommodate 1,000 persons.
我猜这个大厅能容纳 1000 人。

♦ **occupancy** [ˈɒkjʊpənsɪ]
n. 居住，入住
During her occupancy the garden was transformed. 在她居住期间花园改观了。

♦ **tiny** [ˈtaɪnɪ]
adj. 极小的，微小的
The goldfish swam round and round in their tiny bowls. 金鱼在小小的鱼缸里一圈圈地游来游去。

♦ **double as**
兼扮（某个）角色
She doubled as the maid and the secretary in the play. 她在这出剧里兼饰女佣和秘书。

♦ **check in** （在旅馆）登记入住
I'll ring the hotel, telling them we'll check in tomorrow. 我来给旅馆打电话，通知他们我们明天入住。

♦ **kaiseki**
怀石料理，日本怀石料理是日本最悠久的传统料理之一，"不以香气诱人，更以神思为境"，更加体现了日本料理的美轮美奂。相传怀石来自于禅道：为了在长久听禅中抵制饥饿，肚子抱石一块，称为"怀石"；后来就有了给听禅僧人的茶点，再后来有了最负盛名的怀石料理。

Ryokan almost always have an onsen. The onsen is usually separated by gender. Onsen may be indoors, outdoors or both. Many ryokan guests choose to stay at the ryokan all day and night enjoying the onsen, meals and relaxing in common areas or in their room. Large ryokan may offer bars, cafes, games rooms and karaoke. Smaller Ryokan may have none of these things. At very least they're likely to have a beer vending machine. Guests commonly enjoy snacks and drinks in their room throughout the day and night.

07 Japan's Four Great Gates
日本四大鸟居

　　日本的鸟居是一种类似于中国牌坊的日式建筑，常设于通向神社的大道上或神社周围的木栅栏处。主要用以区分神域与人类所居住的世俗界，类似一种结界，代表神域的入口，可以将它视为一种"门"。

　　鸟居的地理位置不一，有的伫立于悬崖之巅，有的建造于湖水中央，但是都会给人一种审美愉悦，自有令人着迷之处。日本的神社就有 9 000 多处，而每一处都至少建有一座鸟居。所以，毫不夸张地说，日本的鸟居成千上万，数不胜数。而这其中，最为著名的有四座——严岛神社的浮动鸟居以及伏见稻荷神社、箱根神社和明治神宫的鸟居。

Torii are gates mark the entrance to Shinto shrines. Passing through a torii represents the transition from the world to a sacred place. They are also placed on the tops of cliffs, in the middle of lakes, in the ocean and anywhere else where they are aesthetically **pleasing**. There is something **enchanting** about a well placed torii.

It's no stretch to **estimate** that there are hundreds of thousands of torii in Japan. There are over 90,000 shrines in Japan each with **at least** one torii. The following are the best known torii gates in the country.

1. Floating Torii of Itsukushima Shrine–The Floating Torii of Itsukushima Shrine on Miyajima Island is one of Japan's

♦ **confirm** [kən'fɜːm]
vt. 确认
The hotel confirmed our reservations by telegram. 旅馆给我们来电确认所订膳宿不作变动。

♦ **torii** ['tɔriː]
n.（日本神社门前的）牌坊，鸟居

♦ **pleasing** ['pliːzɪŋ]
adj. 令人愉快的，满意的，舒适的
Such a view is pleasing. 这样的景色令人心旷神怡。

♦ **enchanting** [ɪn'tʃɑːntɪŋ]
adj. 迷人的
She has the most enchanting smile. 她有着最迷人的微笑。

♦ **estimate** ['estɪmeɪt]
vt. 估计，估算
I estimate that the total cost for treatment will be $12,500. 我估计治疗费用总共会有 12 500 美元。

♦ **at least** 至少
I had other matters to occupy me, during the day at least. 至少白天我还有别的事情要做。

♦ **iconic** [aɪ'kɒnɪk]
adj. 标志性的

♦ **shallow** ['ʃæləʊ]
adj. 浅的；肤浅的
The evening news is often criticized for being shallow. 晚间新闻常因其内容肤浅而受到批评。

♦ **floating** ['fləʊtɪŋ] adj. 漂浮的
Some leaves were floating around

most **iconic** sights. It is also one of Japan's oldest torii (although it has been destroyed and reconstructed many times).

The torii is placed in a **shallow** bit of ocean for the appearance that it's **floating**. It looks **dramatically** different depending on the tide and light. As a result, the torii has **yielded** some of the best known photographs ever taken of Japan.

2. Fushimi Inari Shrine–Fushimi Inari Shrine is the luckiest place in Kyoto. It's dedicated to Inari, the goddess of business, rice and other important stuff.

Business people from all over the Kansai region come to Fushimi Inari to pray for worldly success. Those who are successful, donate a torii to the shrine. It's not cheap.

In return they may win the favor of Inari. They also get to engrave their name (or business name) into the torii. The shrine has collected thousands of torii. It's quite a **stunning** sight.

3. Hakone Shrine–Hakone Shrine's torii in Lake Ashinoko sits in a deep old growth forest. On a clear day Mount Fuji **pops out** of the clouds behind the torii. Lake Ashinoko is a volcanic **crater** lake that always seems to be a different color.

4. Meiji Shrine–Meiji Shrine is an Imperial shrine with an imperial sized wooden torii. If you look at the top of the torii, it's **stamped** with the Chrysanthemum Seal (the seal of the Emperor of Japan). Amongst shrines, a stamp from the Emperor is the ultimate status.

on the still lake. 树叶飘落在平静的湖面上。

♦ **dramatically** [drəˈmætɪkəli]
adv. 极其，极大地
Tourist numbers from across the pond have dropped dramatically. 来自大西洋彼岸的游客数量已急剧减少。

♦ **yield** [jiːld]
vt. 产出，带来
It yielded a profit of at least $36 million. 它带来了至少3 600万美元的收益。

♦ **in return** 作为报答；反过来
I wish I could do something in return for the kindness I have received from him. 我希望我能做点什么事来酬谢他。

♦ **stunning** [ˈstʌnɪŋ]
adj. 令人震惊的，惊人的
The audience was awed into silence by her stunning performance. 观众席上鸦雀无声，人们对他出色的表演感到惊叹。

♦ **pop out** 突出
The surprise made her eyes pop out. 惊讶使她瞪大了眼睛。

♦ **crater** [ˈkreɪtə]
n. 火山口

♦ **stamp** [stæmp]
vt. 刻上……的印记/图章，标记
Please stamp a center mark. 请打一个中心标记。

08 Japanese Cruising in Yakatabune
屋形船中的日式巡游

"屋形船"是日本传统的游船，其历史可以上溯到江户时代。这种船带有顶篷，样子让人不禁会联想起古代的日本，可在河上或海上游览。通常人们会整艘船包下来作为宴会场所，不过也有跟其他客人"合乘"的情况。经营屋形船的设施就叫做"船宿"。船宿会提供很多方案，可以选择不同的游览路线以及饮食的种类。游览时间通常为2~3小时。

乘船游览这种娱乐方式在日本自古就有。7~8世纪的贵族们，据说会乘着画舫，极目远眺，吟咏诗歌，演奏乐器以愉悦身心。再后来出现了装饰俭朴的屋形船，平民百姓也能够乘船游玩了。这就是现在屋形船的原型。

船上设施因船而异，大多数屋形船上都配有冷气和暖气，并设有厕所。船内铺有榻榻米。有的船会为客人准备坐垫，而另一些船上则是日式地坑，相当于坐在凳子上。

屋形船大多选择在晚上出船，但也有在白天出船的。白天看到的景色别有一番风味。乘船在河上或海上游览，能欣赏到不同于平日的景色。尤其是在乘船的同时还可以享受美食的游船方案，非常受人们欢迎。客人可以在船上享用午餐，甚至可以一边欣赏夕阳或夜景一边享用晚餐。

在船中可以感受不同的季节：春天可以欣赏盛开的樱花，夏天可以看烟花，秋天可以赏月，冬天可以看雪。特别是放烟花的日子，屋形船格外火爆。

The "yakatabune" is a traditional **cruising** boat that has been used continuously since the Edo period. Yakatabune have a roof and a style **distinctive** of old Japan. They are a wonderful way to go sightseeing by river or sea. Yakatabune are normally **rented out** for parties, but "noriai" is sometimes available where you can ride with other passengers. Places that manage yakatabune are called "funayado". Funayado offer many different sightseeing courses and dining plans. Cruising normally lasts 2 to 3 hours.

Sightseeing cruises have a long history in Japan. In the 7th and 8th centuries, Japanese **nobility** would ride on decorated boats, read poems, and perform music while enjoying the **scenery**. During the Edo period, rich **samurai** and merchants would compete in making **lavish** yakatabune, and would use them for sightseeing and dining. These lavish lifestyles were then **outlawed**, and extravagant yakatabune disappeared. After this, very basic yakatabune were **constructed** and commoners were able to enjoy cruising. Contemporary yakatabune developed during this time.

As for the Yakatabune Amenities, it depends on the boat,

♦ **cruising** [ˈkruːzɪŋ]
n. 巡航，巡游
They will go cruising in the Mediterranean. 他们将在地中海上巡游。

♦ **distinctive** [dɪsˈtɪŋktɪv]
adj. 有特色的，独特的
Chopsticks, or keizai, are the most distinctive eating tool at the Chinese dining table. 筷子是中餐桌上最有特色的用餐工具。

♦ **rent out** 租出，出租
She decided to rent out a room to get extra income. 她为获得额外收入决定租出一个房间。

♦ **nobility** [nəʊˈbɪlɪti]
n. 贵族（阶级）
Families from these upper classes became the nobility or aristocracy. 这些来自上流社会的家族后来就成了贵族阶级。

♦ **scenery** [ˈsiːnəri]
n. 风景，景色
Sometimes they just drive slowly down the lane enjoying the scenery. 有时他们只是沿着小路慢慢地开车，欣赏两旁的风景。

♦ **samurai** [ˈsæmʊraɪ]
n. 武士，日本的10到19世纪的一个特殊社会阶级，他们一般通晓武艺、以战斗为职业，忠于所效力的封建领主。直到明治维新，武士都是统治日本社会的支配力量，武士的精神被称为"武士道"（Bushido）。

♦ **lavish** [ˈlævɪʃ]
adj. 奢华的，铺张的
They lived a very lavish lifestyle. 他们过着挥霍无度的生活。

♦ **outlaw** [ˈaʊtlɔː]
vt. 宣布……为不合法
To outlaw deficits is a pie in the sky. 宣告赤字非法是空想。

♦ **construct** [kənˈstrʌkt]
vt. 修建，建造
It is proverbially easier to destroy

but many yakatabune have air conditioning and a bathroom. Straw tatami mats are laid out on the floor of the boat. Some boats offer you zabuton **cushions** to sit on, while others have "horigotatsu", which are holes in the floor where you put your legs so you can **sit up** like sitting on a chair.

Most yakatabune **set out** in the evening, but some yakatabune are available in the afternoon. Afternoon cruising offers different scenic views than those at night. Getting on a boat and cruising on a river or sea offers some excellent views you wouldn't normally get to enjoy. Plans where you can drink and eat while cruising are especially popular. In addition to lunch cruises, there are also dinner cruises where you can enjoy the evening and **nighttime** sights.

Enjoy the seasons–spring, with the blossoming cherry trees; summer, with **fireworks** displays; autumn, with beautiful views of the moon; and winter, with beautiful white snow–all of the seasons can be enjoyed while riding on a yakatabune. Yakatabune are especially popular on days when there are fireworks displays scheduled.

than to construct. 谁都知道破坏容易建设难。
♦ **cushion** ['kʊʃən]
n. 垫子，坐垫
♦ **sit up** 端坐，坐起来
The patient was but poorly able to sit up. 病人仅能勉强坐起来。
♦ **set out** 动身，出发
They set out in a westerly direction along the riverbank. 他们沿着河岸向西出发了。
♦ **nighttime** ['naɪttaɪm]
adj. 夜晚的，夜间（发生）的 如：The nighttime air was comfortably cool. 夜晚的空气清新宜人。
♦ **firework** ['faɪəwə:k]
n. （常用 pl.）烟火，烟花
On the stroke of 12, fireworks suddenly exploded into the night. 12:00 的钟声刚敲响，焰火便在夜空中绽放。

09 A Kingdom of Cats
日本：猫的王国

猫是日本民族最喜爱的宠物，在日本人心目中有着特殊的地位。日本人喜欢借助猫来表达自己的感受，在长期的生活中逐渐形成了独树一帜的猫文化。从关于猫的很多传说故事、文学作品中可以看出猫文化的发展及日本人独特的爱猫情结。

1974 年日本艺术家新太郎根据日本短尾猫设计了 Kitty 猫，如今风靡全球。据说能给人带来好运的招财猫，在商店、寺庙中处处都有它的踪影。在东京、大阪和京都等大城市，猫咖啡馆已遍地开花。猫咪咖啡馆是主要以猫咪为主题的咖啡馆。在猫咪咖啡馆里，猫咪是主体。是否拥有金钱，拥有权力对它们来说都不重要，所有人都是平等的。在这里，喝咖啡是其次，最主要的是跟猫咪一起玩耍能缓解压力和孤独。

日本的国土空间虽然狭小，却完全阻挡不了人们对猫的喜爱，人们想尽各种方法"与猫共舞"。在日本国民的关照下，八百万"猫咪军团"可以无忧无虑地过着舒服的生活。

From Hello Kitty designed in 1974 by Japanese artist, Yuko Shimizu, representing the Japanese **bobtail cat**, to Maneki-neko, the beckoning cat that's considered to be a **talisman** or good luck charm, the Japanese love their cats. Because of their easy **maintenance** and ability to thrive in small areas such as apartments, cats are especially popular in Japan. Cats are found everywhere in Japan including cat cafes, where **patrons** pay a fee for the enjoyment of spending time with the **felines**.

Maneki-neko Cats–Maneki-neko, which means "beckoning cat" in Japanese is considered to be a lucky charm or talisman and have **protective** powers. It's often referred to as the happy cat, lucky, welcoming, or fortune cat in English. Maneki-neko was first developed during the Edo period in Japan although the exact origin is unknown. It comes in various colors with some having an electric or battery operated paw action. Along with being found as figurines it's also available as banks, key chains, ornaments, plant **pots**, and more.

Cat Cafes–In Osaka, Japan, many apartment buildings don't allow pets, so cat lovers are forced to get their "kitty fix" someplace else. Enter the Cat's Time Cafe where customers pay a fee to get time to spend time with their favorite feline. The first cat cafe opened in 2004 in Osaka, giving Japanese cat lovers the opportunity to satisfy their cravings for kitty **affection** while enjoying a cup of tea, coffee, or snacks. To ensure cleanliness and safety of the cats, the interactions are closely **monitored** with hand **sanitizing** required, as well as gentle handling of the cats. The cost of visiting with the kitties is approximately $10 an hour and brings joy to both humans and animals. The humans receive **soothing** companionship and the cats get plenty of love and attention so it's a **win-win** all the way around.

Japanese people love cats, but because of space limitations and strict no-pet policies in most apartments many are unable to own one. But that doesn't mean they can't **hang**

♦ **bobtail cat**
短尾猫，日本短尾猫也叫花猫或短尾花猫，是由于基因突变而产生的品种，也是日本土生土长的猫种。日本人认为花猫是幸运的象征，因此有很多家庭饲养。招财猫的样子即来自于日本短尾猫。

♦ **talisman** ['tælɪzmən]
n. 驱邪物；护身符

♦ **maintenance** ['meɪntɪnəns]
n. 维持，保持，此处引申为"饲养"

♦ **patron** ['peɪtrən]
n. 顾客

♦ **feline** ['fiːlaɪn]
n. 猫；猫科动物

♦ **protective** [prə'tektɪv]
adj. 保护的，防护的
Protective gloves reduce the absorption of chemicals through the skin. 防护手套可以减少皮肤对化学物质的吸收。

♦ **pot** [pɒt]
n. 花盆

♦ **affection** [ə'fekʃən]
n. 喜爱
She said goodbye to Hilda with a convincing show of affection. 她和希尔达道别时流露出了明显的爱意。

♦ **monitor** ['mɒnɪtə]
vt. 监督，监控
It would monitor traffic flows and provide feedback to motorists. 它能监控交通状况，然后给司机提供反馈信息。

♦ **sanitize** ['sænɪtaɪz]
vt. 使清洁，进行消毒

♦ **soothing** ['suːθɪŋ]
adj. 使人宽心的，平静的
His soothing words subdued her fears. 他的安慰话减轻了她的恐惧。

♦ **win-win** [wɪn-wɪn]
n. 双赢
This is a win-win situation all around. 这是一个各得其所的局面。

♦ **hang out** 闲逛
We can just hang out and have a good

out with them when the desire strikes. To **compensate for** lack of ownership they just stop by a cat cafe to get their time with kitty. Along with cat cafes there's also a new trend in Japanese architecture with select builders constructing cat friendly **abodes** fit for feline royalty. Sparing no expense, this means the approximately eight million cats that live in Japan no doubt enjoy a very comfortable life.

time. 我们可以只是闲逛一下，开开心。

♦ **compensate** [ˈkɒmpənseɪt]
vi. 弥补，抵补
Nothing can compensate for the loss of a loved one. 失去心爱的人是无法补偿的。

♦ **abode** [əˈbəʊd] n. 住所，公寓
He's of no fixed abode and we found him on the streets. 他居无定所，我们发现他流落街头。

Chapter 3
文化韩国：藏在时光里的繁华

01 Taekwondo: A Martial Art of South Korea
跆拳道：韩国武术

跆拳道，是现代奥运会正式比赛项目之一，是一种主要使用手及脚进行格斗或对抗的运动。跆拳道起源于朝鲜半岛，早期是由朝鲜三国时代的跆跟、花郎道演化而来的。它是国民间普遍流行的一项技击术，被韩国视为国技。"跆拳道"一词，是 1955 年由韩国的崔泓熙将军创造，跆（TAE），意为以脚踢；拳（KWON），以拳头打击；道（DO），则是代表道行、礼仪修炼的艺术。跆拳道是经过东亚文化发展的一项韩国武术，以"始于礼，终于礼"的武道精神为基础。

随着被列为奥运会比赛项目，韩国跆拳道在全世界逐渐流行起来，而且作为一种文化而演化出了多重角色定位。比如，学习跆拳道可以锻炼身体，磨炼耐力，甚至有助于排解压力；跆拳道是一种空手较量的武学艺术，攻守兼备，即便在今天，也可以作为防身的有效手段。

Taekwondo is a martial art form and sport that uses the hands and feet for **attack** and defense. The focus of Taekwondo is on training and **disciplining** the mind along with the body. For those learning the martial art it plays four different roles.

First, Taekwondo as an exercise–Taekwondo is a good exercise for children who are still growing as well as a good way for grown-ups to increase their physical **endurance**. Taekwondo's movements require extensive use of the joints, which increases the **limberness** of one's body. Since there are kicking, jabbing and shouting involved, it's also a great way to relieve stress and get a good **workout**.

Second, Taekwondo as a bare handed martial arts form– Taekwondo learners attack the **opponent** with their bare hands and feet. What sets this apart from other martial arts forms are the powerful and various leg movements involved, and which have enabled it to become a worldwide martial art. Taekwondo's attack is **aggressive**, but at the same time the focus is more on the defense aspect. This can act positively for

---

♦ **attack** [əˈtæk]
n. （队员等的）进攻，攻击

♦ **discipline** [ˈdɪsɪplɪn]
vt. 训练，磨砺
Out on the course you must discipline yourself to let go of detailed theory. 在高尔夫球场上，你必须训练自己做到不拘泥于细枝末节的理论。

♦ **endurance** [ɪnˈdjʊərəns]
n. 忍耐（力），耐久（力）
He showed remarkable endurance throughout his illness. 他在整个生病期间表现出非凡的忍耐力。

♦ **limberness** [ˈlɪmbəz]
n. 柔软，灵活

♦ **workout** [ˈwɜːkaʊt]
n. （体育）锻炼

♦ **opponent** [əˈpəʊnənt]
n. 对手；敌手
The worst thing you can do is underestimate an opponent. 最严重的错误就是低估对手。

♦ **aggressive** [əˈgresɪv]
adj. 进攻性的，攻势的
These fish are very aggressive. 这些鱼极具攻击性。

♦ **category** [ˈkætɪgərɪ]
n. 类型，类别
This book clearly falls into the category of fictionalised autobiography. 这本书很显然属于自传体小说。

those wanting to learn Taekwondo as a way of self defense for practical purposes, even in modern times.

Third, Taekwondo as a sport–Taekwondo is an official competitive **category** in major world sporting events such as the Olympics, Panam Games, Asian Games, All American Games, and South American Games. Competitive Taekwondo involves safety **gear** and set attacks and defenses as to limit the amount of damage possible. This way, competitive martial artists can enjoy the **thrill** of competing with less risk.

Fourth, Taekwondo as an educational method–Taekwondo trains the body, but does as much to develop the mind as well. The objective of learning Taekwondo is to **foster** growth in both areas in order to become a more **mature** human being. Taekwondo learners receive repeated etiquette lessons along with the attack and defense skills to build and strengthen their character.

♦ **gear** [gɪə]
n. （某一特定活动的）设备，装备

♦ **thrill** [θrɪl]
n. 激动人心，兴奋感
His speech caused a thrill among the audience. 他的演说引起了听众的极大兴奋。

♦ **foster** [ˈfɒstə]
vt. 促进，培养
The club's aim is to foster better relations within the community. 俱乐部的宗旨是促进团体内部的关系。

♦ **mature** [məˈtjʊə]
adj.（人、树木、鸟或动物）成熟的
They are emotionally mature and should behave responsibly. 他们在情感上已经成熟，应该负责任地行事。

02 What Is Soju
韩国人的烧酒情结

韩国烧酒是一种酒精饮料。主要的原料是大米，通常还配以小麦、大麦或者甘薯等。韩国烧酒颜色透明，酒精度数一般在 20º—35º 之间不等。现今已知的最早酿造时间是公元 1300 年前后。

韩国烧酒属于清酒类，酒精度数较低，几乎不放香料。特点是入口清新、爽口，刺激性很小，这种特点适合作为烧烤，海鲜生食的配饮。凡是喝过韩国烧酒的人，绝大部分第一次都极不适应，从而放弃再次尝试。但是凡是可以适应韩烧酒的人，都会认为韩烧酒实在可谓是清酒中的极品。

韩国人喝烧酒也有点讲究，最重要的就是那精致的玻璃小酒杯了，用它喝韩烧便有很好的情致。在饮用过程中，也要遵循一些必要的礼节，比如不可以自己给自己倒酒，对长辈要尊敬等。韩国烧酒的价格低廉，在朋友聚会时也是必不可少的。

♦ **distill** [dɪˈstɪl]
vt. 蒸馏，提取
We were asked to distill the crucial points of the book. 我们被要求从这本书中提炼出关键点。

♦ **Mongolian** [mɒŋˈɡəlɪən]
adj. 蒙古的
The plane crashed just after entering Mongolian airspace. 那架飞机刚进入蒙古领空就坠毁了。

♦ **mistakenly** [mɪsˈteɪkənlɪ]
adv. 错误地，被误解地
She accepted that she had acted unwisely and mistakenly. 她承认自己的

Soju is an ancient form of clear alcohol **distilled** from rice and other grains. It was first made in the 1300s in Korea during the **Mongolian** occupation. It remains a popular drink, particularly in South Korea, and is sometimes **mistakenly** called rice wine. In fact, it is quite different from rice wine or sake, since it is not made solely from rice and has a much higher **alcohol content**, about 20%-35% alcohol.

Some compare the taste of soju to vodka, though it tends to have a sweeter finish. The sweetness may come not only from the rice but the addition of grains like wheat, barley and **tapioca**. Soju is usually also sweetened with sugar during the distillation process.

In Korea, soju is served in small shot glasses, or can be used to make mixed drinks. Mixing it with **lemon-lime** sodas is particularly popular among younger Koreans. When consumed in the traditional manner, Koreans have very specific ways of serving and drinking the beverage, and appreciate foreigners who follow these customs.

A few of these rules include never pouring your own glass of soju, and never refilling **a shot glass** with more until it is completely empty. Respect for elders when drinking soju is demonstrated by younger people **turning away** from their elders to drink from their filled glasses, and holding the glass with two hands if a person of superior **stature** is pouring it. Drinkers have the option of either **sipping** soju or taking it in a single shot. Either form is considered polite.

The largest manufacturer of soju is the company Jinro. Doosan is another popular Korean **brand**. The drink is very popular, with several **billion** bottles consumed yearly. A form has also migrated to Japan, where it is called hochu. Koreans, like the Japanese, also are fans of sake, which is known as cheongju.

In South Korea, soju is one of the least expensive types of alcohol to buy, partly **accounting for** its popularity. It also has a **lengthy** history in the Korean culture, and is especially associated with gatherings of friends. Typically, it is consumed in group settings.

举动是不明智和错误的。

♦ **alcohol content**
酒精含量，酒（精）度

♦ **tapioca** [ˌtæpɪˈəʊkə]
n. 木薯

♦ **lemon-lime**
adj. 柠檬味的

♦ **shot glass** 子弹杯

♦ **turn away**
转身，背向；离开；拒绝
A doctor cannot turn away a dying man. 医生是不能见死不救的。

♦ **stature** [ˈstætʃə]
n. 地位，声望
It's a team unrivalled in stature, expertise and credibility. 这个团队的名声、专业技能和信誉都是无可匹敌的。

♦ **sip** [sɪp]
vt. 小口喝，呷，抿
I tried to sip the tea but it was too hot. 我想抿一口茶，可是太烫了。

♦ **brand** [brænd]
n. 品牌，牌子
What is your favourite brand of cigarettes? 你最喜欢哪种牌子的香烟？

♦ **billion** [ˈbɪljən]
n. 十亿

♦ **account for**
导致，是……的原因
Bad weather accounted for the long delay. 糟糕的天气导致了长期的延缓。

♦ **lengthy** [ˈleŋθɪ]
adj. 长的，漫长的；冗长的
After lengthy talks the two sides finally reached a compromise. 双方经过长期的商谈终于达成了妥协。

03 Arirang: A Traditional Korean Song of Joy and Sorrow
《阿里郎》：最熟悉的韩国旋律

广受批评家赞赏的电影导演金基德在获得 2012 韩国大众文化艺术奖的时候演唱了《阿里郎》。他的电影《圣殇》在第 69 届威尼斯电影节中获得金狮奖，在得奖的时候他没有发表获奖感言，仍然是演唱了《阿里郎》。在被问到《阿里郎》对他有着什么意义的时候，金基德称这是表现韩国人的喜悦和悲伤的歌曲。

《阿里郎》始终与韩民族同苦同乐。长期研究阿里郎的金练甲在著作《阿里郎的文化》中称，歌曲阿里郎和电影《阿里郎》均受到日本殖民政府的镇压。日本政府以歌词具有煽动性为由，命令将一部分歌词删除，并没收了 1 万张电影宣传海报。被删除的歌词内容是，"如果我们每次的战斗都是不停的失败，那我们应该点燃火花将世界灭亡。"

但是传单被没收反而引起了大众更多的关注。日本政府甚至启动了骑兵来控制聚在一起的观众。但由于观众人数太多，导致电影院的玻璃窗也碎了，大门也被毁了。而就是因为这个事件，一直以口碑方式流传的"阿里郎"摇身一变成为新民谣和抵抗的象征，并逐渐开始向全国范围扩散。

现在，阿里郎已经成为团结的象征。2000 年悉尼奥运会和 2004 年雅典奥运会的开幕式上，韩朝奥运队代表团联合入场，当时的背景音乐就是阿里郎。2008 年 2 月，纽约交响乐团应朝鲜邀请在平壤进行演出，当时他们就演奏了《阿里郎》。这是韩国战争（1950—1953 年）以后美国的文化团体第一次在朝鲜进行演出，也是第一次有这么大规模的美国人进入朝鲜。

The critically **acclaimed** director Kim Ki-duk sang the Korean folk song Arirang while accepting the 2012 Korea Pop Culture Artist Award, something he had frequently done in the past including the time when he won the Golden Lion award for Best Film for Pieta at the 69th **Venice Film Festival**. Asked what the song means to him, Kim said, "It is an expression of Koreans' joy and sorrow."

Like Kim said, Arirang has shared the pleasures and pains of life in Korea. In The Culture of Arirang, a book by Kim Yeon-gap, the theme song and the movie suffered under the **oppression** of the Japanese colonial government, which

♦ **acclaimed** [əˈkleɪmd]
adj. 广受好评的，赞赏的
♦ **Venice Film Festival**
威尼斯电影节，是每年 8 月至 9 月间于意大利威尼斯利多岛所举办的国际电影节，它与法国的戛纳国际电影节及德国的柏林国际电影节并称为世界三大国际电影节，最高奖项是金狮奖。
♦ **oppression** [əˈpreʃən]
n. 压制，压迫
Wherever there is oppression, there is resistance. 哪里有压迫，哪里就有反抗。
♦ **seditious** [sɪˈdɪʃəs]
adj. 煽动性的
♦ **confiscate** [ˈkɒnfɪskeɪt]
vt. 没收，收缴
No entity or individual shall confiscate or detain any motor vehicle plate. 任何单位和个人不得收缴、扣留机动车号牌。
♦ **flyer** [ˈflaɪə]
n. 传单，海报
♦ **shatter** [ˈʃætə]
vi. 毁灭，粉碎

ordered the omission of certain lyrics due to what was seen as **seditious** and **confiscated** 10,000 advertisement **flyers**. The deleted verse was "if we fail after battle after battle, we shall set a fire and the world will **shatter**."

However, the confiscation stirred so much interest among the public that the mounted police had to be **mobilized** to restore the order. The theater was so packed with viewers that windows were shattered and doors were broken down.

By this stage, Arirang, which was **orally** passed down from generation to generation, became a modern folk song and a symbol of resistance. Then, the song started spreading across the country. "I composed the song," wrote Na in a **memoir**. "My hometown was Hoeryeong on the **border** of Korea and China and when I was a child, they started building a railroad from Cheongjin to Hoeryeong. Laborers from the south sang a sad song with refrains arirang, arirang, arariyo."

"After moving to Seoul, I started **searching for** people who knew the kind of Arirang I heard but my effort was **in vain**. But I could only find Gangwon Arirang from time to time... Even folk music masters did not sing it. So I recalled the melodies and created the lyrics and asked a Dansungsa band to set the song to music."

Since then, Arirang has appeared in various cultural **formats**, though maybe less often as an expression of sorrow. Large groups of cheerleaders for the 2002 FIFA World Cup Korea/Japan sang a version of Arirang by the Yoon Do-hyun Band, regaining heated interest in the song from the general public, especially young people. Olympic champion Kim Yuna skated to the Arirang theme at the 2011 World Figure Skating Championships.

Arirang also became a symbol of harmony. North and South Korean athletes **marched** to Arirang together during the opening ceremonies of the 2000 Sydney and 2004 **Athens** Olympic Games. In February 2008, the New York Philhar-

Such words simply shatter themselves on the hard fact. 这种言论在铁的事实面前碰得粉碎。

♦ **mobilize** [ˈməʊbɪlaɪz]
vt. 动员，使出动
He is trying to mobilize all the supporters. 他正在竭力把所有的支持者动员起来。

♦ **orally** [ˈɔːrəlɪ]
adv. 口头地，口述地
All candidates must first be orally examined. 所有的考生必须先参加口试。

♦ **memoir** [ˈmemwɑː]
n. 回忆录
That volcanologist was busy with memoir after his retirement. 自从退休以后，那位火山学家一直忙于撰写回忆录。

♦ **border** [ˈbɔːdə]
n. 边境，边界
He was never able to get past the border guards. 他从未能够通过边防哨兵的检查。

♦ **search for** 寻找，探寻
His confronting me forced me to search for the answers. 他对我的当面质询迫使我思索如何作答。

♦ **in vain** 没用，徒劳无益
It became obvious that all her complaints were in vain. 很明显她所有的抱怨都是白费口舌。

♦ **format** [ˈfɔːmæt]
n. 格式，版式

♦ **march** [mɑːtʃ]
vi. 前进，行进
The commander waved to the soldiers to march on. 军官挥手叫士兵前进。

♦ **Athens** [ˈæθɪnz]
n. 雅典（希腊首都）

♦ **contingent** [kənˈtɪndʒənt]
n. 代表团
Each nation sent a contingent of athletes to the Olympics. 每个国家都派出了运动员代表团去参加奥运会。

monic played Arirang at the end of their concert in Pyongyang, North Korea, as well. It was the first time an American cultural organization held a concert there, and the largest **contingent** of US citizens to appear since the Korean War (1950–1953).

04 Onggi: Traditional Ceramics in South Korea
韩国传统陶器

今天韩国的陶器，主要延续了朝鲜时代的风格。虽然已经过去了大约 500 年，韩国的陶器不仅生产和制造方式与之前十分相似，而且陶制大型容器的造型和风格也基本没变。多少个世纪过去了，陶制容器仍然是韩国人的居家必备。

在等级分明的古朝鲜时代，制陶工的社会地位十分低下。到了朝鲜王朝时期，随着人口的增加，陶器的使用得到推广，社会开始重视技艺娴熟的制陶大师。到了 19 世纪 70 年代，随着塑料和金属容器的传入，以及蔬菜腌制的减少，许多制陶工们纷纷转行，另谋生路。如今，只有为数不多的大师还坚守着传统的制陶工艺。

The style of pottery **prominent** today has been handed down since the early Joseon era. **Some** 500 years have passed, but production methods, the shape and the style of usage for the large containers all remain largely similar, with records both written and unwritten being kept alive throughout the years. Across the centuries, pottery has remained an essential housekeeping container in many homes.

In the annals of history, however, there is very little about the life of the master potters themselves. During the **class-conscious** Joseon times, pottery craftsmen were generally **disdained** by society **at large** and were treated as **outcasts**.

Originally, potters did not receive much respect for their work. During the later years of the Joseon Dynasty, however, the gradual increase in population lead to a broadening of the uses for pottery. This called for an increase in **artisans** skilled at making pottery.

During the early 20th century and under Japanese occupation, pottery found a place in the modernizing economy and became an industry. There was a great increase in both supply and demand for the large **urns**. Life of the craftsmen,

♦ **prominent** ['prɒmɪnənt]
adj. 重要的，著名的
Each year they compete in a prominent statewide bicycle race. 每年他们都要参加著名的全州自行车大赛。

♦ **some** [sʌm]
adj.（用于数目前）大约的
I have kept birds for some 30 years. 我养鸟大约有 30 年了。

♦ **class-conscious**
adj. 阶级意识强烈的；有强烈社会阶层意识的

♦ **disdain** [dɪs'deɪn]
vt. 鄙视，蔑视
A great man should disdain flatterers. 伟大的人物应鄙视献媚者。

♦ **at large** 一般说来
Did the people at large approve of the government's policy? 一般老百姓赞成政府的政策吗？

♦ **outcast** ['aʊtkɑːst]
n. 流浪的人，被抛弃者
He was treated as a social outcast. 他为社会所摈弃。

however, did not improve and their social status remained on the lower **rungs**. Businessmen owned the ceramic factories and hired **potters** off the streets to mass produce merchandise **wholesale**.

During the war in the early 1950s, the pottery business fell even further. With peace, however, there was a **renewed** demand for ceramic urns, as most of the old ones, in each and every home, had been shattered during the war. Many potters today remember the late 1950s and early 1960s as a time when they could sell their ceramic wares faster than they could make them. The peak of the pottery industry was immediately after the Korean War.

Since the early 1970s, however, plastic and metal containers have been introduced into the modernized economy, and there has also been a broadening of the Korean palette as people **rely** less and less **on** fermented vegetables. Due to these **macro** trends, many potters have left the industry and have **sought** other lines of work.

Today, there are only a few master potters still producing traditional ceramic wares. Among them, Kim Il-man and Jeong Yoon-seok have both been designated as holders of intangible cultural heritage abilities. They have been recognized as true masters of traditional Korean pottery and today act as the vanguard for the restoration of traditional **ceramics**.

♦ **artisan** [ɑːtɪˈzæn]
n. 技工，工匠
♦ **urn** [əːn]
n. 大茶壶，瓮，缸
♦ **rung** [rʌŋ]
n. 阶级
♦ **potter** [ˈpɒtə]
n. 陶工
♦ **wholesale** [ˈhəulseɪl]
adv. 大量地，大批地，大规模地
The fabrics are sold wholesale to retailers, fashion houses, and other manufacturers. 这些纺织品被批发给零售商、时装店和其他制造商。
♦ **renewed** [rɪˈnjuːd]
adj. 复兴的
rely on 依赖于，取决于 如，It would be better to rely on ourselves than on others. 与其求人，何如求己。
♦ **macro** [ˈmækrəu]
adj. 巨大的，特别突出的
♦ **seek** [siːk]
vt. 寻找，探寻（过去式和过去分词为 sought [sɔːt]）
The couple have sought help from marriage guidance counselors. 这对夫妇已经向婚姻指导顾问寻求帮助。
♦ **ceramic** [sɪˈræmɪk]
n. 陶瓷工艺；陶瓷制品

05 Traditional Masks in South Korea
韩国的传统面具

面具是人们内心世界的一个象征，它是一种横遍全球纵观古今的重要文化现象。韩国的面具以纸、木、葫芦、皮毛制成。大多数面具反映出韩国人面部骨骼状貌和面部表情，但有一些则代表现实中的或想象中的动物和鬼神。人带上动物形象的面具来安慰动物的灵魂，戴上面目狰狞的面具来驱逐妖魔鬼怪。

在各种皇宫典礼和民间节日上，传统面具处处可见。韩国面具文化中，最具特色的当属面具舞。由于面具舞过去是在夜间篝火中演出，所以面具十分夸张，显得怪诞，它反映出韩国人民的乐观精神和对生活的热爱。韩国的面具舞蹈是由李氏王朝（1392—1910）的平民百姓发展而来的一种民间艺术。面具舞的主题扎根于平民百姓对现实生活的反抗精神，对人性弱点、社会丑恶现象及特权阶级的讽刺和嘲弄。

韩国的平民利用面具的匿名性和象征性，针对社会的不公正以及道德腐败现象，发表自己的观点。而且在大多数情况下，演出结束时，演员和观众都要一起纵情欢舞，以庆祝演出成功。

Masks, the so-called, "other face of humanity," turn the human being into another character, **veiling** the original face. Throughout the world, masks have been created in a **diverse** range of forms, **embodying** each community's identity and traditions. In Korean, such traditional masks are called tal.

The traditional Korean mask has been used since **prehistoric** times. They were typically worn during royal court ceremonies, during folk festivals and were used for entertainment across the country in times before modern media. The traditional Korean mask dance, the talchum, is a drama that developed as folk festival entertainment played in an open-air theater.

Across the country, the talchum was commonly performed to sharply **criticize** contemporary society and create humorous **satire** that depicted the falsehoods and **hypocrisies** of the upper classes. In addition to cheerful music and energetic dancing, the traditional mask dance has now been recognized as one of the official cultural symbols of Korea.

The word tal refers to a mask that is crafted by shaping wood or sheets of paper into a representation of a human or animal face and which is worn to cover the entire face. The word also includes a second meaning of misfortune, illness and difficulty.

Interestingly, people were reluctant to **hold onto** the word tal in its meaning of a mask. In the past, they believed that if they kept a mask nearby, they would be **in trouble** due to the bad luck **attached** to the mask. Therefore, they stored the masks in a village shrine or burned them immediately after the ritual for which they were created. People regarded masks as religious objects, something that should be feared,

♦ **veil** [veɪl]
vt. 用面纱遮盖；遮盖，掩饰
♦ **diverse** [daɪˈvɜːs]
adj. 不同的，多种多样的
♦ **embody** [ɪmˈbɒdɪ]
vt. 体现，象征
The Constitution and other laws embody the unity of the Party's views and the people's will. 宪法和法律是党的主张和人民意志相统一的体现。
♦ **prehistoric** [ˌpriːhɪsˈtɒrɪk]
adj. 史前的
♦ **criticize** [ˈkrɪtɪsaɪz]
vt. 批评
You were quite right to criticize him. 你批评他批评得很对。
♦ **satire** [ˈsætaɪə] n. 讽刺
Satire is often a form of protest against injustice. 讽刺往往是一种对不公正的抗议形式。
♦ **hypocrisy** [hɪˈpɒkrəsɪ]
n. 伪善，虚伪
♦ **hold onto** 紧抓不放
He was struggling to hold onto a rock on the face of the cliff. 他奋力想要抓住悬崖壁上的一块岩石。
♦ **in trouble** 处于不幸中，有麻烦
He never came except when he was in trouble. 除非有了困难，他从来不到这里来。
♦ **attached** [əˈtætʃt]
adj. 附加的，附属的
More than half of the US elementary schools have kindergarten attached to them. 超过一半以上的美国小学都有其附属的学前班。
♦ **enshrine** [ɪnˈʃraɪn] vt. 供奉

worshiped and **enshrined**.

In ancient times, it was believed that illness was brought by evil spirits and that they could be **repelled** by means of a fearsome-looking mask. Thus, masks were always used in **exorcism** rituals, funerals and communal rites to pay for the well-being of the village. This suggests that tal, as in, "trouble," can only be defeated by using an even more **frightening** tal, or, "mask."

Such exorcism functions are not unique to Korean masks. Various types of masks have long existed all over the world, **originating** in religious or exorcism ceremonies dating back to the earliest times.

In prehistoric times, people wore animal-inspired masks created to **console** the spirit of that animal. They also attached symbolic meanings to terrifying masks in the shape of a god, meant to protect against evil spirits or **external** enemies. It was common to believe one could become an animal or a supernatural being by wearing such a mask.

♦ **repel** [rɪˈpel] vt. 祛除，击退
A country must have the will to repel any invader. 一个国家得有决心击退任何入侵者。

♦ **exorcism** [ˈeksɔːsɪzəm]
n. (以祈祷或符咒) 驱邪

♦ **frightening** [ˈfraɪtənɪŋ]
adj. 令人恐惧的，吓人的
The mask was so lifelike that it was quite frightening. 该面具非常逼真以至看起来有点恐怖。

♦ **originate** [əˈrɪdʒɪneɪt]
vi. 起源于，来自，产生
All theories originate from practice and in turn serve practice. 任何理论都来源于实践，反过来为实践服务。

♦ **console** [kənˈsəʊl] vt. 安慰
Nothing could console him when his wife died. 他妻子去世后，什么事情也不能使他感到宽慰。

♦ **external** [eksˈtɜːnl]
adj. 外面的，外部的

06 Hangeul: Korean Alphabet
韩国人自己的文字

韩文是世宗大王（1397—1450 年）于 1446 年和众学者们一同为百姓读、写方便而创造的文字。全世界有 3 000 多种语言，但拥有自己的文字的只有 100 多种，韩文便是其中之一。特别是不受其他语言的影响，由特定人物独创出新文字的典例在韩文出现之前还没有过。而且，专门出版书籍对新创的文字进行科学性的原理分析和讲解，详细介绍创造此文字的目的、人物、时期、使用方法等，在此之前也是没有过的事情，但是世宗大王和学者们创造的韩文字却做到了这一点。世界语言学者们对韩文给予了高度的评价，在此背景下，1997 年 10 月韩文被登入联合国教科文组织世界遗产纪录。

随着韩国经济的高速发展以及韩流的巨大影响力，全世界对韩国文化的关心度和韩文的学习热潮日渐增长，开设韩国语系的外国大学在日渐增加。韩国政府也在世界各地积极开设韩语教育机关"世宗学堂"，针对各地文化特征，进行韩语初级教材开发、翻译成多种语言的各种普及工作。

Hangeul, the Korean **alphabet**, refers to the series of letters that form **syllables** with which the Korean language is written. The most unique aspect of Hangeul is that it was **intentionally** created by the government as a written means of expressing the Korean language. History states that King Sejong, who was the 4th king of the Joseon Dynasty, sponsored and helped in the scientific creation of the alphabet with the help of a team of **scholars**, making it the most significant invention in Korean history.

Koreans **take pride in** their alphabet. They believe that Hangeul best demonstrates the creativity of Koreans during the past 5,000 years of Korean civilization. Koreans **mark** the 9th of every October as a national celebration to **commemorate** the creation of Hangeul. As the only national celebration for an alphabet in the world, this day reflects the uniqueness of an alphabet created and systematized by a government to reflect the unique sounds of a language.

King Sejong, the **creator** of Hangeul, is regarded as a national hero in Korea. There are in fact only two kings commemorated as truly great kings of Korean history. One is Gwanggaetodaewang of Goguryeo, who ruled over the largest **territory** in Korean history, and the other is King Sejong, who created Hangeul and many other significant inventions. King Sejong appears on the 10,000 won **note** and a statue of him stands at Gwanghwamun Square, which is a symbol of Seoul.

Based on the desire to create a writing system that could be easily learned and **accessed** by all people throughout Korea, King Sejong worked to invent and distribute this alphabet throughout the nation. Because of this, the **illiteracy** rate in Korea is now virtually zero.

Hangeul was named Hunminjungeum at the time of its creation. Hunminjungeum means "Correct Sounds to Instruct the People". The Hunminjungeum Explanation Book King Sejong created has been passed down throughout history; the

---

♦ **alphabet** [ˈɑːlfəbɪt]
n. 字母表，字母系统

♦ **syllable** [ˈsɪləbl]
n. 音节

♦ **intentionally** [ɪnˈtenʃənəlɪ]
adv. 有意地，故意地
She would never intentionally hurt anyone. 她从来不会故意伤害任何人。

♦ **scholar** [ˈskɒlə]
n. 学者

♦ **take pride in**
以……为傲，对……感到自豪
They take great pride in their heritage. 他们为自己的历史传统深感自豪。

♦ **mark** [mɑːk]
vt. 标示，纪念
That programme received critical acclaim and marked a turning point in Sonita's career. 那个项目赢得了评论界的好评，成为索尼塔事业的转折点。

♦ **commemorate** [kəˈmeməreɪt]
vt. 纪念，庆祝
Some galleries commemorate donors by inscribing their names on the walls. 一些美术馆把捐赠者的姓名镌刻在墙上以示纪念。

♦ **creator** [kriːˈeɪtə(r)]
n. 创造者，创作者

♦ **territory** [ˈterɪtərɪ]
n. 领土，版图
This island was once French territory. 这个岛一度是法国的领地。

♦ **note** [nəʊt]
n. 纸币，钞票
Here is a 5 dollars note for you. 给你一张 5 美元的钞票。

♦ **access** [ˈækses]
vt. 使用，获取
Bank customers can access their checking accounts instantly through the electronic system. 银行客户可通过电子系统立即取出活期存款。

♦ **illiteracy** [ɪˈlɪtərəsɪ]
n. 文盲，无知，缺乏教育

Korean government has named it National Treasure No. 70 and it is now housed at the Gansong Art Museum in Sungbuk-dong, Seoul.

The quality of Hangeul has been extensively studied and praised by experts worldwide. In 1989, UNESCO **initiated** the King Sejong Literacy Prize, which is awarded to an individual or group, which contributes to the crusade against illiteracy. This award has been **bestowed** since 1990. In addition, UNESCO selected the Hunminjungeum Explanation Book as a Memory of the World in 1997.

The campaign to wipe out illiteracy launched out with great vigour. 扫盲运动生气勃勃地展开了。

♦ **initiate** [ɪˈnɪʃɪeɪt]
vt. 开始，发起，创始
The trip was initiated by the manager of the community centre. 这次旅行由社区活动中心的经理发起。

♦ **bestow** [bɪˈstəʊ]
vt. 授予，颁发；赠给
The Queen has bestowed a knighthood on him. 女王已经授予他爵士头衔。

07 Hanja: Chinese Characters in South Korea
韩国的汉字文化

韩国受到中华文化很深的影响，同时也是汉字文化圈的一环。大约在 14 世纪时，韩国虽然通行朝鲜语，却没有自己的文字，因而借用汉字，韩国许多宫殿寺庙内的匾额、碑文、经典古籍都以繁体汉字书写。但汉字的使用也只限高官贵族懂汉字而已，后来为了普及文字，才发明古称"谚文"的韩文。韩国有很长一段时间，将两种文字并用，包括韩国宪法，也是由汉字与韩文共同写成。战后韩国脱离日本，开始独尊自己特有的文化，年轻人的教育改以韩文为主，直到 1980 年当时的总统朴正熙下令，将汉字教育从小学课本中删除。

韩国排除汉字教育后，年轻人开始看不懂与汉字有关的文化遗产，以汉字书写的韩国古籍也都成了天书没人懂，废除汉字的政策也使韩国历史与文化陷入严重的危机。现在就有韩国的教育团体，要求政府重视汉字教育。

Hanja are Chinese characters borrowed from and **incorporated** into the Korean language and given uniquely Korean pronunciations. Unlike the Japanese **equivalent**, called kanji, most hanja have not been simplified and remain **identical** to the traditional Chinese characters. Until the late 19th and early 20th centuries, **fluency** in this writing system was necessary to read and write Korean. This writing system based on Chinese characters then **yielded to** a phonetic Korean

♦ **incorporate** [ɪnˈkɔːpəreɪt]
vt. 包含，吸收；把……合并，使并入
The new cars will incorporate a number of major improvements. 新款汽车会有若干重大改进。

♦ **equivalent** [ɪˈkwɪvələnt]
n. 对等物

♦ **identical** [aɪˈdentɪkəl]
adj. 相同的，完全一样的
Nearly all the houses were identical. 几乎所有的房子都一模一样。

alphabet system called hangul that was created in the 1440s but not widely implemented for centuries.

The Korean writing system was once based on Chinese characters. It is believed that the use of these characters was **necessitated** by the introduction of Buddhism. The sixth-century Chinese poem **titled** the Thousand Character Classic, a primer for teaching Chinese characters, also gained popularity in Korea and influenced the development of hanja. By 1583, the poem was being used as a writing **primer** as well. As Korea did not have its own writing system until the 1440s, the Chinese characters were used instead.

Properly literate Koreans thus had to master hanja. Each character is formed using one of 214 radicals, plus additional elements that indicate sound, although a few are **pictographic**. The meaning of these borrowed Chinese characters generally remained the same throughout China, Japan, and Korea, although the pronunciation of each character became uniquely Korean over time.

In the 1440s, King Sejong the Great and his scholars developed a phonetic Korean script now known as hangul that competed with the **logographic** hanja. The promotion of hangul was **spurred** by the fact that the Chinese characters were difficult for most people to master, resulting in a large portion of the population that was illiterate. Hangul was supposed to be easier to learn, and it became part of popular culture despite opposition from the literary **elite**. It did not fully **supplant** hanja until the 20th century.

Hangul is the official written language of both North and South Korea, having been used in official documents since 1894. The old system has never disappeared entirely, however. Hanja were banned in North Korea by Kim Il Sung but reintroduced in 1964 for reasons that are not entirely clear. Students in North Korean elementary and high school learn approximately 2,000 characters.

South Korea has alternatively banned and reintroduced

♦ **fluency** ['fluənsɪ]
n. （尤指语言）流利，流畅
His son was praised for speeches of remarkable fluency. 他儿子因为发言流畅自然而得到了表扬。

♦ **yield to** 让位于，被……接替
The long cruel winter came to an end at last, yielding to a gentle warm spring. 漫长的严冬终于结束，随之而来的是温暖的春天。

♦ **necessitate** [nɪ'sesɪteɪt]
vt. 使……成为必要，需要

♦ **title** ['taɪtl]
vt. 加标题，把…称为
Their story is the subject of a new book titled The Golden Thirteen. 一本题为《金色十三》的新书讲述了他们的故事。

♦ **primer** ['praɪmə]
n. 启蒙读本，入门书

♦ **pictographic** [,pɪktə'græfɪk]
adj. 象形文字的

♦ **logographic** [,lɒgəʊ'græfɪk]
adj. 意音文字的

♦ **spur** [spɜː]
vt. 激励；促进，推动
Even a small success would spur me on to greater effort. 哪怕是微小的成功也会促使我做出更大的努力。

♦ **elite** [eɪ'liːt]
n. 精英
They were, by and large, a very wealthy, privileged elite. 他们基本上是一些非常有钱有势的精英。

♦ **supplant** [sə'plɑːnt]
vt. 取代，代替
By the 1930s the wristwatch had almost completely supplanted the pocket watch. 到了20世纪30年代，手表几乎完全取代了怀表。

♦ **master** ['mɑːstə]
vt. 精通，掌握
Students are expected to master a second language.

these Chinese characters throughout the 20th century. A definitive ban was issued in 1955, but the old system was back by 1964, with more than 1,300 hanja in school textbooks. All school texts were written in hangul by 1970, but middle and high school students continue to be taught around 1,800 hanja as a separate course. Graduate students in Korean language and studies programs are also usually required to **master** these basic Chinese characters.

学生应该掌握一门第二语言。

♦ **predate** ['priː'deɪt]
vt. （在日期上）早于，先于
These mammals predate certain eggs.
这些哺乳动物出现的年代早于某些卵生动物。

Fluency remains necessary for historians and other scholars who study Korean historical documents or literature that **predates** the introduction of hangul. Children are taught some of the old writing system in school, but there is little opportunity to practice reading these characters in daily life. Hangul is now used for native Korean words and even most words native to Chinese. Most hanja continue to appear primarily in personal names and some university textbooks, often with the hangul equivalent.

08 Hanji Paper
韩国纸文化

韩国的传统纸——韩纸，制作方式独特，韧性十足，可以保存千年以上，是制作书本的必备材料。韩纸柔软润滑，通风和保温效果好，糊在窗户和门上，能起到防风的作用，而且阳光可以透过韩纸部分入室内，调节室内温度和湿度，非常实用。此外，由于韩纸的柔韧性和活用性强，韩国人甚至用韩纸制成甲衣，用来防止箭射。被联合国教科文组织指定为纪录文化遗产的4项韩国遗产，也跟韩纸可以保存千年以上这个优点有着密切的关系。

如今，韩纸还将其美丽纹络更多的应用于包装纸，工艺品材料，信纸等方面。特别是，最近用韩纸制成的工艺品、韩纸人木偶等，将韩国元素表现得淋漓尽致。其独特的质感，贴近大自然的设计，日渐受到人们的欢迎。

Hanji literally means "the paper of Korea". The main material is the **fibrous** skin of the **mulberry**. Hanji is not simply paper. It is used in a variety of ways, and has a different name according to its use. If it is **glued** on a door it is called a window paper. It is copy paper if it is used for a family **registry book**, Buddhist **sutra** or old books, while it becomes drawing paper if four gracious plants or birds are drawn upon it.

The strong vitality of Korean paper is the reason it can be used in a multitude of ways. There is an old saying that paper lasts a thousand years and **textiles** (such as silk) last five hundred, reflecting the **superior** strength of paper over cloth. Koreans even used Korean paper as a suit of armor after **varnishing** the lacquer. It is known that the life **span** of Korean paper is 1,000 years. In the West, products made of paper more than 300–400 years old are rare. But Korea has preserved quite a few books and drawings which are almost 1000 years old.

Korean paper was also very famous as much as Sodongpa, a famous Chinese poet in the 11th century, said that he would like to publish his **anthology** with paper produced from Goryeo (The name of the Korean dynasty at that time), which was one of Korea's main export good at that time. Koreans use Korean paper made by traditional methods for government documents or other documents.

The superiority of Korean paper comes from the material with which it is made. The bark of the mulberry is strong and can endure without **decomposition** when it is immersed in the water for 1 year. It allows both air and light through as the fibers are wide. High-quality Korean paper can be produced with trees that are only one year old, while cheaper modern paper must use the pulp from trees 20–30 years old.

The traditional methods for making Korean paper are not being passed down as greatly as before, making the manufacturing process quite challenging these days. And the small quantities, a long production process and distribution limited to specialty markets make it difficult for traditional Korean paper to compete with the mass distribution of cheap easily produced modern paper. The Korean government has therefore appointed the masters of Korean papermaking as intangible cultural **assets** and protects the industry with special care.

The superiority of hanji has endured despite historical and global changes. There is a trend toward using hanji for another purpose, like for **artwork**. Artists for calligraphy and dyeing insist on using Korean paper. Korean paper is used widely in various art industries. Fashion shows for clothing made of hanji have been held on the Champs Elysee in Paris.

♦ **fibrous** [ˈfaɪbrəs]
adj. 纤维的
♦ **mulberry** [ˈmʌlbəri]
n. 桑树
♦ **glue** [gluː]
vt. 粘贴，胶合
Glue the mirror in with a strong adhesive. 用强力胶将镜子固定到位。
♦ **registry book** 登记簿
♦ **sutra** [ˈsuːtrə]
n. 佛经，经典
♦ **textile** [ˈtekstaɪl]
n. 纺织品，织物
♦ **superior** [sjuːˈpɪərɪə]
adj. (在质量等方面) 较好的，先进的，上乘的
Through superior production techniques they were able to gain the competitive edge. 凭借先进的生产技术，他们得以占据竞争优势。
♦ **varnish** [ˈvɑːnɪʃ]
vt. 在 (某物) 上涂清漆
♦ **span** [spæn]
n. 跨度，一段时间
I worked with him over a span of six years. 我和他共事达六年之久。
♦ **anthology** [ænˈθɒlədʒɪ]
n. (诗、文等的) 选集
♦ **decomposition** [diːkɒmpəˈzɪʃən]
n. 分解，腐烂
♦ **asset** [ˈæset]
n. 资产，遗产
The Prime Minister knows that his personal image is his greatest political asset. 总理知道他的个人形象是他最重要的政治资产。
♦ **artwork** [ˈɑːtwɜːk]
n. 艺术品
Their apartment is full of expensive furniture and artwork. 他们的公寓充满了昂贵的家具与艺术品。

A study on potential protective properties of hanji paper for space shuttles is currently underway in a joint study by Korea and the USA.

09 Reasons to Stay at a Hanok
下榻韩屋，歆享自然

恰如英国的村舍、法国的民宿和美国的农场平房，韩国的标志性住房则是韩屋。广义上，韩屋指传统朝鲜族屋子。与自然相融的环保型设计使韩屋正引领一股居室新潮。表面上看，韩屋跟中国唐宋时期传统民居相仿，而事实上却大有不同，这些差异造就了韩屋的宜居性。

当然，在韩屋居住太久，也有不便，比如没有方便的淋浴设施。而对于尚未亲身感受的朋友，不妨先听听这三个理由：第一，利用自然。没有传统墙面赋予韩屋酷爽的夏日，秘密在于其科学的建筑结构。首先，屋檐深长，可以遮挡阳光；不仅如此，冬日太阳高度较低时，阳光进入房子，室温上升；即便被冷空气挤出，屋檐也可以阻挡部分暖气。此外，韩屋有两层，恰似中国的阴和阳，从此可以看出，韩屋确实源于中国唐代建筑；第二，建材原始。即便韩屋因战争或流感爆发而遭废弃，也可整体复归自然，基本不会留下生态足迹。或许你认为毫无必要，但在韩屋里生活，你可以毫无愧疚感，反而很高尚。住在韩屋利于保护环境，还在于其高效的取暖方式（只需地下挖洞生火），因而不需要呼呼作响的空调。当然，从建筑材料本身来说，韩屋的主要材料是石块、木材、粘土和韩纸，不会有现代建筑所产生的污染物；第三，洁净的红土墙。在外行看来，不过一间泥巴小屋；对于韩屋爱好者，则是养生佳所。屋顶、墙壁和地面上都涂满泥巴，扣起字眼来，是金黄色的泥巴或者"红土"。韩屋里除了红粘土冬暖夏凉的功效，使用黄土对居民的健康也是有益的；除了人们熟知的净化和解毒功能，黄土还能释放远红外线。现在已有完整的黄土特效产品生产行业，具有众多保健疗效，比如"黄土枕头"，可以辅助睡眠。

Britain has its cottages, France has its gîtes, the United States has its ranch houses; in South Korea, the **iconic** house is the **hanok**. Broadly defined, hanok can refer to any traditional Korean house. With an environmentally friendly design that's in tune with nature, traditional Korean houses are the new trend in **accommodations**.

As far as appearance goes, what we consider hanok today resembles the residential Chinese architecture of the Tang and Song Dynasties. Hanok, however, differ from their Chinese

♦ **iconic** [aɪˈkɒnɪk]
adj. 图标的，标志性的

♦ **hanok**
韩屋，韩国传统样式房屋，既具有传统美感，又多自然味道，冬暖夏凉，环保宜居。在首尔，韩屋村成为韩国特色景点

♦ **accommodation** [əˌkɒməˈdeɪʃən]
n. 住处，适应
The university is trying to make more accommodation available for students.

counterparts in significant ways. And some of these differences are what **contribute to** the remarkable practical–mental and physical–benefits to sleeping in a hanok.

Sure, there are inconveniences to staying in one for an extended period of time. You will of course have to "give up convenient shower facilities." But for anyone who has not yet felt it, here are at least three reasons you should try:

1. **Harnessing** nature

It's not just the lack of walls that makes this space so cool in the summer. There's a science to it. The secret lies in the architecture. First, there is the depth of the **eaves**, which act as a shade from the summer sun. But the eaves do more than simply act as beach umbrellas. In the winter, the sun, which is low in the sky, enters and warms the rooms. And even if the warm air is pushed out by the colder air, the deep eaves act as a blockade, and the warm air lingers. Hanok are also characterized by their dual flooring, which fit together like yin and yang. This dual floor design marks how hanok deviates from the typical Chinese architecture of the Tang era.

2. Primary materials

If hanok are ever abandoned in a war or killer flu panic, they will return to the earth, leaving little to no **ecological footprint**. Not that we would ever wish this upon such a pretty little place. At hanok you can think about it, because the conclusion won't make you feel guilty, but on the contrary, **virtuous**. We can already **surmise** that hanok are good for the environment because the houses have efficient heating (you just build a fire under the floor) and you don't need wheezing air conditioners. But there are also the ingredients of the hanok itself. The primary materials used to build hanok are stone, wood, clay and paper, producing none of the same **pollutants** that arise from modern architecture.

3. Purifying red clay walls

To the untrained eye: a hut made of mud. To the hanok enthusiast: a well-being wonder house. The floors, walls and roofs of hanok are all **grouted** with mud, and not just any mud, but

大学设法为学生提供更多的住处。

♦ **contribute to**

促成，有助于；捐献；投稿

Smoking is a major factor contributing to cancer. 吸烟是致癌的一个重要因素。

♦ **harness** [ˈhɑːnɪs]

vt. 统治，支配；利用

♦ **eave** [iːv]

n. 屋檐

♦ **ecological footprint**

生态足迹，又称生态占用，就是能够持续地提供资源或消纳废物的、具有生物生产力的地域空间，此处指，处理废弃的韩屋基本不用占生态资源。

♦ **virtuous** [ˈvɜːtjʊəs]

adj. 善良的，有道德的

♦ **surmise** [ˈsɜːmaɪz]

vt. 猜测

There's so little to go on, we can only surmise what happened. 几乎毫无凭据，我们只能猜测发生了什么。

♦ **pollutant** [pəˈluːtənt]

n. 污染物

♦ **grout** [graʊt]

vt. 用薄泥浆填塞

♦ **hwangto**

n. 黄土

♦ **proximity** [prɒkˈsɪmɪtɪ]

n. 接近，亲近

Families are no longer in close proximity to each other. 各家不再像以前一样比邻而居。

♦ **detoxify** [diːˈtɒksɪˌfaɪ]

vt. 使解毒

Vitamin C helps to detoxify pollutants in the body. 维生素 C 可以帮助解除体内污染物的毒性。

golden mud, or "red clay", if we are being literal with the translation.

Besides the heating and cooling benefits of red clay in the architecture, **hwangto**'s **proximity** to the residents is also believed to be beneficial to their health. Hwangto is known to have purifying and **detoxifying** properties, as well as emitting far infrared rays. There are entire lines of hwangto wonder products with a variety of health benefits, such as the "hwangto pillow", which is supposed to aid in comfortable sleep.

Chapter 4
寻味日本：穿越时空的味蕾盛宴

01 A Travel to Sushi
令人回味的寿司盛宴

寿司文化深深扎根于日本数千年的历史与传统中，通常选用海苔、生鱼、大米制成，被视为一种饮食艺术。在日本，人们只在特殊场合食用;寿司而近年来在美国广受欢迎，餐馆的寿司价位从中等到昂贵的都有。

在日本文化中，寿司被视为一种艺术的原因是，它的外观跟口感同样重要。日本各地的厨师做卷和摆盘的方式各具风格，他们要用数年时间学习如何制作寿司。

几千年前，日本人发明了寿司来保存收拾干净的生鱼。把鱼放在大米和食盐中间，用沉重的石块压上几个星期，等到鱼发酵以后再用海苔之类的轻质食材包住。到18世纪，一名来自东京的厨师洋平，制作寿司时，去掉了发酵过程，新鲜寿司大受欢迎，因而出现了两种不同风格的寿司——大阪的关西派和东京的江户派。江户派主要包括调过味的米饭和其他配料，关西派则是在一层米饭上加一点海鲜，美国人熟知的主要是江户派寿司。

加利福尼亚大学贝克利分校东亚图书馆日本书籍负责人 Yuki Ishimatsu 指出，日本只在特殊场合才吃寿司的原因是价格昂贵，"而在美国却截然不同，但也分传统日本寿司和加州寿司两种。"其中，加州寿司更敢于尝试，里面有鳄梨和其他一些蔬菜类原料，而传统寿司主要是生鱼片。

Sushi **is rooted in** thousands of years of Japanese history and tradition. It is made with seaweed, fish and rice, and is considered to be an art form. Eaten on special **occasions** in Japan, it has become popular in the United States in recent years. Sushi restaurants can **range** in price from moderate to very expensive.

In Japanese culture, sushi is considered to be an art form, because its appearance is just as important as how it tastes. Chefs from different regions of Japan roll it and arrange it on the plate according to their own styles, and they spend years learning the **craft** of sushi-making.

Sushi was invented thousands of years ago in Japan as a way to **preserve** raw, cleaned fish. It was pressed between rice and salt by a heavy stone for a few weeks and then covered with a lighter material like **seaweed** until the fish had **fermented**.

♦ **be rooted in** 深植于，根源在于
I can't pull this bush up, it's firmly rooted in the ground. 这棵矮树我拔不起来，它的根在地里生得很牢。

♦ **occasion** [əˈkeɪʒən]
n. 场合，时机，机会
fit the occasion 适合这种场合

♦ **range** [reɪndʒ]
vi. 在……范围内变动
ages that ranged from two to five 两岁至五岁年龄段

♦ **craft** [krɑːft] n. 艺，手艺
light crafts 手工艺

♦ **preserve** [prɪˈzɜːv]
vt. 保护，保持，保存，保藏

♦ **seaweed** [ˈsiːwiːd]
n. 海草，海藻，海苔

♦ **ferment** [ˈfɜːment]
vi. (使)发酵

In the 18th century, a chef from Tokyo named Yohei Hanaya decided to forget about the fermentation process and **serve** it on its own. Fresh sushi became very popular, and two distinct styles emerged–the Kansai style from Osaka and the Edo style from Tokyo. The edo style consists primarily of **seasoned** rice mixed with other **ingredients**, and the Kansai style is made with **a small bit of** seafood on a pad of rice. Most people in the United States are familiar with the edo style.

Yuki Ishimatsu, the head of the Japanese collection at the UC-Berkeley East Asian Library, said Japanese people mostly eat sushi for special occasions because it is very expensive. "The sushi here in the States is very different, but it's divided into two types–traditional Japanese and California style." The California style is more **experimental** and includes **avocados** and other **vegetarian** ingredients, and the traditional style is mostly fish.

♦ **serve** [sɜːv]
vt. 服务
serve tea 上茶

♦ **season** ['siːzn]
vt. 调味

♦ **ingredient** [ɪnˈɡriːdɪənt]
n. 成分，因素，配料

♦ **a small bit of** 一点点，一星半点

♦ **experimental** [ˌeksˌperɪˈmentl]
adj. 实（试）验（性）的
an experimental farm 试验农场

♦ **avocado** [ˌævəˈkɑːdəʊ]
n. 鳄梨，又称牛油果，生长在热带和亚热带的中美洲等地，果实为营养价值很高的水果，有"森林奶油"的美誉。

♦ **vegetarian** [ˌvedʒɪˈteərɪən]
adj. 素食的，蔬食的

02 Sashimi: Traditional Japanese Cuisine
日本传统菜肴生鱼片

日本料理以生鱼片最为著名，它堪称是日本菜的代表作。生鱼片在日语中写作"刺身"，而生鱼片则是中国人对它的称呼。日本北海道渔民在供应生鱼片时，由于去皮后的鱼片不易辨清种类，故经常会取一些鱼皮，再用竹签刺在鱼片上，以方便大家识别。这刺在鱼片上的竹签和鱼皮，当初被称作"刺身"，后来虽然不用这种方法了，但"刺身"这个叫法仍被保留下来。

生鱼片是将新鲜的鱼、贝等原料，依照适当的刀法加工，享用时佐以酱油与山葵泥调出来的酱料的一种生食料理。原料以深海产的鱼类及其他海产品为主。生鱼片的选料非常严格，应保证原料的新鲜、洁净、无污染。在生鱼片制作过程中，也采用透明化的管理方法，即厨师在食客的眼皮底下制作生鱼片，以此保证原材料的新鲜和洁净。

♦ **compare** [kəmˈpeə]
vt. 比较，对照
compare to/with 与……相比
Cast iron cannot compare with steel in strength. 铸铁在强度方面比不上钢。

♦ **garnish** [ˈɡɑːnɪʃ]
n. 配菜

♦ **saltwater** [ˈsɔːltˌwɔːtə(r)]
adj. 盐水的，海产的
The water in the ocean is all saltwater. 海洋中的水都是盐水。

♦ **freshwater** [ˈfreʃwɔːtə(r)]
adj. 淡水的

♦ **parasite** [ˈpærəsaɪt]
n. 寄生虫，寄生物
I don't want to be a parasite. I must earn

Sashimi is an important element in Japanese cuisine, where it is often served at the beginning of a meal as an appetizer. It is often **compared** to sushi, another popular Japanese dish, although the two are actually different. Sashimi is raw fish sliced very thin and served with a variety of **garnishes** and sauces. Sushi is served with rice, and often appears wrapped in specially treated seaweed known as nori.

Saltwater fish is always used to make sashimi because many **freshwater** fish species contain **parasites** that could cause **intestinal distress** if eaten. In addition, the fish is fresh and of the highest quality to **ensure** its optimum flavor and healthiness. Many restaurants keep their fish alive in saltwater **tanks**, ensuring that the fish can be prepared to order. When going out for this cuisine, diners should pick a **reputable** restaurant with an obvious supply of fresh, high quality fish. When preparing it at home, cooks should make sure that the **fishmonger** knows that they intend to eat the fish raw, so that he or she can recommend the safest and freshest **specimens**.

Sashimi is often prepared at a **bar** so that customers can watch the chef. This tradition probably **stems from** a desire to make sure that the fish being used is fresh and of the highest quality, but it is also very interesting to watch. Chefs use a very sharp knife to **fillet** the fish, removing potentially dangerous bones along with the skin. Then the fish is sliced very fine and beautifully laid out on a **platter** along with the garnishes and sauces of choice.

Common garnishes include pickled vegetables such as **ginger**, shredded radish, and toasted nori. Sashimi is usually also served with soy sauce and wasabi, and some cooks add ground ginger root to the soy sauce for an extra dimension of flavor. The fish and condiments are arranged so that consumers can easily pick up pieces and garnish with chopsticks before dunking them in the sauce.

Seafood used for sashimi commonly includes bluefin tuna, snapper, abalone, bass, fish roe,

my own way in life. 我不想做寄生虫，我要自己养活自己。
♦ **intestinal distress** 肠胃不适
♦ **ensure** [ɪnˈʃʊə]
vt. 确保
We will be going all out to ensure it doesn't happen again. 我们要全力保证此事不再发生。
♦ **tank** [tæŋk]
n. （盛放液体或气体的）箱，缸
♦ **reputable** [ˈrepjʊtəbl]
adj. 声誉好的，有信誉的
We prefer to deal only with reputable companies. 我们只喜欢和有声誉的公司打交道。
♦ **fishmonger** [ˈfɪʃmʌŋɡə(r)]
n. 鱼贩子，鱼商
♦ **specimen** [ˈspesɪmɪn]
n. 样品
They are very interested to receive a specimen of the new type. 他们很想得到一份新型号的样品。
♦ **bar** [bɑː(r)]
n. 酒吧
♦ **stem from** 来自，起源于
Correct decisions stem from correct judgments. 正确的决定来源于正确的判断。
♦ **fillet** [ˈfɪlɪt]
vt. 把（鱼、肉）切成片
Please fillet it for me. 请替我把它切成片。
♦ **platter** [ˈplætə]
n. 大浅盘
♦ **ginger** [ˈdʒɪndʒə]
n. 姜，生姜
♦ **octopus** [ˈɒktəpəs]
n. 章鱼
One octopus has eight tentacles. 一条章鱼有八根触角。

prawns, mackerel, bonito, shad, octopus, and squid. The fatty part of tuna, known as toro, is particularly prized because it has a creamy, melt in the mouth flavor. Western consumers often enjoy this dish made with tuna and mackerel, and they sometimes have difficulty with the rubbery texture of raw squid and **octopus**.

03 Ramen in Japan
香喷喷的日本拉面

说到日本料理，人们比较熟悉的有生鱼片、寿司之类的传统美食。但是，日本拉面与日本高级传统料理相比，可以说是一项大众美食，时至今日甚至已经发展成了日本一项独具特色的饮食文化。日本拉面发展的历史相对不长，它源于中国的面食，从上世纪初传入日本，经过其独特的演变，逐渐成为日本人餐桌上一道必不可少的佳肴。

不论是日式拉面或中华拉面，都是品尝其面条和汤汁，中华拉面保留了中国正统的汤面形式，以配料来展现其独特的味道，而日式拉面配料较少改变，一般都是以玉米、叉烧、海苔、笋干、蛋、豆芽、海鲜等为基础再做变化，不过拉面本身并不会因为这些配料的不同而有所变化，因为汤头及面条的融合才是绝佳拉面的重头戏。

在日本，吃拉面的最佳场所当属拉面馆，这在日本遍地都是，车站、娱乐街等等。由于日本跟中国文化的渊源关系，在食用日本拉面时也使用筷子，在日本的中国游客会倍感亲切，价格也相对便宜。另外，各种类型的拉面吃法，保证让你大快朵颐。

Ramen is a noodle soup dish that was originally imported from China and has become one of the most popular dishes in Japan in recent decades. Ramen are inexpensive and widely available, two factors that also make them an ideal option for **budget** travelers. Ramen restaurants, or ramen-ya, can be found in **virtually** every corner of the country and produce countless regional variations of this common noodle dish.

The second key aspect of ramen is the noodles, which are made of wheat and come in many different types. Typical Ramen noodles are long and elastic, but countless varieties exist that vary from thin and straight to thick and **wavy**. Some ramen-ya allow you to **customize** your noodle order **to some extent** such as by allowing you to select a thickness (thin, regular or thick) or doneness (regular or firm).

♦ **budget** [ˈbʌdʒɪt]
adj. 预算少的
♦ **virtually** [ˈvɔːtjuəlɪ]
adv. 几乎；实际上，事实上
He knew virtually nothing about music but he could smell a hit. 他对音乐几乎一窍不通，却预感到它将会大受欢迎。
♦ **wavy** [ˈweɪvɪ]
adj. 波状的
♦ **customize** [ˈkʌstəmaɪz]
vt. 定制，定做
They wanted to customize a sign outside each conference room. 他们想在每间会议室外面定制一个电子标牌。
♦ **to some extent** 在一定程度上
Language is a reflector of a society to some extent.

Though ramen can be considered a one dish meal, many ramen-ya also serve a selection of side dishes in addition to their noodles. The offerings vary from shop to shop but virtually all ramen-ya serve gyoza (potstickers). These Chinese style, pan fried dumplings come five or six to an order and are eaten after being **dipped** in a mixture of soy sauce, **vinegar** and rayu (hot chili oil). And of course, nothing **complements** a steaming hot bowl of ramen like an ice cold beer.

The best place to eat ramen is at **specialized** ramen restaurants, which are commonly found around busy locations such as train stations, entertainment districts and along busy roads. Ramen-ya are usually **sit-down** restaurants with a **counter** and some tables, although smaller ones may only have a single counter. In busier locations, some ramen-ya may only offer standing counter space.

Ramen are also often featured on the menus of other restaurants that serve a wider range of dishes such as common **eateries** found at tourist sites, izakaya, family restaurants and food stalls. Hot ramen dishes can also be purchased around the clock at convenience stores and at some vending machines.

Ramen are eaten with chopsticks which are usually available at the table. A Chinese style spoon is often provided as well to help with small toppings and for drinking the soup. It is also alright to lift up the bowl to drink the soup directly from the bowl.

Ramen noodles get **soggy** quickly and should be eaten immediately after they are served. As with other noodle dishes in Japan, a **slurping** sound is made when eating ramen. The slurping enhances the flavors and helps cool down the piping hot noodles as they enter your mouth. At the end of the meal, it is alright to leave some unfinished soup in the bowl. You do not need to drink the whole bowl to be polite, although it is considered a compliment to the chef to do so.

Ramen are also available in several prepared forms that are quick and easy to make at home or in your hotel room. A wide range of **instant ramen** products are sold in cups and packets at supermarket, convenience store and some vending machines. The simplest require only the addi-

---

从某种程度上来说，语言反映了社会。

♦ **dip** [dɪp]
vt. 蘸，浸
I'll allow the children to dip their bread into the soup. 我让孩子们把面包浸在汤里吃。

♦ **vinegar** [ˈvɪnɪɡə]
n. 醋

♦ **complement** [ˈkɒmplɪmənt]
vt. 与……相辅相成，补充
The two suggestions complement each other. 这两条建议相互补充。

♦ **specialized** [ˈspeʃəlaɪzd]
adj. 专门的

♦ **sit-down**
adj.（餐饭）由侍者送上餐桌的，坐在桌前吃的

♦ **counter** [ˈkaʊntə]
n. 柜台
The customer cast his money on the counter and left. 那位顾客把钱扔在柜台上就离开了。

♦ **eatery** [ˈiːtərɪ]
n. 餐馆，饭店

♦ **soggy** [ˈsɒɡɪ]
adj. 浸透的，过分浸泡的
The ground was soggy after the heavy rain. 大雨过后，地面湿透了。

♦ **slurp** [slɜːp]
vt. 啧啧地吃
You may not slurp your soup. 喝汤不可发出声音。

♦ **instant ramen** 速食拉面

tion of hot water, which is sometimes supplied at the store or machine where they are sold. Hotels in Japan almost always provide hot water on their rooms, making these types of instant ramen an easy, hot meal choice for tourists, as well.

04 Washoku: An Intangible Cultural Heritage
日本传统和食：世界级的享受

和食，即日本料理，起源于日本列岛，逐渐发展成为独具日本特色的菜肴。和食要求色自然、味鲜美、形多样、器精良，而且材料和调理法重视季节感。当提到日本料理时，许多人会联想到寿司、生鱼片，或是摆设非常精致，有如艺术的怀石料理。

和食的主食以米饭、面条为主，因为靠近大海所以副食多为新鲜鱼虾等海产，常配以日本酒。日本和食以清淡著称，烹调的特色着重自然的原味，不容置疑，"原味"是日本料理首要的精神。其烹调方式，十分细腻精致，从数小时慢火熬制的高汤、调味与烹调手法，均以保留食物的原味为前提。

最能直接展现日本和食文化的场合时每年的新年节日，在除夕之夜的家庭团圆饭上，不仅有我们熟知的寿司和生鱼片等传统美食，还包括寓意长寿的松果和面条，以及象征好运的甜黑豆等过年特供。2013年12月，和食作为非物质文化遗产被联合国教科文组织收入世界遗产名录。

The traditional cuisine of Japan, called Washoku, is unique in its combination of **seasonal** and regional variation served in an aesthetic presentation. Washoku was named in December 2013 to UNESCO's list of Intangible Cultural Heritage.

The core ingredient of Japanese food is rice, but it's **enhanced** with a multitude of main and side dishes that include regional fish, meat and many vegetables and **pickles**, as well as soup. Noodles are also a traditional ingredient in a meal, including the thin soba noodles, often made of **buckwheat**, or the thicker udon wheat noodles.

But Washoku isn't just about the ingredients. It's also in the **presentation** of each meal, with individual dishes served in their own plate or bowl, like a carefully composed work of art laid out on the table in front of the diner.

♦ **seasonal** ['siːzənl]
adj. 季节的，时令的
The beauty of the lake is no way diminished by seasonal change. 湖的美丽不会由于季节的更迭而逊色。

♦ **enhance** [ɪn'hɑːns]
vt. 提高，增进，增加（价值、质量、吸引力等）
The games have enhanced friendship and unity among the people and athletes of various countries. 这次运动会增进了各国人民和运动员之间的友谊和团结。

♦ **pickle** ['pɪkl]
n. 腌菜，泡菜；腌制食品

♦ **buckwheat** ['bʌkwiːt]
n. 荞麦

♦ **presentation** [ˌprezen'teɪʃn]
n. 展现；演出；颁发

A Japanese meal can be presented all together with multiple dishes in front of you **at once**, or more formally, the main dishes are brought out in a **predetermined** order to take the diner on a **culinary** journey, not just a meal.

As UNESCO explained in its citation for awarding Washoku with its "Intangible Cultural Heritage" designation, "Washoku is a social practice based on a set of skills, knowledge, practice and traditions related to the production, processing, preparation and consumption of food. It is associated with an essential spirit of respect for nature that is closely related to the **sustainable** use of **natural resources**."

Washoku is a **feast** of many courses. Anyone who has sat through a traditional "Kaiseki" meal in a Japanese restaurant, sitting on a "zabuton" pillow on a tatami floor in a private room with your family or friends, will never forget the Washoku experience. You're served course after course of dishes in small **portions** until you're stuffed by the end. The flavors and textures are all uniquely Japanese and delightful.

In some meals, the final course can be a bowl of rice with tea poured over it. It's called "ochazuke", and it's a way to clear your palate and help digest the feast you've just eaten.

The best-known showcase for Washoku, mentioned by UNESCO in its **award**, comes every New Year. In Japan, the big day for celebrations isn't New Year's Eve like in the west, but instead New Year's Day. It's marked with a family feast of traditional food, including dishes familiar to Westerners like sushi and sashimi, but also special items cooked up just for the New Year, including food that represent symbols like noodles (for long life), or sweet black beans (for good luck).

Japanese also eat special New Year's sweet rice cakes that are **pounded** with traditional wooden **mallets** and steamed then grilled to a crunchy exterior and hot **gooey** inside.

There is a presentation of a new play tonight. 今晚有一场新戏演出。
♦ **at once** 一起，同时
Suddenly, a lot of these bills have come due at once. 突然，许多账单都一起到期了。
♦ **predetermined** [priːdɪˈtɜːmɪnd]
adj. 预定的，预先确定的
♦ **culinary** [ˈkʌlɪnərɪ]
adj. 烹饪的，厨房的
She is studying culinary arts. 她正在学习烹调。
♦ **sustainable** [səˈsteɪnəbl]
adj. 可持续的
Brazil's farms are sustainable, too, thanks to abundant land and water. 幸亏有丰富的土地和水源，巴西的农场也是可持续的。
♦ **natural resources** 自然资源
♦ **feast** [fiːst]
n. 盛宴；盛会，宴会
The scene was a feast for the eyes. 这景色令人赏心悦目。
♦ **portion** [ˈpɔːʃən]
n. （饭菜的）一份，一客
She ordered a portion of fried eggs. 她点了一份煎蛋。
♦ **award** [əˈwɔːd]
n. 颁奖（典礼或致辞）
♦ **pound** [paʊnd]
vt. 连续重击
Somebody began pounding on the front door. 有人开始不停地猛敲前门。
♦ **mallet** [ˈmælɪt]
n. （长柄）木槌，大锤
♦ **gooey** [ˈguːɪ]
n. 蜜糖，胶粘物

05 Japanese Curry
无处不在的日式咖喱

除了印度及与其邻近的各国外，日本也是酷爱咖喱的国度，看看现在摆在超市货架上出售的各种咖喱粉、咖喱块，绝大多数的外包装上都打着日本风味的印记，差点要让人误以为日本才是咖喱的发祥地。其实，日本与印度虽然同处于亚洲，但日本人吃的咖喱却是到了明治维新时期才由欧洲传入的。似乎无论什么东西，一经传到日本，便转型为更加精致、细腻、温和的事物，与其本土文化巧妙地融为一体。咖喱传到日本后，也得到了新的发展。

日本咖喱一般不太辣，因为加入了浓缩果泥，所以甜味较重。虽然日式咖喱又称欧风咖喱，事实上还是由日本人所发明的。咖喱除了可以拌饭吃外，还可以作为拉面和乌龙面等汤面类食物的汤底，这方面和其他地方的咖喱有较大分别。北海道札幌地区还有一种汤咖喱。

咖喱传入日本后，出现了可以大规模生产的咖喱粉与咖喱块。虽然不再像印度家庭自制的咖喱那样味道千变万化、自在随心，但胜在够方便，节省时间。不必上餐馆，不必费力气学厨艺、买材料，只要稍微加热，淋在米饭上即可食用。咖喱也因此成为了一种普通人可以随时享用的美味。

If Japan has a cultural equivalent of the American **Hamburger** it's Japanese Curry Rice. Curry powder was introduced to Japan from India (**via** the British) by the mid 19th century. It immediately **caught on**. Originally considered a Western dish (British Navy curry), Japanese curry was **adapted** to local tastes with time.

It is considerably **blander** than a typical Indian curry. Westerners might compare it to a spicy **gravy**. Spicier variations are available but are typically a **disappointment** for spicy food enthusiasts.

Japanese curry has a thick texture and is usually served with vegetables and meat. Vegetarian curries are relatively rare in Japan. Vegetables are usually of the basic variety (onions, **carrots** and potatoes). Beef and pork are the most common meats used. Beef is popular in Osaka and pork in Tokyo. And Japanese short grain rice is the preferred rice for curry in Japan.

♦ **hamburger** [ˈhæmbɜːgə]
n. 汉堡包

♦ **via** [ˈvaɪə]
prep. 经过，通过

♦ **catch on** 变得流行
It's hardly surprising his ideas didn't catch on.
他的想法没有被广泛接受，这并不足为奇。

♦ **adapt** [əˈdæpt]
vt. 改变……以适合

♦ **bland** [blænd]
adj.（食物）淡而无味的（blander 是其比较级形式）

♦ **gravy** [ˈgreɪvɪ]
n. 肉汁，肉卤

♦ **disappointment** [ˌdɪsəˈpɔɪntmənt]
n. 失望，扫兴
to one's disappointment 令某人失望的是

♦ **carrot** [ˈkærət]
n. 胡萝卜

Curry is **practically** a Japanese staple and many people eat it at least once a week. The average person in Japan eats more Japanese curry than sushi. It's that big.

There're plenty of places where you can find curry. Curry rice is found in supermarkets and convenience stores in **vacuum sealed** packages complete with meat and vegetables. Most supermarkets carry more than a **dozen** varieties.

Curry fast food chains such as Curry House CoCo Ichibanya and Go! Go! Curry! are **ubiquitous** throughout Japan. Curry rice is also served by hotels, tourist food courts and company **cafeterias**. The Japanese Navy serves curry rice every Friday.

Japanese curry rice is one variation of Japanese curry. In Japan, curry (with the same basic taste) is served in every **imaginable** way. Popular varieties include: Kare Pan-buns (bread) stuffed with curry, Dorai Kare-literally "dry curry", including curry fried rice and curry with a thick, dry meat sauce, and Yaki Kare-literally "baked curry", curry rice topped with a **raw** egg and baked, popular in Osaka.

Practically every prefecture in Japan lays claim to some local variation of Japanese curry. In some cases, these aren't popular with the locals but are sold to tourists. Food based domestic tourism is big in Japan. Every prefecture is engaged in intense competition to have interesting food.

♦ **practically** [ˈpræktɪkəlɪ]
adv. 实际上
There is practically no plant cover on the deserts. 沙漠实际上没有植物层。
♦ **vacuum sealed** 真空封闭的
♦ **dozen** [ˈdʌzn]
n. 一打，十二个
He sat behind a table on which were half a dozen files. 他坐在一张放有6个文件夹的桌子后面。
♦ **ubiquitous** [juːˈbɪkwɪtəs]
adj. 无处不在的，普遍存在的
The apple is undoubtedly the most ubiquitous of all fruits. 苹果无疑是所有果树中栽培最广泛的一种。
♦ **cafeteria** [ˌkæfɪˈtɪərɪə]
n. 自助餐厅
♦ **imaginable** [ɪˈmædʒɪnəbl]
adj. 能想象到的，可能的
The house has the most spectacular views imaginable. 从这所房子可以看到所能想象的最壮丽的景色。
♦ **raw** [rɔː] adj. 生的，未做熟的
The meat was black and scorched outside but still raw inside. 那块肉外表焦黑，但里面仍是生的。

06 Natto: The Bad Tasting Food
日本纳豆：难闻的健康食品

纳豆是日本常见的传统发酵食品，由黄豆通过纳豆菌（枯草杆菌）发酵制成豆制品，具有黏性，不仅保有黄豆的营养价值、富含维生素K2、提高蛋白质的消化吸收率，更重要的是发酵过程产生了多种生理活性物质，具有溶解体内纤维蛋白及其他调节生理机能的保健作用。日本人食用纳豆的历史已超过一千年。日本料理中也经常用到纳豆，甚至会把纳豆加入西餐中，比如制成纳豆意大利面。

有医学研究证明了纳豆的一些健康价值，日本的媒体就经常吹捧纳豆的功效，比如可以

降低胆固醇，治疗癌症等等，几乎到了神乎其神的程度。2007年1月7日，日本关西电视台生活资讯节目《发掘！真有其事大百科Ⅱ》宣称"根据美国专家的饮食研究，进食纳豆可以有效减肥"。随后，该段内容被日本《周刊朝日》发现内容不实。2007年1月21日，关西电视台社长千草宗一郎为此公开道歉。

Natto is made by fermenting soya beans. It smells bad and is extremely **slimy**. It also has a very strong taste. It's generally unpopular amongst foreigners in Japan. Japanese people in Kansai (Osaka, **Kobe**, Kyoto) are also not particularly fond of Natto.

Natto has been around since 300 BC. In **feudal** times, it was an important source of protein in the Japanese **diet**. Traditionally it's a breakfast food that's eaten with rice and miso soup. Hot **mustard** (karashi) and soy sauce are often mixed in to natto. A raw **quail egg** is also sometimes mixed in.

Natto is a common ingredient of Japanese cuisine. For example, it's used in sushi such as this natto maki. Natto is also incorporated into Japanese style western cuisine such as this natto **spaghetti**.

The Japanese media often **touts** the health benefits of natto. Natto has been **credited** with almost magical health benefits. It's supposed to reduce cholesterol, blood clots, **heart attacks**, **pulmonary embolisms** and strokes. It's also said to prevent balding in men, **Alzheimer's disease**, osteoporosis and cancer. Other claims include that it reduces excessive immune reactions (e.g. allergies), is good for your skin and generally makes you younger.

Some of these claims are **validated** by **preliminary** medical research. Natto is chocked full of protein, probiotics, vitamin K and vitamin PQQ. It also contains a unique **enzyme** called nattokinase.

The possible health benefits of natto tend to be exag-

♦ **slimy** [ˈslaɪmɪ]
adj. 粘糊糊的，黏滑的
The steps were slimy with moss. 台阶因长满苔藓而发黏。
♦ **Kobe** 神户，日本本州岛西南岸港市。
♦ **feudal** [ˈfjuːdl] adj. 封建的
♦ **diet** [ˈdaɪət] n.（日常）饮食
It makes sense to eat a reasonably balanced diet when slimming. 在减肥过程中保持饮食的营养相对均衡是明智的。
♦ **mustard** [ˈmʌstəd] n. 芥末，芥菜
♦ **quail egg** 鹌鹑蛋
♦ **spaghetti** [spəˈɡetɪ]
n. 意大利面条
♦ **tout** [taʊt] vt. 吹捧
♦ **credit** [ˈkredɪt]
vt. 相信，认为……有（某种品质）
I wonder why you can't credit him with the same generosity of spirit. 我想知道你为什么不认为他具有同样崇高的思想境界。
♦ **heart attack** 心力衰竭，心脏病发作
♦ **pulmonary embolism** 肺栓塞
♦ **Alzheimer's disease**
阿尔茨海默氏病（简称AD），一种中枢神经系统变性病，起病隐袭，病程呈慢性进行性。临床上以记忆障碍、失语、失认、视空间技能损害等全面性痴呆表现为特征，病因迄今未明。65岁以前发病者，称早老性痴呆；65岁以后发病者称老年性痴呆。
♦ **validate** [ˈvælɪdeɪt] vt. 证实，确认
Additional studies and tests have tended to validate this conclusion. 进一步的研究和试验有助于确认这个结论。
♦ **preliminary** [prɪˈlɪmɪnərɪ]
adj. 初步的，初级的
They are taking preliminary steps in preparation for a possible war. 他们正在为应付一场可能的战争做初步的准备。
♦ **enzyme** [ˈenzaɪm] n. 酶
♦ **spike** [spaɪk]
vi.（价格、数量等）突然上升，剧增

gerated by the Japanese media. In 2007, natto sales **spiked** after one television program reported that natto has dramatic weight loss benefits. They later admitted that they had **falsified** their data and apologized.

Besides, natto is a common ingredient in Japanese dog food because people also feel it's good for their pets.

07 Edamame: Twig Beans in Japan
日本枝豆：喝酒好伴侣

日本枝豆，又称日本青豆或毛豆，餐馆里常吃的毛豆其实就是未成熟的大豆。一般呈青绿色，豆荚和豌豆同形，但是比较硬，而且外皮有很多细毛。一个豆荚内通常有二到三颗豆子，但也有只有一个豆子或四个豆子以上的少数情况。毛豆一般用盐水煮熟，现剥现吃。这种吃法在日本和中国很常见，之后传入夏威夷及美国。

日本居酒屋里，点一份枝豆，服务员会顺便送上海盐，顾客可以根据自己的口味来添加海盐。同样是枝豆，日本人更喜欢非转基因的豆子，甚至会满世界的进口非转基因大豆，比如乌克兰和北美地区。其实，对日本民众来说，对未成熟枝豆的喜好也没那么痴迷，很多的豆类食物更多地使用成熟大豆做原料。

Edamame (literally: twig beans) are steamed young **soybeans** typically served with sea salt. They're a magic food for **izakaya** because they encourage customers to drink more. They are salty but not particularly **filling** (as compared with the oily foods commonly served by Izakaya). As one of the many aspects of Japanese culture that **invoke** feelings of nostalgia for people, edamame are a social food that remind many of the **blurry** izakaya nights of the past.

There's a big difference from one edamame to the next. Edamame are "young" soybeans in the sense that they are harvested while they are still soft and **supple** (before full maturity). The best edamame are fresh, local varieties that are

---

♦ **falsify** ['fɔːlsɪˌfaɪ]
vt. 篡改，伪造；歪曲
She had to falsify the daily accounts so you wouldn't know about it. 为了不让您发现，她还得在日用开支账上做点手脚。

♦ **Edamame**
n. 日本毛豆，日本青豆
♦ **soybean** ['sɔɪbiːn]
n. 大豆，黄豆
The last houses give way to soybean fields. 最后一批房子也被拆掉用作了大豆地。
♦ **izakaya**
n. 居酒屋，既是日本传统的小酒馆，也是具有日本特色的饮食料理店，提供比较有质量的饭菜。随着时代的推移，居酒屋也逐渐成了日本文化不可缺少的组成部分，日本的电影和电视剧中也往往会出现居酒屋的场景。
♦ **filling** ['fɪlɪŋ]
adj. (食物) 令人感到饱足的
Although it is tasty, crab is very filling. 螃蟹虽然好吃，却容易让人感到饱足。
♦ **invoke** [ɪn'vəʊk]
vt. 引起，唤起，激发 (感情等)
♦ **blurry** ['blɜːrɪ]
adj. 模糊的，朦胧的
My blurry vision makes it hard to drive. 我的视力有点模糊，开起车来相当吃力。
♦ **supple** ['sʌpl]
adj. 柔软的
He has nothing of the supple form or slippery manner of the modern Greek

picked by hand in Japan. Top izakaya will only serve edamame when they are locally **in season**. However, edamame that are harvested by machine, frozen and imported from overseas just don't taste the same.

Compared with **GM** soybeans, many Japanese consumers have a strong preference for non-GM soybeans. The majority of soybeans grown in North America are GM. Japanese buyers search the world for non-GM soybeans and buy from producers such as the **Ukraine**.

The preferred salt for Edamame is Arajio (a lumpy, mineral rich, slightly fishy sea salt). Some restaurants will provide you with unsalted edamame and salt. This allows you to salt your edamame to your taste. After salting edamame you should wait 2 or 3 minutes before eating. Let them absorb the salt. Edamame are eaten by hand. The beans can be squeezed out of the **pod** into your mouth.

The soybean is used in a great number of Japanese dishes such as deep fried edamame wrapped in yuba. Young soybeans (edamame) are **not nearly** so important to Japanese cuisine. Most soy foods such as tofu, yuba, miso and shoyu are made with mature soybeans.

about him. 他没有一点当今希腊人那种柔软的身段和圆滑世故的神态。

♦ **in season** 当季
Strawberry is in season now. 草莓现在已上市了。

♦ **GM**
adj. 转基因的
全称：Genetically Modified
Top supermarkets are to ban many genetically modified foods. 大品牌超市即将下架许多转基因食品。

♦ **Ukraine** [juː(ː)'kreɪn]
n. 乌克兰，位于东欧，是欧洲除俄罗斯外领土面积最大的国家。作为作为世界上重要的市场之一和世界上第三大粮食出口国，乌克兰有着"欧洲粮仓"的美誉。

♦ **pod** [pɒd]
n. 荚，豆荚
They're as alike as two peas in a pod. 他们非常相像，就像一个豆荚里的两颗豌豆。

♦ **not nearly** 远非，远不能
Tom has not nearly corrected his shortcomings in work. 汤姆远远没有改正自己在工作中的缺点。

08 Why the Japanese Are Patriotic about Rice
日本人为何对水稻如此钟爱

日本的大米十分昂贵，出口率不到 1%，几乎所有的自产大米都在国内消费掉。其实，日本的农业生产规模一直在缩减。19 世纪 60 年代，日本还能自己供应本国 79% 人口的需求，时至今日已经降低到了 40%。随着 60% 的日本农民超过 65 岁，日本的水稻种植形势不断恶化。日本政府也认识到国家食物供应保障的问题，采取了保护措施。而尽管日本大米很贵，民众仍然热于购买本国大米，认为这是爱国的表现。日本人对本国大米可谓是钟爱有加。

日本的大米在质量和安全上声誉很高，民众对国产大米十分有研究，能够根据大米的外表、味道等迅速辨别真伪。在神道教文化中，好有专门的谷物之神——稻荷神。传说他有时以男人形态出现，有时以女人的形态出现，甚至会变幻成蜘蛛等其他形态。他还有两个随从，是白色的狐和狸猫。

Japanese rice is expensive. It's rarely exported (less than 1%). In Japan, domestic rice is popular despite the price. Almost all the rice consumed in the country is Japanese. Japan is so **patriotic** about rice that there's a rice dish called hinomaru designed to look like the Japanese **flag**.

Japanese agriculture is fading into the past. In 1960, Japan produced 79% of the food required to feed its population. Today, it only produces 40%. The situation is going to **get worse**. Over 60% of Japanese farmers are over 65 years of age.

Japan is worried that its **idyllic** countryside of green rice farms will soon be a thing of the past. The government also worries that Japan will be **at the mercy of** other countries for its food supply. People are aware of the crisis and **pitch in** with their yen to help. It's considered patriotic to buy Japanese rice and produce despite the fact it's expensive.

In the countryside, there are rice shops and rice vending machines. Rice can be purchased unpolished (brown) from the machine. You feed the rice into a **polisher** for a separate fee.

Japanese agriculture has an excellent reputation for quality and safety. Japanese rice is a short-grain variety characterized by a slightly sticky **texture**. Most Japanese people (and some long term residents of Japan) can tell you **right away** if rice is Japanese from the texture, taste and consistency. California rice farmers produce a grain called Nishiki that's similar to Japanese rice (Japonica). It hasn't caught on in Japan. However, it was a **commercial** success due to demand from Japanese restaurants around the World.

Actually, the Japanese diet has westernized. In Japan, rice consumption **per capita** has fallen for many years. In 1965, the average person consumed 118 kilograms (260 pounds) of rice a year. Today, that has dropped to 60 kilograms (132 pounds).

Rice is important to Japanese culture. Historically, rice

♦ **patriotic** [ˌpætrɪˈɒtɪk]
adj. 爱国的，有爱国心的
His speech was full of patriotic sentiments. 他的演说充满了爱国之情。

♦ **flag** [flæg]
n. 旗，旗帜
A flag was flying on the new military headquarters. 一面旗帜在新的军事指挥部上空飘扬着。

♦ **get worse**
恶化，变得更糟
The nurse on duty was fearful that the patient should get worse. 值班的护士担心病人的病情会恶化。

♦ **idyllic** [aɪˈdɪlɪk]
adj. 田园的，诗情画意的
I saw before me an idyllic life. 展现在我眼前的是充满诗情画意的生活。

♦ **at the mercy of**
任……摆布，受……支配
I shouldn't like to be at the mercy of such a cruel man. 我可不愿受这样残酷的人摆布。

♦ **pitch in** 参与，协力
We needed everybody to pitch in and help decorate. 我们需要每个人打起精神去帮忙装修。

♦ **polisher** [ˈpɒlɪʃə]
n. 抛光机

♦ **texture** [ˈtekstʃə]
n. （摸上去的）质地，质感
We could feel the smooth texture of silk. 我们能感觉出丝绸的光滑质地。

♦ **right away** 立刻，马上
I am getting in touch with him right away. 我马上和他进行联系。

♦ **commercial** [kəˈmɜːʃəl]
adj. 商业的
There has always been a difference between community radio and commercial radio. 社区广播电台和商业广播电台一直是有区别的。

♦ **per capita** 人均，每人
Ethiopia has almost the lowest oil con-

cultivation was key to survival. Japan is a small island nation with a high population. Due to its mountainous geography only 11% of land is arable. Japanese history is dotted with terrible **famines**.

In this **context**, it's no surprise that Japan's most important god is Inari–the androgynous (god or goddess) of rice. Shinto gods often have more than one responsibility. Inari is also the god/goddess of fertility, agriculture, foxes and business success. Inari is said to transform into a fox from time to time. So in Japan, foxes get a lot of respect. There are shrines to Inari all over the country.

sumption per capita in the world. 埃塞俄比亚的人均石油耗费量几乎是全世界最低的。
♦ **famine** [ˈfæmɪn]
n. 饥荒，饥饿
We're collecting for the famine victims. 我们正在为遭受饥荒的灾民募款。
♦ **context** [ˈkɒntekst]
n.（想法、事件等的）背景，环境
It was this kind of historical context that Morris brought to his work. 莫里斯的作品正是基于这样一种历史背景。

Chapter 5
爱上韩味：唯美食与文化不可辜负

01 Korean Bulgogi Insight
透视韩式烤肉

　　韩式烤肉原来叫做"mac-jok"，是人们用酱汁和大蒜将牛肉腌泡后放在火上烤制而成的肉食。"mac"是指"高句丽"（位于朝鲜半岛北部的古朝鲜王国）地区。传统上，中国人烤肉前并不腌泡，传到朝鲜王国后加上了腌泡环节，包括用酱汁和大蒜等，这便是韩式烤肉的早期做法。

　　韩式烤肉广受欢迎的秘密很可能在于牛肉鲜嫩。这其中，牛肉品质固然重要，但真正的秘密在于厨师师傅精湛的刀工和全心的准备。韩式烤肉一般使用鲜嫩低脂的牛肉里脊，要仔细剔去肉里的肥肉和肌腱。为了使牛肉变嫩，要用刀背朝着与肉的纹理相反的方向拍打精肉，要费一番功夫使牛肉味道更佳。经过一番切割和拍打，肉质更嫩，腌制时更容易入味。

　　制作韩式烤肉当然要从腌制开始。牛肉的腌制材料包括酱油、蜂蜜或糖、切细的青葱、大蒜、加盐的芝麻面和黑胡椒。腌制过程中，所有的成分充分发酵，使烧烤中产生的有害物质减少。一篇发表在《农业和食品杂志期刊》上的研究报告指出，用酱油或糖腌泡可以抑制食物烹制过程中胆固醇物质的产生。

　　The original form of **Bulgogi** was called "mac-jok." It was a type of meat dish where people **marinated** the beef with sauce and garlic before barbecuing it over the fire. The term "mac" indicates the region of **Koguryo**, an ancient Korean kingdom that was located in the northern part of Korea. Traditionally, Chinese people did not marinate their meat before **grilling**. However, Mac-jok, which was developed in Korea, consisted of marinating meat before grilling. It involved marinating beef in Korean sauce and garlic; this became the early form of Bulgogi.

　　The Secret of Taste: The reason that Bulgogi has become so popular everywhere is probably because of its tender beef that almost melts in one's mouth. Of course, the quality of the beef would be important in creating such effect, but the true secret is in how well the beef is cut and how devoted the cook is in preparing the food. Traditionally, tender and less fatty portion of **sirloin** is used for Bulgogi. Also, the fat and

♦ **Bulgogi**
韩式烤肉，肉质鲜嫩多汁，口味醇香浓厚，具有韩国特有的香甜口味，可做成肉串或直接烧烤。

♦ **marinate** ['mærɪneɪt]
vt.（将肉等放在调味汁中）浸泡，腌制

♦ **Koguryo**
高句丽，公元前一世纪至公元七世纪在中国东北地区和朝鲜半岛存在的一个民族政权，与百济、新罗合称朝鲜三国时代。

♦ **grill** [grɪl]
vi. 烧烤，严加盘问

♦ **sirloin** ['sɜːlɒɪn]
n. 牛肉里脊（牛的上部腰肉）

♦ **tendon** ['tendən]
n. 肌腱

♦ **tenderize** ['tendəraɪz]
vt. 使嫩化

♦ **texture** ['tekstʃə]

the **tendon** between the meats have to be carefully removed. To **tenderize** the beef, one has to carefully pat the lean meat in the opposite direction of the meat's **texture** with the back of a knife. Even if it takes a while, it makes Bulgogi taste better. During this process of cutting and tenderizing, the meat becomes tender and the marinating becomes more effective.

The preparation of Korean beef dish always **begins with** marinating. The beef is marinated with thick soy sauce, honey (or sugar), finely chopped green onion, garlic, powdered sesame mixed with salt, and black pepper. During this process, all the ingredients ferment and help reduce the amount of harmful **compounds** that are formed during the cooking process. A study published in the **Journal of Agricultural and Food Chemistry** concluded that **marinades** containing soy sauce or sugar **inhibit** the development of so-called cholesterol oxidation products (**COPs**) during cooking.

n. 质地，纹理，肌理

♦ **begin with**
以……开始；开始于……
The English alphabet begins with A. 英语字母表的第一个字母是 A。

♦ **compound** ['kɒmpaʊnd]
n. 混合物，化合物

♦ **Journal of Agricultural and Food Chemistry**
《农业和食品杂志期刊》，美国化学协会主办的关于农业科学的期刊，半月一期。

♦ **marinade** [,mærɪ'neɪd] n. 腌泡汁

♦ **inhibit** [ɪn'hɪbɪt] vt. 抑制，约束
inhibit wrong desires 抑制邪念 inhibit sb. from doing sth. 禁止某人做某事

♦ **COPs**
全称：cholesterol oxidation products。胆固醇氧化物，肌肉组织的一种成分，近年来生物医学研究表明，COPs 具有很强的细胞毒害性和致突变性，可能致癌。

02 Korean Gimjang: The Making of Kimchi
泡菜：忘不了的韩国味道

　　Gimjang 是指韩国冬天腌制咸菜的风俗，历经多年一直保存至今。因冬季 3~4 个月间，大部分蔬菜难以耕种，咸菜腌制一般都在初冬进行。

　　历史上，蔬菜难以保存过冬，因此在入冬之前，人们会把蔬菜腌制成泡菜来存储。季节一到，全国上下，不管是城市还是乡村，社区里的各家各户聚集在一起，赶在一场雪之前，把泡菜腌制出来。虽然如今新鲜蔬菜已经可以全年供应，但是腌制泡菜的传统一直延续着。

　　韩国还有许多专门介绍泡菜腌制场景的录像资料。比如，上世纪五六十年代，人们把成罐的泡菜往市场上运；晚秋的阳光下，一排身着韩服的妇女在等待购买泡菜的过往顾客。再如，八十年代的资料显示，随着核心家庭的增多和泡菜工厂的产生，人们集体腌制泡菜的现象有所减少。尽管如此，腌制泡菜的传统在韩国人的日常生活中仍然占据着不可替代的地位。

As temperatures continue to drop, people in Korea have begun preparations for the long winter ahead. The days from mid-October to late November, **in particular**, marked a spe-

♦ **in particular** 尤其，特别
She likes fruit and apples in particular.
她喜欢水果，尤其是苹果。

cial time of year known in Korea as gimjang season.

Gimjang refers to the long tradition of preparing large quantities of kimchi, Korea's staple food, before the start of winter. Before the **advent** of modern **refrigeration**, fresh produce and other ingredients were hard to **come by** during the winter, and cooler temperatures also made the **labor-intensive** process of kimchi-making considerably more grueling. For these reasons, families and communities in the countryside and cities alike made a practice of gathering together, usually before the first snowfall, to make enough kimchi to last the winter. And while both kimchi and fresh vegetables are now widely available all year round, many in Korea still continue the gimjang tradition.

Among the **documentary** pieces dating back to the 1950s and 1960s, several show scenes of produce-growers transporting their wares to the marketplace. A photo from 1957 shows a woman in the countryside balancing a large basket of freshly picked **cabbage** on her head, to be unloaded onto a cart **piled** high with the same round produce. A cow waits to pull the cart. Another photo from the same year shows a similar cart full of long-stemmed radishes instead of cabbage. In another, a line of women in Hanbok sit squinting under the rays of the late autumn sun, waiting for passersby to buy their goods.

In a video from the 1960s, a group of women packed freshly-made kimchi into traditional jars. According to gimjang practice, the jars would be **buried** underground, where the cool dirt would provide the **optimal** temperature to store kimchi throughout the winter, warm enough to prevent freezing yet cool enough to prevent the stock from going **sour**.

The records from the 1980s hint at the gradual decline of the gimjang tradition, due in part to the rise of the nuclear family and also the opening of kimchi factories. Images from these factories show mechanized **assembly lines** and uniformed workers **churning out** mass quantities of kimchi.

♦ **advent** [ˈædvənt]
n. 出现，到来
Swallows come by groups at the advent of spring. 春天来临时燕子成群飞来。
♦ **refrigeration** [rɪˌfrɪdʒəˈreɪʃən]
n. 冷藏，冷冻（技术）
♦ **come by** 得到，弄到
How did you come by that cheque? 你是怎么弄到那张支票的？
♦ **labor-intensive**
adj. 劳动密集型的
♦ **documentary** [ˌdɒkjʊˈmentəri]
adj. 记录的，纪实的
We have documentary evidence that they were planning military action. 我们有书面证据证明他们正在策划军事行动。
♦ **cabbage** [ˈkæbɪdʒ]
n. 甘蓝（洋白菜、卷心菜）
♦ **pile** [paɪl] vt. 堆起，堆叠
The usual way to reclaim land is to pile sand rock on to the seabed. 开垦陆地的通常做法是在海床上堆起沙石。
♦ **bury** [ˈberi] vt. 埋藏，遮盖
The pirates would often bury gold in the cave and then failed to collect it. 海盗常把金子埋藏在山洞里，而后来又没能取走。
♦ **optimal** [ˈɒptɪməl]
adj. 最佳的，最优的；最理想的
Can the market economy of private ownership deploy resources with an optimal way? 私有制的市场经济能以最优的方式配置资源吗？
♦ **sour** [ˈsaʊə]
adj.（牛奶等食物）变质的，馊的
In hot weather the milk easily goes sour. 在炎热的天气牛奶很容易变坏。
♦ **assembly line**
（工厂产品的）装配线，流水线
♦ **churn out** 快速生产，大量生产
He began to churn out literary compositions in English. 他开始用英文创作大量的文学作品。

Amid all the changes that have visited Korea over the past decades, gimjang still plays an important role in their food culture and in daily lives.

03 Korean Seaweed Spreads Around the World
走向世界的韩国紫菜

在韩国人的餐桌上，紫菜是最常见的小菜之一。紫菜的用途很多，可以和鸡蛋烤成"紫菜鸡蛋卷"；可以和虾、银鱼等一起放在油里炸成"腌咸鱼"；还可以跟又甜又咸的酱料一起制成"调味紫菜"，做法非常多样。

韩国人喜欢吃的下饭小菜——紫菜在海外主要作为零食受到人们的喜爱。东远F&B公司制作的橄榄油紫菜、芥末紫菜与泡菜味紫菜等各种味道的紫菜深受外国人的喜爱。现在，紫菜不仅出口到日本、中国、泰国等亚洲国家，还出口到了美国、加拿大、欧洲等地。其中，紫菜在美国的消费量最大。

紫菜是一种生长在水下石头等物体上的海藻类植物。因为它看起来就像"大海的衣服"，所以过去也被叫做"海衣"。朝鲜半岛全罗南道莞岛是出产紫菜最多的地方，该地区出产的海藻类产品占韩国全部海藻类产品生产量的五分之四。

在制作紫菜时，一般会把从海里采集上来的紫菜在180至200的高温下烤制5至30秒，然后将再进行加热与干燥。紫菜不仅味道好，营养也非常高。

随着全世界"紫菜之爱"的愈加浓烈，全罗南道的许多养殖场与韩国食品企业正在尝试开发更为多样的韩国紫菜种类，向更加宽广的领域进行挑战。

Gim, or laver, a type of edible seaweed, is one of the staple side dishes found on the Korean table. It is a very **versatile** ingredient, as it can be cooked in a variety of forms. It can come as gim gyeranmari, a rolled egg omelette in seaweed, or it can be fried along with dried shrimp or fish. Sometimes, it can come as gim muchim, mixed with a sweet and salty sauce. Seaweed is **capable of** many transformations, bringing variety, color and texture to the meal.

As one of Korean cuisine's favorite side dishes, laver is now being loved in markets beyond the **peninsula**, if not necessarily as a traditional Korean side dish then certainly as a snack. Dongwon F&B, a food producer, markets a variety of

♦ **versatile** [ˈvɜːsətaɪl]
adj.（指工具、物品等）多用途的
Pork is also the most versatile of meats. It can be roasted whole or in pieces. 在肉类中，猪肉的做法也是最多的，可以整块烤来吃，也可以切片烤来吃。

♦ **capable of** 能够，具有
The car was capable of 110 miles per hour. 该车时速能达到110英里。

♦ **peninsula** [pɪˈnɪnsjʊlə]
n. 半岛
The Arab live on the Arabian Peninsula. 阿拉伯人居住在阿拉伯半岛上。

♦ **olive** [ˈɒlɪv]
n. 橄榄

flavored seaweeds, including **olive**, wasabi and spicy kimchi, all gaining popularity among foreign consumers. Sea Veggies, Dongwon's brand of flavored laver, in particular is known as a **snack** that is low in calories but rich in taste, and finds its place in the **grocery carts** of parents concerned for their children's health. Considered to be a healthy **marine** snack, earlier this year Sea Veggie products began to be distributed in more than 2,700 grocery stores managed by the Kroger Company, a US-based retailer. According to Dongwon, many types of its seasoned seaweed are being sold at snack bars in a number of public schools in the US.

Laver has been exported to the US, but also to Canada and Europe, having already **swept through** Japan, China and Thailand. Nowadays, the US is regarded as a new **emerging market** when it comes to edible seaweed, as it can now be found on shelves at Whole Foods Market and Costco. The **retailers** are normally supplied with Korean laver through a Korea-based producer, and they then sell it onward in their local markets with their own brands.

Laver, a type of marine seaweed, grows on rocks **underwater**. In the past, it was called haeui, as it makes the sea look like it's wearing a garment. Most of the gim in Korea comes from Wando County in Jeollanam-do (South Jeolla Province), a famous region for various types of marine **algae**. The seaweed grown in Wando makes up as much as **four fifths** of the total laver harvested across the country.

Seaweed collected from the sea is commercialized as it is processed, being dried and heated to around 180 or 200 degrees **Celsius** for around 5 to 30 seconds. Laver is great both in taste and nutrients. A serving of laver has less than 1 percent of the fat recommended in a standard daily diet, but contains as much as 30 to 40 percent of a day's needed proteins and **carbohydrates**. Moreover, a single piece of laver has Vitamin A, equivalent to that provided by two eggs, as well as Vitamin B1, B2, C and D. Seaweed is also rich in **calcium**, po-

Smear a little olive oil over the inside of the salad bowl. 在色拉碗的内壁上抹一点橄榄油。

♦ **snack** [snæk]
n. 小吃，点心，快餐
I only have time for a snack at lunchtime. 中午，我的时间只够吃点心。

♦ **grocery cart** 购物车

♦ **marine** [məˈriːn]
adj. 海产的，海的
Bezanik is diving to collect marine organisms. 贝扎尼奇正在潜水采集海洋生物。

♦ **sweep through** 席卷，风行
The disease can sweep through whole populations in a very short time. 这种病可以在很短的时间里在全体人口中流行开来。

♦ **emerging market** 新兴市场

♦ **retailer** [riːˈteɪlə]
n. 零售商
Take the goods back to your retailer who will refund you the purchase price. 把商品退还给你的零售商，他们会按原价退款的。

♦ **underwater** [ˈʌndəˈwɔːtə]
adv. 在水下，在水中
Some stretches of beach are completely underwater at high tide. 海滩上有些地方在涨潮时完全淹没在水中。

♦ **algae** [ˈældʒiː]
n. 水藻，藻类

♦ **four fifths** 五分之四

♦ **Celsius** [ˈselsjəs] n. 摄氏
The star's surface temperature is reckoned to be minus 75 degrees Celsius. 这颗恒星的表面温度估计在零下75摄氏度左右。

♦ **carbohydrate** [ˈkɑːbəʊˈhaɪdreɪt]
n. 碳水化合物，糖类

♦ **calcium** [ˈkælsɪəm]
n. 钙

tassium, iron and phosphorus.

Encouraged by the worldwide popularity of laver, many seaweed farms in Wando County, as well as larger corporations, have started to widen their business scope these days, investing in new domestic breeds of seaweed.

04 Songpyeon: Korean Tastes for Chuseok
了解美味的韩国松饼

从很久以前开始，韩国人就将农作物收获的时节阴历八月十五看作是和春节一样重要的节日。中秋节当天，全家人聚在一起行茶礼，然后分享祭礼饮食。人们会分享用当年收获的新米做成的米饭与年糕，到了晚上，还会对着圆月许愿。除了新米米饭、新米松饼、芋头汤以外，祭礼饮食还包括菠菜、绿豆芽、桔梗三色凉拌菜、各种煎饼、排骨等肉类与烤鱼等多样的美食。其中，松饼是韩国人中秋丰盛的餐桌上不可缺少的代表性美食。

祖先茶礼桌上的松饼是对一年丰收的感谢，同时也含有对驱逐家中厄运进行祈愿的意义。在制作松饼时，要把新收获的大米和谷物放在松叶上，再加入馅儿后捏成松饼。

韩国各地的中秋饭桌各有特色，这一点在松饼的制作上也体现了出来。

在首尔，五色松饼最为常见。首尔松饼用五味子、栀子、艾草等天然材料进行染色，个头儿不大，可以一口而入。忠清道的南瓜松饼非常著名。将秋季刚收获的南瓜与新大米粉和在一起制成面团，在其中加入大枣或芝麻馅儿，然后捏成南瓜的模样。在全罗道的灵光与高兴地区，人们喜欢制作添加苎麻叶的苎麻松饼。

除此以外，全罗道的梅花松饼、庆尚道的葛藤松饼、济州岛的豌豆松饼等也都非常著名。味道与形状丰富多样的松饼可以满足人们的味觉与视觉。与要趁热吃的普通年糕不同，松饼要晾凉了才好吃。

As autumn has come with its cool **breeze** to blow away the scorching heat of summer, Chuseok, a Korean holiday equivalent to Thanksgiving, is **around the corner**. Historically, Koreans have regarded Chuseok, also known as hangawi, the 15th day of August on the lunar calendar, as one of the largest holidays along with Seollal (Lunar New Year's Day).

On the day of Chuseok, Korean families gather to celebrate the year's harvest by **conducting** jesa (ancestral rites), eating food made with newly harvested crops and fruits, and **making wishes** at night under the full moon. Along with steamed rice, toran guk (taro soup), namul (herb dishes like

♦ **breeze** [briːz]
n. 微风
The sun went in, and the breeze became cold. 云层遮住了太阳，微风有了些凉意。

♦ **around the corner**
即将来临，在拐角处
The Spring Festival is just around the corner. 春节即将来临。

♦ **conduct** [ˈkɒndʌkt]
vt. 举行，组织，安排
Scientists would conduct the second study in five southern African nations.

spinach and bean sprouts), meat, and seafood, one of the most popular Chuseok **delicacies** on the table is songpyeon, or half-moon-shaped rice cakes.

Songpyeon is traditionally put on the ancestral rites table on Chuseok day to show appreciation for the year's harvest and ask one's ancestors to help avoid misfortune. It is made with newly harvested rice and crops and cooked with pine tree leaves.

Each of the provinces in Korea has their own unique songpyeon varieties made with local **specialties**.

In Seoul, people make small **bite-sized** songpyeon in various colors like green, yellow, red, and white. Natural ingredients like fruit herb omija, gardenia seeds, and **mugwort** are used to make these rice cakes.

Gamja songpyeon or songpyeon made with potato is popular in Gangwon-do (Gangwon Province), as potatoes are one of the local specialties of the region. These rice cakes are made with potato starch with powdered rice and red bean or **kidney bean** filling. Some people leave their **handprints** on the cakes to give them a shape.

Hobak songpyeon or pumpkin-shaped songpyeon is popular in the Chungcheong region. Made with dried or powdered **pumpkin** and powdered rice, these rice cakes are filled with jujube or sesame seeds.

People in Yeonggwang or Goheung in the Jeolla region enjoy mosi songpyeon or songpyeon made with **ramie** leaves. These rice cakes are made with boiled water with ramie leaves, non-glutinous rice, red beans, beans, chestnuts, jujube, and sesame. They are very chewy and don't **go stale** at room temperature.

Flower-shaped songpyeon also known as maehwa (apricot flower) songpyeon is also popular in the Jeolla area as songpyeon made with kudzu roots or green beans are also popular in Gyeongsang province and on Jeju Island, respectively. Songpyeon varieties **amuse** food lovers with their beautiful shapes and good flavors. Unlike typical rice cakes that are advised to be eaten when hot, songpyeon is more delicious when **cooled off**.

科学家打算把第二项研究安排在非洲南部的五个国家进行。

♦ **making wishes** 许愿

♦ **delicacy** [ˈdelɪkəsɪ]
n. 精美的食物，美味佳肴
A pheasant is a delicacy we seldom can enjoy. 野鸡是我们很少能品尝到的美味。

♦ **specialty** [ˈspeʃəltɪ]
n. 特色，特性

♦ **bite-sized**
adj.（食物）一口大小的，很小的

♦ **mugwort** [ˈmʌgwɔːt]
n. 艾叶

♦ **kidney bean** 菜豆

♦ **handprint** [ˈhændprɪnt]
n. 手印，手纹
How do you explain the half handprint by a wall? 你怎么解释那边上靠墙的半个手印？

♦ **pumpkin** [ˈpʌmpkɪn]
n. 南瓜
Pumpkin pie is a traditional American dish served on Thanksgiving. 南瓜馅饼是美国传统的感恩节食物。

♦ **ramie** [ˈræmɪ]
n. 苎麻

♦ **go stale** [steɪl]
（食物）变味的，不新鲜的

♦ **amuse** [əˈmjuːz]
vt. 使高兴，逗乐
The boys felt amused by the clown. 孩子们被滑稽演员逗得发笑。

♦ **cool off** 变凉，凉一凉
Maybe he's trying to cool off out there in the rain. 可能他是想在雨里凉快一下。

05 Samgyetang: Korean Ginseng Chicken Soup
参鸡汤：韩国夏日必备

参鸡汤是韩国一道非常著名颇具特色的菜肴名汤，肉类食品和滋补类食品的完美组合，最具代表性的韩国宫中料理之一。参鸡汤不仅不油腻，且清爽鲜美，营养价值极高，带有一股药香。鸡肉炖得极烂，筷子一夹之下骨肉分离，肉香中还带有米香、药香。鸡肚里面填着满满的糯米，汲取鸡汤精华的糯米比嫩鸡肉更要美味。同时鸡肚里面还有大枣、板栗、枸杞、高丽参等配料营养丰富。

它以做法简便、滋味香浓而广受人们的喜爱。对于女性来说，食用参鸡汤好处很多，可以滋补、养生、美容、去燥，而且在补养的同时，又不必担心发胖。因为鸡肉的热量极低，参鸡汤的做法又较为天然，使得汤清无油，非常健康。

食用参鸡汤是个精细的过程，得慢慢品尝，急不得。如今，具备美味和健康价值的参鸡汤，不仅广受韩国民众的喜爱，而且已经随着韩国饭馆走向世界。

Long before the Western tradition of Campbell's Chicken Soup as a cure for sickness, the Korean version was a prevention, cure, and a summertime **rejuvenation** dish. Its bone-in chicken method with sticky rice, **ginseng**, **jujubes**, and garlic is a gigantic bowl of Korean comfort food that must be exported.

For its medicinal benefits and traditional herbal **additives**, the soup is generally considered a summertime meal served hot and meant to **replace** the lost energy and vitamins taken by the summer heat. But the preventive and **curative** ginseng, along with the "stick-to-your-ribs" feel, makes it a year-round soup.

Samgyetang, the Korean ginseng chicken soup, is typically made with a young chicken (under 50 days old) stuffed with rice, **peeled** chestnuts, and jujubes, or Korean dates. It's then boiled in a ginseng **broth**. What is added in the broth is what separates a standard samgyetang from an exceptional one. The general mix of salt, pepper, whole garlic, and green onions is the standard. However, each recipe has medicinal

---

♦ **rejuvenation** [rɪˌdʒuːvɪˈneɪʃən]
n. 恢复活力，复兴

♦ **ginseng** [ˈdʒɪnseŋ]
n. 人参，高丽参

♦ **jujube** [ˈdʒuːdʒu(ː)b]
n. 枣

♦ **additive** [ˈædɪtɪv]
n. 添加物，添加剂

♦ **replace** [rɪ(ː)ˈpleɪs]
vt. 替换，代替
Who do you suppose will replace her on the show? 你觉得谁会代替她参加这场演出？

♦ **curative** [ˈkjʊərətɪv]
adj. 能治病的，有疗效的
Ancient civilizations believed in the curative powers of fresh air and sunlight. 远古文明相信新鲜的空气和阳光有治病的功效。

♦ **peeled** [piːld]
adj. 去皮的

♦ **broth** [brɒ(ː)θ]
n. 肉汤

additives which can separate it from the competition: gingko nut, milkvetch root and **wolfberry**.

The soup is most popular in the summer when the combination of heat and **monsoon** rains can make it hard to keep moving. Sambok, the Korean word for the three hottest days of the year falling between July and August, and the **downpours** of rain in June keep samgyetang restaurants in Korea **packed**. Most restaurants that serve samgyetang serve only just that, making a long-lasting business on a secret, generational recipe. **On top of** serving the roughly $10 soup, restaurants will offer a small **complimentary** bottle of insangju, ginseng alcohol. As is the case with most ginseng-based foods in Korea, it's also meant to strongly boost physical and sexual **stamina**.

Samgyetang is not a quick meal either. The chicken is whole, and there is a bit of separation to be done. A large stone pot is served alongside a smaller bowl with a ladle. The ladle is meant to **scoop** small servings into the bowl, or to separate the bones from the soup. It's served with the traditional side dishes and garlic chicken gizzards (usually misidentified as chicken rectum).

For Koreans who are heavy on traditional medicine, the health benefits are obvious for them. The Chosun Ilbo, a Korean newspaper, reported that: "According to oriental medicine guides, garlic **detoxifies** the body, jujube quenches thirst, and ginkgo nut protects lungs that are apt to be weakened by low energy levels. All of these ingredients are then cooked with chicken, rich in protein and essential amino acids."

Beyond the medicinal benefits, the food deserves a more international presence in foreign Korean restaurants, even if it's not served in its traditional big bowl. Regardless of one's health, samgyetang's presence should not be confined to sweaty Koreans hovering over a bowl in the summer heat. It deserves to be an international cuisine.

♦ **wolfberry** [ˈwʊlfbɜri]
n. 枸杞

♦ **monsoon** [mɒnˈsuːn]
n.（夏季）季风，季风

♦ **downpour** [ˈdaʊnpɔː(r)]
n. 倾盆大雨

♦ **packed** [pækt]
adj. 拥挤的，塞满了……的
His room was packed with fruit, flowers, gifts etc. 他的房间里堆满了水果、鲜花及礼品等。

♦ **on top of**
除……之外
He lost his job and on top of that his wife left him. 他失业了，不仅如此，他妻子也离开了他。

♦ **complimentary** [ˌkɒmplɪˈment(ə)rɪ]
adj. 赠送的

♦ **stamina** [ˈstæmɪnə]
n. 体力，耐力，持久力（stamen 的名词复数）

♦ **scoop** [skuːp]
vt.（用勺子等）舀
Use both hands to scoop up the leaves. 用双手捧起叶子。

♦ **detoxify** [diːˈtɒksɪˌfaɪ]
vt. 清除（体内）的毒素，（使）解毒，（使）排毒
Seaweed baths can help to detoxify the body. 海藻浴有助于身体解毒。

06 Uijeongbu Budae Jjigae: Soup for Koreans
部队汤：没有华丽外衣的韩国美食

韩国最棒的美食其实并不华丽。在美食连载报道第一篇中介绍的烤鸡排在过去也被称作"平民的排骨"。烤鸡排等代表韩国的众多饮食都是在食物短缺的时期产生的，随着周边环境的改善，这些饮食也得到了发展。部队汤就是可以充分说明那段历史的一种食物。

部队汤的诞生要追溯到朝鲜战争以后，当时韩国刚刚开始重建。由于食物短缺，那时的人们都在为了寻找食物而徘徊，在议政府、松炭、汶山等美军部队曾经驻扎过的地区，可以找到一些美军的剩余食品。最早的部队汤也被叫做"约翰逊汤"，这一名字取自林登·贝恩斯·约翰逊。

部队汤与美军有很大的联系，这一点从食材上也可以分辨出来。部队汤的材料中包含热狗火腿、午餐肉和培根等西洋食品。当时，这些食物都是部队里常吃的肉类食品，因此也被叫做"部队肉"。

把相互不太搭配的食物放在一起煮着吃，这对于西方人来说可能一开始会觉得有点奇怪，但是部队汤却将这些食材很好地结合在一起，变成一种美食。虽然其中加入了很多西洋食材，但是部队汤还是成为了具有代表性的韩国饮食。部队汤是过去韩国作为贫困国家的象征，汤中融入了为国家重建而努力的人们的灵魂。

Many of Korea's finest **culinary** inventions hide humble origins. Many of Korea's best-known dishes were created during times of **scarcity**, then continued to develop as **societal** conditions improved around them. Perhaps the best example of this is budae jjigae, or "army base stew".

The origins of budae jjigae date back to end of the Korean War when the country was beginning the long process of **recovery** and rebuilding. Due to food shortages, the people ate whatever they could get, and **surplus** army food from US bases was common in areas like Uijeongbu, Songtan, and Munsan where there were many US bases. One of its original **nicknames** was "Johnson tang," combining then-President Lyndon B Johnson with "tang," a Korean word for soup.

Still today, budae jjigae is considered a staple of Uijeongbu cuisine, where foodies can discover the city's dedi-

---

♦ **culinary** [ˈkʌlɪnəri]
adj. 烹饪的，厨房的

♦ **scarcity** [ˈskeəsɪti]
n. 物资匮乏，萧条
The scarcity of fruit was caused by the drought. 水果供不应求是由于干旱造成的。

♦ **societal** [səˈsaɪətəl]
adj. 社会的
The societal attribute and the natural attribute are the duality of education. 自然属性和社会属性是教育的二重性。

♦ **recovery** [rɪˈkʌvəri]
n. 恢复，复原
In many sectors of the economy the recovery has started. 许多经济领域已经开始复苏。

♦ **surplus** [ˈsəːpləs]
adj. 多余的，过剩的

cated food alley. Found right next to Jungang Station on the Uijeongbu LRT Line, Uijeongbu Budae Jjigae Street **boasts** a collection of restaurants specializing in this delicacy. It's a small **stretch** of road featuring not more than ten specialty restaurants, and it can be hard to find. Owners stand outside their shops inviting passers-by to enter. Most restaurants have floor seating only, **prompting** diners to take off their shoes to sit down. Many of the restaurants display posters on the wall detailing the humble roots of their signature dish.

The connection with the American military can still be seen in the ingredients in budae jjigae, including distinctly American ingredients such as hot dogs, Spam, and **bacon**—which at the time were called "budae gogi", or "army base meat". Add to the mix more processed and canned American foods such as baked beans, macaroni, and sliced American cheese. In the **postwar** era, this was the first introduction for most Koreans to these processed Western foods. They may have seemed too salty or greasy for Korean tastes, so they were **sliced up** and boiled.

Over the years as food supplies stabilized, more distinctly Korean ingredients have been added to the recipe to enhance its flavor for Korean **palates**. It's now common to have budae jjigae with tteok (rice cakes), kimchi, red pepper paste, and various types of noodles including both ramen and cellophane noodles.

While the idea of eating a mixture of such vastly incompatible ingredients might be **unsettling** to most Westerners at first, budae jjigae attains a very comfortable balance of flavors. Despite its many American ingredients, budae jjigae is a distinctly Korean culinary invention. Budae jjigae remains a symbol of the **impoverished** country that Korea once was, as well as the tremendous spirit of the Korean people that helped them to rebuild their country.

The manufacturers in some countries dumped their surplus commodities abroad. 一些国家的制造商向国外倾销过剩产品。

♦ **nickname** ['nɪkneɪm]
n. 别称，绰号
She delighted in the nickname, the "iron lady". 她喜爱这个昵称——"铁娘子"。

♦ **boast** [bəʊst]
vt. 以有……而自豪，自负

♦ **stretch** [stretʃ]
n. (路等) 一段，(土地等) 一片，(水域等) 一泓

♦ **prompt** [prɒmpt]
vt. 提示，促使
Japan's recession has prompted consumers to cut back on buying cars. 日本经济的不景气使得消费者在购买车辆上减少了开支。

♦ **bacon** ['beɪkən]
n. 培根，熏猪肉，腊肉，咸肉

♦ **postwar** ['pəʊst'wɔː]
adj. 战后的
The increase in postwar borrowing by developing countries has recently excited interest. 战后发展中国家借款的增加，近来已引起人们的关注。

♦ **slice up** 切片
First slice all the fruit up, then add the ice cream. 先把水果切成薄片，然后放入冰淇淋。

♦ **palate** ['pælɪt] n. 味觉，嗜好
The new flavour pleased his palate. 这种新的调味品满足了他的口味。

♦ **unsettling** [ʌn'setlɪŋ]
adj. 使人不安的，混乱的
All these changes are so unsettling. 这些变化都使人心神不定。

♦ **impoverished** [ɪm'pɒvərɪʃt]
adj. 贫穷的，穷困的
He came from an impoverished background. 他出身贫寒。

07 Patbingsu: A South Korean National Dessert
红豆刨冰：韩国的国民甜点

红豆刨冰是一种韩国的夏日甜点，由刨冰制成，并配有红豆酱、炼乳、新鲜水果、奶油以及谷物。韩国顶级快餐连锁店，侬特利还在此基础上增加了南瓜子、菠萝、迷你棉花糖大小的糍粑。首尔柏悦酒店提供的甜点还有黑巧克力酱和蜜饯橙片口味。当然，不同的咖啡馆也有自己独特口味的甜点，不过最常见的还是抹茶或咖啡冰淇淋。

这种甜点耐嚼、香脆、奶香浓郁，当刨冰融化后就变成冰凉香甜的汤汁。在韩国，老少男女一个夏天都离不开红豆刨冰。它也是情侣们的最爱，两只勺子一盘刨冰，一起享受甜蜜浪漫的时刻。

Patbingsu is a South Korean **dessert** made with shaved ice and a variety of other ingredients. The name means "red bean rice" and is sometimes rendered as "pat bing su" in English. Originally the recipe was fairly simple, containing just shaved ice and sweetened red beans with small rice cakes and, often, **ground** nuts. That version can still be found, but some recipes have become much more **elaborate**. Patbingsu is served as a composed dish, where each ingredient is displayed in a distinct layer, while custom **dictates** that it be stirred together just before eating.

The original dish was sold as street food, appearing sometime in the late 1950s or early 1960s. Both patbingsu and ice pops appeared during that time. South Korea has very hot, humid, summers and ice was not readily available on the **residential** level until the mid-1960s, so these new, cooling treats were very popular.

From its beginnings as a simple street treat, patbingsu has grown into a national favorite. Modern versions are sold by restaurants ranging from fast food places to gourmet establishments, though they continue to be sold at street **stalls**. Soon after it first appeared, the ingredients list started to grow. The standard presentation now includes shaved ice, sweetened red beans or bean paste. Sweetened condensed

♦ **dessert** [dɪˈzɜːt]
n. 餐后甜食，甜点
♦ **ground** [graʊnd]
adj. 碾碎的
♦ **elaborate** [ɪˈlæbərət]
adj. 复杂的，精心制作的
According to the prosecution, the officers manufactured an elaborate story. 根据控方意见，官员们精心编造了事情经过。
♦ **dictate** [dɪkˈteɪt]
vt. 要求；命令
What right has one country to dictate the environmental standards of another? 一个国家有什么权力强行给另一个国家制定环境标准？
♦ **residential** [ˌrezɪˈdenʃəl]
adj. 居民的，住宅的
The town is a residential suburb. 这个小镇是市郊住宅区。
♦ **stall** [stɔːl]
n. 货摊
He sold boots on a market stall. 他在集市上摆摊卖靴子。
♦ **nugget** [ˈnʌgɪt]
n. 小块东西
a useful nugget of information 一条有用的信息

milk, ice cake **nuggets**, canned fruit cocktail, and corn flakes are also commonly used.

Possible other ingredients now include ice cream and frozen yogurt. **Vanilla**, or fruit flavors, such as strawberry, is popular, as are coffee or green tea flavors. Some recipes include fresh fruit such as bananas or strawberries. **Chocolate** chips or small jelly candies are another popular addition.

Two ingredients not familiar to many in North America or Europe are sweetened red beans and rice cakes. The red beans are red azuki beans, a very small bean with a slightly sweet natural flavor. They are commonly cooked with sugar and used in sweets throughout East Asia. Some patbingsu recipes use whole beans in sweet **syrup**, while others use sweet red bean paste.

Korean rice cakes are made from **glutinous** rice which has been **pounded** into a sticky paste and formed into various shapes. Those used in patbingsu are small and **plump** and have a neutral rice flavor. The rice cakes are prized for their texture, and the way they pick up other flavors as they mix with the many ingredients of patbingsu.

♦ **vanilla** [vəˈnɪlə] n. 香草
♦ **chocolate** [ˈtʃɒkəlɪt] n. 巧克力
♦ **syrup** [ˈsɪrəp] n. 糖浆，糖汁
♦ **glutinous** [ˈɡluːtɪnəs] adj. 黏的
glutinous rice 糯米
♦ **pound** [paʊnd] vt. 连续重击或拍打
Pound the roots with a heavy flat stone. 用又重又平的石头拍打树根。
♦ **plump** [plʌmp] adj. 蓬松的，松软的
The grains are quite plump. 谷粒很饱满。

08 Characteristics of Hansik Cuisine
到了韩国吃什么

韩食即韩国人的饮食，和西洋、中餐不同的是韩国饮食限制肉类的使用，多以发酵食品、蔬菜和米饭为主，这对健康和瘦身都很有好处，因此格外受到全世界的关注。

此外，餐桌上摆好主食和副食后，全家人及朋友们围坐一起，除了各自的米饭和汤外，所有的饮食都会共同分享。这充分体现了无论什么都要共同分享、共同担当的韩国民族的特点，也是韩国饮食文化的特征。

韩食的核心是米饭和泡菜，同时搭配以多种多样的副食。泡菜在韩国饮食上的意义十分重要，被选为世界五大健康饮食之一。除了泡菜以外，拌饭、排骨、烤肉、韩定食等也是在韩流旋风之下，走向世界的韩国代表性饮食。特别是在亚洲掀起韩流热潮，被称为宫廷料理连续剧的《大长今》，使得韩国饮食更加备受瞩目。

Korean food is referred to in Korean as **Hansik**. While many other Asian **ethnic** foods such as Chinese or Japanese food have become popular throughout the world, Korean

♦ **Hansik** n. 韩食
♦ **ethnic** [ˈeθnɪk] adj. 种族的，某文化群体的

food has yet to reach its peak. The Korean government is **crusading** for the globalization of hansik **in cooperation with** companies, **civic** groups and the mass media. As the people of the world gain a better understanding of Korean food, its flavors, and its roots, Korean food will undoubtedly become a global commodity like the food of Korea's neighbors.

The key to Hansik is **fermentation**. Every nation has their unique fermented foods such as cheese, yogurt or natto. There are many kinds of fermented foods in Korean cuisine. The purpose of fermentation is to purposely break down foods into more **digestible** components through the natural use of the bacteria that exists all around us. Unlike food simply going bad, fermentation represents a useful and practical change. So the Korean says not seokhinda (to be spoiled) but "sakhinda" (to be fermented). The kimchi that is preferred most by Korean people contains salted **shrimp** and has aged underground for at least a year in a jangdokdae (large clay jar). Like a fine wine, the process of **aging** gives kimchi its deep taste.

Another feature of hansik is that it is strongly based on vegetables. The basic composition of a table serving is steamed rice, soup and a variety of side dishes. All of them are traditionally vegetable-based; in fact, a side dish of meat was typically a rare sight on the dining table of common people. The cow in Korea, which has long been an agricultural society, was regarded as a **tool** of labor rather than mere food.

Hansik is fundamentally a slow food, a cuisine well suited to health and well being, because it is mostly based on vegetables grown locally and aged and fermented sauces. One of the best opportunities for visitors to Korea is the Temple Stay. The most popular type of Temple Stay is one that includes the true temple dining experience, which **prohibits** the use of meat and of artificial flavors.

As the unique taste and **undeniable** health benefits of hansik are becoming more widely known, the day is surely not far off where everyone will be able to enjoy hansik at home or at their neighborhood Korean restaurant.

◆ **crusade** [kruːˈseɪd]
vi.（长期坚定不移地）奋斗，争取
We must crusade for world peace. 我们必须为世界和平而奋斗。

◆ **in cooperation with** 与……合作
The TV play was produced in cooperation with CCTV. 这部电视剧是与中央电视台合作制作的。

◆ **civic** [ˈsɪvɪk]
adj. 公民的，市民的

◆ **fermentation** [ˌfɜːmenˈteɪʃən]
n. 发酵
Alcohol may be made by fermentation of many plants. 许多植物经过发酵可以提炼出酒精。

◆ **digestible** [dɪˈdʒestəbl]
adj. 易消化的

◆ **shrimp** [ʃrɪmp]
n. 虾，小虾
Shall we get some shrimp and prawns? 我们要不要买些小虾和对虾？

◆ **aging** [ˈeɪdʒɪŋ]
n.（酒等）陈化，熟化

◆ **tool** [tuːl]
n. 器具，工具；（有助于做工或完成某事的）用具

◆ **prohibit** [prəˈhɪbɪt]
vt. 禁止，不准许
The government introduced a law to prohibit tobacco commercials on TV. 政府采用新法律来禁止电视上播放烟草广告。

◆ **undeniable** [ˌʌndɪˈnaɪəbl]
adj. 不可否认的，无可争辩的
What was undeniable was the wide appeal of this popular humour. 无可否认的是这种大众幽默非常受人欢迎。

09 Eating Out in South Korea
外出就餐去哪里

除了各种特色韩国料理，餐馆是韩国人的饮食文化中不可忽略的一环。韩国的餐馆种类繁多，从不起眼的路边摊贩，到高大上的奢华场所，应有尽有。餐馆中提供的食物能够充分满足不同人群的口味，既有传统韩食，也有西式餐点和快餐。几个人一块出去聚餐吃个饭价格不贵，而且韩国人经常加班到很晚，因此去韩国人经常外出去餐馆吃饭。

韩国也不乏外国特色的餐馆，比如最常见的中国和日本餐馆，最近兴起的快餐连锁店，还有美国、意大利和印度等国经营的特色餐馆，都是很吸引人的去处。另外，若果想去体验韩国料理特色，不妨去烧烤店品尝一下韩式烧烤。

There are restaurants of all types in South Korea from street vendors to expensive formal establishments. There are many restaurants in between these two **extremes**, which offer traditional Korean food, fast food and western dishes. Eating out is very popular as it is **relatively** cheap and due to the fact that many people **work late**.

The most common foreign restaurants are Chinese or Japanese, although in recent years there has been a huge expansion in the number of recognizable fast food **chains** opening in the country. There are more **nationalities** represented in Seoul where there are a number of American, Indian and **Italian** restaurants to be found.

Korean barbecue restaurants, where the food is cooked at the table, are a popular way to try local cuisine. A **barbecue** meal typically involves sharing **marinated** meats, fish and vegetables with a selection of sauces and **side dishes**. The food is grilled on an iron basket filled with **charcoal**, allowing diners to cook what they want in the style they want. The barbequed meat and vegetables are wrapped in a lettuce leaf to make a **sandwich**, and are then eaten.

Street food is **enormously** popular in South Korea with a large variety **on offer**. It tends to be seasonal, which makes

---

♦ **extreme** [ɪksˈtriːm] n. 极端
We should not go to extremes in doing anything. 我们做任何事都不能走极端。

♦ **relatively** [ˈrelətɪvlɪ]
adv. 相对地，比较地
Con-struction remains a relatively labour-intensive industry. 建筑业相对来说依然是劳动密集型的行业。

♦ **work late** 工作到很晚

♦ **chain** [tʃeɪn]
n. 连锁店，连锁集团

♦ **nationality** [ˌnæʃəˈnælɪtɪ]
n. 国家，国籍

♦ **Italian** [ɪˈtæljən] adj. 意大利的

♦ **barbecue** [ˈbɑːbɪkjuː]
n. 烤肉，烧烤野餐
He was invited to attend a barbecue social last Saturday afternoon. 上星期六下午他应邀去参加一个烤肉聚餐会。

♦ **marinated** [ˈmærɪneɪtɪd]
adj. 腌制的

♦ **side dish** 配菜，正菜外的附加菜

♦ **charcoal** [ˈtʃɑːkəʊl] n. 木炭
They broiled turkey over a charcoal flame. 他们在木炭上烤火鸡。

♦ **sandwich** [ˈsænwɪdʒ] n. 三明治
He satisfied his hunger with a sandwich and milk. 他以三明治和牛奶充饥。

it a fun way to experience local eating habits. **Pojangmacha** are street carts which sell foods and are popular for lunches or quick snacks. A popular snack is twigim which are deep fried **squid**, dumplings, or vegetables which are similar to tempura. Other popular choices are dak-kkochi, spicy grilled chicken and waffles. There are also shik dangor hole-in-the-wall restaurants which sell cheap noodle or soup dishes.

♦ **enormously** [ɪˈnɔːməslɪ]
adv. 极其，巨大地
This book was enormously influential. 这本书极具影响力。
♦ **on offer** 在出售中，供出售的
That shop has chairs on offer at 10 dollars. 那家商店里有椅子廉价出售，每把十美元。
♦ **pojangmacha** n. 路边小吃摊
♦ **squid** [skwɪd] n. 鱿鱼

Chapter 6
街拍日本：独具一格岛国风

01 Karaoke in Japan: Nothing But for Fun
日本卡拉 OK：开心去唱

卡拉 OK 起源于日本，这种享受音乐的方式已经享誉全球，并成为了世界上不少推崇者喜爱的娱乐休闲活动。卡拉 OK 在日本仍不停更新、进化，越来越多的卡拉 OK 机现在装有联网技术，通过使用视频等工具让卡拉 OK 的乐趣不仅限于唱歌而已，还能表演吉他等乐器，模仿流行偶像的舞蹈动作。据说日本目前已经有超过 9000 多个卡拉 OK 机构。最典型的就是家庭成员或朋友们租一间科技新潮的卡拉 OK 房，唱自己熟记于心的歌曲。

日本人对于卡拉 OK 只有一个态度：唱歌就是为了快乐，无所谓好听与否！即便有人因为唱得不好，也绝对不要捂住耳朵或者夺走歌唱者的话筒，这是极其无礼的行为；因为在卡拉 OK 里，每个人都是自己的"超级巨星"。

Virtually everyone in Japan likes karaoke–from high school kids to **old folks**. It's a highly recommended experience for visitors to Japan. Karaoke is essentially a space to have a private party (groups small and large). Couples also enjoy karaoke. Karaoke brings out the wild side in almost everyone. **Seemingly** shy people are the most likely to be wild at karaoke.

Karaoke can be found in entertainment **neighborhoods** in major cities such as Tokyo and Osaka. They're very common. Shinjuku alone has more than 40 karaoke locations. They are usually large buildings with 4–12 floors of karaoke boxes. Karaoke are also widely available in small towns and the countryside. In some cases, countryside karaoke boxes are small **cottages**.

Karaoke is cheap in the afternoons and more expensive at night. Prices also vary by location and how modern the karaoke is. Japan built a lot of karaoke boxes in the 1980s and 1990s–many karaoke are showing their age. You will be asked how long you need the room. This can usually be **extended**. All night plans are often available after a certain time of night (e.g. a flat rate per person for midnight to 5 am). The karaoke

♦ **old folk** 老年人
♦ **seemingly** [ˈsiːmɪŋli]
adv. 表面上看来，貌似
She was rich, beautiful and seemingly ageless. 她富有而美丽，永远显得那么年轻。
♦ **neighborhood** [ˈneɪbəhʊd]
n. 地区，社区，街区
The whole neighborhood have been hunting for the missing child. 整条街的人都在寻找那个失踪的孩子。
♦ **cottage** [ˈkɒtɪdʒ]
n. 小屋，村舍
♦ **extend** [ɪksˈtend]
vt. 延长
Can you extend your visit for a few days more? 你能把你的访问再延长几天吗？
♦ **up** [ʌp]
adj.（时间）结束的，用完的，到点的
When the six weeks were up, everybody was sad that she had to leave. 6 周过去了，大家都为她不得不离开而难过。
♦ **remote** [rɪˈməʊt]
n. 遥控器

will call you 10 minutes before your time is **up** to remind you.

Karaoke **remotes** are somewhat difficult to use. They have an option to display English song titles but menu **buttons** often remain in Japanese at all times. Somehow most people manage to **figure it out**. If you understand the remote you'll be popular. There's a phone on the wall you use to order food and drinks. Staff can help you with the remote and any problems you may have.

There are also karaoke machines for adding **echo** to your voice. This can be turned up and down with controls on the karaoke machine itself. For whatever reason, **gaijin** have something of a reputation–gaijin dislike echo (generally). The machines also **rate** your singing. Many new machines rate how many calories you burned with your song. The machine is always right.

One should be clear about one thing: Nobody can sing. Karaoke fans aren't beautiful **vocalists**– they're party people. Join a karaoke party even if you don't sing. It's unlikely anyone will pressure you to sing–people are usually fighting over the mic. If someone sings badly it's impolite to cover your ears or take the mic from them. Everyone is a superstar at karaoke.

♦ **button** [ˈbʌtn]
n. 按钮，电钮
He reached for the remote control and pressed the "play" button. 他伸手拿过遥控器，按下"播放"键。
♦ **figure out** 搞清楚，弄明白
I can't figure out what he was hinting at. 我想不出他在暗示什么。
♦ **echo** [ˈekəʊ]
n. 回声，回响
There was an echo on the line and I couldn't hear clearly. 电话里有回音，我听不清楚。
♦ **gaijin** [ˈɡaɪdʒɪn]
n. （日本人眼里的）外国人
♦ **rate** [reɪt]
vt. 评价，评级
♦ **vocalist** [ˈvəʊkəlɪst]
n. 声乐家，歌手
This girl works as a part-time vocalist in a bar before becoming famous. 这个女孩成名之前，在一个酒吧作兼职歌手。

02 Izakaya: Japanese Style Bar
日本酒吧：居酒屋

居酒屋，指日本传统的小酒馆，是提供酒类和饭菜的料理店。起源于江户时期，据说最初是酒铺经营者为了使客人在买酒之后，能当即在铺内饮用而提供一些简单的菜肴开始的。随着时代的推移，居酒屋也逐渐成了日本文化不可缺少的组成部分，日本的电影和电视剧中也往往会出现居酒屋的场景。

在日本，居酒屋很容易就能找到。有时外面悬挂着大红灯笼，上面写着"居酒屋"的字样；有些连锁店干脆没有红灯笼。居酒屋一般有两种：传统的和现代的。传统的一般只提供啤酒和清酒，现代的更像个小餐馆。居酒屋里环境比较随和，没必要穿得太正式。

What is an "izakaya" and how do you know where to find one? It is primarily a drinking establishment with mostly Japanese alcohol and it serves **light food**. Once catering strictly to businessmen, it has become popular among women and students as well. Similar to the American bar, **appetizers** and light foods are served along with various beers, wines and of course, sake.

How do you know where to find an izakaya? They are advertised with red **lanterns** with the word "izakaya", "yakitori", **and so on**. Some izakaya chains do not have the red lanterns but they have "izakaya" on their signs. They are fairly easy to **locate** and always fun to visit.

There are two types of izakaya: the old and the modern. The old one is **set up** more like an American diner, with a counter and chairs or stools. They often they have only sake and beer, although there are some that have alcohol from western countries. (Please note that the older izakaya is still much cleaner than the typical American diner!) The modern izakaya looks like a nicer restaurant with proper sit-down tables and chairs. Some even offer the low tables and tatami mats upon which to sit.

So what foods can you order at the izakaya? It all depends on your mood and the type of izakaya you visit. When visiting an izakaya, you will always be served otooshi, which is a small dish of food that varies by establishment. The otooshi is served without ordering, much how most restaurants in the US serve you bread without having to order separately.

There are of course many other types of izakaya. There are chains that offer a more extensive menu and are better for larger parties. The robatayaki offers grilled seafood and vegetables, which are grilled in front of the customer on an open hearth. This is **recommended** for vegetarians and because they can choose the ingredients (point and nod) they want grilled.

The izakaya offers traditional Japanese foods, such as udon, yakitori, sushi, sashimi, etc. For those who are not very **adventurous** and want to **stick to** more familiar American food, there is always pizza and French fries. But be warned, pizza in Japan is not like pizza in the US!

The atmosphere at the izakaya is very casual and friendly. There's no need to **dress up**

♦ **light food** 清淡食物
♦ **appetizer** [ˈæpɪtaɪzə(r)]
n. 开胃菜；开胃食品，开胃物
♦ **lantern** [ˈlæntən]
n. 灯笼
There is an ice lantern show in Harbin every year in winter. 每年冬天，哈尔滨都举行一次冰灯展。
♦ **and so on** 等等，诸如此类
They increased their income by raising silkworms and so on. 他们靠养蚕等增加了收入。
♦ **locate** [ləʊˈkeɪt]
vt. 查找……的地点，确定……的位置，找到
Rescue teams are using thermal imaging to locate survivors of the earthquake. 救援队伍正利用热成像确定地震幸存者的位置。
♦ **set up** 建立
The city police set up roadblocks to check passing vehicles. 该市警察设置了路障以检查过往车辆。
♦ **recommend** [rekəˈmend]
vt. 推荐
Though ten years old, this book is highly recommended. 尽管是10年前出版的，这本书仍值得大力推荐。
♦ **adventurous** [ədˈventʃərəs]
adj. 大胆的，爱冒险的
Warren was an adventurous businessman. 沃伦是个敢于冒险的商人。
♦ **stick to** 坚持，忠于
Stick to your principles, and you will win through. 坚持你的原则，就会胜利。
♦ **dress up** 打扮
Little girls dress up as angels for festivals. 小女孩们在节日里扮成天使的样子。

though many people will be dressed in business attire after having left from work. Be prepared for politeness and lots of good food and alcohol!

03 Capsule Hotels: Japanese Life in the Tube
日本胶囊旅馆："管子"里的生活

胶囊旅馆是日本极具特色的，充分体现日本资源节约与空间创意的便捷式旅馆。这种胶囊旅馆大多只有在繁忙的都市地区才有，因为日本可怕的加班文化，促使了胶囊旅馆的诞生。这种旅馆是几十个整齐摞起来的"胶囊"。每个胶囊"盛放"一个顾客。有人说它很像宇宙飞船的太空舱，也有人说像棺材。1979年，第一家胶囊旅馆诞生于日本大阪，随后迅速遍及日本，甚至走向世界。

"胶囊"卧室一般刚好容得下一人居住，通常配有一台电视，当然还有一部让人眼花缭乱的遥控器。在公共区设有食品和饮料自动售货机，十分人性和方便。虽然日本文化以开放著称，但是对于胶囊旅馆这个新潮的发明，男女住客一般还是要分层而居，文身的房客很难入住。虽然胶囊旅馆对于上班族来讲很是便宜，对于一般人来说，可以当作一种旅行体验住上一晚，但就舒服程度来说，却不宜长居。

The great capsule hotel building boom is over. The first capsule hotel opened in Osaka in 1979. It immediately received national and international press **coverage**. Within a few short years there were capsule hotels all over Japan.

Capsule hotels offer rooms that are similar to **torpedo tubes**. They're for travelers who just need a place to sleep. Capsule hotels are conveniently located and cheap (2,000–4,000 yen), and their rooms are surprisingly comfortable. They're usually about 2 meters long (6 feet 7 inches). Most people can **stretch out** in one. The rooms have a television and a central remote control that controls everything you can imagine. Besides, the hotels provide **lockers** for luggage. They either have **communal** baths or shower rooms. Some have swimming pools and **saunas**.

Some capsule hotels have different floors for men and women. Many capsule hotels are men-only or women-only. Men are far more likely to stay in a capsule hotel. Salary men who miss their last train sleep at a capsule hotel and then go

---

♦ **coverage** [ˈkʌvərɪdʒ]
n.（新闻）报导，采访
There's little coverage of foreign news in the newspaper. 报纸上几乎没有国外新闻报道。

♦ **torpedo tube** 鱼雷发射管

♦ **stretch out** 伸直身子躺下

♦ **locker** [ˈlɒkə]
n. 寄物柜，储物柜

♦ **communal** [ˈkɒmjʊnl]
adj. 公共的，公用的
We each have a separate bedroom but share a communal kitchen. 我们各有一间独立的卧室，但共用一个厨房。

♦ **sauna** [ˈsaʊnə]
n. 桑拿浴室，桑拿房

♦ **tattoo** [təˈtuː]
n. 纹身，刺青
I've decided to get my tattoo removed. 我已经决定去掉我身上的纹身。

♦ **organized crime**
有组织的罪行，犯罪集团（的活动）

directly back to work in the morning. Staying at a capsule hotel is often far cheaper than a taxi home (after the trains stop running).

Customers with **tattoos** are (often) not accepted. Tattoos are widely associated with **organized crime** in Japan. It's also not possible to bring outside food to your room. Common areas usually include food and drink vending machines and PCs. Capsule hotels often provide **pajamas** to wear. Most Japanese guests wear the pajamas. Tourists are less likely to try them. Some old capsule hotels have vending machines that are used to pay for your stay.

In the 1990s, unemployed (or casually employed) Japanese **urbanites** were living in capsule hotels. For more than 10 years, capsule hotels have faced increased competition from manga cafes. Manga cafes are cheaper, more flexible and (generally) have more services than a capsule hotel. Manga cafes are only mildly less private than a capsule hotel. As the case goes, this social problem has generally shifted to manga cafes. There are Japanese youth living in manga cafes.

Modern capsule hotels are designed to compete with manga cafes. For example, rooms have free **WiFi** and the ability to charge a wide range of mobile devices. They may also include entertainment such as games and video **on demand**.

Capsule hotels are a recommended Japan travel experience. However, it's not recommended to stay in a capsule for more than a night or two. It's difficult to live out of a locker for too long. Other types of Japanese budget accommodations are far more comfortable for longer stays.

♦ **pajama** [pəˈdʒɑːmə]
n. 睡衣
♦ **urbanite** [ˈɜːbənaɪt]
n. 城市居民，都市人
More and more urbanite begin to pay attention to mental health. 越来越多的都市人，开始注重心理健康。
♦ **WiFi** 无线局域网
♦ **on demand** 一经要求

04 Mansions in Japan: Apartments for Residence
日本的特色公寓

日本的"mansion"并不是我们常说的名流富贵们所居住的宽敞的房宅，而是普通人生活的狭小的单元公寓。人们可以买来居住，也可以用于出租。日本的这种公寓小的可能只有三个单元，大的甚至会成为地标性建筑。

除了个别奇特的建筑外，日本大部分单元公寓的造型设计千篇一律。尽管空间比较狭小，但是利用率很高。小小的空间里却常常配置有奢华的浴室，西式地板房中总有一件铺着榻榻米的传统住房，这些奢华的配置也会大大提高公寓的售价。

♦ **smallish** [ˈsmɒlɪʃ]
adj. 略小的，较小的
The pool is smallish and more crowded than most. 这个池子略微小些，比大多数的池子更挤。
♦ **condominium** [ˌkɒndəˈmɪniəm]
n. 单元式公寓
Are there any other condominium association dues? 业主是否须缴纳其他附加公寓相关费用？
♦ **suburb** [ˈsʌbɜːb]

In Japan mansions aren't massive houses and estates for the rich and famous but **smallish** apartments for regular people. Japanese mansions are the equivalent of **condominiums**. People buy them to live in or rent out. They range from massive landmark buildings to small 3 unit buildings.

In small towns and distance **suburbs** of major cities such as Tokyo, they're still building new areas of houses. In urban areas, houses are often replaced with **concrete** mansions. For the past 30 years there's been a migration of urban people from houses to mansions.

Tokyo, Osaka, Sapporo and Fukuoka are still in a mansion building boom (that has lasted at least 30 years in the case of Tokyo). Units **depreciate** quickly. Rent drops with each year added to a mansion's age. In Japan's boom years it was possible to view mansions as an **appreciating asset**. These days, they (generally) deprecate with wear and tear on the building and interior.

Some buildings have unique architecture but the vast majority are **cookie-cutter** designs. Mansions range from large multi-floor units to tiny one room **studios**. Generally, mansions are small but efficient. However, there are several areas where buyers look for luxurious features.

Firstly, mansions tend to have large bathrooms **relative** to apartment size. In Japanese culture, bathing is a **recreational** activity. People **splurge on** unusually large **bathtubs**. Bathtubs have advance control systems that keep the water at a particular **temperature** or automatically pour a bath for a pre-scheduled time (they can also sing).

Bathrooms often have a separate Japanese style shower area. It's also common to have a dressing room **adjoining** the bath area. Toilets are usually in a separate small room.

Mansions usually have western style flooring. Many have one Japanese room with tatami floors. Tatami rooms (washitsu) are another luxury. Japanese people are generally **nostalgic** about traditional Japanese rooms. Many people dream to

n. 郊区，城郊

♦ **concrete** [ˈkɒnkriːt]
adj. 混凝土制的

♦ **depreciate** [dɪˈpriːʃɪeɪt]
vi. 贬值
The house begins to depreciate from the moment it is bought. 房子从被买下的那一瞬间起价值就开始下跌。

♦ **appreciating asset** 升值的资产

♦ **cookie-cutter**
adj. 千篇一律的
Handmade goods appeal to those who are tired of cookie-cutter products. 手工制品受到那些已厌倦整齐划一产品的消费者的欢迎。

♦ **studio** [ˈstjuːdɪəʊ]
n. 工作室
I cut it out and pinned it to my studio wall. 我把它剪下来钉在我工作室的墙上。

♦ **relative** [ˈrelətɪv]
adj. 比较而言的，相对的

♦ **recreational** [ˌrekrɪˈeɪʃənəl]
adj. 消遣的，娱乐的
These areas are set aside for public recreational use. 这些地方已经划出来用于公共娱乐。

♦ **splurge on** 挥霍；浪费
Let's splurge on a fried chicken for one time. 我们就奢侈一次买只炸鸡吧！

♦ **bathtub** [ˈbɑːθtʌb]
n. 浴缸

♦ **temperature** [ˈtemprɪtʃə(r)]
n. 温度，气温
The star's surface temperature is reckoned to be minus 75 degrees Celsius. 这颗恒星的表面温度估计在零下75摄氏度左右。

♦ **adjoin** [əˈdʒɔɪn]
vt. 邻近，毗连
Canada and Mexico adjoin the United States of America. 加拿大与墨西哥临近美国。

have one of their own. The other luxury people look for in a mansion is a shower toilet with lots of buttons.

Small luxuries affect the price of a mansion very little, as in most real estate markets–Japanese mansion prices are driven by location. There aren't very many dangerous neighbourhoods in Japan so that's not a big concern. Buildings in popular neighbourhoods or that are convenient for commuting to work are most expensive. It's possible to pay 30,000 USD / month in Tokyo for a medium size 3 bedroom mansion in a **posh** building / location.

♦ **nostalgic** [nɒˈstældʒɪk]
adj. 怀旧的
He made a nostalgic return visit to Germany. 他满怀怀旧之情重访德国。

♦ **posh** [pɒʃ]
adj. 豪华的，精美的
I was once having dinner with him in a posh restaurant. 我曾经与他在一个豪华的餐厅共进晚宴。

05 Japanese Furniture
日本家庭里的独特家具

现在日本的家居中，西洋家具也非常普遍的被使用。比如：床、桌子、椅子和沙发。与此同时，传统形式的家具也仍然被人们喜爱和使用。

日本家居设计中，既有传统的榻榻米日式房间，也有铺木地板的现代式房间。榻榻米是日本式草席，由秸秆制成，尺寸大致是长180厘米，宽90厘米。在坐到榻榻米草席上的时候，一般都要脱下拖鞋，除了礼仪方面的原因之外，还可以保护草席。传统日式榻榻米房间有壁龛，上边可以装饰挂轴画、插花、陶瓷等。房间入口处有纸做的拉门和拉窗，都是可以移动的。

日本的厨房，基本上都装有燃气炉、电饭锅、微波炉和冰箱。至于日式房间的卧室，里边基本不设有床。所谓的床，是晚上铺在地板上而白天收在壁橱里的被褥。所以，晚上的卧室，在白天就是客厅或者餐厅。

普通的日本房间内没有中央暖气设备。冬天人们使用天然气、石油或者电做燃料的暖气，空调来取暖。此外，到了冬天，人们喜欢围着一个可以取暖的矮桌子坐，这在寒冷的季节里非常流行。

Western style furniture, including beds, tables, chairs and sofas, are found in most Japanese **households** today. In addition, uniquely Japanese style furniture and household devices have survived or been introduced into the Japanese home.

♦ **household** [ˈhaʊshəʊld]
n. 家庭，户
I grew up as part of a large household. 我生长在一个大家庭。

♦ **consist of** 由……组成，包括
The atmosphere consist of more than 70% of nitrogen. 大气中含有70%以上的氮气。

♦ **tile** [taɪl]
vt. 用瓦片、瓷砖等覆盖
The roof is ready to be tiled. 屋顶可以盖瓦了。

Japanese households often **consist of** both Japanese style rooms with tatami floors, and modern rooms with wooden or **tiled** floors. Tatami mats are made of **straw** and measure roughly 180 cm x 90 cm. You should always take off your slippers when stepping on tatami mats in order to protect them from damage.

Traditional tatami rooms have an alcove (tokonoma) in which a hanging **scroll** (kakejiku) and a flower arrangement (ikebana) or piece of pottery is displayed. The room entrances are **sliding** paper doors (fusuma) and sliding paper screens (shoji) which can be removed completely.

Most Japanese kitchens are equipped with a **gas stove**, rice cooker, microwave oven, and **refrigerator**. The traditional Japanese bed is a **futon** which is laid on the floor only during the night and kept in a **closet** (oshiire) during the daytime. Consequently, the bedroom can then also function as a living or dining room.

Most houses in Japan do not have **central heating**. Instead, gas, oil and electric ovens and air conditioners are used to heat single rooms. The heating devices are **turned off** during the night and when nobody is in the room. In addition, heated tables (kotatsu) are a popular piece of furniture during the winter.

◆ **straw** [strɔː]
n. 稻草，麦秆
The old peasant is twisting pieces of straw into a rope. 这位老农民正把稻草搓成绳子。

◆ **scroll** [skrəʊl]
n. 画卷，卷轴

◆ **sliding** ['slaɪdɪŋ]
adj. 滑行的

◆ **gas stove** 煤气炉

◆ **refrigerator** [rɪ'frɪdʒəreɪtə]
n. 冰箱
The refrigerator is reasonable in price. 这种电冰箱价格公道。

◆ **futon**
n. 日本床垫，蒲团

◆ **closet** ['klɒzɪt]
n. 壁橱
The closet is full of broken toys and other nonsense. 壁橱里都是些破损的玩具及其他无价值的东西。

◆ **central heating**
中央暖气系统

◆ **turn off**
（把……）关掉
The boy had the presence of mind to turn off the gas. 那男孩子镇定地关掉了煤气。

---

06 Department Stores in Japan
日本百货公司

日本有几家连锁百货公司，主要集中在新宿区、银座与涩谷。日本第一间百货公司于20世纪初成立，起初是和服店，同时提供各类奢侈品。日本百货业几十年来颇为成功的。然而泡沫爆破，雷曼事件，大型商场与大卖场的出现及网上购物的竞争下，百货店业绩每况愈下。

大多数百货公司的许多楼层以女性服饰为号召。人流最多的是美食部门的地下楼层，而在大楼顶端的某个或多个楼层有餐厅，并有不同的餐厅种类可供选择日式、中式或西式等等。日本百货公司的服务无微不至。店员各随时随地等候呼招，以接待顾客。许多电梯由电梯小姐播报楼层以及开关门。商品陈列优美而且购买的商品会得到细心的包装，当然价格也会偏高。

In Japan, department stores typically operate in buildings five to ten stories high. They provide for a **one-stop** shopping experience with a wide **range** of products available, mostly better known brands and high quality goods. Accordingly, prices are generally on the expensive side.

The first department stores in Japan were founded during the early 1900s. Their **predecessors** were kimono stores, which supplied various types of luxurious goods during the Edo and Meiji periods. Japanese department stores were largely successful for decades. However, they have been **undergoing** difficult times in recent years due to the economic **slowdown** since the 1990s, as well as increased competition from supermarkets and mass consumer retailers.

At a department store, shopping is divided into levels. The food department is almost always in the basement and can be an attraction by itself due to the wide variety of Japanese delicacies, sweets, desserts and other **consumables** on display. At ground level is usually the cosmetics department, where many famous international and local brands of cosmetics are represented.

Moving up, the first few levels are often women's fashion, while men's fashion and the sports department tend to be on the next couple of levels. Located above are usually one or two levels dedicated to interior and lifestyle goods, **stationery** and toys.

The top level is usually the restaurant floor, where **multiple** restaurants serving different types of Japanese and international cuisine, can be found at a reasonable price. Some department stores also have **rooftop** gardens open to customers, which may be used as beer gardens in summer.

♦ **one-stop** [ˈwʌnˌstɒp]
adj. 一站式的，一条龙的，单独一处就可以提供各种服务的

♦ **range** [reɪndʒ] n. 范围，类别
She is a beautiful boat, but way, way outside my price range. 这条船很漂亮，但价格却远远超出我能承受的范围。

♦ **predecessor** [ˈpriːdɪsesə]
n. 前身，原有事物
It was the home to the League of Nations, the predecessor of the United Nations. 它曾是联合国的前身——国际联盟的所在地。

♦ **undergo** [ˌʌndəˈɡəʊ] vt. 遭受，经历
If the world is to avoid environmental catastrophe, advanced economies must undergo a profound transition. 世界若要想避免环境灾难，经济发达的国家必须进行深刻变革。

♦ **slowdown** [ˈsləʊdaʊn]
n. 减速，放缓
This readjustment, when it comes, will inevitably lead to a slowdown in economy. 一旦启动这种再调整，必然会导致经济减速。

♦ **consumable** [kənˈsjuːməbl]
n. 消费品
the sales mode of perdurable consumable 耐用消费品销售模式

♦ **stationery** [ˈsteɪʃ(ə)nərɪ]
n. 办公用品，文具
She has bought paper, pens, and other such stationery. 她买了纸、笔以及诸如此类的文具。

♦ **multiple** [ˈmʌltɪpl] adj. 多种多样的
The government performed competently in the face of multiple challenges. 面临多种挑战，政府表现得非常出色。

♦ **rooftop** [ˈruːftɒp] n. （外部的）屋顶
shout sth. from the rooftops 公开宣布，使人尽皆知

♦ **unparalleled** [ʌnˈpærəleld]
adj. 无与伦比的，无双的
It was an unparalleled opportunity to de-

Japanese department stores are famous for their **unparalleled** customer service. The constant greeting by the staff is a distinguishable feature. If you visit a big department store just before it opens, you would usually see its employees **lined up** neatly, waiting to welcome customers. The moment the second hand of the clock hits the opening time, the doors will be **punctually** opened, and customers can make a grand entrance being **flanked** by bowing and greeting staff.

The elevator girls are another unique characteristic. They are female staff, neatly dressed in uniform with the task to tend to the elevators. They provide relevant information to customers as the elevator goes through the different levels and act according to requests by customers to **alight** at specific floors. Unfortunately, the number of elevator girls has decreased in recent times, **presumably** due to cost cutting measures, but they can still be found at some of the bigger stores in Tokyo and Osaka.

velop her career. 这是她发展事业的绝好机会。

♦ **line up** 排成一行，排队等候
Line up the glasses and I'll fill them. 把玻璃杯排好，我来把它们倒满。

♦ **punctually** [ˈpʌŋktjʊəlɪ]
adv. 如期地，准时地
Computerized payroll systems are used to ensure that employees accounts are credited punctually. 采用计算机付薪制度确保工薪准时地存入职工的帐户。

♦ **flank** [flæŋk]
vt. 侧面有，位于……之侧面
Bookcases flank the bed. 床的两侧有书柜。

♦ **alight** [əˈlaɪt] vi. 走下来
Prepare to alight, for we are almost there. 我们马上要到了，准备下车吧。

♦ **presumably** [prɪˈzjuːməblɪ]
adv. 据推测；大概，可能
Presumably this is where the accident happened. 这大概就是事故现场。

07 Combini: Convenience Stores in Japan
日本便利店成功的秘密

日本的便利店叫做 Combini，对于那些忙于工作甚至无暇买菜做饭的日本人来说，没有便利店的日子实在是难以想象的事情。日本便利店不仅具备超市的货物齐全功能，而且方便顾客可以随时去购买。与美国的便利店相比，日本便利店物品种类更加丰富齐全，甚至包括刚刚包装的食物，供作午饭或者晚饭食用。

日本的便利店之所以能够取得巨大成功，原因就在于 Combini 经营者们能够及时捕捉到顾客需求，充分利用最新科技管理商品存储和订购。甚至有些日本 Combini 还采用提供额外服务的方式吸引顾客。

It's hard to **imagine** modern life in the Japan without

♦ **imagine** [ɪˈmædʒɪn]
vt. 想，设想，想像
I would imagine she's quite lonely living on her own. 我猜想她一个人过肯定很孤独。

♦ **carton** [ˈkɑːtən]
n.（尤指装食品或液体的）硬纸盒，塑料盒

♦ **grocery** [ˈɡrəʊsərɪ]
n.（食品）杂货店
He was employed at the local grocery store as a delivery boy. 他受雇于当地杂货店当送货员。

♦ **given** [ˈɡɪvn]
adj. 指定的；假设的，假定的

convenience stores like 7-Eleven, Circle K or Lawson's. They truly are convenient for busy folks who need a **carton** of milk or other **grocery** item. They may not carry everything that a supermarket would, but they have what you need at any **given** moment.

Convenience stores in Japan serve a similar function, as a quick stop for essential items. But Japan's "combini", as they're called, are **stocked** with a much wider array of items than their American **counterparts**, including lots of fresh-packed food for lunch or dinner **on the go**.

Japanese convenience stores have great Japanese food. You can pick up an array of traditional Japanese fare such as sushi, Japanese-style fried chicken, as well as more modern, Americanized food such as spaghetti and even sandwiches such as egg salad and **ham** and cheese.

The first 7-Elevens opened in the 1970s, but the Japanese public didn't **embrace** the concept of a neighborhood store at first. In the mid-1970s there were just 1,000 convenience stores throughout the country. An April, 2013 article in Japan Times reported that there were 50,000 convenience stores throughout Japan. Like in the US, 7-Eleven is the largest chain of convenience stores in Japan. The next two are Lawson's and Family Mart.

In Japan, 7-Eleven has become so **dominant** over the decades that its **parent company**, Seven & I Holdings Ltd. Co., was able to buy the US chain of 7-Eleven stores from its original owner, Southland Corporation in 1991.

The reason that Japanese combinis have been so successful has been these stores' attention to customers' needs and the use of the latest technology to manage the ordering and stocking. Because of the need to **conserve** space, combinis have less storage for stock than their American counterparts, so they evolved a system of tracking customers' needs and ordering only as stocks run low. So the **onigiri** and other prepared foods are delivered multiple

We will meet at a given time and location. 我们将在指定的时间和地点见面。

♦ **stock** [stɒk] vt. 备有，提供货物
We stock a wide range of cards and gift wrap. 我们备有各种各样的贺卡和礼品包装材料。

♦ **counterpart** [ˈkaʊntəpɑːt]
n. 相对物，（功能或性质）极相似的物或人

♦ **on the go** 忙个不停，活跃着
I've been on the go ever since eight o'clock this morning. 我从早晨 8:00 起就一直忙个不停。

♦ **ham** [hæm] n. 火腿

♦ **embrace** [ɪmˈbreɪs]
vt. 接受，接纳

♦ **dominant** [ˈdɒmɪnənt]
adj. 占优势的，主导的
The firm has achieved a dominant position in the world market. 这家公司在国际市场上占有举足轻重的地位。

♦ **parent company** 母公司，总公司

♦ **conserve** [kənˈsɜːv]
vt. 节约，节省
He writes on both sides of the sheet to conserve paper. 他在纸张的两面都写字以节省用纸。

♦ **onigiri**
n. （日本）饭团，一种日本民间传统美食，在日本战国时代，饭团曾经作为古代日本士兵行伍军打仗时的干粮。传统的日本饭团是三角状，饭团中裹上一颗腌制的酸梅（超酸无比），外面裹上一片干海苔包裹，携带十分方便。饭团的可口与其便于携带的优点，使它至今仍然很受欢迎。

♦ **airline** [ˈeəlaɪn] n. 航线，航空公司
This year the airline will be hard-pressed to make a profit. 今年该航空公司将很难赢利。

♦ **novel** [ˈnɒvəl] adj. 新颖的，新奇的
She come up with a novel solution to the problem. 她想出了一个解决问题的新奇的办法。

times a day.

Some combinis' focus on customer service has led to the addition of services such as package delivery and pickup, payment centers for customers' bills, concert tickets and even **airline** tickets.

Convenience stores in Japan came after the chains in the United States, but they have evolved in **novel** ways that suit the culture and the customers in Japan. Any American who visits a combini in Japan will be pleasantly surprised at the similarities–and the differences.

08 Takkyubin: Efficient Delivery in Japan
日本宅急便：高效的快递

宅急便是日本的大和运输所建立的宅配服务品牌，借由各种交通工具的小区域经营及转运系统，经营户对户小包裹的收取与配送。由于其市场占有率大，因此也成为宅配的代名词。与邮局寄送最大的差别是，邮局仅能在平日上班时间亲自到邮局或是邮政代办所付费寄送，宅急便是可以到包括便利商店等代收通路，或是打电话请宅急便直接到家里收取包裹。

日本的大和运输株式会社（Yamato Transportation）成立于 1919 年，是日本第二古老的货车运输公司，也日本最大的宅急便公司。大和运输的象征商标，是一个黑猫叼着小猫的图案。大和运输认为，图案中那种小心翼翼、不伤及小猫、轻衔住脖子运送的态度，仿佛是谨慎搬运顾客托运的货物，这种形象正和公司的宗旨相符合。

Japan is a comfortable country. The case in point should be Japan's famously efficient, cheap and reliable delivery service (takkyubin). In many countries, sending something as small as an envelope by **express delivery** can be expensive. In Japan, large **parcels** can be sent for a reasonable price (e.g. suitcases and sports equipment). Takkyubin is registered and fast (often same day or next day).

Takkyubin matches the Japanese lifestyle. People take trains instead of cars. It's a terrible experience to try to carry huge **suit-**

♦ **express delivery**
快递，限时专送

♦ **parcel** [ˈpɑːsl]
n. 包袱，包裹
I reached up and put the parcel on top of the cupboard. 我伸手托起包裹将它放到了柜子顶上。

♦ **suitcase** [ˈsjuːtkeɪs]
n. 手提箱，衣箱
He picked up his suitcase and climbed the stairs.
他拎起手提箱，爬上了楼梯。

♦ **stimulate** [ˈstɪmjʊleɪt]
vt. 刺激，推进
These proteins stimulate the production of blood cells. 这些蛋白质会刺激血细胞的产生。

♦ **access** [ˈækses]
n. 接近或使用的机会
Mr. Dennis said he had requested access to a telephone. 丹尼斯先生说他已经请求使用电话。

♦ **handle** [ˈhændl]
vt.（成功地）处理，应付
Don't take on more responsibilities than you can handle. 不要承担过多的责任。

♦ **wrinkle** [ˈrɪŋkl]
vt. 使起皱纹
Too much sunbathing will wrinkle

cases on a Tokyo rush hour train. So, it's popular to send bags to/from the airport. It's also possible to send bags from one hotel to the next. All major hotels offer takkyubin. Good hotels will put your takkyubin bags in your room before you arrive.

Access to cheap takkyubin has **stimulated** web businesses in Japan. If you order something online (even at night) it often arrives the next day. Free shipping is common with purchase. Over 99% of Japanese people with **access** to the internet say they regularly make purchases online.

One of the great things about takkyubin is that they can **handle** a wide range of goods. If you want to send electronics–no problem; if you want to send a suit that can't be **wrinkled**–no problem. It's also possible to ship refrigerated foods. The common term for this is cool takkyubin.

Some delivery companies in Japan have a policy that delivery persons should run when they're not in their **truck**. They park their truck and run to your door. If they have something to deliver to your neighbors they'll run down the street. It's something to see.

Takkyubin will **pick up** from your home. It's also possible to send takkyubin from most convenience stores. If you're not home when a delivery comes, you can usually call to **reschedule**. No matter how many times you miss delivery–you can reschedule (some companies may have limits but it's fairly high). In any case, there's no need to drive to a **depot** to pick up your items.

Yamato Transport is Japan's largest takkyubin company. In fact, "takkyubin" is their trademark. The **generic** Japanese term for delivery service is takuhaibin. The trademark has been so successful that it's replaced the real word in common usage. Yamato Transport is commonly known as "kuro neko" (black cat)–their **logo** features a black cat carrying a black **kitten** in its mouth. This logo is one of the most recognizable logos in the country (right up their with McDonald's Golden Arches).

your skin. 晒太阳过多会使你的皮肤起皱纹。

♦ **truck** [trʌk] n. 货车，卡车
Now and then they heard the roar of a heavy truck. 他们不时地听到大卡车的轰鸣声。

♦ **pick up**
（通常指开车）取走，接载
We drove to the airport the next morning to pick up Susan. 我们第二天早晨开车去机场接苏姗。

♦ **item** ['aɪtem]
n.（一件）物品，商品
If you buy more than one item. the shipping cost will be combine. 如果你不止买一件商品，送货费用将会更加便宜。

♦ **reschedule** [riːˈʃedjuːl]
vt. 重新安排……的时间，将……改期
Would you like me to reschedule you for another time? 要不要我再另外为你安排别的时间？

♦ **depot** [ˈdepəʊ]
n. 仓库，库房
They leased the building as a depot. 他们租用这栋大楼作仓库。

♦ **Yamato Transport**
大和运输，在1970年代开始服务，一直以来居于宅急便（Takkyubin）服务市场的领导地位。虽然宅急便（Takkyubin）是其注册商标，这个字已经成为宅配服务的通称。

♦ **generic** [dʒɪˈnerɪk]
adj. 通用的，一般的
Generic drugs are usually cheaper than branded drugs. 一般的药品通常比品牌药品便宜。

♦ **logo** [ˈlɒgəʊ]
n.（某公司或机构的）标识，标志
You can use the logo in all your promotional material. 你们可以将这个标志用在所有的宣传材料中。

♦ **kitten** [ˈkɪtn]
n. 小猫

09 Train Culture of Japan
日本的列车文化

日本的列车文化常常受到人们的曲解，比如有人说东京的火车太拥挤，一团糟。其实，拥挤的背后，是日本人对列车的痴迷和钟爱，是一种正面的文化现象。日本的列车价格便宜而又方便，极大地改变了人们的生活。比如，人们晚上不用驾车便可随意出门去转转，也避免了酒驾的问题，因此人们可以开怀畅饮，夜生活也变得更加丰富。

日本的列车公司，一方面因为列车的准点到达而闻名，另一方面因为公司的员工而著称。员工们穿着整洁的制服，秉持专业素养与顾客至上的服务意识。在日本乘坐火车旅行的速度甚至比得上开车。另外，日本通过子弹头列车，既促进了旅游业的繁荣，又提高了经济效益。

Japan's train culture is often **portrayed** negatively. People think of Tokyo trains as a big **crush**-train pushers packing into overcrowded trains. It's true that Japanese trains are **overcrowded** but there's another side to the story. Most people in Japan like trains (some are even **obsessed** with trains).

Japanese trains are affordable and convenient. They've transformed Japanese culture in numerous ways. They have also dramatically improved quality of life in Japan.

Trains allow people to go out at night without worrying about driving. Tokyo people both young and old have active social lives. Tokyo **nightlife** wouldn't be the same if everyone was driving home. And also it's possible to read or study on the most crowded of trains. Virtually all Tokyo commuters study, play games, sleep or access social networks during their daily commute.

Most companies pay for employee train passes (a tax free benefit). Workers in Japan typically have zero costs related to their daily commute. As the train schedules are so accurate that Tokyo workers are rarely late, so even if they're late for work (due to train delay) they can get an **excuse** slip from their train company.

Apart from its **on-time** culture, Japanese train company

♦ **portray** [pɔːˈtreɪ]
vt. 描述，描绘

♦ **crush** [krʌʃ]
n. 拥挤（的人群）

♦ **overcrowded** [ˌəʊvəˈkraʊdɪd]
adj. 挤满的，过度拥挤的
The assembly hall was overcrowded long before the performance began. 演出开始前，大会堂里早已挤得水泄不通了。

♦ **obsessed** [əbˈsesd]
adj. 着迷的
We live in a society which is obsessed with slimming. 我们生活在一个热衷于减肥的社会。

♦ **nightlife** [ˈnaɪtlaɪf]
n. 夜生活
Tokyo is a huge city and has an impressive nightlife. 东京是一个大城市，有着令人印象深刻的夜生活。

♦ **excuse** [ɪksˈkjuːz]
n. 借口，托辞
National security is the stock excuse for keeping things confidential. 国家安全常被用作对一些事情保密的挡箭牌。

♦ **on-time** [ˈɒnˌtaɪm]
adj. 准时的，按时的

♦ **trim** [trɪm]
adj. 整齐的，整洁的

staff also wear **trim** and tidy uniforms. They're known for their professionalism and customer service excellence. Train travel is far safer than traveling by car. For this reason, some Japanese companies don't allow employees to drive to work (**contractual** agreement). According to Japanese labor law companies are responsible if an employee is **injured** on the way to work.

Japan's excellent **intercity** bullet train system makes it easy to travel within Japan. This helps to fuel tourism and make Japanese business more efficient. And tourism by train is also relaxing. It's common for friends to have a little party on shinkansen (bullet) trains. Staff come by regularly with drinks and food for purchase. The most popular food item is always ekiben (train lunch boxes)–ekiben have a rich culinary tradition and often **resemble** fine food.

Trim lawns and gardens are everywhere in evidence. 到处都能看见整齐的草地和花园。

♦ **contractual** [kənˈtræktjʊəl]
adj. 合同的，契约的
The builders failed to meet their contractual obligations. 建筑商没能履行合同中规定的义务。

♦ **injured** [ˈɪndʒəd]
adj. 受伤的
Try to rest the injured limb as much as possible. 尽量不要活动受伤的手臂。

♦ **intercity** [ˌɪntəˈsɪti]
adj. 城际的，城市间的
The company plans to run trains on key intercity routes. 公司计划在主要城际路线上开通火车。

♦ **resemble** [rɪˈzembl]
vt. 与……相像，类似于

10 Bicycles in Japan
日本的自行车文化

在日本，自行车被所有年龄段和社会身份的人广泛使用于日常生活中。学校、上班的往返或从家到电车站，从幼儿园接送孩子或日常杂货的采购等都离不开自行车。

日常使用的最普通的自行车一般装备有一个车筐，有的还装有一个（或者两个）儿童自行车座椅，一把简单的锁，与中国最常见的自行车没有什么区别。可折叠的自行车、登山车和比赛用自行车变得越来越普遍，但从数量来讲，远低于日常使用的自行车。

理论上，自行车应该行驶在街道而不是路边人行道，除了道路标志表明路边人行道是步行者和骑自行车者共同使用之外。但实际上骑自行车者倾向于一直使用人行道。由于自行车的高度普及，在多数铁路站和购物中心附近有专用的自行车停车场。在一些地方，错误停放的自行车可能会被地方街道管理部门拖走，缴纳罚款后才可取回，罚款一般在3000日元左右。

在日本，自行车被偷窃的现象不很多，但是也会偶尔出现。为了与自行车偷窃做斗争，在日本每辆自行车都应该向警察局登记，费用是一次性的并且数目很小。如果购买一辆新自行车，注册过程有可能由商店处理，但如果从他人手里购买一辆二手车，应该向当地警察局以本人的名字重新登记自行车以避免误解。

Bicycles are widely used in Japan by people of all age groups and social **standings**. Tourists will find that **rental** bicycles are available in many tourist destinations as an alternative means of **getting around**.

The most common bicycle type in Japan and at rental shops are simple bicycles for everyday use, called mamachari ("mom's bicycle"). Mamachari are typically equipped with a basket and/or a child seat, a simple lock, a **kickstand** and just one gear. More advanced models with multiple gears or electric assistance are gradually becoming popular. **Foldable** bicycles, **mountain bikes** and road racing bicycles are rarely available for rent and on the streets are vastly **outnumbered** by the inexpensive mamachari.

Rental bicycles are available in many tourist destinations. They can be an inexpensive and convenient way to get around relatively compact cities or towns, where distances between attractions are slightly too far to **cover** on foot. Rental shops can usually be found at train stations. Some shops require a deposit and/or photo identification for rentals. They might also ask for the address and phone number of your accommodation.

The majority of bicycles available for rental are the typical mamachari. Rental fees are usually 100–300 yen per hour, 400–800 yen for half a day, and 1000–1200 yen for an entire day. On rare occasions, road bicycles, mountain bikes or electric-assisted bicycles (no license required to ride them) are offered at higher rental rates. Most shops do not allow overnight rentals. In cycling-friendly areas, some accommodations provide staying guests with bicycles **for free**, although some also charge a fee.

Of course there're certain rules for **cyclists** to follow. In theory, cyclists are supposed to use the streets and not the **sidewalks**, except when signs indicate that the sidewalks are for use by both **pedestrians** and cyclists. In practice, however, cyclists tend not to follow this rule and use the

---

♦ **standing** ['stændɪŋ]
n. 身份，地位
♦ **rental** ['rentl]
adj. 租用的，出租的
♦ **get around**
随意走走；到处旅行，游历
Does Abell get around a great deal? 艾贝尔常出去走动吗？
♦ **kickstand** ['kɪk,stænd]
n. (慢车停车的) 支架，撑脚架
♦ **foldable** ['fəʊldəweɪ]
adj. 可折叠的；可合拢的
The foldable powered cycle is one safe and light riding tool. 可折叠动力车是非常安全、轻便、实用的代步工具，方便出行。
♦ **mountain bike**
山地车，山地自行车
♦ **outnumber** [aʊt'nʌmbə]
vt. 数量多于，超过，比……多
♦ **cover** ['kʌvə]
vt. 行走（一段路程）
I want to cover 100 miles before it gets dark. 在天黑之前我想走完100英里。
♦ **for free** 免费
At first, we had to play for free. 开始，我们不得不免费演出。
♦ **cyclist** ['saɪklɪst]
n. 骑自行车（脚踏车）的人
♦ **sidewalk** ['saɪdwɔːk]
n. 人行道
♦ **pedestrian** [pe'destrɪən]
n. 行人，步行者
♦ **helmet** ['helmɪt]
n. 头盔，安全帽
Miners wore a helmet as a guard against falling rocks. 矿工头戴钢盔，以防落石。
♦ **optional** ['ɒpʃənəl]
adj. 可选择的，非强制的
♦ **multi-storey** [mʌl'tɪst'ɔːrɪ]
adj. 多层的
That new multi-storey carpark is a real eyesore.

sidewalks out of convenience. **Helmets** are **optional** and are not usually provided by rental shops.

In many big cities, there are dedicated bicycle parking areas near railway stations and shopping centers. Here and there you may even find **multi-storey** parking garages for exclusive use by bicycles. Where there is a lack of **designated** parking space, do not follow bicycles that are ruthlessly parked even in clearly designated non-parking zones. Illegally parked bicycles may be removed by the local authorities and can only be **retrieved** by paying a fine. Park instead at a location where your bicycle will obviously not be a **hindrance**.

那座新的多层停车场实在难看。

♦ **designated** ['dezɪgneɪtɪd]
adj. 指定的，选定的
The hotel was appointed a designated hotel by the Beijing Travel and Tourism Administration. 该旅馆是北京旅游局的定点旅馆。

♦ **retrieve** [rɪ'tri:v]
vt. 取回，重新得到
He was determined to retrieve his honor. 他决心恢复名誉。

♦ **hindrance** ['hɪndrəns]
n. 障碍，障碍物

Chapter 7
邂逅韩国：开启韩式真生活

01 Traditional Markets: The Lifestyle of the Koreans
韩国传统市场：韩国人的生活视窗

现代化的市场具有交通便利，物品种类俱全等特征，虽然方便购买物品，但每个市场从形态上看都大同小异，毫无个性而言。而韩国的传统市场，则可在空地上摆摊，瞬间搭建成一个小店铺，不管认不认识的人之间都会相互微笑着问好。

韩国传统市场物品的价钱也并非明码标价，是通过买家与卖家的讲价而实现的，如果是个砍价能手的话，会得到意想不到的折扣哦。在这样的传统市场里，到处都充满了人情味，是一处感受韩国人日常生活最好的空间。如果您想在都市之中，在感受韩国美景的同时，品尝美食，参观特别的街区，那么不妨到传统市场里走一遭吧。

Koreans use the expression, "the smell of the people" to express the feeling of being **surrounded** by **humanity**. This sense of being together as one with a crowd, even **in the absence of** a relationship between each individual, is an important part of Korean culture. When people seek this **scent** of humanity, one of the first places they go to is the local sijang, or market.

Markets have always been a gathering place where people engage with each other, whether it's by trading tales or trading **merchandise**, and Korea's markets remain a **vibrant** part of the social and commercial scene today. From the **gigantic** Jagalchi Seafood Market in Busan to the technology-driven Yongsan Electronics Market in Seoul to the tiny neighborhood markets that dot cities and towns all across Korea, they are the place to truly appreciate the "smell of the people." By bringing together the people who grow and make things with the people who will use them, markets build a sense of unity and **tie** together people and products into one community.

♦ **surrounded** [səˈraʊndɪd]
adj. 被……环绕着的（后面常与 by, with 连用）
In the cosy consulting room the children are surrounded by familiar objects. 在温馨的诊疗室里，孩子们周围摆满了亲切熟悉的东西。

♦ **humanity** [hjʊ(ː)ˈmænɪtɪ]
n. 人性，人文
For him, the place is fairly boiling with humanity. 对他来说，这个地方充满了人情味。

♦ **in the absence of**
缺乏……时，当……不在时
In the absence of actual data no reliance can be placed on such figures. 在缺乏实际资料的情况下，这样的数据不可靠。

♦ **scent** [sent]
n. 气味，痕迹
Many kinds of insect find their mates by scent. 许多昆虫通过气味找到交配对象。

♦ **merchandise** [ˈmɜːtʃəndaɪz]
n. 商品，货物
Retailers can return defective merchandise. 零售商可以退回有缺陷的商品。

♦ **vibrant** [ˈvaɪbrənt]
adj. 充满活力的
Tom felt himself being drawn towards her vibrant personality. 汤姆感觉自己被她充满朝气的个性所吸引。

♦ **gigantic** [dʒaɪˈɡæntɪk]
adj. 巨大的，庞大的
The earth may be thought of as a gigantic magnet. 整个地球可以想象为一块硕大无朋的磁石。

♦ **tie** [taɪ]
vt. 连接，（用线、绳等）系

Korean markets, whether large or small, require some special skills. As fixed prices have become the **norm** and big box stores can be found everywhere, the art of bargaining may not be exercised much in contemporary life. However, it's alive and well in the **marketplace**. Instead of being an **adversarial** encounter, though, it's usually a friendly exchange. A good but not greedy **haggler** commands respect, and merchants enjoy the **back-and-forth** as they explain their wares and justify their prices. Sellers can also offer suggestions, whether it's the right **fabric** for a suit or the best kind of bean paste for a particular sauce. The social nature of the marketplace brings both sides together as friends for a few moments, and many merchants reward repeat shoppers with the pick of the lot or a little extra thrown in.

He tied the ends of the plastic bag together. 他把塑料袋的两头系在了一起。
♦ **norm** [nɔːm] n. 标准，规范
♦ **marketplace** [ˈmɑːkɪtˌpleɪs] n. 集市
Peasants sell vegetables and eggs in the marketplace. 农民在集市卖蔬菜和鸡蛋。
♦ **adversarial** [ˌædvəˈseərɪəl] adj. 敌对的，对抗性的
That doesn't sound adversarial to me. 我觉得，这听上去并没有敌对的意味。
♦ **haggler** [ˈhæɡlə] n. 很会砍价的人
♦ **back-and-forth** 来回（的过程）
♦ **fabric** [ˈfæbrɪk] n. 织物
You can hang lengths of fabric behind the glass. 你可以在玻璃后面挂几条织品。

02 South Korea Media
韩国媒体大观

韩国的新闻出版业已有一个多世纪的历史。1896 年，韩国创办了全国第一份报纸——《独立报》，每周发行三次，共分四页，包括韩英双语报道（前三页是韩文，第四页是英文），首次发行 300 份。随后，韩国报业在现代化的潮流中，更新设备和传播技术，促进了自身的发展的同时，更重要的是，媒体时刻都在为维持民族精神做贡献，而且开拓人们的视野，把瞬息万变的世界形势展现在人们的面前。

除了报纸，韩国的媒体还包括迅速发展的电视行业。从 1956 年在首尔设立的首个商业化电视台开始，到电视娱乐化的潮流，如今，在信息技术革新的引领下，韩国的电视业获得举世瞩目的骄人成就。

The modern Korean **press** is well over a century old. Korea's first modern newspaper, the Dongnipsinmun (Independence Newspaper), was founded in 1896 by Dr. Philip Jaisohn (Seo Jae-pil in Korean). The Dongnipsinmum was a **bilingual** paper with 300 copies of four tabloid pages printed three times a week, the first three pages in Korean and the last page in English.

♦ **press** [pres] n. 报纸，报刊；媒体
The government says it will not be bullied by the press. 政府声称不会屈服于新闻媒体的压力。
♦ **bilingual** [baɪˈlɪŋɡwəl] adj. 双语的，两种语言的

Over the following decades, Korean newspapers found their greatest challenge in **upholding** the **nationalistic** spirit of the Korean people and opening their eyes to the rapidly changing world. The newspapers played an important role in independence movements during the Japanese **colonial** period (1910-1945). The Chosun Ilbo and the Dong-a Ilbo are the two oldest newspapers in Korea, both were **inaugurated** in 1920 **in the wake of** the March First Independence Movement.

Korean newspapers have made significant investments in modern press facilities and equipment in recent years. Most national **dailies** operate **computerized** typesetting and editing systems with multicolor printing capability.

The first edition of the Dongnipsinmum (The Independent) Published on April 7, 1896, it was Korea's first privately-owned, all-Hangeul newspaper. In addition, Yonhap News Agency maintains 49 overseas **bureaus** in Europe, North America, the Middle East, Southeast Asia, and South America.

Television broadcasting in the Republic of Korea began in 1956 with the opening of a privately-owned and commercially operated station in Seoul. This first TV station, however, was destroyed by fire in 1959. In December 1961, KBS-TV was inaugurated by the government as the first **full-scale** television service in Korea. The Munhwa Broadcasting Corporation established MBC-TV, another nation-wide **network** in August 1969. SBS (the Seoul Broadcasting System), a private channel, began broadcasting in 1990.

The KBS, MBC, SBS and EBS television networks launched digital broadcasting in the Seoul **metropolitan** area in the latter half of 2001. The service was expanded to the greater Seoul and surrounding areas in 2002.

Cable TV started experimental services in 1990. As public demand for more information and a greater variety of entertainment increased, demand for cable TV has been **on the increase**. At the end of 2009, 15.2 million **subscribers** were

---

♦ **uphold** [ʌpˈhəʊld]
vt. 支持；维持
Frankly speaking, I cannot uphold such conduct. 坦白地说，我不能支持这样的行为。

♦ **nationalistic** [ˌnæʃənəˈlɪstɪk]
adj. 民族主义的，国家主义的

♦ **colonial** [kəˈləʊnjəl]
adj. 殖民（地）的，殖民主义的
His guerrillas defeated the colonial army in 1954. 1954 年他领导的游击队打败了殖民军队。

♦ **inaugurate** [ɪˈnɔːgjʊreɪt]
vt. 开创，创始

♦ **in the wake of**
在……之后的；尾随，紧跟
The company is in bankruptcy proceedings in the wake of a strike that began last spring. 去年春天开始的罢工一结束，这家公司就进入了破产程序。

♦ **daily** [ˈdeɪlɪ]
n. 日报

♦ **computerized** [kəmˈpjuːtəraɪzd]
adj. 计算机化的
The factory has been fully computerized. 这家工厂已完全计算机化了。

♦ **bureau** [bjʊəˈrəʊ]
n. （提供某方面信息的）办事处

♦ **full-scale** [ˈfʊl-ˈskeɪl]
adj. 全面的；彻底的
The fighting is threatening to turn into full-scale war. 这场战斗有可能会演变为全面的战争。

♦ **network** [ˈnetwəːk]
n. 网，网络，网状物

♦ **metropolitan** [metrəˈpɒlɪt(ə)n]
adj. 大都会的，大城市的

♦ **on the increase**
正在增加之中，不断增加
Vegetarianism is on the increase in Britain. 素食主义在英国越来越盛行。

♦ **subscriber** [sʌbsˈkraɪbə]
n. 用户，订户

able to view about 120 cable channels broadcasting programs.

The development of IPTV (Internet Protocol Television) has also **paved the way for** Korea to become one of the leaders in the field of information technology. According to the Korea Communications Commission (KCC), there were 3.086 million IPTV service subscribers as of the end of 2010.

♦ **pave the way for**
为……铺平道路，为……做好准备
The mushroom development of technology will pave the way for improving our economy. 科学技术的迅猛发展将为我们改善经济状况铺平道路。

03 An All-Mobile Life in South Korea
韩国人的移动生活

在今天的韩国，"以手机为主导的数字生活"已经开始变得触手可及，并进入实际商用阶段。很多家庭已经安装上了"手机钥匙"、"手机电器开关"、"手机取钱卡"等，而安装的价格也并非高不可攀。随着手机和网络技术的日益进步，在明日的韩国，手机将极有可能掌控人们日常生活的一切！从三星和乐金等大型科技公司便可一瞥韩国的科技实力，可以预言，韩国的未来将是移动生活。

韩国的手机非常普及，许多韩国人在乘坐地铁时，都会沉浸在手机中，比如用手机看电视剧；而且韩国也是世界上最早用手机接收电视信号的国家。人们可以通过手机听音乐、看视频、订阅电子报刊，甚至是支付各种费用。

It has been a while since the mobile phone became **more than** just a phone, serving as a texting device, a **camera** and a digital music player, among other things. But experts say South Korea, because of its high-speed wireless networks and top technology companies like Samsung and **LG**, is the test case for the mobile future.

With young South Koreans changing mobile phones once a year, according to consumer groups, it is virtually impossible to **keep track of** what they can do with the latest models. But the use of mobile devices is so widespread that at any given time, you will see South Koreans of all ages sitting in subways and buses **engrossed** in watching a television soap opera on **hand-held** devices, very often their mobile phones. They talk on the phone and at the same time read

♦ **more than** 不只是
♦ **camera** ['kæmərə]
n. 照相机；摄像机
♦ **keep track of**
了解；跟踪；与……保持联系
As a doctor, Brooks has to keep track of the latest developments in medicine.
作为一名医生，布鲁克斯必须了解医学的最新发展动态。
♦ **engrossed** [ɪn'ɡrəʊst]
adj. 全神贯注的，专心致志的
The student is engrossed in his book.
这名学生正在专心致志地看书。
♦ **hand-held** ['hænd,held]
adj. 便携式的，掌上型的
♦ **vibrate** [vaɪ'breɪt] vi. 振动，颤动
The ground shook and the cliffs seemed

comic books on its screen. And these comics have sound effects: Phones **vibrate** when a bomb explodes.

In 2005, South Korea became the first country in the world where mobiles could receive digital television **signals**–something Americans with their latest iPhones are just beginning to get used to. Like many other places these days, the phone is also a calculator, dictionary and **stopwatch**; a television remote control and **navigator** for your car. Newspapers are **delivered** to mobile phones. Some even get fired by mobile: In March, a group of taxi drivers rallied after their company sent them a text message of dismissal–a practice that gained **notoriety** as the country's economic **downturn** deepened.

Here, people sometimes even raise pets by phone, part of a global fad that began in the late 1990s with the Japanese invention of the Tamagotchi digital pet. You feed, walk and clean up behind the digi-dog that lives inside your mobile. If you neglect it, it **sulks**, withers and dies.

Each month last year, four million South Koreans bought music, videos, ring tones, online game subscriptions and articles from newspaper archives and other online items and charged them to their mobile phone bills, without **going through** any bank or credit card. South Koreans have done this since 2000.

to vibrate.
大地在摇晃，悬崖好像在颤动。
♦ **signal** ['sɪɡnl] n. 信号
The red signal means you can shoot. 红色信号表示可以射击。
♦ **stopwatch** ['stɒpwɒtʃ]
n. (赛跑等记时用的) 秒表，跑表
♦ **navigator** ['nævɪɡeɪtə]
n. 导航 (仪)
♦ **deliver** [dɪ'lɪvə]
vt. 递送，交付，发表
My master ordered me not to deliver the message except in private. 我的主人命令我务必私下里传递消息。
♦ **notoriety** [ˌnəʊtə'raɪətɪ]
n. 恶名，丑名
His daring escape from prison gained him a certain notoriety. 他大胆的越狱使他臭名昭著。
♦ **downturn** ['daʊntɜːn]
n. (经济等) 衰退，低迷
They predicted a severe economic downturn. 他们预言会有严重的经济衰退。
♦ **sulk** [sʌlk] vi. 生气，愠怒
He went off to sulk in his room. 他回到自己屋里，生起闷气来。
♦ **go through** 经历，通读
How long will it take to go through the book? 读完这本书要多少时间？

04 Hiking in South Korea
徒步游韩国

在韩国，徒步旅行是种非常受民众喜爱的休闲娱乐活动，人们可以徒步探索韩国的魅力山色和乡村风景，其中，比较典型的徒步旅行是从山脚的寺院开始的。

韩国的国家公园风景秀丽，在 20 个国家公园中，有 15 个是依山而建，其中有很多路标明晰的徒步路线。而且，游客可以根据自己的时间和体力选择不同的路线。在徒步中，各种风景美不胜收，比如可欣赏到连绵起伏的山脉、幽深神秘的山谷和令人惊叹的悬崖峭壁。

♦ **countryside** ['kʌntrɪsaɪd]
n. 乡村，郊野
I've always loved the English countryside. 一直以来我都很喜欢英国的乡间。
♦ **pastime** ['pɑːstaɪm]
n. 消遣，娱乐
His favourite pastime is golf. 他最喜欢的消遣是打高尔夫。
♦ **at the foot of**
在……的底部 / 脚下

Hiking and walking are very popular ways to explore South Korea's beautiful mountain **countryside**. Hiking is a national **pastime**. Many walks start from temples which are often located **at the foot of** a mountain.

The country's many national parks offer **spectacular** walking **trails**. Songnisan National Park is one of the best places to hike in South Korea. The main peaks in the park are Cheonwangbong, Birobong, and Munjangdae. The Beopjusa Temple, which has a large golden **Buddha statue**, is a popular place to start a walk.

Seoraksan National Park, which is home to many rare species, is in the northeast of the country near the fishing city of Sokcho. The Biryong Falls and Baekamsa Temple are popular **destinations** for walks. The park is a mixture of stone **forts**, Buddhist **monasteries**, forests and large waterfalls, all set among **rugged granite** peaks. This park is popular for walks of all lengths, including multi-day **trek**.

Juwangsan National Park is another park which is a good hiking destination. It is famed for its deep **gorges** and thick forests. The Jubong trail is the most popular walk in this park.

South Korea's national parks are all very beautiful. Of the 20 national parks, 15 of them are mountain parks. They all have plenty of walking and hiking trails which are usually clearly signposted. It is possible to do easy to moderate day walks, as well as some longer and more physically demanding hikes. The parks cover a range of different **landscapes** from rolling hills to deep valleys and rugged cliffs.

Some of the parks have camping facilities, though they are often basic and only open in the summer. Some of the larger parks, such as Seoraksan and Jirisan, have mountain huts where people doing long-distance walks can stay overnight. The Korean National Parks Service (KNPS) sometimes closes trails temporarily to allow wildlife to recover.

There lies a small town at the foot of the mountain. 山脚下有一个小镇。

♦ **spectacular** [spek'tækjʊlə]
adj. 壮观的，引人注目的
The house has the most spectacular views imaginable. 从这所房子可以看到所能想象到的最壮丽的景色。

♦ **trail** [treɪl]
n. 小径，路线
I vote that you try to pick out the trail for us. 我提议由你来选我们该走哪条小路。

♦ **Buddha statue** 佛像

♦ **destination** [ˌdestɪ'neɪʃn]
n. 目的地，终点
The troops rushed to their destination without a single halt. 部队马不停蹄地赶到了目的地。

♦ **fort** [fɔːt]
n. 堡垒，要塞
No one can get into the fort without a pass. 没有通行证，任何人不得进入要塞。

♦ **monastery** ['mɒnəstri]
n. 修道院，寺院

♦ **rugged** ['rʌɡɪd]
adj. 崎岖的，凹凸不平的
The Rocky Mountains have rugged mountains and roads. 落基山脉有崇山峻岭和崎岖不平的道路。

♦ **granite** ['ɡrænɪt]
n. 花岗岩，花岗石

♦ **trek** [trek]
n. 长途跋涉，艰难的旅程
It's a long trek into town. 进城去要走很长的路。

♦ **gorge** [ɡɔːdʒ]
n. 山峡，峡谷
East of the gorge leveled out. 峡谷东面地势变得平坦起来。

♦ **landscape** ['lændskeɪp]
n. 风景，景观

05 Skiing in South Korea
一起去韩国滑雪

韩国的滑雪场位于美丽的山林中，拥有各种滑雪道和现代化便利设施，有专为孩子们准备的雪橇场，还有可以欣赏冬季美景的凤尾船，从初学者到滑雪爱好者，不论是谁都可以使用。另外还有温泉和散步路等除滑雪以外仍可尽情娱乐的设施。韩国人就不用说了，滑雪场还有很多从没有冬季的国度来的以家庭为单位的游客前来游玩，是冬季代表性的旅游地。

韩国的滑雪场主要集中在冬季降雪量丰富的江原道地区和可利用周末游玩的首尔近郊一带。江原道作为韩国最先降雪的地区，高山众多，是滑雪和单板滑雪的最佳去处。拥有滑雪场的度假村大部分是四季型的综合休养地，住宿设施齐全，而且被舒适清新的大自然所包围。

There are **ski** resorts all around South Korea and new ones are continually being developed. Many are in Gangwon-do Province, as it has the highest annual **snowfall** in the country. Most of the resorts are well equipped and offer luxury **accommodation** and all modern **amenities**. It is possible to rent equipment at the resorts. Many of the resorts also have **spas** and a variety of other sports and **leisure** facilities on offer. Most of the resorts can be reached by bus from Seoul. Some of them have artificial snow machines to allow visitors to make the most of the winter season. Lessons for people of all levels are available at the resorts.

The biggest resort in the country is Yongpyong at the foot of Palwang Mountain. It is about 200 km east of Seoul and receives an average of 250cm of snow each year. Skiing and **snowboarding** are possible at the resort from mid-November until April. As well as traditional **slopes**, some of which are of international competition standard, the resort has half pipes, ramps, and a **terrain** park which has received

---

♦ **ski** [skiː]
n. 滑雪

♦ **snowfall** ['snəʊfɔːl]
n. 降雪，降雪量

♦ **accommodation** [ə,kɒmə'deɪʃn]
n. 住处，住所

♦ **amenity** [ə'miːnɪti]
n. 便利设施
The town offers various entertainment amenity for children. 这座城镇为孩子们提供了各种各样的娱乐设施。

♦ **spa** [spɑː]
n. 温泉疗养院；温泉疗养中心
Bath in Britain is Eruope's famous spa town. 英国的巴思是欧洲著名的矿泉疗养地。

♦ **leisure** ['leʒə]
n. 悠闲，休闲
Finally she sat down with a sigh; this she could eat at her leisure. 终于，她叹着气坐下来了，到了现在，她才可以悠闲地吃东西。

♦ **snowboarding** ['snəʊbɔːdɪŋ]
n. 滑板滑雪

♦ **slope** [sləʊp]
n. 斜坡，山坡
The slope increases as you go up the curve. 上了弯道以后，路越来越陡。

♦ **terrain** ['tereɪn]
n. 地形，地势
It took us the whole day to trek across the rocky terrain. 我们花了一整天的时间艰难地穿过那片遍布岩石的地带。

♦ **skier** ['skaɪə(r)]
n. 滑雪者

♦ **resort** [rɪ'zɔːt]
n. 度假胜地，度假村

very good reviews.

Muju, or Deogyusan, is also a major ski resort with slopes for **skiers** of all levels. It is in Deogyusan National Park and is one of the most important resorts in Asia. The resort is home to both the longest (the Silk Road) and steepest (Raiders) slopes in the country. There are also dedicated sledging runs.

The Alpensia **resort** is small and has six skiing, snowboarding and sledging slopes connected via high speed lifts. The resort also has a dedicated area for experienced snowboarders and areas for **biathlon** and cross country skiing. It will be the main **venue** for the 2018 winter Olympics and new facilities are currently under construction.

There are free buses around the resort and plenty of nightlife. 这个游览胜地到处都有免费大巴，夜生活也很丰富。

♦ **biathlon** [baɪˈæθlən]
n. 现代冬季两项，是一种滑雪加射击的比赛。

♦ **venue** [ˈvenju]
n. 会场，（尤指）体育比赛场所
The date and venue of the game must remain under wraps. 比赛的时间和地点必须保密。

06 Water Sports in South Korea
韩国的激情水上运动

韩国是个临海国家，有各种水上运动，比如帆板、冲浪、潜水和皮划艇运动等等，设备齐全，是个体验水上激情的好去处。

被誉为"水上休闲运动"之花的"帆板运动"当然不能错过。帆板运动是在冲浪板上装上帆船的帆，依靠风的力量来航行的水上休闲运动。抓住风帆，根据风向和风力大小来保持平衡航行是它的趣味所在。在韩国，去汉江体验帆板运动是个不错的选择。

韩国的潜水运动之所以流行，在于它的独特自然条件。韩国是亚热带气候，沿海有许多有趣的观赏鱼类，众多火山小岛下有许多软珊瑚等。而且韩国还有专门的潜水学校可以学习潜水技术。此外，江原道的皮划艇活动也是很出名的哦。

South Korea is a coastal nation and offers **plenty of** opportunities for water sports. **Facilities** are available for **windsurfing**, surfing, diving, **canoeing**, **kayaking** and rafting in South Korea.

Windsurfing is a popular and well-established sport in

♦ **plenty of** 很多，大量的
She is in the fortunate position of having plenty of choices. 好在她有很多选择。

♦ **facility** [fəˈsɪlɪtɪ]
n.（供特定用途的）场所，设备

♦ **windsurfing** [ˈwɪndsɔːfɪŋ]
n. 帆板运动

♦ **canoeing** [kəˈnuːɪŋ]
n. 皮划艇运动

♦ **kayaking** [ˈkaɪækɪŋ]
n. 皮艇运动

♦ **circuit** [ˈsɜːkɪt]
n. 巡回
Smith was subpoenaed as a witness to appear in the circuit court. 史密斯被传作证人在巡回法院出庭。

♦ **spot** [spɒt]
n. 地点，场所
The doctor was on the spot a few minutes after the accident. 医生在事故发生几分钟后就赶到现场了。

♦ **body** [ˈbɒdɪ]

South Korea. The country hosts an event in the professional windsurfing **circuit**. Ulsan, a city in the southeast of the country, is a major windsurfing destination and JinHa, a quiet town half an hour from the city, is home to one of the best surfing beaches in South Korea. Jeju Island is also popular and has many windsurfing beaches with good waves and plenty of remote **spots**. In Seoul, it is possible to windsurf on the Han River.

The Korean Windsurfing Association is the national **body** for the sport. They offer lessons at locations around the country. There are also **regional** windsurfing associations around the country which offer lessons and run clubs. Surfing is a growing sport in South Korea. Although the country lacks **reliably** good conditions, there are locations where excellent waves can be found. Jeju and Pusan are good choices.

As for diving, Jeju Island is a popular location with divers in South Korea. The **subtropical** waters are home to many interesting fish and there are soft **corals** to be seen on the walls of the area's many small volcanic islands. Seogwipo is another good diving spot where there are large **kelp** forests, dolphins, lots of fish and beautifully-colored soft corals. A particular feature of diving in the region is the unusual mix of tropical and temperate fish **species**. There is an international diving school on Jeju Island which offers lessons and tours for people of all levels.

There is also an English-speaking dive school in Seoul which **caters for** foreigners living in the country. They offer courses for everyone from complete beginners to those who want to make a **career** out of diving.

For canoeing, kayaking and rafting, Inje in Gangwon-do is the most popular location in South Korea. The Naerincheon Stream has many **rapids** and is set in beautiful mountain scenery. There is a canoe school in Inje which runs courses in English, and the town also hosts festivals which attract many top level kayakers.

n. 团体，机构，组织

♦ **regional** [ˈriːdʒən(ə)l]
adj. 地区的，区域的

♦ **reliably** [rɪˈlaɪəblɪ]
adv. 可靠地，确实地

♦ **subtropical** [sʌbˈtrɒpɪkəl]
adj. 亚热带的，亚热带特点的
They are more prevalent in soils of the tropical and subtropical regions. 它们在热带和亚热带地区的土壤中较为普遍。

♦ **coral** [ˈkɒrəl]
n. 珊瑚

♦ **kelp** [kelp]
n. 大型褐藻，巨藻，海带

♦ **species** [ˈspiːʃɪz]
n. 物种，种类（单复同形）
Are we the only thinking species in the whole of creation? 我们是万物中惟一有思想的物种吗？

♦ **cater for**
迎合，满足（口味、需求等）
Retailers have to cater for very different tastes around the country. 零售商们必须迎合整个国家人与人之间差异巨大的口味偏好。

♦ **career** [kəˈrɪə]
n. 职业，事业
Talent, hard work and sheer tenacity are all crucial to career success. 事业要成功，才能、勤奋和顽强的意志都至关重要。

♦ **rapid** [ˈræpɪd]
n. 急流

07 A Better Understanding of South Korea
多了解一下韩国

经过几十年的发展，韩国的经济实力在全球占据着举足轻重的地位，在科技领域更是引领世界。比如像三星这样的科技公司，不仅在韩国本土雄踞一方，即便是在国际市场上也是日益繁荣。在全球化的今天，你在不经意之间便很可能遇到跟韩国相关的产品或服务，所以不妨多掌握一些韩国常识，以备不时之需。

处于东亚文化圈的熏陶下，即便韩国曾经长期受到西方文化的影响，韩国国民的集体意识要远远重于个人主义。比如说，有时韩国人虽然知道对方的名字，却也要称呼对方为"我的同事"或者"我的妻子"。

在韩国教育体制下，孩子们除了要上公立学校读书，还要参加数学、音乐等各种课外辅导课程，整天忙忙碌碌，一直到晚上 10:00 才休息。在日常交流中，韩国人毫不避讳各种私人问题，这可能会让西方人大跌眼镜。

Over the past few decades, South Korea has become a significant force in the global economy, particularly in the **tech** sector. Korean tech **giants** like Samsung not only maintain huge sales figures in their home market, but enjoy increased market share in international markets. A land of huge **metropolises**, strong talent, and rapid growth, Korea is a place you're likely to **encounter** in one way or another during your lifetime. Even if you never visit South Korea yourself, you may meet Koreans who have come to your country to visit or do business. If and when that happens, knowing a thing or two about Korean culture might **come in handy**.

Many East Asian cultures have a strongly collectivist **mindset**. This is even true in South Korea, which has long been governed democratically and has a more westernized culture than some Asian nations. Although South Koreans may adapt more readily than some, to **individualistic** cultures of the west, they still display certain habits and opinions that may be foreign to westerners. For example, when referring to their **coworkers** or family members, Koreans rarely

♦ **tech** [tek]
n. 技术
♦ **giant** [ˈdʒaɪənt]
n. 巨人，卓越人物，巨头
♦ **metropolis** [mɪˈtrɒpəlɪs]
n. 大都市，大都会
Shanghai is a metropolis in China. 上海是中国的大都市。
♦ **encounter** [ɪnˈkaʊntə]
vt. 不期而遇，遇到
If you undertake the project, you are bound to encounter difficulties. 如果你承接这项工程的话，免不了会遇到许多困难。
♦ **come in handy**
有用，派得上用处
That key will come in handy if you lock yourself out. 要是你把自己锁在了屋外，那把钥匙就派上用场了。
♦ **mindset** [ˈmaɪndset]
n. 思维模式，心态
I can't take their mindset anymore. 我再也不能容忍他们的心态。

use others' names unless they are present. A Korean will say "my colleague" or "my wife" even if he knows that you know that person's name.

Another interesting **facet** of Korean culture is the education system. In the United States and other western countries, children attend school for only 6 to 8 hours per day, and although they may participate in one or two **extracurricular** activities, they still have **ample** free time for playing and socializing. In Korea, by contrast, children rarely have free time. In fact, they often have even less free time than adults. The reason for this is that Koreans value both **breadth** and depth in education. A typical Korean student will attend public school for a few hours per day, and will then spend several more hours at a specialized school for math, music, or another subject. Sports practice, language lessons, or other activities follow, so that children's days often do not end until 10 pm.

When learning about another culture, it's always important to **get a sense** for what that culture sees as proper in conversation. In conversations between Koreans and Americans, for example, or between Koreans and British, this is especially important. Unlike Japanese culture, Korean culture is very open and friendly. Koreans feel comfortable discussing aspects of their personal lives that would embarrass many westerners, especially those from the US and UK For example, bodily functions like **menstruation** and **lactation** are not openly discussed with strangers in many western cultures, but Koreans do not **shy away** from these subjects. In addition, it is often considered **rude** or inappropriate for westerners to discuss financial issues like salaries and debt. These topics are not taboo for Koreans, however.

♦ **individualistic** [ˌɪndɪˌvɪdjuəˈlɪstɪk]
adj. 个人主义的
♦ **coworker** [ˈkəʊˌwɜːkə]
n. 同事，共同工作的人
♦ **facet** [ˈfæsɪt]
n. 侧面，方面
Being a well-paid business woman is only one facet of her life. 高薪阶层职业妇女的身份只是她生活的一个方面。
♦ **extracurricular** [ˌekstrəkəˈrɪkjʊlə(r)]
adj. 课外的，学校课程以外的
We have spent a lot of time on the extracurricular exercise. 我们在课外练习上花了很多时间。
♦ **ample** [ˈæmpl]
adj. 足够的，充足的
There was ample time to get to the airport. 有足够的时间到达机场。
♦ **breadth** [bredθ]
n. 宽度，（知识、兴趣等）广泛
♦ **get a sense** 了解
I get a sense that people are feeling better about themselves. 我觉得现在人们的自我感觉更好了。
♦ **menstruation** [ˌmenstruˈeɪʃən]
n. 月经
♦ **lactation** [lækˈteɪʃ(ə)n]
n. 哺乳（期）
♦ **shy away** 避开，回避
We frequently shy away from making decisions. 我们常常害怕作出决定。
♦ **rude** [ruːd] adj. 粗鲁的
They had called her rude names. 他们用粗鲁的言语谩骂她。

08 A New Attitude to Divorce
韩国离婚新变化

十年前，在韩国一所大型的婚姻介绍机构——Sunoo，还没有牵手客户离婚的记录；即便有那么一些离婚的，也会因为世俗的偏见而过着孤独的生活。而今天，韩国的离婚率已是世界最高，Sunoo 的会员的离婚率竟达到 15%。

韩国人在坚守传统价值的同时，却也面临着离婚率屡创新高的现实。儒家传统文化与现代西方文明在今天的韩国社会激烈碰撞。随着时代进步和妇女社会地位的升高，韩国妇女开始勇敢地追求自己的幸福，他们不再对丈夫的出轨忍气吞声。这也是离婚率升高的原因之一。

Only a decade ago, Sunoo, one of South Korea's largest **matchmaking** services, had no **divorced** clients. Few Koreans divorced anyway, and deep social **prejudice** forced those who did to **resign** themselves to a life of **solitude**.

Today, with a **surging** divorce rate that now ranks among the world's highest, divorced clients account for 15 percent of Sunoo's membership. But as with other agencies that match people looking to marry, Sunoo keeps its divorced members in a largely separate category.

They are **adhering to** traditional values. At the same time, it's a reality that divorce is rising and will probably continue to rise. Rapidly changing attitudes toward divorce show a South Korea **in the throes of** a social transformation. Still **anchored** in Confucian values of family and **patriarchy**, South Korea is fast becoming an open, Westernized society—with the world's highest concentration of Internet broadband users, a pop culture that has recently been breaking taboos left and right, and living patterns increasingly focusing on individual satisfaction.

Social changes that took decades in the West or Japan, **sociologists** here like to point out, are occurring here in a matter of years. In the last decade, South Korea's divorce rate swelled 250 percent, in keeping with women's rising social

---

♦ **matchmaking** [ˈmætʃˌmeɪkɪŋ]
n. 做媒，婚姻介绍

♦ **divorced** [dɪˈvɔːst]
adj. 离婚的

♦ **prejudice** [ˈpredʒʊdɪs]
n. 成见，偏见，歧视
I've spent a lifetime fighting against racism and prejudice. 我一辈子都在同种族主义和偏见作斗争。

♦ **resign** [rɪˈzaɪn]
vt. 屈从，勉强接受

♦ **solitude** [ˈsɒlɪtjuːd]
n. 孤独
She went out little, and affected a life of solitude and simplicity. 她很少出门，喜爱一种孤独而简单的生活。

♦ **surging** [ˈsɜːdʒɪŋ]
adj. 激增的，急剧上升的

♦ **adhere to** 遵循，坚持
They failed to adhere to our original agreement. 他们未能遵守我们原定的协议。

♦ **in the throes of**
处于……困境（或痛苦）中
This country is in the throes of war. 这个国家处于战争的痛苦中。

♦ **anchor** [ˈæŋkə]
vt. 使扎根，使固守；与……有紧密联系

status. But it shot up even more after the economic crisis of 1997, which caused widespread unemployment and shook men's basic standing in the society and family.

Also, the marriage rate–lower than the United States' and higher than Europe's and Japan's–has been declining. People are marrying later and having fewer children.

In addition, more young couples are defying a longtime taboo against living together, though they largely keep the fact hidden from their parents and co-workers. Moving in together has become such a phenomenon that a recent television series became a hit by **tackling** the issue.

South Korean popular culture, perhaps like America's in the 1970's, is overflowing with taboo-shattering shows. Another hit television show, "The Woman Next Door"–which has been called the Korean "Sex and the City" –focuses on the marriages and **extramarital** affairs of three women in their 30's. The show describes a radical departure, social critics have pointed out, from the days when men engaged in affairs and wives endured in silence.

Over the years, divorce laws that discriminated against women were also changed. But the surge in divorce in the 1990's came as women became better educated and more of them held jobs. Now women are more likely to feel that they are **entitled** to seek personal happiness. The majority of divorces are initiated by women, and personality conflict is the reason cited most often.

Talking openly about one's divorce is something Koreans still seldom do, and doing so brought tears to Ms. Yoo's eyes. "My husband was **irresponsible** toward the family," she said. "I was hoping that he would change–he is my children's father, after all."

The roots anchor the plant in the earth. 根部使植物固定在土壤中。

♦ **patriarchy** ['peɪtrɪɑːkɪ]
n. 父权制（社会），家长制

♦ **sociologist** [ˌsəʊsɪəˈlɒdʒɪst]
n. 社会学家
A sociologist named David has studied school uniform policies since 1998. 社会学家大卫自从1998年开始研究校服制度。

♦ **tackle** ['tækl]
vt. 着手处理，解决
Poverty and unemployment are frustratingly hard to tackle. 贫穷和失业是难以解决的问题，这常常让人泄气。

♦ **extramarital** [ˌekstrəˈmærɪtəl]
adj. 婚外的，私通的
We should discourage extramarital affairs. 我们应该遏止婚外情。

♦ **entitled** [ɪnˈtaɪtld]
adj. 被赋予权力的，有资格的
The fans are entitled to their opinions but booing doesn't help anyone. 粉丝有权表达他们的观点，但起哄对任何人都没有好处。

♦ **irresponsible** [ˌɪrɪsˈpɒnsəbl]
adj. 不负责任的，缺乏责任心的

---

09 Decline in the Old Way of Business Culture
职业女性大翻身

几十年前，韩国的女性白领人数稀少，地位也不高。晚上公司部门聚餐之后，如果有男同事轮流拽着她们去舞池陪跳，即便不情愿，女同事也没人敢抱怨。如果有主管在，那么饭桌上最漂亮的两位女性必须坐在他的左右，斟酒相伴。而传统上，韩国公司里，受到儒家文化里等级尊卑思想的影响而形成的下级与辈分区分明显等商业文化，到如今，开始逐渐瓦解。

1997年的席卷亚洲的经济危机，同样波及韩国。韩国民众大量失业，以往的雇主关系遭受质疑和挑战。在全球化的潮流下，韩国的大型财阀们也开始意识到，陈旧的管理模式和理念也严重阻碍了企业的创新发展。同时，妇女开始争取自己的经济和社会权益；在生意场上，女性的社会地位逐渐上升。

When Hwang Yong Taek, a 43-year-old marketing chief at Hyundai Card, began his career at another big South Korean company 18 years ago, women in the office were few and low in **status**. No woman could complain when the department went out to dinner and ended up in a **nightclub**, with men taking turns **dragging** reluctant female colleagues to the **dance floor**. If an **executive** attended the dinner, the two prettiest women had to sit on either side of him, filling his glass.

So the message was clear when Hyundai Card, one of the leading credit card companies in South Korea, fired a senior manager last year for sexual **harassment** during such a dinner.

Across major South Korean businesses, the old male-oriented and rigidly **top-down** corporate culture is **crumbling**. The shift signals an end to a regimen that served South Korea well when military **strongmen** and the **paternalistic** chairmen of its conglomerates **spearheaded** the country's economic growth.

Office workers came to work and stayed as long as their bosses. They raised and emptied their glasses when their section chief said, "Bottoms up!" They seldom **spoke up** during meetings or challenged their superiors' decisions. They all got the same raises and were promoted at the same time. They

♦ **status** ['steɪtəs]
n. 社会地位；(在公众或某一团体中的) 威望，地位，身份

♦ **nightclub** ['naɪtklʌb]
n. 夜总会

♦ **drag** [dræg] vt. 拖拽，拉扯
He hates parties; we had to drag him into going. 他不喜欢参加聚会，我们必须拉他去。

♦ **dance floor** 舞池

♦ **executive** [ɪgˈzekjutɪv]
n. 经理，主管
He had been granted his own TV show by some demented executive. 某个愚蠢的主管已经批准他自己来做一个电视节目。

♦ **harassment** [ˈhærəsmənt]
n. 骚扰
They have a policy of zero tolerance for sexual harassment. 他们对性骚扰采取绝不容忍的政策。

♦ **top-down** [ˈtɒpdaʊn]
adj. 自上而下的，组织管理严密的

♦ **crumble** [ˈkrʌmbl]
vi. 瓦解，崩裂
I will love you until the seas run dry and the rocks crumble. 我将爱你直到海枯石烂。

♦ **strongman** [ˈstrɒŋmæn]
n. 强人，大力士；铁腕人物

♦ **paternalistic** [pəˌtɜːnəˈlɪstɪk]
adj. 家长式的

♦ **spearhead** [ˈspɪəhed]
vt. 当……的先锋，带头
He seemed to spearhead every important city so fearlessly and successfully. 每次进攻重要城市，他似乎都以大无畏的精神充当先锋，而且攻无不克，战无不胜。

♦ **speak up**
畅所欲言，清楚地表明看法
Please speak up so that the people at the back of the room can hear you. 请大点声讲，让屋子后面的人也能听

didn't know whether they were to be transferred until it was announced. If a woman refused to "voluntarily retire" when she got married, it was considered a **scandal**.

It was comfortingly Confucian in its respect for patriarchy and **hierarchy**, and it suited the mind-set of men who, almost without exception, had served as **conscripts** in the military. But a series of shocks have forced a rethinking of this once-successful model.

The 1997 Asian financial crisis brought job layoffs that undermined old assumptions of what employer and employee owed each other. Women pushed into the **workplace** by the economic uncertainty became newly **assertive** about their rights.

Above all, there was the growing realization among the top conglomerates that the old management style stood in the way of what they needed to do most to survive: innovate and globalize.

Women still account for less than 13 percent of the work force at the 100 largest South Korean businesses, according to the Federation of Korean Industries. Still, the status of women in the workplace is rising, as reflected in a popular television commercial. The ad, for an LG Electronics cellphone, shows male office workers scrambling to please their demanding female boss.

见你的声音。

♦ **scandal** [ˈskændl]
n. 丑闻，丑事，丢脸的事件
This drugs scandal is another blot on the Olympics. 这次的兴奋剂丑闻又给奥林匹克运动会抹了黑。

♦ **hierarchy** [ˈhaɪərɑːkɪ]
n. 等级制度或体系

♦ **conscript** [ˈkɒnskrɪpt]
n. 被征入伍者

♦ **workplace** [wɜːkpleɪs]
n. 工作场所；车间，工厂
Workplace safety remained a serious problem, particularly in the mining industry. 工作场所安全仍然是个严重问题，采矿业尤为如此。

♦ **assertive** [əˈsɜːtɪv]
adj. 肯定的，自信的
They begin to mute their voices, not be as assertive. 他们开始压低嗓门，不再那么肯定了。

Chapter 8
古老文明：追觅历史的沧桑

01 Imperial Palace of South Korean
韩国故宫：魅力昌德宫

公元 15 世纪早期，太宗皇帝下令在吉祥之地再修建一座新的宫殿，于是成立了修建宫殿的队伍来执行这项命令，新的宫殿占地 58 公顷，内有处理政务的宫殿和皇族的寝宫，整个宫殿完美地适应了当地的崎岖地形，与四周的自然环境和谐地融为一体，成为远东地区宫殿建筑设计的典范之作。

宫殿布局包括宫殿公共区、一座皇族寝宫和后花园。后花园，作为国王休息之所，内有一株 300 多年的参天大树，一口小池塘，还有楼阁。花园修建力求接近自然，而且如非必须连手也不能触摸。院中遍布人工喷泉和亭台楼阁。观赏园林的最美时节，当属秋季草木茂盛，叶儿初落时分。

世纪轮回，昌德宫一直被韩国人视为珍宝，但直到 1997 年 12 月才被世界文化遗产委员会收录为世界文化遗产。昌德宫是 2010 年 11 月首尔二十国集团会议期间，各国第一夫人游览的场所之一，也是能代表韩国之美的历史名胜之一。

In the early 15th century, the **Emperor T'aejong** ordered the construction of a new palace at an **auspicious** site. A Bureau of Palace Construction was set up to create the **complex**, consisting of a number of official and residential buildings set in a garden that was cleverly adapted to the uneven **topography** of the 58-ha site. The result is an exceptional example of Far Eastern palace architecture and design, blending harmoniously with the surrounding landscape.

The palace grounds **are comprised of** a public palace area, a royal family residence building, and the rear garden. Known as a place of rest for the kings, the rear garden **boasts** a gigantic tree that is over 300 years old, a small pond, and **pavilions**. Changdeokgung's rear garden was constructed during the reign of King Taejong and served as a resting place for the royal family members. The garden was kept as natural as possible and was touched by human hands only when ab-

---

◆ **Changdeokgung Palace**
昌德宫，又名东阙，位于韩国首都首尔，是朝鲜王朝时期五大宫之一，也是朝鲜王宫里保存得最完整的一座宫殿。

◆ **Emperor T'aejong**
朝鲜太宗李芳远（1367—1422），李氏朝鲜第三代君主，朝鲜王朝第一任国王，庙号太宗。曾以两次王子之乱的方式，铲除异己，进而继位。

◆ **auspicious** [ɔːsˈpɪʃəs]
n. 吉兆的，幸运的

◆ **complex** [ˈkɒmpleks]
n. 综合体，复合体，此处指宫殿。

◆ **topography** [təˈpɒɡrəfi]
n. 地形，地势

◆ **be comprised of** 由……组成
The United States is comprised of 50 states. 美国是由 50 个州组成的。

◆ **pavilion** [pəˈvɪljən]
n. 亭，阁

◆ **boast** [bəʊst]
vt. 包含，拥有（常指令人满意的事物）

◆ **foliage** [ˈfəʊlɪdʒ]
n. 树叶，植物

◆ **World Cultural Heritage**
世界文化遗产，全称为"世界文化

solutely necessary. Many pavilions and fountains occupy the garden. The most beautiful time to see the garden is during the fall when the autumn **foliage** is at its peak and the leaves have just started to fall.

Though it has been treasured by Koreans for centuries, the Changdeokgung Palace was not **designated** a World Cultural Heritage by the World Cultural Heritage Committee until December of 1997.

The Changdeokgung Palace was one of the places visited by the "first ladies of the Seoul G20" during the **G20** conference in Seoul in November 2010. It is one of the historic **attractions** that represent the beauty of Korea.

和自然遗产"，属于世界遗产范畴，1972 年联合国教科文组织在巴黎通过了《保护世界文化和自然遗产公约》，成立联合国教科文组织世界遗产委员会，旨在于保护全人类共同的遗产

♦ **designate** ['dezɪgneɪt]
vt. 命名，指定，指派

♦ **attraction** [əˈtrækʃən]
n. 吸引，吸引力，吸引人的事物

♦ **G20**
二十国集团，全称 Group 20，是当前全球主要的经济合作论坛，旨在推动已工业化的发达国家和新兴市场国家之间就实质性经济合作。

02 Gyeongju: A Museum Without Walls
韩国庆州市：没有围墙的博物馆

庆州市是韩国庆尚北道的市。庆州曾是新罗王朝的首都，也是韩国古代文明的摇篮，现有人口约 28 万，是一座恬静的城市。举凡山地、溪谷，都有王陵、石塔、佛像、寺庙遗址。不赴博物馆探古，只游览庆州古都，也就等于在探索古代灿烂文化的遗址，故庆州有"无围墙的博物馆"之称。主要旅游景点包括古坟公园、佛国寺、瞻星台、庆州民俗工艺村、五陵等，其中佛国寺已被列为世界文化遗产。

佛国寺是一座上规模的古刹，内供奉着栩栩如生的菩萨塑像等，作为新罗时代（公元前 57—935 年）的国寺，经历了新罗近千年灿烂佛教文化的洗礼，是一处珍贵的佛教遗迹。穿过佛国寺，沿着吐含山岭（海拔 745 米）前行 8 公里左右，就可看到几乎处于吐含山顶的石窟庵。庵内供奉的是 8 世纪统一新罗时期，运用佛教美术的最高工艺，雕塑而成的本尊佛像。石窟庵本尊佛像面朝太阳升起的东海，韩国人将沐浴在晨光里的这座微笑着的佛像称为"新罗人的微笑"。

庆州有着丰富的文化遗产，庆州地区的文物占全国的 5.5%，庆尚北道的 30%。另外，庆州的文化设施比较完善，文化生活也很丰富，具有很大的文化潜力。从首尔出发，仅需四五个小时的车程即可到达。

Situated in the **southeastern** part of Korea, Gyeongju in Gyeongsangbuk-do Province was the capital of the **Silla Kingdom** (57 BC–AD 935), which was ruled by 56 kings over 992 **years**, the longest period of any dynasty in the history

♦ **southeastern** [sauθˈiːstən]
adj. 东南的，东南部的
Florida, in the southeastern United States, is called the Sunshine State. 位

of Korea. Over the **course** of almost a thousand years, Silla transformed itself from a small tribal nation to a kingdom occupying more than half of the Korean Peninsula. During that time, Gyeongju had **steadfastly** remained its capital.

Gyeongju had previously been called Seorabeol and Gyerim, and the name Gyeongju first appeared on record in AD 935. These days, Gyeongju continues to show its importance even though more than a thousand years have passed since the **fall** of the Silla Kingdom.

Buddhism, which the Silla Kingdom adopted in the 6th century, helped **strengthen** the royal power and unite the people. The Buddhist religion also left **fascinating** cultural heritages. For this reason, Gyeongju features numerous Buddhist cultural relics, and is the top destination for school trips in Korea. The Bulguksa Temple and Seokguram **Grotto** are major historical sites in Gyeongju and the **essence** of Korean Buddhist culture. In 1995, both became the first sites in Korea to be designated a UNESCO World Cultural Heritage. In 2000, five historical sites in downtown Gyeongju became UNESCO World Cultural Heritages under the name of the Gyeongju Historic Areas. Thanks to this mass of culturally rich heritage, Gyeongju must continue to be preserved and recognized both at the national and global level.

Gyeongju can be reached by train or bus in four to five hours from Seoul. Home to the capital of the Silla Dynasty, Gyeongju has so many things to see that the whole city is often referred to as a museum without walls. **In terms of** city or population size, Gyeongju is just a small city. But having been the capital of a thousand year kingdom, Gyeongju cannot be **viewed** in just a few days.

于美国东南部的佛罗里达州被称作是阳光之州。
♦ **Silla Kingdom**
新罗，朝鲜历史上的南部邦国。
♦ **course** [kɔːs] n. 进程，过程
in the course of 在……的过程中
I hope the problem could be settled in the course of nature. 我希望这个问题能够自然而然地解决。
♦ **steadfastly** [ˈstedfəstlɪ]
adv. 不变地，坚定地
She steadfastly refused to look his way. 她坚决拒绝朝他那边看。
♦ **fall** [fɔːl] n. 衰落，灭亡，崩溃
♦ **strengthen** [ˈstreŋθən]
vt. 加强，巩固
His visit is intended to strengthen ties between the two countries. 他此次访问旨在增进两国间的关系。
♦ **fascinating** [ˈfæsɪneɪtɪŋ]
adj. 迷人的，有极大吸引力的
The changing vivid colours of the sunset are really fascinating. 日落时变化多端的色彩确实使人心醉神迷。
♦ **grotto** [ˈgrɒtəʊ] n. 石窟，洞室
Water trickles through an underground grotto. 水沿着地下岩洞流淌。
♦ **essence** [ˈesns] n. 精华，精髓
♦ **in terms of**
就……而言，从……的角度来说
It cannot be measured in terms of money. 这是不能用金钱衡量的。
♦ **view** [vjuː]
vt. 观看，观赏
You need to log onto the site to view the clips. 你要登录这个站点才能观看这些剪辑。

03 Suwon Hwaseong Fortress
小城故事：水原华城

说到白天去首尔的游玩之地，恐怕位于京畿道水原华城最令人难忘了。1997 年联合国教科文组织将其收入世界遗产名录时，指出它巧妙融合了东西方的建筑风格。公元 16 世纪，日本入侵朝鲜王朝，宏伟的宫殿寺庙大都损毁，朝鲜王朝因而修建了水原华城，并于 1796 年世宗大王（1752—1800）在位时期完成。

水原华城依靠 5.7 公里长、5 米高的城墙设计，护卫国王的临时宫殿和村落，防御外敌入侵。水原华城除了石砌城墙、警戒塔、军事要塞角楼等特色景点外，更有设计精妙、异彩纷呈的建筑结构，是朝鲜王朝时代宫殿建筑的典型，各种风格的和谐融合。

据说华城建设是世宗大王从首尔迁都计划的一部分。究其缘由，在于首尔承载了世宗对于父亲庄献世子许多悲戚的记忆，父亲被祖父英祖所杀。当时，英祖听闻庄献精神失常，滥杀无辜，就将世子锁在米柜，八天而亡。结果，世宗在位期间大都在修复有关父亲回忆的遗产。迁都水原，世宗可以逃离首尔的勾心斗角，走近父王陵寝，而且可以实施自己的改革蓝图。

世宗颇有远见，在位期间复兴了朝鲜王朝。实学派协助世宗开展了一系列社会改革和技术创新。比如，建城的市民有酬劳，发明的机械可吊起七吨多重的建材。

历经两个世纪战乱风雨，约有 75% 的城墙保留下来。从水原火车站步行前往，你会先看到北大门，然后是朝鲜史上最大的南大门，两门都环有有半月形石质防御工事——瓮城。

In terms of day trips from Seoul, I can't think of a better place than Suwon Hwaseong Fortress in the city of Suwon, Gyeonggi Province. In 1997 when the United Nations designated the Suwon Hwaseong Fortress a part of the world's cultural heritage, they cited its unique blend of eastern and western **architectural** styles. Completed in 1796 by the great **Joseon Dynasty**, king Jeongjo (1752–1800), its construction was inspired by the 16th century Japanese invasions, which destroyed most of Korea's grand palaces and temples.

In a break with the past, Suwon Hwaseong Fortress was designed to protect both a **temporary** palace for the king and a village from foreign invaders, **by means of** a 5.7-kilometer long, 5-meter high fortress wall. But while Suwon Hwaseong Fortress **features** the stone walls, sentry towers and turrets of a military **stronghold**, it's also enhanced by

♦ **in terms of**
在……方面，用……的话，根据，按照
It can not be measured in terms of money. 这是不能用金钱衡量的。

♦ **architectural** [ˌɑːkɪˈtektʃərəl]
adj. 建筑上的，建筑学的

♦ **Joseon Dynasty**
朝鲜王朝，又称李氏朝鲜（1392—1910），朝鲜半岛历史上的一个封建王朝。

♦ **by means of**
用……的方法，凭借……
He succeeded by means of perseverance. 他通过坚持获得成功。

♦ **temporary** [ˈtempərəri]
adj. 暂时的，临时的
The government will provide tempo-

the delicate and colorful architecture typical of Joseon-era palaces. The result is an unusually harmonious integration of styles.

It's been said that the fortress was part of King Jeongjo's plan to move the capital away from Seoul. Why the move, you ask? Well, Seoul bore bad memories for the king, whose father, Prince Sado, was murdered by his grandfather, King Yeongjo. Upon hearing that Sado was mentally ill and **indiscriminately** killing people, Yeongjo locked the prince in a rice chest for eight days until he died. As a result, Jeongjo spent much of his **reign** trying to repair his father's legacy. If he moved the capital to Suwon, the new king could escape the fractious **strife** of Seoul palace life, he would be closer to his father's grave, and he could realize his reformist **agenda**.

King Jeongjo is remembered as a visionary whose reign was a **renaissance** for Joseon-era Korea. Silhak, a new school of philosophy that emphasized scientific and practical learning, helped Jeongjo launch both progressive social and technological innovations. For example, the citizens who built Suwon Hwaseong Fortress were paid, and new inventions, including a machine that could lift over seven tons, were employed.

Despite two centuries of war and conquest, about 75% of the fortress wall remains. If you walk there from the Suwon train station, you'll reach Paldalmun gate first. The name of the fortress's 2-story tall south gate means, "gate open in all directions". The north gate, or Janganmun, is the largest gate ever built in Korea. Destroyed during the Korean War, it was rebuilt in 1979. Both gates are surrounded by an **ongseong**, which is a protective stone semicircle.

rary accommodation for up to three thousand people. 政府将给多达3 000人提供临时住处。

♦ **feature** ['fi:tʃə] vt. 以……为特色
The show featured dogs of every description. 展览会中展示了各式各样的狗。

♦ **stronghold** ['strɒŋhəʊld]
n. 要塞，据点
You are to take the enemy stronghold before dawn. 你们必须在凌晨前攻下敌人的堡垒。

♦ **indiscriminately** [ˌɪndɪsˈkrɪmɪnɪtlɪ]
adv. 不分皂白地，不加选择地

♦ **reign** [reɪn]
n. 统治，统治时期，支配
More and more nobles made Moscow their home during Catherine's reign. 在叶卡捷琳娜大帝统治时期，越来越多的贵族移居莫斯科。

♦ **strife** [straɪf] n. 斗争，冲突
The country was torn apart by internal strife. 这个国家被内部纷争搞得四分五裂。

♦ **agenda** [əˈdʒendə]
n. 议程，议事日程
What's on your agenda for tomorrow? 你明天的日程是怎么安排的？

♦ **renaissance** [rəˈneɪsəns]
n. 复兴，复活，新生
Popular art is experiencing a renaissance. 通俗艺术正在复兴。

♦ **ongseong**
瓮城，为加强城门防守而修建的护门小城，用砖砌成，呈半月形，从而使其军事防御能力增强了两倍。

04 Beauty of Gochang
魅力高敞郡

全罗北道的高敞郡地区被联合国教科文组织指定为生物圈保护区。继雪岳山国立公园、济州岛、全罗南道新安多岛海、光陵树林之后，高敞成为韩国第五大生物圈保护区，高敞郡整个行政区域（671.52平方公里）都被列入了生物圈保护区，这还是韩国有史以来的第一次。

联合国教科文组织生物圈保护区的选定是对在保护生物与文化多样性的同时，对居民们还在持续利用的地区进行的一种鼓励制度。被指定为核心保护区的地方，生态系统保护做得更为彻底。高敞泥滩、云谷湿地、支石墓世界文化遗产、禅云山道立公园与东林水库野生动物保护区等都被联合国教科文组织指定在核心保护区域内。

如果来到全北高敞郡，还有一处一定不能错过的景点，那就是在2000年被列入世界文化遗产的支石墓遗址。在全罗北道高敞郡的官网上写道："至今为止，在高敞地区共发现了1600多座支石墓。高敞是支石墓分布最密集的地区。"

位于高敞邑西侧3公里以外的岛山村，以及位于岛山村西侧1.2公里以外的梅山村是全世界最大的支石墓密集地。在这里可以了解到支石墓的变迁史。在看似平凡的田地上冒出了几块巨石，站在这些巨石前，仿佛看到先史时代的部族为了追思族长而将巨大的石头搬到这里的场景。

The southern county of Gochang has been designated as a UNESCO **biosphere** reserve. With the new designation as of May 28, Gochang in Jeollabuk-do (North Jeolla Province) became Korea's fifth region to make the list following Seoraksan National Park, Jeju Island, Dadohae, and Gwangneung Forest. Also, this is the first time in Korea that an entire county that **stretches** 671.52 square kilometers has been designated as a protected area.

Chosen by the UNESCO's Man and the Biosphere (MAB) program, the biosphere reserves are globally recognized for their preservation values for **biological** and cultural diversity that **harmonize** with economic and social development.

Among the regions within the county are core-protected areas which will come under the closer **scrutiny** of UNESCO. Gochang's core-protected regions include Gochang Tidal Flat, Ungok Wetland, Goindol Village, Seonunsan Provincial Park,

---

♦ **biosphere** [ˈbaɪəsfɪə]
n. 生物圈

♦ **stretch** [stretʃ]
vi. 延伸，绵延
The tea plantations stretch far into the distance. 茶园一直延伸到很远的地方。

♦ **biological** [baɪəˈlɒdʒɪkəl]
adj. 生物的，生物学的

♦ **harmonize** [ˈhɑːmənaɪz]
vi. （与……）融洽，和谐，与……协调一致
The new building does not harmonize with its surroundings. 那栋新楼与周围环境不协调。

♦ **scrutiny** [ˈskruːtɪnɪ]
n. 监督；检查
Public scrutiny had brought civil servants out from the backroom and into the spotlight. 公众监督把公务员

and Donglim Reservoir Wildlife **Sanctuary**.

Gochang Tidal Flat was added to the Ramsar List of Wetlands in 2010. Ramsar wetlands are selected based on the Ramsar Convention that provides the **framework** for national action and international cooperation for the conservation and wise use of wetlands and their resources. The 40.6-square-kilometer-sized Gochang flat, the largest among the Ramsar wetlands in Korea, is famous for its diverse **array** of natural monuments and **endangered** wildlife including the Kentish Plover, Eurasian Oystercatcher, red-backed sandpiper, and whooper swan.

Gochang has another Ramsar designated wetland, Ungok Wetland. Compared to Gochang Tidal Flat which is a coastal wetland, Ungok is an **inland** wetland. The 1.797 square kilometers that make up Ungok Wetland were formed as a result of being surrounded by mountains on all sides. Water collected in the middle of the land, causing new life to emerge. Today, the Ungok Wetland is also a **habitat** for numerous legally protected living creatures such as the buzzard, otter, and kestrel.

The World Heritage Goindol (**dolmen**) village, the 2000 installment, is a must-see tourist attraction in Gochang. "Gochang County has the largest number of dolmens throughout the world," writes the county's official website. "More than 1,600 dolmens have been discovered to this day."

Dosan Village (three kilometers west of Gochang-eup) and Maesan Village (1.2 kilometers west of Dosan) are two of the world's largest dolmen-concentrated regions. Visitors to the villages, accordingly, can have a **glimpse** of changing history through diverse types of dolmens. Standing in front of the large stones dotted **sparsely** throughout the farmlands, one can almost picture the scenes that would have unfolded during prehistoric times, when tribes would have set up a dolmen in respect of a deceased **chief**.

从幕后带到了公众关注之下。

♦ **sanctuary** [ˈsæŋktjuəri]
n. 保护区

♦ **framework** [ˈfreɪmwəːk]
n. 构架，框架
It's a bridge of steel framework. 那是座钢铁结构的桥梁。

♦ **array** [əˈreɪ]
n. 一大批

♦ **endangered** [ɪnˈdeɪndʒəd]
adj. 濒危的，快要绝种的
This island is maintained as a sanctuary for endangered species. 那个岛继续作为濒危物种的保护区。

♦ **inland** [ˈɪnlənd]
adj. 内地的，内陆的
The idea to have the capital moved so far inland will have a great effect on the future of Brazil. 把首都远迁内地的这一主张对巴西的未来将产生巨大的影响。

♦ **habitat** [ˈhæbɪtæt]
n.（动物的）栖息地，住处
The panda's natural habitat is the bamboo forest. 大熊猫的天然栖息地是竹林。

♦ **dolmen** [ˈdɒlmen]
n. 支石墓，（用石架成的）史前墓
石牌坊

♦ **glimpse** [glɪmps]
n. 一瞥，一看
have/get/catch a glimpse of 一瞥……
She catches a glimpse of a car in the distance. 她一眼就瞥见了远处的汽车。

♦ **sparsely** [ˈspɑːsli]
adv. 稀疏地，稀少地
Rural areas are sparsely populated.
乡村地区人烟稀少。

♦ **chief** [tʃiːf]
n. 族长，酋长，首领

05 The Jongmyo Shrine: A Priceless for the World
韩国宗庙：无价的世界遗产

　　韩国宗庙为供奉朝鲜时期历代王和王妃以及被推崇的王和王妃神位的祠堂，寺庙建筑由正殿和永宁殿组成。宗庙是韩国儒家传统的表现、流传至今的礼仪遗产以及建筑的价值体现，1995 年 12 月被评定为世界文化遗产。由于宗庙为举行祭礼的地方，所以其建筑不能奢华。正因为如此，建筑高度节制而简练，装饰、色彩和花纹也尽量单纯而简洁，以突出必要的空间。布局、结构、装饰、色彩的简洁和单纯把宗庙建筑升华为象征的高度。

　　目前，在正殿的 19 个龛室里供奉着 19 位王和 30 位王后的神位，在正殿西边永宁殿的 16 个龛室里供奉着从正殿移来的 15 位王和 17 位王后，以及英王和王妃的神位。宗庙的祭礼每年定期举行 5 次，如国家有特殊的变化可随时举行，以告知神灵。祭礼伊始，大王会亲自到各神室前行大礼四次、敬酒，对所有神位一视同仁，不敢有所疏漏。

　　Jongmyo is the royal shrine where the memorial services for the kings and queens of the Joseon Dynasty were performed. The structure represents the greatest religious **implications** from a Confucian perspective. Since the principal **ideology** of the Joseon Dynasty was based on Confucianism, the services performed in Jongmyo must also be viewed as an extension of political activities.

　　The Jongmyo Shrine was one of the first Korean national **monuments** listed as a UNESCO World Heritage Site in 1995. The Jongmyo Shrine, however, is relatively small compared to Gyeongbokgung Palace, the main palace of the Joseon Dynasty, and has less aesthetic value than other structures like, for example, Changdeokgung Palace.

　　This demonstrates that the Jongmyo Shrine has an **indigenous** value that has been largely neglected by the Korean people. The value of the shrine does not come from the structure itself, but rather from its historical background. The real value of the Jongmyo Shrine is in its excellent preservation of the history of the Joseon Dynasty through its dedication to all the **deceased** kings and queens over 500 years in one place.

♦ **implication** [ˌɪmplɪˈkeɪʃən]
n. 含意，言外之意
The clear implication is these are things that any educated person ought to know. 其中含意不言而喻：任何受过教育的人都应当知道这些事情。

♦ **ideology** [ˌaɪdɪˈɒlədʒɪ]
n. 思想（体系）

♦ **monument** [ˈmɒnjumənt]
n. 纪念碑

♦ **indigenous** [ɪnˈdɪdʒɪnəs]
adj. 固有的，生来的
Indians were the indigenous inhabitants of America. 印第安人是美洲的土著居民。

♦ **deceased** [dɪˈsiːst]
adj. 已故的，已死的

♦ **justify** [ˈdʒʌstɪfaɪ]
vt. 证明（决定、行为或想法）正当；表明……必要
We'll always justify our actions with noble sounding theories. 我们总会用听起来非常高尚的理论为我们的行动辩护。

As more is learned about the Jongmyo Shrine, more values are discovered that **justify** the **legitimacy** of it as one of most precious national monuments in Korea.

In 1394, King Taejo, the founder of the Joseon Dynasty, ordered that the capital should be moved to Hanyang, present-day Seoul. King Taejo ordered the building of the Jongmyo, the royal shrine for the memorial service, to the left of Gyeongbokgung Palace and the Sajikdan, the **altar** for the god of the earth and grain, to the right of the palace. The Jongmyo Shrine was completed in 1395, one year after moving the capital and before the completion of the construction of Gyeongbokgung Palace itself.

What was the reason behind building the Jongmyo and Sajikdan on each side of the main palace? The Jongmyo is the royal shrine **dedicated** to the memorial services for deceased kings and queens of the Joseon Dynasty, and the Sajikdan is the altar for the god of the earth and grain. Having these two structures on each side of the main palace implies that the legitimacy and authority of founders of the Joseon Dynasty had been **approved** by the divinely sanctioned.

The Jongmyo Shrine is regarded as a sacred ground of Confucianism. Since Confucianism does not worship a **deity** or God as in Christianity or Buddhism, the legitimacy that runs from the ancestors becomes the sacred ideology of Confucianism. That is why the shrine was the first royal structure built by King Taejo, founder of the Joseon Dynasty. Not surprisingly, the Jongmyo Shrine was the first building structure to be **rebuilt** after the complete destruction of all the palaces and the main building structures during the Japanese invasion of 1592. This **suggests** that the Jongmyo Shrine had the greatest religious and political significance within the Joseon Dynasty.

♦ **legitimacy** [lɪˈdʒɪtɪməsɪ]
n. 合理（性），合法（性）
Legitimacy and justice are the two cardinal principles in public administration. 合法性和公正性是公共管理的两个最基本原则。

♦ **altar** [ˈɔːltə]
n. 祭坛

♦ **dedicated** [ˈdedɪkeɪtɪd]
adj. 专用（于……）的
These gases are generally stored in a dedicated high-pressure gas cylinders in. 这些气体一般都是贮存在专用的高压气体钢瓶中。

♦ **approve** [əˈpruːv]
vt. 批准，承认
About ninety-five percent of those who cast their votes approve the new constitution. 参加投票的人中有大约95% 支持新宪法。

♦ **deity** [ˈdiːɪtɪ]
n. 天神，上帝

♦ **rebuild** [riːˈbɪld]
vt. 重建
The company is making every effort to rebuild its business. 这家公司正在尽一切努力重建自己的企业。

♦ **suggest** [səˈdʒest]
vt. 表明，暗示
The signs suggest that the elections will be non-violent and fair. 种种迹象表明选举将会是非暴力的、公正的。

06 Historical Villages in Korea
韩国的历史村落

韩国的历史村落中，有氏族村落、邑城村落等多种类型，其中氏族村落占到全部历史村落的 80%，可谓是韩国代表性的历史村落类型。韩国的氏族村落形成于朝鲜时代 (1392~1910 年) 初期，到了朝鲜时代后期，80% 的村落都是氏族村落，甚至有的村落一直延续到今天。

河回村和良洞村既是韩国具有代表性的氏族村落，又是两班 (朝鲜时代统治阶层的身份) 贵族村落。这两处在朝鲜时代两班文化大放异彩的历史村落位于韩半岛的东南部 (岭南地方)，依山傍水，村落建筑是为了适应夏天高温多湿，冬天低温干燥的气候而建造，房屋构造也遵循着儒教礼法。

两处村落作为两班氏族村落，其代表性建筑构造为宗家、住宅、亭子、书院、书堂等。周边的农耕地与自然景观依然美丽如画，并且与之相关的许多礼仪、游戏、著作、艺术品等文化遗产也完好地流传至今。

河回村和良洞村是韩国氏族村落中历史最悠久的，也是朝鲜前期氏族村落形成期的典型代表。两个村落遵循着传统风水的原则，村子的构造充分把功能性和观赏性结合于一体。另外，这里还完整地保存了朝鲜时代儒学家们的学术古文献和文化艺术品，以及传统的家庭礼仪和富有特色的村落仪式等文化遗产，备受世人瞩目。2010 年，在巴西召开的第 34 届联合国教科文组织世界文化遗产委员会上，河回村和良洞村作为"韩国的历史村落"被载入世界文化遗产。

Although there are numerous historical villages in Korea, the most **representative** are "clan villages". In Korea, a **clan** is a social group comprised of people of the same **paternal** line, family name, and ancestral home; it also includes women who have entered into the clan by marriage. Consequently, the term "clan village" refers to a village in which one or two clans form the majority of the village's residents and play a central role in making decisions about village life.

Though the entire Korean peninsula is scattered with historical neighborhoods and cultural **gems**, clan villages **make up** 80% of all historical villages, a major spread since their establishment in the early part of the Joseon Dynasty (1392–1910). Of these pockets of **time-honored** beauty, Hahoe

♦ **representative** [ˌreprɪˈzentətɪv]
adj. 典型的，有代表性的
♦ **clan** [klæn]
n. 宗族；氏族
♦ **paternal** [pəˈtɜːnl]
adj. 父系的，父方的
♦ **gem** [dʒem]
n. 精华，宝石
♦ **make up** 组成，构成
Women officers make up 13 percent of the police force. 女警占警力的 13%。
♦ **time-honored** [ˈtaɪmˌɒnəd]
adj. 历史悠久的
♦ **surviving** [səˈvaɪvɪŋ]
adj. 幸存下来的，继续存在的
She was the last surviving member of the

and Yangdong are Korea's longest **surviving** and most well-preserved traditional clan villages. Both villages were home to the yangban (ruling noble class) during the Joseon and together are regarded as the **epicenter** of Korea's Confucian culture.

Hahoe and Yandong face outward towards quietly flowing river waters and are guarded by forested mountains at the **rear**. Long ago, each village was constructed with sensitivity to the unique mountain and waterside climate. Not only built to **be able to** withstand temperature and **humidity** changes throughout the year, village houses, pavilions, study halls, and Confucian academies were specially constructed and arranged so as not to violate Confucian etiquette and the principles of Feng shui.

In addition to their unique **spatial** arrangements, the villages hold priceless **archives** and artwork from Joseon Era Confucianists and are some of the few remaining places that strictly observe traditional family and community rituals and events. **In recognition of** these attributes, the UNESCO World Heritage Committee officially put these historical villages of Korea on the UNESCO World Heritage List at its 34th convention meeting in Brazil.

family. 她是这家人中仅存的一员。
♦ **epicenter** [ˈepɪsentə(r)]
n. 中心，集中点
♦ **rear** [rɪə]
n. 后部，背面
A trailer was attached to the rear of the truck. 卡车后面挂了一辆拖车。
♦ **be able to** 能够
I do hope you'll be able to come to the wedding. 我确实希望你能来参加婚礼。
♦ **humidity** [hjuːˈmɪdɪti]
n. 湿度；潮湿，湿热
The humidity of soil helps plants to grow. 土壤潮湿有助于植物生长。
♦ **spatial** [ˈspeɪʃəl]
adj. 空间的
An article can be written in chronological, spatial or logical order. 文章可以按时间、空间或逻辑顺序来写。
♦ **archive** [ˈɑːkaɪv]
n. 档案（文件）
She went to the city archive this morning. 她今天上午去了市档案馆。
♦ **in recognition of**
认识到，承认……

07 Joseon Wangjo Sillok: Memory of the World Register
世界记忆遗产：《朝鲜王朝实录》

朝鲜王朝实录是把自朝鲜王朝始祖太祖至哲宗的 25 代 472 年（1392－1863）按年月日记录的编年史，共 1893 卷 888 册，是最古老且庞大的史书。实录函盖朝鲜年代的政治、外交、军事、制度、法律、经济、产业等各个方面的史实，是在世界上罕见的宝贵历史记录。它的意义还在于记录历史的真实性和可信性。

朝鲜王朝实录从基础资料的起草到实际编述和刊行，所有工作由春秋馆的史官负责，此官职的独立地位和对记述内容的保密，得到了制度上的保障。实录是在下一代王即位后开设实录厅、安排史官编撰的，其史草连国王也不能随意阅读，保障高度秘密，以确保实录的真实性和可信性。

实录编成后，把实录分送到在全国各地要地设置的史库各一份保存。遇壬辰倭乱和丙子胡乱曾被火烧毁，每当此时，重新出刊或进行补修。朝鲜王朝实录留传至今的有：鼎足山本 1181 册、太白山本 848 册、五台山本 27 册、其他散本 21 册，共 2077 册。这些留存本一并被指定为国宝第 151 号，1997 年 10 月又被联合国教科文组织登记为世界纪录遗产。

Joseon Wangjo Sillok (Annals of the Joseon Dynasty) **covers** 472 years (1392–1863) of the history of the reigns of 25 kings, from the dynasty's founder King Taejo to King Cheoljong. In **chronological** order, the king's everyday affairs, court **functionaries'** everyday reports to the king, the king's commands, and other daily matters dealt with in the public offices are **compiled** in 1,893 chapters in 888 books.

To keep up the compilation of Joseon Wangjo Sillok involved many historians, **historiographers**, and censors, who were responsible for writing daily drafts, editing them, and printing the resulting **volumes**. These writers participated in every national conference and kept records of the actual details of national affairs that were decided in discussion between the king and officials. Their freedom of expression and of maintaining secrecy was constitutionally **guaranteed**. Their daily records were placed in the **custody** of the Chunchugwan Office of Annals Compilation. Except for the historians, nobody was allowed to read them, not even the king. Any historian who disclosed the contents was severely punished as a **felon**. The regulations and ordinances governing historiography were very strict.

When a king died, a temporary office of annals compilation was set up and the **annals** of his reign were published **posthumously** and preserved in the historical archives under **rigorous** management. To further safeguard them, a set of the annals was deposited in each of the four archives located in four key mountainous locations nationwide: the Jeongjoksan, Taebaeksan, Jeoksangsan, and Odaesan Archives. Some were reduced to ashes during the Japanese and Qing invasions but were reconstructed and reprinted.

There are 2,077 existing volumes that were collected

◆ **cover** ['kʌvə]
vt. 涉及，包括
The talks are expected to cover other topics too. 会谈估计还会涉及别的问题。

◆ **chronological** [ˌkrɒnə'lɒdʒɪkəl]
adj. 按时间顺序的，编年的

◆ **functionary** ['fʌŋkʃənərɪ]
n. 公职人员，官员

◆ **compile** [kəm'paɪl]
vt. 收集，编制
It takes years of hard work to compile a good dictionary. 编辑一部好词典需要数年的艰苦工作。

◆ **historiographer** [ˌhɪstɔːrɪ'ɒgrəfə]
n. 史官，史料编纂者

◆ **volume** ['vɒljuːm]
n. 卷册

◆ **guaranteed** [ˌgærən'tiːd]
adj. 受到保障的

◆ **custody** ['kʌstədɪ]
n. 监管，监督；保管，照管
in the custody of 受……的监管
When his parents die, he is placed in the custody of his aunt. 他的父母去世以后，他就交由姑妈照管。

◆ **felon** ['felən]
n. 重罪犯

◆ **annals** ['ænəlz]
n. 编年史，年鉴

◆ **posthumously** ['pɒstjuməslɪ]
adv. 于死后，于身后
After the war she was posthumously awarded the George Cross. 战争结束后，她被追授乔治十字勋章。

◆ **rigorous** ['rɪgərəs]
adj. 严格的

from the archives: 1,181 from the Jeongjoksan Archive, 848 from the Taebaeksan Archive, 27 from the Odaesan Archive, and 21 scattered copies called Sanyeopbon. They were all **registered** in UNESCO's Memory of the World in October 1997.

The Joseon Wangjo Sillok covers the historical and cultural aspects of the Joseon Dynasty including politics and **diplomacy**, military affairs, law, economics, industry, transportation, communications, social systems, customs and manners, arts and crafts and religion. These enormous historical and cultural resources, of **unprecedented** accuracy, serve as an **encyclopedia** of the Joseon society. Their beautiful font types also show the advanced printing methods of Korea from early on. Today they are indispensable materials for the study of Korean history while providing diverse resources for the study of other East Asian countries including Japan, the China, and Mongolia.

Vigorous youth is subjected to rigorous discipline. 活泼的年轻人须受到严格的纪律约束。
♦ **register** [ˈredʒɪstə]
vt. 登记；注册
♦ **diplomacy** [dɪˈpləʊməsɪ]
n. 外交
♦ **unprecedented**
[ʌnˈpresɪdəntɪd]
adj. 前所未有的，空前的
The pace of agricultural growth since the reforms began has been unprecedented. 改革以来的农业增长速度是前所未有的。
♦ **encyclopedia**
[enˌsaɪkləʊˈpiːdɪə]
n. 百科全书

08 Joseon Dynasty Through Films
在电影中相遇朝鲜时代

以朝鲜时代为素材的韩国电影非常多。仅 2014 年一年，就有好几部以朝鲜时代为背景的电影上映，其中包括描写朝鲜正祖时代的《逆鳞》、以正祖的祖父英祖时代为背景的《思悼：8 天的记忆》，以及描写哲宗时代的《群盗》等。

电影《逆鳞》主人公的正祖是一位改革君主，自称"万川明月主人翁"的正祖认为王之下的万物都是平等的。他推行与百姓直接对话并交流的政治理念。一生热爱读书与写作的正祖虽然不到 50 岁就英年早逝，但是他创下了无法想象的业绩。电影《群盗》讲述了在两班与腐败官吏极其专横暴戾的朝鲜哲宗 13 年，为百姓打抱不平的智异山义贼们的故事。

以朝鲜时代为背景的作品不断出现的原因是什么？首先，朝鲜时代拥有长达六百多年的历史，其间发生了很多故事。特别是每天都记录国情的《朝鲜王朝实录》，这本书可谓是一本故事宝典。包括王的一举手一投足、在全国发生的各种琐事，以及自然现象等在内，该书对朝鲜时代的五百多年进行了详细记录；其次，朝鲜时代与现在不同，那是一个将人分为两班、平民与奴婢的身份社会。人与人之间存在着严格的身份区别，因此也出现了很多矛盾。平民与奴婢常常对支配阶层的两班进行抵抗。这种抵抗发挥了巨大的力量，这也成为迎接近代化到来的背景。

存在于大韩民国诞生之前的朝鲜王朝是一个与 21 世纪截然不同的王朝国家，但朝鲜时代人物所经历的问题与现在没有什么差别。应该如何让国家富饶安定，应该如何解决民生问题，朝鲜时代是一个忧苦不堪并充满矛盾的时期。以朝鲜时代为背景的这些影片为生活在当下的我们带来了感动与教训。

The Joseon Dynasty (1392–1910) ruled over Korea for more than 500 years. The lives and times of the 27 **monarchs** are some of the most widely used material in Korean film. In 2014 alone, a couple of films set with the royal dynasty as background will be released. Earlier this year, theaters saw the release of "The Fatal Encounter," a film which deals with the times of King Jeongjo (1776–1800). Two more films are set to be released later this year. They are "Sado: Memory of Eight Days," which **revolves** around King Yeongjo (1724–1776), grandfather to Jeongjo, and "Group of Robbers," which **focuses on** King Cheoljong (1849–1863).

King Jeongjo (1752–1800), the **protagonist** of "The Fatal Encounter," was a strong monarch. He has often been compared to Louis XIV of France, widely known as "The Sun King." Defining himself as the Man-cheon-myeong-wol-ju-in-ong, or, "Master of Ten Thousand Rivers and the Moon," meaning that he can **shed light on** all creatures, King Jeongjo believed that all were equal under the king. This was reflected in his willingness to communicate and listen. He was always **willing** to have a conversation with the public.

The movie "Group of Robbers" is set in the 13th year of King Cheoljong's reign, 1862, when **rampant** corruption among the upper classes and government officials reached its peak. The **Robin Hood**-like story **pivots around** a group of **bandits** who lived on the slopes of Jirisan Mountain and who pursued **righteousness** and justice, fighting for the poor, helpless people.

As seen with the two films above, movies set during the Joseon Dynasty are released again and again. What could be the reason?

♦ **monarch** [ˈmɒnək]
n. 国王，君主
To his own people, Solomon was a wasteful and oppressive monarch. 在本国人民眼里，所罗门是个挥霍、残暴的君主。

♦ **revolve** [rɪˈvɒlv]
vi. 围绕
revolve around 围绕
The planets revolve around the sun. 行星绕着太阳运转。

♦ **focus on**
关注，以……为中心 如 Their talks are expected to focus on arms control. 他们的会谈预计会集中讨论军备控制问题。

♦ **protagonist** [prəʊˈtæɡənɪst]
n. 主人公

♦ **shed light on**
照亮，施恩于
A government report shed light on the causes of local floods. 政府所提出的报告说明了本地水灾发生的原因。

♦ **willing** [ˈwɪlɪŋ]
adj. 乐意的，愿意的

♦ **rampant** [ˈræmpənt]
adj. 蔓延的，猖獗的

♦ **Robin Hood**
罗宾汉，英国民间传说中著名的英雄形象，行侠仗义、劫富济贫的绿林好汉。

♦ **pivot around**
围绕，以……为核心

♦ **bandit** [ˈbændɪt]
n. 土匪，强盗

♦ **righteousness** [ˈraɪtʃəsnɪs]
n. 正义

First of all, the Joseon Dynasty has 518 years of history and, subsequently, an abundant range of stories related to the period. In particular, the Annals of the Joseon Dynasty, a daily record of national affairs, is the source of many such stories, **handed down** over the generations. It depicts the daily royal details of more than 500 years of history, including every single movement of the king, trivial incidents that **occurred** across the country and even natural phenomena. The massive amount of historical records must be attractive source material for a number of directors.

Second, Joseon society was extremely **hierarchical**. People were classified as either ruling yangban, the **aristocrats**, as pyeongmin, the middle class, or as nobi, the slaves. There was strict classification, with **stringent** discrimination between the strata. Conflicts between them were unavoidable. The resistance of the middle classes and slaves against the aristocrats could often be observed. Social movements developed huge power, laying the ground work for the modernization of the nation.

The Joseon Dynasty, existent for half a millennium before the birth of the Republic of Korea, must have been different from the 21st century. However, the problems people had to endure do not show any particularly differences. It was a period of contemplation and deliberation, as the nation sought prosperity, stability and the well-being of the people.

The treasured experiences of previous generations are **reenacted** and brought life through movies, touching the modern viewer's heart and giving lessons to the people of today.

Our allies are the millions who hunger and thirst after righteousness. 那成千上万如饥似渴追寻正义的人是我们的联盟。
♦ **hand down**
遗留，把……传递下来
♦ **occur** [əˈkɜː]
vi. 发生，出现
♦ **hierarchical** [ˌhaɪəˈrɑːkɪkəl]
adj. 按等级划分的，等级（制度）的
♦ **aristocrat** [ˈærɪstəkræt]
n. 贵族
♦ **stringent** [ˈstrɪndʒənt]
adj. 严格的
He announced that there would be more stringent controls on the possession of weapons. 他宣布将对武器的持有实行更严格的控制。
♦ **reenact** [riːˈnækt]
vt. （使）再现，重演

09 Himeji-jo Castle
日本第一名城：姬路城

作为日本第一个登录的世界遗产，姬路城外观一片洁白，加上白色的灰泥墙面，仿佛一只展翅舞蹈的白鹭，因而得名"白鹭城"。不像日本其他古城，姬路城堡因没有遭受战争等灾难的损坏而保存完好。城内有 74 处建筑被日本政府确立为重要的文化遗产。

城堡始建于1346年，后来军阀丰臣秀吉（1537—1598）统治时期，组织大规模的城墙建设，奠定了今天姬路城的基础。江户时代初期，经过九年的精心修复，才有了我们看到的宏伟城堡。

如果你体格足够强健，受得了爬上爬下，那就到城堡里面转转，欣赏美景从来不是权贵的特权。城堡内复杂的构造，特别是那三座高耸的瞭望塔靠柱子和迷宫似的通道蜿蜒相接，依然是打仗的绝好堡垒，隐蔽的布局可以拖住敌军的入侵，让他们晕头转向。这种设计是为了防止敌人进入城堡中央的最高瞭望塔和主楼，所以，去那里要带上地图，当心迷路！

众多的城门上，有城堡保卫的构造遗迹，万一敌人攻入，可以投掷石块打击敌人；还有些城门的通道极其狭窄，一次允许通过的人数不多，城墙上挖有无数的孔洞用来射击，还有许多窗格用来投掷巨石。里面竟然建有厨房，以防遭围攻时城堡倒塌，饿死城内居民的企图也不会得逞。此外，外面墙上厚厚的白泥不仅好看，更能有效阻挡敌军的子弹和炮火。

城堡主楼矗立于太姬山巅，总高32米，建于高约15米的巨石之上，从楼顶观望，景色颇为壮丽。晴日里，不难想象，封建领主伫立楼顶，胸怀一统河山的豪情壮志。夜晚，整个城堡灯火通明，强烈推荐日落以后前去游览。

Because its pure white appearance with white plaster coating looks like a dancing **Shirasagi (Egret)** with wings spread, this famous castle is also called the "Shirasagi-jo". It **was spared from** damage during the war and from many other disasters and is in a remarkably preserved state compared to other castles. Seventy-four structures within the castle site including a tower and gate are designated as important cultural assets of Japan.

The year of establishment was 1346. Later, the warlord **Toyotomi Hideyoshi** (1537-1598), who ruled over most of Japan, built a full-scale castle wall, which became the base for present-day Himeji-jo. At the start of the **Edo period**, the castle underwent considerable **renovation** over a 9-year period to create the magnificent appearance we see today.

If you are confident in the strength of your legs and back to climb up and down, you should take a look around the inside of the castle. Clearly, beauty was not the only priority of those **in power** throughout the ages. Its complicated structure, particularly the three tall watchtowers connected by columns and winding maze-like passages, functions well as a war fort and **conceals** a mechanism to halt the invasion of enemies and throw them into confusion. The design is intended to prevent access to the tallest watchtower and castle keep, situated at the heart of the castle, which functions as a center, so beware if you go there without a map, you may get lost!

♦ **Shirasagi (Egret)**
n. 白鹭，一种鸟类，因体羽全白而得名。

♦ **be spared from**
幸免于，免于遭受（痛苦、折磨等不好的事情）
Northern Somalia was largely spared from the famine. 索马里北部的大部分地区逃过了这场饥荒。

♦ **Toyotomi Hideyoshi**
丰臣秀吉（1537—1598），日本战国时期的著名封建领主，继室町幕府之后，近代首次统一日本的日本战国三英杰（与同时代的织田信长、德川家康并称）之一。在位时强化武士阶层，晚年发动朝鲜战争。

♦ **Edo period**
江户时代（1603—1867），是德川幕府统治日本的年代，是日本封建统治的最后一个时代。

♦ **renovation** [ˌrenəʊˈveɪʃən]
n. 整修，修复；革新
The building has undergone major renovation. 这座大楼已进行大整修。

♦ **in power**
当权的，在位的；执政，掌权

♦ **conceal** [kənˈsiːl]
vt. 隐藏，隐蔽，隐瞒

♦ **under siege**
被包围，围困
The city was under siege. How could

Among the many gates are the remains of gate mechanisms for dropping stones on the enemy if they manage to enter, or gates with an extremely narrow passageway so that not many people could pass at once. Numerous holes to shoot from are made in the castle wall and there are windows from which to drop gigantic stones on the enemy, too. It is very interesting that there is a kitchen in the inner court in case the castle falls **under siege** or an attempt is made to starve out the **occupants**. By the way, the thick coating of white plaster on the outer surface is not just there for **aesthetic** purposes but also for defense, because of its excellent resistance to fire and bullets.

they helplessly wait for death? 兵临城下，岂能束手待毙？
♦ **occupant** [ˈɒkjuːpənt]
n. 占有者，居住者
♦ **aesthetic** [iːsˈθetɪk]
adj. 美学的，审美的，美感的
aesthetic standard 审美标准
♦ **approx.**
abbr. (approximately) 近似地，大约
♦ **feudal** [ˈfjuːdl]
adj. 封建(制度)的 封地的 常见搭配：
feudal lord 封建主，诸侯。

The castle keep rising from the peak of Mt. Hime-yama is built with a total height of 32m on a stone wall **approx.** 15 m high, and the view from the top of the keep is spectacular. On a fine day, you can imagine the emotions of a **feudal** warlord with his ambitions to dominate the whole country. At night, the entire castle is lit up, so a visit after sunset is highly recommended as well.

10 Senso-ji Temple
东京最古老的寺庙

　　浅草寺是东京都内最古老的寺庙。相传，在推古天皇三十六年（公元 628 年），有两个渔民在宫户川捕鱼，捞起了一座高 5.5 厘米的金观音像，附近人家就集资修建了一座庙宇供奉这尊佛像，这就是浅草寺。其后该寺屡遭火灾，数次被毁。到江户初期，德川家康重建浅草寺，使它变成一座大群寺院，并成为附近江户市民的游乐之地。除浅草寺内堂外，浅草寺院内的五重塔等著名建筑物和史迹、观赏景点数不胜数。每年元旦前后，前来朝拜的香客，人山人海。

　　寺院的大门叫"雷门"，正式名称是"风雷神门"，是日本的门脸、浅草的象征。门内有长约 140 米的铺石参拜神道通向供着观音像的正殿。作为了解日本民族文化的旅游名胜，来自世界各国的游客，络绎不绝。

　　寺西南角有一座五重塔，仅次于京都东寺的五重塔，为日本第二高塔。火烧后使用近代技术改建而成，建筑物本身虽失去了历史价值，但作为当地居民的心灵支柱一直活跃至今。直通寺院的内侧门。左右是守护佛教的一对仁王像。守护神一个横眉竖目、紧闭双唇、威武强壮。另一个威猛雄伟、叱咤邪恶。

Early in the morning of March 18, 628, when the capital of Japan was Asuka (present-day Nara **Prefecture**, two fishermen, Hinokuma Hamanari and his brother Takenari, were fishing in the Sumida River. Suddenly **sensing** something, they pulled up their net to find a statue of **Bodhisattva Kannon**. When Haji no Nakatomo, village headman of Asakusa, heard about this, he immediately realized that the object was a statue of the important Buddhist deity Bodhisattva Kannon. Taking vows as a Buddhist priest and remaking his home into a temple, he spent the rest of his life in **devotion** to Bodhisattva Kannon.

In 645, **renowned** Buddhist priest Shokai Shonin built Kannondo Hall upon visiting the Asakusa district during his travels. Following a **revelation** he received in a dream, Shokai decided that the image should be hidden from human view, and this tradition has remained in place ever since.

Asakusa began as an **obscure** fishing village along an **estuary** of Tokyo Bay, part of the vast **wilderness** of the area known as Musashi. The district later **thrived** as people arrived in increasing numbers to worship. When Ennin (794–864), the highest-ranking priest of Enryaku-ji (head temple of the Tendai School of Buddhism) visited Senso-ji in the mid-ninth century, he created a statue identical to the hidden one that could be viewed and worshipped by the people.

During the Kamakura period (1192–1333), the shoguns, who held the true power in Japan during this time, demonstrated great devotion to Senso-ji. Gradually, other historically prominent figures including military commanders and the **literati** came to follow their example. Enjoying the protection of these **illustrious** individuals, the temple buildings were refined. During the Edo period (1603–1867), first Edo shogun Tokugawa Ieyasu deemed Senso-ji the temple where prayers for the aspirations of the shogunate would be offered. As a result the buildings **were imbued with** still greater dignity, and the temple complex flourished as the center of Edo (pres-

---

◆ **prefecture** [ˈpriːfektjʊə]
n. （日本）县，辖区
Nara Prefecture 奈良县

◆ **sense** [sens]
vt. 感觉到，觉察到，意识到
Amy could sense his liveliness even from where she stood. 埃米从她所站的位置都能感到他活力逼人。

◆ **Bodhisattva Kannon**
观音菩萨，从字面解释就是"观察（世间民众）声音"的菩萨，是佛教四大菩萨之一。她相貌端庄慈祥，经常手持净瓶杨柳，具有无量的智慧和神通，大慈大悲，普救人间疾苦。

◆ **devotion** [dɪˈvəʊʃən]
n. 献身，奉献
He is adorable for his devotion to science. 他献身科学的精神令人敬佩。

◆ **renowned** [rɪˈnaʊnd]
adj. 有名的，享有声誉的；有声望的

◆ **revelation** [ˌrevɪˈleɪʃən]
n. （宗教中的）天启，启示

◆ **obscure** [əbˈskjʊə]
adj. 不著名的，无名的
He is an obscure poet. 他是一个不著名的诗人。

◆ **estuary** [ˈestjʊərɪ]
n. 港湾；（江河入海的）河口
We moored in the estuary, waiting for high tide. 我们在港湾停泊，等待涨潮。

◆ **wilderness** [ˈwɪldənɪs]
n. （草木丛生的）荒地，荒野

◆ **thrive** [θraɪv]
vi. 兴盛，兴隆起来
His company continues to thrive. 他的公司一直在蓬勃发展。

◆ **literati** [ˌlɪtəˈrɑːtiː]
n. 知识界，文人学士（literatus 的名词复数）

◆ **illustrious** [ɪˈlʌstrɪəs]
adj. 著名的，显赫的；杰出的
Washington and Lincoln are illustrious Americans.

ent-day Tokyo) culture.

Senso-ji is Tokyo's oldest temple. Known affectionately to people all over Japan as the temple of the Asakusa Kannon, it draws some 30 million visitors every year, remaining an important center of worship. Amongst the many Buddhas, Bodhisattva Kannon is known as the most **compassionate**, relieving beings of their suffering and responding to prayers with great **benevolence**. This Bodhisattva Kannon, the principle image of Senso-ji, has been an unparalleled source of benefits and miracles, saving and protecting countless people over the course of the 1,400 years since its appearance in the world.

华盛顿和林肯都是杰出的美国人。
♦ **be imbued with** 充满
Her voice was imbued with an unusual seriousness. 她的声音里充满着一种不寻常的严肃语气。
♦ **Senso-ji**（日本）浅草寺
♦ **compassionate** [kəmˈpæʃənɪt]
adj. 有同情心的
One could tell at a glance that she was a compassionate person. 一眼就能看出她很有同情心。
♦ **benevolence** [bɪˈnevələns]
n. 仁慈，善举

11 Buddhist Monuments in the Horyu-ji Area
佛教圣地法隆寺

公元 680 年法隆寺的原始建筑毁于火灾，但随后重建。西院首先重建，包括主要寺庙，随后是东院。随着僧侣集聚，公元 11 世纪寺庙扩建。19 世纪后期的日本明治维新收到神道教影响，这些佛寺渐渐荒废，直到 1897 年再次大规模重建，重现昔日辉煌，自此保存完好。

法隆寺地区建筑群主要由两部分构成。西院包括金堂和五重塔，东院建有梦殿，一座八角形建筑，建于公元 739 年，用以纪念圣德太子。这些寺庙外观与中国建筑风格相似，是因为它们建设时正逢佛学从中国传播而来。正如中国寺庙那样，法隆寺的宝塔留有圣迹，而金堂内的宗教塑像风格各异。

公元七世纪到八世纪之间，中国僧侣经由朝鲜半岛来到日本，在佛学影响下，日本建造了法隆寺佛教建筑群。伸手素我氏影响的圣德太子，把它作为日本佛学中心，开始建造建筑群。顶峰是在他去世时捐献的东院土地上建造的梦殿。镰仓时代，圣德太子成为佛教徒崇拜的偶像，进一步确保了寺庙建筑群能一直保存到明治维新神道教兴起时。

1993 年，法隆寺地区及其建筑群被联合国教科文组织列入世界文化遗址，包括 38 处日本国宝。其中，五重塔在 2011 年被认定为现存最早的木质建筑，该寺庙被日本帝国当作国家的守护神，因此保存了它的历史原貌。

The original buildings at **Horyu-ji** were destroyed by fire in 680, but were rebuilt almost immediately. The Western Precinct, which contains the main temple, was built first, followed by the Eastern Precinct after the land was donated by **Prince Shotoku** upon his death. Buddhist priest communities began to form within the temple complex, which were further expanded by temple construction in the 11th century. The buildings **fell into disrepair** during the Shinto-influenced **Meiji Restoration** in the late 19th century, but a major reconstruction effort in 1897 restored the structures to their former glory and they have been carefully maintained ever since.

There are two main sections to the Horyu-ji complex. The Western Precinct consists of the Kondo or Golden Hall, and the "Goju-no-tou" pagoda. The Eastern Precinct contains the Yumedono or Dream House, an **octagonal** structure that was built in 739 to **hold a memorial service for** Prince Shotoku. The **exterior** of the monuments bear a **resemblance** to Chinese architecture, due to Buddhism's spread from China at the time of its construction. As with Chinese Buddhist temples, the pagoda in the Horyu-ji complex houses holy **relics** while the Kondo contains various religious statues.

The monuments at Horyu-ji were built in the 7th and 8th centuries as a result of the spread of Buddhism by Chinese monks who entered the country via the **Korean Peninsula**. Prince Shotoku of the influential Soga clan began construction of the complex as a focal point of Buddhism in Japan, which **culminated** in the Yumedono being erected at his death upon the land he donated in the Eastern Precinct. A **cult** treating Prince Shotoku as a Buddhist icon was established during the **Kamakura period**, which further ensured that the temple complex was maintained until the rise of Shintoism in the Meiji Restoration.

In 1993, the Horyu-ji area and its structures were listed as a World Heritage Site by **UNESCO**. It houses 38 of Japan's national treasures, and the Goju-no-tou pagoda within the complex is considered to be the oldest standing wooden structure as of 2011. The Japanese Empire believes it is guarded by this temple, and as a result preserves its historical architecture.

♦ **Horyu-ji**
法隆寺，又称斑鸠寺，位于日本奈良生驹郡斑鸠町，是圣德太子于飞鸟时代建造的佛教木结构寺庙，1993年与其中建筑群列入世界文化遗产。

♦ **Prince Shotoku**
圣德太子，公元7世纪的著名政治家，是日本第一部宪法的制定者。

♦ **fall into disrepair** 失修，荒废

♦ **Meiji Restoration**
日本资本主义现代化的改革运动，始于1868年明治天皇新政府时期，这次改革使日本跻身于世界强国之列。

♦ **octagonal** [ɒkˈtæɡənl]
adj. 八边形的，八角形的

♦ **hold a memorial service for**
纪念，追悼

♦ **resemblance** [rɪˈzembləns]
n. 类同之处

♦ **exterior** [eksˈtɪərɪə]
n. 外部，外表，外貌

♦ **relic** [ˈrelɪk]
n. 遗物，遗迹，废墟，纪念物

♦ **Korean Peninsula**
朝鲜半岛，与中国东部接壤，包括现在的朝鲜和韩国。

♦ **culminate** [ˈkʌlmɪneɪt]
vi. 达到顶点，高潮
culminate in/with + 时间或事件

♦ **cult** [kʌlt] n.（对宗教等的）崇拜
a cult figure 崇拜偶像

♦ **Kamakura period**
镰仓时代（1185—1333），日本历史中以镰仓为全国政治中心的武家政权时代，镰仓幕府的建立标志着日本中世纪封建时代的开始。

♦ **UNESCO**
（全称：United Nations Educational, Scientific, and Cultural Organization）联合国教科文组织，联合国旗下专门机构之一，成立于1946年，总部设在法国巴黎，旨在促进教育、文化、科学方面的文化合作以及各国人民的相互了解。

Chapter 9
悠游日韩：一景一色一芳华

01 Mount Fuji: A New World Cultural Heritage
世遗新宠富士山

2013 年 6 月 22 日，正在柬埔寨首都金边举行的第 37 届世界遗产大会批准将富士山列入联合国教科文组织《世界遗产名录》，富士山从而成为日本的第 17 处世界遗产。

富士山是日本的象征之一，影响着日本的自然和人文地理以及国民的精神家园。

作为日本最高峰，富士山海拔 3776 米（12380 英尺），是一座活火山。山体位于三大板块交界处：阿穆尔板块（同欧亚板块相连）、鄂霍次克板块（与北美洲板块相连）和菲律宾板块都在富士山地区之下汇聚。富士山距离日本首都同时也是日本最大的城市东京仅仅 100 公里（62 英里），事实上，上次 1707 年爆发时火山灰有落到东京，烧过的碳灰喷洒如雨。1708 年以来，还未发现再次爆发的迹象，爆发的危险变小。

富士山气候极冷山上一年里大部分月份都覆盖着积雪，最冷时有 -38.0 ºC (36.4 ºF)，最热时达 17.8 ºC (64.0 ºF)。攀登富士山是一项富有冒险的运动，从 6 月 1 日到 8 月 27 日。作为最受国内外游客欢迎的旅游景点，每年有超过 200 000 人登上顶峰，大部分是在相对暖和的夏季。沿途山路上的小屋提供饮料，基本医疗用品和休息的房间，很受登山者喜爱。许多人晚上登山，是为了到山顶看日出，毕竟，日本号称"日出之国"，富士山上的日出有个专门的名字，"御来光"。

至少从公元 7 世纪开始，富士山一直是神道人士的圣地。神道是日本的本土信仰，从富士山山下沿途而上，尽是神社，供奉着神道教信仰的神灵，在富士山上的神灵是木花开耶姬公主，她的标识是樱花，许多神社供奉木花开耶姬，叫做"祈福"神社，主要分布在富士山下和山顶，然而放眼全日本，竟有 1 000 多座。

Mount Fuji is a symbol of Japan. The mountain contributes to Japan's physical, cultural, and spiritual **geography**.

As the tallest mountain in Japan, standing at 3,776 meters (12,380 **feet**), it is an active **volcano**, sitting on a "triple junction" of **tectonic** activity: the Amurian plate (associated with the Eurasian tectonic plate), the Okhotsk plate (associated with the North American plate) and the Filipino plate all **converge** in the region beneath Mount Fuji. It is only 100 kilometers (62 miles) from Tokyo, Japan's capital and largest city. In fact, the last time Mount Fuji **erupted**, in 1707, volcanic ash fell on Tokyo. During that time, burned pieces of coal and

♦ **geography** [dʒɪˈɒgrəfi]
n. 地理学，地理，地形；（房屋）布局
♦ **foot** [fʊt]
n. 英尺
♦ **volcano** [vɒlˈkeɪnəʊ]
n. 火山
active/extinct volcano 活火山 / 死火山
♦ **tectonic** [tekˈtɒnɪk]
adj. 构造的，建筑，地壳构造上的
tectonic movement 构造运动，地壳运动
♦ **converge** [kənˈvɜːdʒ]
vi. 聚合，集中于一点

ashes came out like rain. Ever since 1708, no eruption signs have been discovered and today, this mountain has a less risk of volcano's eruption.

The climate is extremely cold as the surface of the mount **is covered with** snow for most of the months during the calendar year. The coolest temperature here was -38.0 ºC (36.4 ºF) and the hottest temperature was 17.8 ºC (64.0 ºF). Climbing Mount Fiji is an adventurous sport and it starts from July 1st to August 27th.

Mount Fuji is the single most popular tourist site in Japan, for both Japanese and foreign tourists. More than 200,000 people climb to the summit every year, mostly during the warmer summer months. "Huts" on the route up the mountain **cater to** climbers, providing **refreshments**, basic medical supplies, and room to rest. Many people start climbing Mount Fuji at night, as better to experience sunrise from the summit–Japan, after all, is **nicknamed** "the Land of the Rising Sun." The sunrise from Mount Fuji has a special name, Goraiko.

Mount Fuji has been a sacred site for practicers of **Shinto** since at least the 7th century. Shinto is the **indigenous** faith or spirituality of Japan. Many Shinto shrines dot the base and ascent of Mount Fuji. Shinto shrines honor Kami, the supernatural **deities** of the Shinto faith. The kami of Mount Fuji is Princess Konohanasakuya, whose symbol is the cherry blossom. Konohanasakuya has an entire series of shrines, called Segen shrines. The main Segen shrines are at the base and summit of Mount Fuji, but there are more than 1,000 across all of Japan.

The avenues converge at a central square. 道路汇聚在中央广场。
♦ **erupt** [ɪˈrʌpt]
vi.（火山，情感等）爆发
My neighbor erupted in anger over the noise. 噪声使我的邻居勃然大怒。
♦ **be covered with**
覆盖着……
♦ **be covered with frost/moss**
被冰霜覆盖／长满苔藓
♦ **cater to**
满足（需要），投合（喜好）
Our literature and art ought to cater to popular taste. 我们的文艺必须为大众所喜闻乐见。
♦ **refreshment** [rɪˈfreʃmənt]
n. 恢复，精神爽快
♦ **nickname** [ˈnɪkneɪm]
vt. 给……取绰号，给……起诨名
♦ **Shinto** [ˈʃɪntəʊ]
n. 神道教，日本的传统民族宗教，属于泛灵多神信仰（精灵崇拜），视自然界各种动植物为神祇。1945年前为日本国教。
♦ **indigenous** [ɪnˈdɪdʒɪnəs]
adj. 本土的
♦ **deity** [ˈdiːɪti]
n. 神，神灵

02 Osorezan: Entrance to the Hell in Japan
日本地狱之门：恐山

恐山位于日本青森县，在本州最北端，与高野山、比睿山并为日本三大灵场之一。灵场内有许多种类的温泉，属于下北半岛国家公园。

由于以前的火山活动而形成硫气孔，会喷出弥漫着混集了蒸气与硫磺臭气，整座山被硫磺臭气所笼罩，而形成肃杀的景象。但在前方的破火山口湖畔，则是一个一望无际，纯白的沙滩，呈现一片平静的风景。虽说如此，但是恐山的风景还是很美丽的，并且有很多的寺庙。

在那个不知是地狱还是天堂的奇异世界里，你会发现不少死人墓。由于这个山是现世为故人而设的地方，所以改了现在的名字。那里是失去藏身之所的幽灵们最后去的地方，是连接这个世界和"黄泉"的山。

根据佛教信仰，人们死后会根据生前的"业"从三祖河上三座桥中的一座上走过，决定死后的命运，因此佛教文化在此十分盛行。恐山脚下建有菩提寺，佛教是能够解决人们死后归宿的地方，附近住有传统的日本招魂师——市子。此外，对于那些夭折或者比父母早逝的孩子，据说，在过桥时会有儿童的保护神jiso相助。恐山因此受到失去孩子的父母的格外关注。

Osorezan (fear mountain) is considered the entrance to hell according to Japanese legend. It's an **active volcano** in Aomori prefecture that has a burnt, **barren** landscape. Osorezan (Mount Osore) sits on the shores of a **poisonous** lake, smells of **sulphur** and has a bitterly cold winter. Nevertheless, it's a popular tourist destination.

According to Japanese Buddhist belief, when we die we must cross Sanzu River (three crossing river) into the **afterlife**. According to legend, this afterlife crossing (Sanzu River) is the narrow brook that leads from Osorezan to Lake Usori. This is based on **geographical** similarities with descriptions in ancient Buddhist writings.

There are 3 crossings over the river. If you've lived a good life you can take a bridge. If you've lived a **mediocre** life you can cross at a ford (a shallow path across the river). If you've lived a bad life you must walk through the waters of the river filled with demons and unspeakable **terrors**. A female and a male demon stand on the banks of the Sanzu River. The female demon (named Datsueba) **strips** the clothes of the dead. The male demon (Keneo) weights the clothes on branches to judge their **karma**.

The vast majority of Japanese funerals are Buddhist ceremonies that adhere to this belief. For example, it's believed that the departed make the crossing 7 days after they die–a special ceremony is typically held on this day to pray for a successful crossing.

♦ **active volcano** 活火山

As an active volcano may erupt at any time, it is most risky to go and examine an active volcano. 活火山会随时喷发，去探察活火山是件非常危险的事情。

♦ **barren** ['bærən]

adj. 荒芜的，贫瘠的

The place used to be a stretch of barren land. 早先这里是一片不毛之地。

♦ **poisonous** ['pɔɪznəs]

adj. 有毒的，有害的

Some mushrooms are good to eat; some are poisonous. 有些蘑菇可食用，有些则有毒。

♦ **sulphur** ['sʌlfə]

n. 硫磺，硫

♦ **afterlife** ['ɑːftəlaɪf]

n. 来世，来生

♦ **geographical** [ˌdʒɪəˈɡræfɪkəl]

adj. 地理的

These birds have a wide geographical distribution. 这些鸟的地理分布很广。

♦ **mediocre** [ˌmiːdɪˈəʊkə]

adj. 普通的，平庸的

I think of myself a mediocre writer. 我认为我自己只是个普通的写作者。

♦ **terror** ['terə]

n. 恐怖，恐怖的事物

Those rebels are a terror to the entire town. 那些反叛者使全城的人感到恐惧。

Bodaiji is the sole temple and main attraction at the foot of Osorezan. It's built around pools of bubbling hot sulphuric water. It stems from a branch of Japanese Buddhism that has played a traditional role helping the dead to negotiate the afterlife.

Traditionally, blind female **shaman** known as **Itako** practiced in the area. They claim to be able to communicate with the dead. In the past, Itako numbered in the hundreds. Today, this tradition has faded and their numbers have dwindled. The local authorities regard them as a **fraud**. Even the temple maintains their distance—saying that they tolerate the Itako but aren't associated with them.

It's said that children and the unborn who die before their parents cross the river by building bridges with pebbles. It's also said that demons **disrupt** this effort on a regular basis. However, there are many jiso placed in the area to help children who must make the crossing. Jiso are the traditional protectors of children in Japan. Therefore, Osorezan attracts parents who've recently lost children. Such parents care for the area's many jiso, giving them clothes for the winter.

♦ **strip** [strɪp]
vt. 除去，剥去
The doctor told me to strip down to my shorts. 医生让我脱得只剩一条短裤。
♦ **karma** [ˈkɑːmə]
n.（佛教和印度教的）业；因果报应，因缘
♦ **Bodaiji** 菩提寺
♦ **shaman** [ˈʃæmən]
n. 招魂巫师
♦ **Itako**
n. 市子，招魂者，并且只有青森的恐山招魂者才叫市子；其他地区虽然也有招魂者，但是并不叫市子。
♦ **fraud** [frɔːd]
n. 欺诈；骗子
Her assistant was accused of theft and fraud by the police. 她的助手被警方指控犯有盗窃和欺诈罪。
♦ **disrupt** [dɪsˈrʌpt]
vt. 扰乱，破坏，使瓦解
Slavery seemed likely to disrupt the Union then. 当时，奴隶制似乎有可能分裂美国。

03 Kiyomizu-dera Temple
日本清水寺

清水寺是京都最古老的寺院，被列为日本国宝建筑之一。清水寺因寺中清水而得名，顺着奥院的石阶而下便是音羽瀑布，清泉一分为三，分别代表长寿、健康、智慧，被视为具有神奇力量，游客路经此地一定会来喝上一口水，据说可预防疾病及灾厄。相传寺院为公元 798 年由延镇上人所建造，为平安时代之代表建筑物，后来曾多次遭大火所焚毁，现今所见为 1633 年德川家光依原来建筑手法重建。清水寺自古以来作为日本为数不多的观音灵地而闻名，平安时代以来，经常出现于日本文学作品当中。1994 年，作为古京都文化遗产的一部分登录于世界遗产名录上。

♦ **alluring** [əˈljʊərɪŋ]
adj. 迷人的，吸引人的
The life in a big city is alluring for the young people. 大都市的生活对年轻人颇具诱惑力。
♦ **sect** [sekt]
n. 宗派，教派
♦ **supposedly** [səˈpəʊzɪdlɪ]
adv. 据说，据认为
The novel is supposedly based on a true story. 据说这部小说是以一个真实的故事为依据的。

寺院周围是京都的名胜古迹，春天樱花盛开，秋天红叶似火，也是著名的赏枫及赏樱景点。宛如古都的风物诗般，清水寺外围的一景一色，完完全全地将京都的风采表露无疑，无论是春天的樱花，夏天的瀑布，秋天的红叶或是冬天的细雪，清水寺都仿佛是为了证明京都而存在的一般，无时无刻吸引着人们流连忘返。清水寺朴素的正殿阳台突出于断崖之上，因为环境优美而成为跳楼自杀者的首选之地。

Kiyomizu-dera is an **alluring** place. It's owned by an independent Buddhist **sect** that has mysterious rituals. It's one of the largest temple complexes in Kyoto, and also the most visited Kyoto attraction.

Kiyomizu-dera temple has a fascinating history. People used to jump off its 13 meter (42 feet) high stage. Anyone who survived the fall was **supposedly** granted a wish. Of the 234 people who tried it 200 survived. Today this practice is strictly forbidden.

The temple was established in 778. The buildings of the temple have been destroyed many times by earthquake or fire. The present buildings were constructed in 1633. They don't contain a single **nail**. This is a novel architectural **technique** for such large wooden structures. It's a 17th century attempt to earthquake-proof the temple. The brackets used in the construction provide far more flex (as compared to nails) **in the event of** an earthquake. This is all **theoretical**—no one actually knows how the structure would perform in a large earthquake.

There's a three streamed waterfall at Kiyomizudera that feeds a small **pond**. The water at Kiyomizu-dera is said to be lucky (or grant wishes). Tourists line up for a chance to drink the water. Kiyomizu-dera is one of the few Kyoto temples that are open at night. The temple looks particularly brilliant **lighten up** at night.

♦ **nail** [neɪl]
n. 钉子
A mirror hung on a nail above the washstand. 脸盆架上方用钉子挂着一面镜子。

♦ **technique** [tek'niːk]
n. 技巧，技术
This musician has perfect technique but little expression. 这位音乐家技巧极好，但表现力不足。

♦ **in the event of**
万一，如果……发生
Airbags protect the driver in the event of a severe frontal impact. 汽车若遇到正面猛烈撞击，安全气囊可以保护驾车者。

♦ **theoretical** [θɪə'retɪkəl]
adj. 理论上的
There was undeniably a strong theoretical dimension to his thinking. 不可否认，他的思想很有理论深度。

♦ **pond** [pɒnd]
n. 池塘，水塘
His pond has been choked by the fast-growing weed. 他的池塘里长满了恣意蔓生的杂草。

♦ **light up**
照亮，(使)变得喜悦
Tom will really light up when he sees his new bike. 汤姆看见他的新脚踏车时，一定会十分高兴。

♦ **exit** ['ekzɪt]
n. 出口
They escaped through an emergency exit and called the police. 他们从紧急出口逃脱，并报了警。

♦ **confuse** [kən'fjuːz]
vt. 混淆，搞错
I think it's a serious mistake to confuse books with life. 我认为把书本同生活混为一谈是大错特错。

The temple serves Buddhist vegetarian food and beer near the **exit**. There's also a crowded shopping street near the temple. There are several shops in the area that dress tourists as Maiko (Geisha). The shops do a good job of it–foreign tourists often **confuse** them for the real thing.

04 Tokyo Sky Tree
东京晴空塔

东京晴空塔是位于日本东京都墨田区的电波塔。由东武铁道株式会社和其子公司东武塔天空树共同筹建，于 2008 年 7 月 14 日动工，2012 年 2 月 29 日竣工，同年 5 月 22 日正式对外开放。其高度为 634 米，于 2011 年 11 月 17 日获得吉尼斯世界纪录认证为"世界第一高塔"，成为全世界最高的自立式电波塔。

东京晴空塔的建造目的，是为了降低东京市中心内高楼林立而造成的电波传输障碍，因此特地建在开阔的地区。如今，晴空塔已经成为东京吸引游客的风景地标。在晴日里，登上观景台，整个东京的风光尽收眼底。

Tokyo Sky Tree is the tallest **structure** in Japan at 634 meters (2,080 feet). It's designed as a **landmark** to attract tourists and as a broadcasting tower.

It **dominates** Tokyo's **skyline** and can be seen from all over the city. Like Mount Fuji, Sky Tree can suddenly appear in the skyline on a clear day from remarkable distances. Locals generally consider it aesthetically pleasing. Its **dynamic** lighting is often themed for holidays and events.

The tower is the tallest building in Tokyo by far. On a clear day it's possible to see most of Tokyo **in the distance** from its **observation deck**. Tokyo is incredibly spread and dense. The view from Sky Tree gives you a good sense of the city.

So the Sky Tree is reasonably expensive and attracts large crowds on weekends and holidays. It should be noted that Tokyo has several free observation decks including the massive Tokyo City Hall building.

Sky Tree has observation decks at 350 and 450 meters. **By comparison**, the Tokyo City Hall building is below 250

♦ **structure** [ˈstrʌktʃə]
n. 建筑物；结构，构造
The house was a handsome four-story brick structure. 这所房子是一幢造型美观的四层砖砌建筑。

♦ **landmark** [ˈlændmɑːk]
n. 地标，路标；里程碑
There was a conspicuous landmark ahead. 前面有一个显著的路标。

♦ **dominate** [ˈdɒmɪneɪt]
vt. 耸立于，俯临

♦ **skyline** [ˈskaɪlaɪn]
n.（建筑物在天空映衬下的）轮廓线，天际线

♦ **dynamic** [daɪˈnæmɪk]
adj. 动感的，动态的；充满活力的
Are you looking for a dynamic salesperson? 你们需要充满活力的销售人员吗？

♦ **in the distance**
在远处，在很远的地方
The wail of the bagpipe could be heard in the distance. 远远地能听到风笛的呜咽。

meters. The Sky Tree observation deck has a glass floor area. There's a restaurant and cafe at the 350-meter level. Entrance in included with your meal at the restaurant with **courses** starting at 6,000 yen for lunch and 12,000 yen for dinner.

Tokyo Sky Tree's design is inspired by the architecture of Japanese **pagodas**. In Japan, Pagodas were designed to hang from a central **support beam**. They are known to be extremely **resilient** to earthquakes. It's a design that has stood up for over 1,000 years. The tower took four years to construct and cost around 40 billion yen. It incorporates innovative wind and earthquake proof features including 100 ton tuned mass **dampers**.

When Sky Tree opened in 2012 it replaced Tokyo Tower as Tokyo's primary broadcasting tower. As Tokyo Tower is now surrounded by too many skyscrapers to transmit a quality signal, it was deliberately built in a **low-rise** area to improve its broadcast signal. Tokyo Sky Tree is almost twice as high as Tokyo Tower (At 333 meters Tokyo Tower is little more than half the height of Sky Tree).

♦ **observation deck** 观景台
♦ **by comparison** 相比之下
This dress is really cheaper by comparison. 比较起来，这件衣服确实便宜。
♦ **course** [kɔːs]
n. 一道菜
♦ **pagoda** [pəˈɡəudə]
n. 塔，宝塔
Regardless of danger, he climbed the pagoda. 他不顾危险地爬上了高塔。
♦ **support beam** 支撑梁
♦ **resilient** [rɪˈzɪlɪənt]
adj. 弹回的，有弹性的；能复原的
Rubber is a resilient material. 橡胶是有弹性的材料。
♦ **damper** [ˈdæmpə]
n. 减震结构
♦ **low-rise** [ˈləu,raɪz]
adj.（建筑物等）低矮的，不高的
The high and low-rise apartment blocks built in the 1960s are crumbling. 20世纪60年代建造的高低不一的公寓楼群正在逐渐破损坍塌。

05 A Mansion and a Brilliant Political Family
鸠山会馆：别样政治家宅邸

"鸠山会馆"作为第52—54代内阁总理大臣的私邸于1924年（大正13年）建成。这里还因为是鸠山一郎的孙子——前首相鸠山由纪夫和众议院议员鸠山邦夫成长的摇篮而声名远播。这里也被称为"音羽御殿"，美丽的欧风设计是出自鸠山一郎的友人，代表大正、昭和时代的日本建筑家——冈田信一郎的杰作。一楼的第一会客厅到第二会客厅及餐厅的门打开后，即成为连通的一间，这是采用了日本建筑风格的设计。可以看得出为了使亲朋好友生活得方便舒适，连细节部位也作了精心的设计。

战后不久，即昭和20年代后半，由于党的设施不足，第二会客厅成为进行日苏谈判等决定日本未来的重要会场。即使现在，前首相鸠山由纪夫、代议士邦夫好像也经常在这里召开各种会议。

馆内到处装饰着以鸟、鹿为主题的艺术品和彩绘玻璃。装饰楼梯平台的彩绘玻璃上展现的是奈良的法隆寺。从不同的视角观看可以产生立体效果。鸠山一郎过去的书房现作为一郎纪念馆对大众开放。除了大礼服、石膏像、勋章等，还展示着写给薰夫人的情书。能够一窥大政治家鲜为人知的一面是一件很有趣的事情！

Hatoyama Hall was built in 1924 as the private **residence** of Ichiro Hatoyama, the 52nd, 53rd and 54th Prime Minister of Japan. It is also known as the home where his grandsons, former Prime Minister Yukio Hatoyama and Kunio Hatoyama, a member of the House of Representatives, grew up.

The western-style building, also called the Otowa Palace, was designed by Shinichiro Okada, a friend of Ichiro Hatoyama and leading Japanese **architect** in the Taisho and Showa eras. In the building, Japanese architectural style is incorporated. For example, one continued room appears by opening all of the doors of the 1st and 2nd **reception** rooms and dining room on the first floor. You can learn that Mr. Okada paid attention to even the finest details so that his **intimate** friend would be able to stay comfortably.

The land area of the **estate** is approximately 6,600 square meters. In this place, the address of the front entrance is different from that of the rear entrance.

During the latter half of Showa 20's (1945 to 1954), not far away from the end of the war, the facilities for the political parties were **insufficient**. Because of this, the second reception room of the hall was used for important meetings that would determine Japan's future, including Japan–**Soviet** negotiation. It seems that the room is still used today by former Prime Minister Yukio Hatoyama and diet member Kunio Hatoyama for various meetings.

Objects of art and **stained glasses** based on bird and deer **motifs** are decorated in various areas of the building. The stained glass that decorates the staircase landing depicts Horyuji Temple in Nara, which looks **three-dimensional** depending on the viewing angle.

The room that used to be Ichiro Hatoyama's study is **on**

♦ **residence** ['rezɪdəns]
n. 住处，住宅
♦ **architect** ['ɑːkɪtekt]
n. 建筑师，设计师
♦ **reception** [rɪ'sepʃən]
n. 接待，招待
He had gone to the reception desk, presumably to check out. 他已经去前台了，可能是要办理退房手续。
♦ **intimate** ['ɪntɪmɪt]
adj. 亲密的，亲近的
♦ **estate** [ɪ'steɪt]
n. 庄园，地产
♦ **insufficient** [,ɪnsə'fɪʃənt]
adj. 缺乏的，不足的
The case was thrown out of court because of insufficient evidence. 由于证据不足，法庭对此案不予受理。
♦ **Soviet** ['səʊvɪet]
n. 苏联（人），苏维埃
♦ **stained glass**
彩色玻璃（常于镶嵌在教堂的窗户）
♦ **motif** [məʊ'tiːf]
n. （文艺作品等的）主题，主旨
Love is an eternal motif in art and literature. 爱情是文学艺术中的永恒主题。
♦ **three-dimensional**
[θriː'dɪmenʃənəl]
adj. 三维的，立体的
♦ **on display** 在展览，展出
Many exhibits with characteristics of the Chinese art are on display. 许多具有中国艺术特色的展品陈列出来。
♦ **bronze** [brɒnz]
adj. 青铜制的
♦ **restoration** [,restə'reɪʃən]
n. （规章制度等的）恢复，复原
The restoration took almost 4,000 man-hours over four years.

display as the Ichiro Memorial Room. In addition to his court uniform, death mask and medals, also on display are the love letters sent to his wife, Kaoru. Have fun getting a glimpse into an unknown side of the powerful politician!

Besides, there is a **bronze** statue in the garden blooming with beautiful roses, which Ichiro Hatoyama loved. This statue was given to the estate from Russia in 2006 to commemorate the Soviet-Japan Joint Declaration of 1956 and the 50th anniversary of the **restoration** of **diplomatic** relations between the two countries. The statue faces in the direction of Moscow to express the passionate desire to **conclude** the peace treaty.

修复工作历时4年，耗费近4 000工时。

♦ **diplomatic** [ˌdɪpləˈmætɪk]
adj. 外交上的
He envisages the possibility of establishing direct diplomatic relations in the future. 他设想在未来可以建立直接的外交关系。

♦ **conclude** [kənˈkluːd]
vt. 缔结
conclude a treaty 缔结条约
The two countries is reported to have conclude a military convention. 据报导，这两个国家已缔结军事协约。

06 Ameyoko: Candy Alley in Tokyo
东京的商店街

Ameyoko 商店街是台东区的JR 御徒町站到上野站间的高架西侧沿线，南北长约四百米左右的商店街，一般称作"Ameyoko"。战后，由于食品极度匮乏此处诞生了自然形成的黑市（非法开设的市场），据说就是 Ameyoko 的雏形。

现在这里则集中了海产类、干货等食品、以及服装、杂货、珠宝饰品等各行业店铺，可以与店员讨价还价是 Ameyoko 的特征，也是一大妙趣。店员的揽客声、与店员的讲价声等，高昂的声音此起彼伏，总是充满活力。年末有很多人来此求购过年用的生鲜食品等，愈发地混杂，热闹的景象还作为季节风情诗被新闻节目报道过。

Ameyoko (Candy Alley) is a busy shopping **bazaar** in downtown Tokyo between Ueno and Okachimachi. It's not like most Tokyo shopping districts. Ameyoko sales people are aggressive and willing to **negotiate**. This attracts **bargain** hunters from all over the city.

Sales **tactics** often include ridiculously low prices if

♦ **bazaar** [bəˈzɑː] n. 街市，市场
Chickens, goats and rabbits were offered for barter at the bazaar. 在集市上，鸡、山羊和兔子被摆出来作物物交换之用。

♦ **negotiate** [nɪˈɡəʊʃɪeɪt]
vi. 谈判，协商
negotiate peace 议和 negotiate a peace treaty 议订和约
It is difficult to negotiate where neither will trust. 双方彼此不信任便很难进行协商。

♦ **bargain** [ˈbɑːɡɪn]
n. 特价商品，便宜货，廉价货
At that low price the house is a bargain. 按那样低的价钱出售，这房子是便宜的。

♦ **tactic** [ˈtæktɪk]
n. 手段，策略
a delaying tactic 拖延的战术
Echolocation is a highly technical and interesting tactic. 回声定位是一项具有高度技术性和趣味性的手段。

you're willing to buy at **bulk** (e.g. 10 identical pairs of shoes). These are usually one time offers that resemble an **auction**.

Ameyoko shops sell everything you can imagine—fish, food stuffs, fruits and vegetables, clothing, fashion accessories, shoes, **cosmetics**, toys, **housewares**, heath goods and sports equipment. It's known as a good place to find rare and unusual stuff. Some Ameyoko shops sell traditional foods, wares and decorations for Japanese New Years. The market is extremely crowded in December.

First developed as a candy market in the early 20th century, the area became a **black market** as Japan's economy collapsed after WWII. When the economy recovered (in the 1950s) Ameyoko regained its **legit** status. The police still **keep a close eye on** the area. Ameyoko has an underworld feel. There's some candy but it's certainly not a candy market anymore.

Many shopkeepers in Ameyoko have been here for generations. The area has character. It's great for a walk or photo tour. Ameyoko is approximately 3 blocks long and 2 blocks wide. It's **crammed** against the JR Yamanote line train tracks between Ueno and Okachimachi station. Also there are plenty of small restaurants and food stalls in Ameyoko.

♦ **bulk** [bʌlk] n. 大量，大块
The bulk of the population lives in cities. 大多数人口居住在城市里。

♦ **auction** [ˈɔːkʃən] n. 拍卖，竞卖
Thirteen per cent of Christie's coin and banknote auction went unsold. 佳士得13%的硬币和纸币拍卖流拍。

♦ **cosmetic** [kɒzˈmetɪk]
n. 美容品，化妆品
These black models are moving in on what was previously white territory: the lucrative cosmetic contracts. 黑人模特正逐步涉足曾是白人主宰的领地：签约获利丰厚的化妆品行业。

♦ **houseware** [ˈhaʊsweəz]
n. 家庭用品，家用器皿

♦ **black market** 黑市，非法市场
During the war, there was a thriving black market in food. 战争期间，黑市买卖食品十分盛行。

♦ **legit** [ləˈdʒɪt] adj. 合法的
The business seems legit. 这笔生意看起来是合法的。

♦ **keep a close eye on**
密切注视，留心瞧着
We should keep a close eye on new technology. 我们应该密切新技术。

♦ **cram** [kræm]
vt. 拥挤，挤在，塞在
The room's full; we can't cram any more people in. 屋里满满的，再也挤不进去人了。

07 Tokyo vs. Osaka
从东京到大阪

就如同中国的北京和上海一样，作为关西地区人口最多的都市，大阪常被拿来与作为关东之代表的东京比较。比如，乘坐扶梯时东京站左边，大阪则站右边；东京饮食味道较重，大阪则喜欢清淡爽口；在棒球队里，东京人多支持巨人队，大阪人则几乎都是阪神虎队的粉丝；东京人说话含蓄绕弯，大阪人说话直接爽快；东京人嘲笑大阪人购物时斤斤计较地讲价，大阪人则反讥东京人打肿脸充胖子；东京人觉得大阪人太自我，喋喋不休，花里胡哨，而大阪人则认为东京人装清高、沉闷无聊、单调乏味……

日本和大阪分别作为日本第一和第二大城市，地理距离仅为 60 公里，两座城市实际上共处一个城市圈。本文会带领你了解日本和东京的一些不同，让你对两个城市有一个更加清晰的轮廓。

There's an intense **rivalry** between Tokyo and Osaka as the 1st and 2nd biggest cities in Japan. They are very close (within 60 kilometers or 37 miles). In fact, physically they form one **contiguous** urban area.

The citizens of Osaka tend to **complain about** Tokyo. The two primary complaints are that Tokyo people are a little cold and that the Tokyo dialect of Japanese is **weird**. Tokyo residents are largely quiet on the subject of Osaka. They might politely say it's a nice place.

The primary **stereotype** about Tokyo is that people are cold (shy and reserved). This is sometimes extended to suggest that Tokyo is full of **snobs**. However, Osaka is **reputed** to be more outgoing and aggressive. For example, Osaka motorists are said to be ultra-aggressive and willing to break the rules. It's hard to generalize about cities of over 10 million individuals. However, there is certainly **a grain of** truth to both stereotypes.

Osaka people are outgoing and **passionate**. They're willing to **strike up** a conversation with a stranger or rebel against parking regulations. Tokyo people have a bubble of privacy in public but once you get to know them you'll find they are just as outgoing. The shyness of Tokyo people can make the city feel cold at times–this phenomenon is known as the Tokyo desert.

In terms of dialects, Osaka has a strong dialect known as Osaka-ben. Osaka-ben sounds both more **melodic** and harsher than standard Japanese. It has pronunciation, grammar and vocabulary differences. As a foreigner, if you learn to speak with a strong Osaka dialect the locals will **adore** you. Likewise, Tokyo also has a dialect, Tokyo-ben. However, Tokyo dialect is widely considered "standard" Japanese. Many peo-

♦ **rivalry** ['raɪvəlrɪ]
n. 竞争，对抗，对立
♦ **contiguous** [kən'tɪɡjʊəs]
adj. 临近的，共同的
They are two immediately contiguous areas. 这两个地区紧密接邻。
♦ **complain about** 抱怨
People usually complain about having to deal with too much bureaucracy. 人们经常抱怨不得不应付太多的繁文缛节。
♦ **weird** [wɪəd]
adj. 怪异的，怪诞的
The altered landscape looks unnatural and weird. 改造后的景观看起来很不自然，极其怪异。
♦ **stereotype** ['stɪərɪəʊtaɪp]
n. 刻板印象
♦ **snob** [snɒb]
n. 势利小人，势利眼；附庸风雅之徒
♦ **repute** [rɪ'pju:t]
vt. 把……称为，认为
♦ **a grain of** 一点点，一些
Our observations may contain a grain of truth for you to refer to. 我们的意见也许会有千虑一得之处，供你参考。
♦ **passionate** ['pæʃənɪt]
adj. 热情的，热衷的
He is very passionate about the project. 他对那个项目非常热心。
♦ **strike up**
开始（交谈）
strike up a conversation with sb. 开始与某人交谈
I hope you will strike up a lasting friendship. 我希望你们将建立起永久的友谊。

ple in Osaka would disagree.

Besides, both cities own their own baseball team. The Tokyo Giants (Yomiuri Giants) are the most successful team in Japanese professional baseball. They've won 21 Japan Series titles. They are so successful that people all over Japan dislike them. Many baseball fans in Japan don't **cheer for** any particular team to win–they just cheer for the Giants to lose. These fans are known as Giants Haters. Although the Osaka Tigers (Hanshin Tigers) have only won the Japan series once in the 76 year history of the club, they're known to have the wildest fans (who are always jumping off a bridge).

As a **cosmopolitan** city, Osaka is too often overlooked by tourists. It's friendly and there's plenty to do and see. If you visit–don't be shy to talk to the locals. Osaka residents tend to have a lot of character and a good sense of humor.

♦ **melodic** [mɪˈlɒdɪk]
adj. 有旋律的
Wonderfully melodic and tuneful, his songs have made me weep. 他的歌旋律优美、悦耳动听，让我潸然泪下。

♦ **adore** [əˈdɔː]
vt. 敬佩，非常喜欢
We adore them for their generosity. 我们钦佩他们的慷慨。

♦ **cheer for**
为……喝彩叫好，为……鼓劲加油
Let's hurry and cheer for them. 我们快点给他们加油去。

♦ **cosmopolitan** [ˌkɒzməˈpɒlɪtən]
adj. 世界性的，国际化的
London has always been a cosmopolitan city. 伦敦一直是一个国际化都市。

08 Jeju Island with Unique Costal Culture
游览济州岛，领略海岸美景

济州岛，又叫蜜月之岛、浪漫之岛，位于朝鲜半岛的南端，隔济州海峡与半岛相望，是韩国最大的岛。这是120万年前火山活动而形成的岛屿，火山被誉为世界新七大自然奇观之一，这里气候温和，有韩国夏威夷之称。椭圆形的岛屿由火山物质构成，数以百计的丘陵、滨海的瀑布、悬崖和熔岩隧道吸引着世界各地的游人。

济州岛古代建有名为"耽罗国"的独立王国，因此保有本岛独有的风俗习惯、方言与文化等。自古以来，这个岛一直以"三多三无三丽"而闻名，这些都反映了济州岛上朴实的民俗风情。济州岛可谓是风景与文化兼具，是旅游与度假的不错选择。

Located southwest of the Korean Peninsula, Jejudo Island is a volcanic island **in the shape of** an oval that measures 73km from west to east, and 31km from north to south. As Korea's most southern region, the weather on Jejudo Island **remains** significantly warmer than the mainland even during the cold winter months. Jejudo Island is sometimes **referred to** as "Samdado Island" (meaning the "three many")

♦ **in the shape of** 呈……的形状
The pool was in the shape of a heart. 游泳池呈心形。

♦ **remain** [rɪˈmeɪn]
vi. 保持
It remains below 13℃ for about five months of the year. 一年约有五个月气温保持在摄氏13度以下。

because of its **abundance** of rocks, women, and wind. Wind from the ocean blows steadily throughout the year and past volcanic activity has littered the island with an assortment of beautiful and unusually-shaped black rocks. The island's reputation of having an abundance of women points back to the time when fishing was the primary means of income and many men were lost at sea.

Before the invention of modern means of transportation, travel to and from the mainland was often a difficult and dangerous journey that few **attempted**. Since the island was **cut off** from the mainland in this way, the people on the island developed their own unique culture and dialect.

Out of this culture was born a set of unusual icons that **demonstrate** the uniqueness of the island: "Haenyeo", "Dolhareubang", "Galot", and "Bangsatap".

Back in the days when Jejudo Island was a land of fishing villages, the local women were responsible for a large part of the family's income. "Haenyeo" (female divers) often went diving to collect **shellfish** and edible seaweed, filling the quiet sea air with whistles announcing their **catch**.

Every visitor to Jeju is sure to see their fair share of Dolhareubang (literally "old grandfather stone statues"). Sometimes serious-looking, sometimes almost comical, these statues **dot** the **landscape** and have become one of the most widely-recognized symbols of the island.

The word "Galot" refers to traditional Jeju clothing that is **dyed** with persimmon juice. Often associated with the area's agricultural way of life, these orange-hued, lightweight pieces of clothing are a trademark of Jeju.

Another special sight are the Bangsatap piled all around the island: at houses, beaches, and even tourist attractions. These small, round towers made of many stones were thought to **ward off** evil, protect the village, and bring prosperity to the people. It is because of this deep-seated belief that one can still see Bangsatap near the **entranceways** of many buildings.

♦ **refer to** 涉及，指的是
The new law does not refer to land used for farming. 那条新法律并不涉及耕种用地。

♦ **abundance** [əˈbʌndəns]
n. 丰富，充裕；大量，极多

♦ **attempt** [əˈtempt]
vt. 尝试，试图
He is attempting a difficult task. 他正在试图完成一项困难的任务。

♦ **cut off** 隔断，隔离
Light and water in embassy buildings were cut off. 大使馆内的水电都被切断了。

♦ **demonstrate** [ˈdemənstreɪt]
vt. 显示，展示
Thousands have braved icy rain to demonstrate their support. 数千人在寒冷的天气中冒雨赶来以示他们的支持。

♦ **shellfish** [ˈʃelfɪʃ]
n.（海生）贝类，甲壳类海生动物

♦ **catch** [kætʃ]
n. 抓住，捕获量

♦ **dot** [dɒt]
vt. 散布于，点缀
Small coastal towns dot the landscape. 这一地区滨海小镇星罗棋布。

♦ **landscape** [ˈlændskeɪp]
n. 风景，景观
He was lost in the contemplation of the landscape. 他对着眼前的景色沉思起来。

♦ **dye** [daɪ]
vt. 染色，给……染色
Black will dye over other colours. 黑色能把大多数其他颜色盖住。

♦ **ward off** 避开，挡住
He managed to free one hand to ward off a punch. 他设法挣脱出一只手来挡住了一拳。

♦ **entranceway** [ˈentrəns,weɪ]
n. 入口，大门

♦ **breathtaking** [ˈbreθ,teɪkɪŋ]
adj. 激动人心的，惊人的，惊险的

In addition to having its own unique culture, Jeju is full of **breathtaking** sights and unusual attractions: World Heritage Sites (such as Hallasan Mountain and Seongsan Ilchulbong Peak) and sandy beaches alongside **turquoise** waters. Small mountains (called oreum in Jeju dialect) are found all across the island. There are said to be more than 365 oreums, more than one for each day of the year! The "Jeju Olle" paths offer a great opportunity to explore this unique landscape, leading visitors among quiet places off the **beaten path**.

Jeju's phenomenal natural beauty, historical legacies, **quirky** museums, and array of water sports make it one of the best vacation spots in Korea.

Our car was driving at a breathtaking speed down the expressway. 我们的车子以惊人的速度沿着高速公路行驶。
♦ **turquoise** [ˈtɜːkwɑːz]
adj. 青绿色的
♦ **beaten path**
常走的路；常规，惯例
♦ **quirky** [ˈkwɔːkɪ]
adj. 诡诈的，离奇的
We've developed a reputation for being quite quirky and original. 我们因为风格奇特又独具创意而名声在外。

09 Korean Buddhist Temples: A Journey to Peace
韩国佛寺：一次平静之旅

作为韩国历史悠久的宗教教派，佛教一直对韩国的政治、经济、文化产生巨大的影响。现在韩国佛教共有26个宗派，9 200多座寺庙和1 100多万名信徒，是信徒最多的宗教。遍及韩国的佛寺是韩国佛教文化的珍贵财富，其中不乏各种佛教雕塑、绘画等宝贵遗产。

韩国佛寺一般建于深山之中，那里有山谷、溪流等自然美景，自然成为人们远离世俗、修身养性的去所，其中住着众僧人和信徒。除此之外，世俗的游人访客如今也可以申请参与寺庙住宿（Temple Stay）项目，通过在佛寺中短住，体验佛寺生活，净化心灵，发现自我。

With 1,700 years of Buddhist history, Korea is home to numerous temples scattered around the nation that preserve a rich, ancient heritage of Buddhist culture. Each temple has its own interesting history as well as a variety of Buddhist statues, paintings, **pagodas**, bells, and other valuable cultural relics.

Korean Buddhist temples are often **nestled** deep in mountainous regions, and set near the natural beauty of rivers, valleys, or the sea. Their locations offer a great refuge for those seeking peace of mind or a quiet place to **meditate**. Temples also serve as residences for monks and **devotees**

♦ **pagoda** [pəˈɡəʊdə]
n. 塔，宝塔
The lofty pagoda stands like a giant at the top of the mountain. 巍巍宝塔屹立在山巅。
♦ **nestle** [ˈnesl]
vt.（使）置于，坐落在（安全、有遮蔽之处）
On this breezy idyllic retreat, 36 beachfront bungalows nestle amidst lush vegetation. 在这个清风拂恬淡怡人的去处，36座海滨别墅坐落在枝叶繁茂的草木间。

who practice or share the teachings of Buddha.

Every day, Korean Buddhist culture meets the modern world at the gates outside every temple. But these temples are not merely tourism and sightseeing spots; rather they are fully functioning places of learning and spiritual practice that **carry out** the 1,700-year-old teachings and traditions. Everything in a temple has meaning which helps provide visitors with an **introspective**, calm, peaceful, and meditative atmosphere. Outsiders can also find **solace**, refuge, and rest at a temple as they are filled with **sanctity**, purity, and **authenticity**.

Recently, a growing number of temples have developed Temple Stay programs for meditation, rest, or just to experience temple life, drawing increasing numbers of visitors every year.

First started in 2002, Temple Stay is a unique opportunity to experience Korean Buddhism, its lifestyle, rituals and spirituality. It generally **entails** staying at a traditional Buddhist temple, and engaging in daily **monastic** activities. Between 2002 and 2011, more than 750,000 Koreans and 110,000 foreign nationals participated in Temple Stay programs across the country. Today, Temple Stay remains one of the most popular programs among **locals** and foreigners for experiencing Korean Buddhism.

Temple bell sounds **resonate** throughout the mountains, **rendering** peace in the hearts of temple visitors. Temple Stay provides refuge from the city life, as well as time and space for meditation and healing. As a popular Korean traditional cultural experience program, Temple Stay is indeed a journey to self-discovery.

♦ **meditate** [ˈmedɪteɪt]
vi. 沉思，冥想
It is important to meditate on the meaning of life. 思考人生的意义很重要。
♦ **devotee** [ˌdevəʊˈtiː]
n. 信徒；皈依者，献身者
♦ **carry out** 执行，施行
The Navy is to carry out an examination of the wreck tomorrow. 海军明天将对失事船只进行细查。
♦ **introspective** [ˌɪntrəʊˈspektɪv]
adj. 反省的，内省的
This matter forces me to become introspective. 这件事迫使我变得自省。
♦ **solace** [ˈsɒləs]
n. 安慰，慰藉
The news brought no solace to the grieving relations. 这个消息并未给悲痛的家属带来什么安慰。
♦ **sanctity** [ˈsæŋktɪtɪ]
n. 圣洁，神圣
There was an air of sanctity in the old church. 这所古老的教堂内有一种神圣的气氛。
♦ **authenticity** [ˌɔːθenˈtɪsɪtɪ]
n. 真实
There has been some debate over the authenticity of his will. 对于他的遗嘱的真实性一直有争论。
♦ **entail** [ɪnˈteɪl] vt. 需要
This job would entail your learning how to use a computer. 这工作将需要你学会怎样用计算机。
♦ **monastic** [məˈnæstɪk]
adj. 庙宇的，修道院的
♦ **local** [ˈləʊkəl]
n. 当地人，当地居民
♦ **resonate** [ˈrezəneɪt]
vi. 回响，共鸣
♦ **render** [ˈrendə] vt. 给予
We are going to render them economic assistance. 我们打算向他们提供经济援助。

10 Gwangjang Market with History and Culture
传承至今的广藏市场

在首尔市内有很多观光胜地，但是最能体验首尔文化的要数各式各样的市场了。其中，最能展现典型首尔样貌的是广藏市场。

1905年建成的广藏市场是韩国历史最悠久的市场，位于首尔市中心的东侧，离东大门不远。虽然不像东大门、南大门市场那样被外国游客所熟知，但东大门和南大门市场的商人都会到广藏市场来进货。在广藏市场不仅可以购买到布料、旧衣服，还可以定制韩服，市场内挤满了销售多种商品的商贩。

广藏市场最有名的东西就是小吃了。在贯穿市场中心的两条小道上，排满了销售韩国街头小吃的店铺与摊位。叫卖声喧闹的市场内人流不息。对于第一次来到这里的人来说，可能会觉得有些不知所措，但是在适应了这种喧杂之后，就会发现这里是既温暖又热情的地方。

在市场内伸向两侧的长椅上，一年四季都坐满了品尝小吃的客人。2005年市场安装完玻璃屋顶之后，这里成为了可以阻挡风雪的好地方。在天寒地冻的冬季，制作食物时升起的袅袅热气将寒冷赶走。虽然设施改造使市场的样子发生了一点点变化，但是这里依旧保留了古老的气息，这也是广藏市场的魅力所在。

Of all the attractions found in Seoul, perhaps none offer a more authentic cultural experience than the city's **myriad** markets. And of those, perhaps none offer the **quintessential** Seoul experience quite like Gwangjang Market.

First established in 1905, Gwangjang Market is Korea's oldest remaining daily market. It can be found east of downtown Seoul, not far from Dongdaemun Market. Although not as well known among foreign tourists as the markets in Dongdaemun and Namdaemun, many **vendors** from both those markets come to Gwangjang Market to buy their products. The market has an **extensive** selection of vendors offering silks, tailored Hanbok, and second-hand clothes.

But Gwangjang Market is most **famed** for its food selection. Running through the heart of the market are two **crisscrossing** corridors stuffed full of booths, stalls, and **storefronts** offering a variety of Korean street foods. The market

---

♦ **myriad** ['mɪrɪəd]
adj. 无数的，各式各样的
Myriad stars are twinkling in the night sky. 无数的星星在夜空中闪烁着。

♦ **quintessential** [ˌkwɪntɪ'senʃəl]
adj. 典型的，精髓的
Everybody thinks of him as the quintessential New Yorker. 大家都视他为典型的纽约人。

♦ **vendor** ['vendɔː]
n. 摊贩，小贩

♦ **extensive** [ɪks'tensɪv]
adj. （范围）广泛的
This is an insurance policy with extensive coverage. 这是一项承保范围广泛的保险。

♦ **famed** [feɪmd]
adj. 著名的，出名的
The king was famed for his cruelty. 那个国王以残暴出名。

is a bustle of activity and loud noise, but once a newcomer **gets over** the sensory overload it is quite a warm, welcoming place.

"Gwangjang Market's main attractions are the varieties of traditional foods and the very warm people's feel," said Shin Jaeeun, a 21-year-old Yonsei University student. "I'd passed by Gwangjang Market numerous times **on my way to** school but looks are definitely deceiving. Never would I have imagined a whole other culture that gives off such a traditional **vibe**."

Korean workers flock to the market all year round to sit at the benches lining each of the booths and **sample** the foods. It is enjoyable all year round thanks to the glass roof added to the market in 2005 to protect the stalls from rain and snow. Even during the coldest days of winter, the amount of food being cooked in this steam-filled passageway **staves off** the cold. Despite the occasional improvements to the facilities, the market maintains an atmosphere that has mostly gone unchanged over the past century.

♦ **crisscrossing** [ˈkrɪskrɒsɪŋ]
adj. 纵横交错的
♦ **storefront** [ˈstɔː frʌnt]
n. 店面，铺面
♦ **get over** 渡过，克服
We are certain that he will get over his illness. 我们相信他一定会战胜病魔的。
♦ **on one's way to**
在去往……的路上
A truck driver saw the fire when he was on his way to the town. 一位正赶往城中的卡车司机看到了燃起的大火。
♦ **vibe** [vaɪb] n. 氛围，感觉
It gave me a nostalgic vibe. 它引起了我的怀旧情绪。
♦ **sample** [ˈsæmpl] vt. 品尝
She made us sample her cooking. 她让我们品尝她做的饭菜。
♦ **stave off** （暂时）挡住，避开
Water rationing was implemented in order to stave off a water shortage. 实施限水措施是为了延缓缺水的现象。

11 Trickeye Museum: Visitors as Heroes
独特的特丽爱美术馆

中世纪的骑士穿过画框将矛高高举起；凶恶的鱼张开大口好像要吞掉一切；佩戴一对天使的翅膀；以跏趺坐的姿势浮在空中。这些画已经不再是"困在"框架里的插画，参观者们也不再只是欣赏，而成为了作品的主角。

特丽爱美术馆位于首尔弘大附近，这里的作品都有一个共同点，那就是只有人"进入"到作品当中，作品才算完成。"特丽爱"是美术技法"视觉陷阱"英语表达方式"Trick of the eye"的缩写，它利用错视让人们把平面上的图案看成立体的图案。美术馆的另一大看点就是冰雪美术馆。这里温度保持在零下4度，电视、马车、电冰箱、滑梯与冰屋等全部设施都是用冰打造而成的。参观者们可以利用各种冰制的设施享受一次冰雪体验。

特丽爱美术馆自2010年开馆以后，通过人们口头相传与SNS（社交网络服务）渠道等，受到了海外游客们的喜爱。

A **medieval** knight comes out from the frame and holds his **lance** at head height, aiming at his target. A giant, scary fish opens its mouth as wide as it can, to swallow everything in sight. People have **angelic** wings **sprouting** from their back and look like they've descended from the sky, or else they sit with legs crossed in a **yoga** position and **levitate** above the floor. They are not merely onlookers, but are the heroes of the pictures.

All the pictures at the Trickeye Museum, located along the broad double **esplanade** in the Hongdae neighborhood of Seoul, require people to take part in the painting to complete the artwork. "Trickeye" is a **fabricated** English word based on the French word "trompe-l'œil," an art technique that uses realistic **imagery** to create an **optical** illusion and which depicts the objects in three dimensions. Unlike other museums or art galleries, this place has no taboos. It allows people to touch and take photos of each of the displayed works. The audience can also take part in the artwork by feeling it and communicating with it. The pictures are displayed on the wall or on the floor, to create artwork along with the audience by maximizing the 3D effect.

The museum has a total of eight exhibition halls, including an ice museum and a permanent exhibition hall. It shows not only well-known pictures from around the world, but also has pictures the museum created itself. In its theme-based exhibition halls, the museum recently introduced new paintings of China and of famous Dutch painter **Vincent van Gogh** (1853–1890).

Some noticeable pictures include a scene from a famous Chinese movie featuring kung fu master Jet Li, a panda hanging from a bamboo tree, "The Starry Night" and "Terrace of a Cafe on Montmartre". In the permanent exhibition hall, people can appreciate scenes from **fantasy**, adventure, travel, **safari** and romance movies. Visitors can pose for a photo in front of a giant, scary fish. One of the most favorite pictures has sets of

---

♦ **medieval** [ˌmedɪˈiːvəl]
adj. 中世纪的
Marriages in medieval Europe were customarily arranged by the families. 在中世纪的欧洲，婚姻通常是由双方的家庭安排的。

♦ **lance** [lɑːns]
n. 长矛，标枪

♦ **angelic** [ænˈdʒelɪk]
adj. 天使的

♦ **sprout** [spraʊt]
vi. 长出，发芽
The seeds sprout into small, hairlike seedlings. 种子发育成小小的、毛茸茸的幼苗。

♦ **yoga** [ˈjəʊɡə]
n. 瑜伽（术）

♦ **levitate** [ˈlevɪteɪt]
vi. 轻轻浮起，飘浮空中
I often dream that I can levitate. 我经常梦想我能够飞起来在空中飘浮。

♦ **esplanade** [ˌespləˈneɪd]
n. 海滨大道，游憩场，散步路

♦ **fabricated** [ˈfæbrɪkeɪtɪd]
adj. 编造的
The evidence was totally fabricated. 这个证据纯属伪造。

♦ **imagery** [ˈɪmɪdʒərɪ]
n. 意象，肖像
Most of her poems abound in imagery. 她的诗歌大多意象丰富。

♦ **optical** [ˈɒptɪkəl]
adj. 视觉的，眼睛的
He has optical trouble. 他的视力有问题。

♦ **Vincent van Gogh**
文森特·梵高，荷兰后印象派画家。

♦ **fantasy** [ˈfæntəsɪ]
n. 幻想
She clings to a romantic fantasy of wedded bliss. 她沉醉于婚后幸福的浪漫幻想。

♦ **safari** [səˈfɑːrɪ]
n. 野生动物园

angelic wings against a blue wall. It attracts so many people that there's always a long queue, waiting to take their photo there.

♦ **must-see**
adj.（影片等）必须看的，应当看的
♦ **igloo** [ˈɪgluː]
n. 雪块砌成的圆顶小屋

The Ice Museum is another **must-see** attraction at the museum. The room maintains a temperature of minus 4 Celsius. Everything inside is made with ice, including an ice TV, an ice fridge, an ice carriage, an ice slide and an **igloo**. Visitors are advised to bring a jacket.

Since opening in 2010, the Trickeye Museum has become really popular among tourists who visit Seoul and through social networking channels. The Trickeye Museum ranked at the top of the list of the most popular museums or galleries in Korea, as announced in March by TripAdvisor, a worldwide online travel community. The National Museum of Korea and the Leeum, Samsung Museum of Art, took second and third places on the list, respectively.

12 Pimatgol: Korean Food Alleys
吃货福音：避马胡同

人们有的时候会被首尔城市中心熙来攘往的景象"压得"喘不过气来，这也可能是"避马胡同"这样的休息空间存在的原因。"避马"是指躲开马的意思，这条狭窄的小巷历史悠久，很多不被人们所熟知的韩国 600 年的传统文化在这里被完好地保存了下来。

避马胡同是朝鲜时代为平民百姓打造的一条小巷。在存在"两班"这种上层阶级的当时，社会身份最低的平民百姓有义务要遵守很多习惯。上层阶级的人们骑着马在路上经过时，平民百姓要缩起身子躲起来。为了不与两班迎头碰面，减少时间的消耗，平民百姓在与钟路中心街平行，并位于稍北侧一点的地方打造出一条小巷。这条小巷就是避马胡同。

随着时间的流逝，避马胡同的景象根据韩国人的需要逐渐发生了改变。韩国社会再也没有骑马的两班，这条小巷成为了从城市中心复杂的交通状况中逃离出来的休息空间。

2012 年 1 月刊的首尔杂志介绍了首尔的小吃胡同名单，避马胡同也被列入其中。在避马胡同，布满了各式各样的韩国传统饮食专营餐厅，从价格非常低廉的啤酒到韩国产的传统茶，种类多样，极具魅力。

现在，尽管避马胡同的痕迹只留下了一小部分，但在现代社会，如果对不被人们所熟知的韩国平民百姓文化感到好奇的话，这里依旧是非常值得一去的地方。

The **bustle** of downtown Seoul can be overwhelming at times, leaving one feeling **trampled**. That's why there are **alleys** of refuge such as Pimatgol. Meaning "Horse-Avoiding Alley," this narrow alleyway preserves a lesser-known side of Korean culture through its 600-year-old history.

Pimatgol was first created during the Joseon Dynasty by the peasant class, known as sangmin. As the lowest class of Korean society, they were **subject to** many customs and obligations in the presence of aristocrats, known as yangban. Travel along the main street of Jongno was tedious, as the sangmin would often be required to **prostrate** themselves every time a nobleman passed, usually on horseback. To escape this time-consuming ritual, the sangmin constructed a small alleyway that runs **parallel** to Jongno, just a little north of the major **thoroughfare**, so they wouldn't have to encounter aristocrats during their travels.

Over time, Pimatgol evolved and adapted to the needs of the Korean people. With aristocrats on horseback no longer a concern, the alley has become a refuge from downtown traffic. During the Imperial Japan era, organizers of the Samil (March 1) Movement gathered in Pimatgol in the **basement** of Seungdong Church the night before the famous reading of the Korean Declaration of Independence. During the politically unstable '80s it was a refuge for student demonstrators escaping from the police.

Originally, Pimatgol was 2.5 kilometers in length, able to convey pedestrians from inside Dongdaemoon gate all the way to Gwanghwamun, **terminating** behind present-day Kyobo Building. Urban redevelopment has claimed all but one central leg of the historic alley, located between Tapgol Park and the YMCA. It is easy to find from the southern end of Insadong, provided you're willing to brave the mysterious **winding** alleyways.

Stepping into Pimatgol takes the visitor into a completely different environment. During the day it's a **near-deserted** channel for pedestrians and delivery **scooters** in a hurry, and at night segments of the alley come alive with workers toasting the end of another long work day. Many of the restaurants in the alley are **adorned** with **grotesque** Hahoe yangban masks, a well-known creation of

◆ **bustle** [ˈbʌsl]
n. 喧闹，忙乱；匆匆忙忙
I sat in a café, watching the bustle of the street outside. 我坐在咖啡馆里，望着街上忙碌的景象。

◆ **trampled** [ˈtræmpld]
adj. 无所适从的
It is easy to feel trampled by the relentless march of technology. 随着科技发展的日新月异，人们容易感到无所适从。

◆ **alley** [ˈælɪ]
n. 胡同，小巷
We live in the same alley. 我们住在同一条小巷里。

◆ **subject to** 须服从……的
Their participation is subject to a number of important provisos. 他们的参与受一些重要条款的限制。

◆ **prostrate** [prɒsˈtreɪt]
vt. 使俯伏，使拜倒

◆ **parallel** [ˈpærəlel]
adj. 平行的，并列的
Parallel lines will never meet no matter how far extended. 无论延伸多长，平行线永不相交。

◆ **thoroughfare** [ˈθʌrəfeə]
n. 通道，大道，大街
Don't park your car on a busy thoroughfare. 不要把你的车停在繁忙的大街上。

◆ **basement** [ˈbeɪsmənt]
n. 地下室

◆ **terminate** [ˈtɜːmɪneɪt]
vi. 结束，到达终点（站）
You have no right to terminate the contract. 你无权终止合同。

◆ **winding** [ˈwaɪndɪŋ]
adj. 蜿蜒的，弯曲的
We climbed up a winding track towards a mountain refuge. 我们沿着一条蜿蜒的小道爬向山上的一处避难所。

◆ **near-deserted** [nɪədɪˈzɜːtɪd]
adj. 空荡荡的，几乎废弃的

◆ **scooter** [ˈskuːtə]
n. 小型摩托车

Joseon-era sangmin culture. Although the **blind** corners might first alarm newcomers, the friendly atmosphere of the alley soon appears.

During lunch break, patrons gather in Bullojujeom (Fire Bar), a cozy place with a **rustic** wooden interior and murals displayed on the walls. One of the regulars is Shin Chang-han, an architect and artist who has contributed several wall murals to the area. He is quick to welcome visitors with a cup of coffee and show off his artwork.

It is because of this friendly, disarming atmosphere that Pimatgol represents an **oasis** of calm in the ever-developing downtown district. The January 2012 issue of Seoul Magazine included Pimatgol in its list of Seoul's top food alleys, recommending the tea house Ssarypmoon, "where you may just catch the owner giving a performance on the daegeum, a large bamboo flute." There are many other delightful secrets hidden away in the depths of this back-alley **labyrinth**.

Although only a small stretch of Pimatgol remains today, it is still worth visiting to get a rare look at Korea's sangmin culture. To get there, head out Jonggak Station Exit 3, and you will find the entrance to the alley behind Pizza Hut.

♦ **adorn** [ə'dɔːn]
vt. 装饰
Water lilies adorn the tops of columns. 莲花用来装饰石柱顶部。

♦ **grotesque** [grəu'tesk]
adj. 怪诞的，奇异的
a grotesque distortion of the truth 对事实的荒诞歪曲

♦ **blind** [blaɪnd]
adj. 隐蔽的，看不清的

♦ **rustic** ['rʌstɪk]
adj. 质朴的，朴素的
When he came to decorate the kitchen, Kenneth opted for a friendly rustic look. 装修厨房的时候，肯尼思选择的是一种亲切质朴的田园风格。

♦ **oasis** [əu'eɪsɪs]
n.（困苦中）令人快慰的地方（或时刻），（沙漠中的）绿洲
They stopped for the night at an oasis. 他们在沙漠中的绿洲停下来过夜。

♦ **labyrinth** ['læbərɪnθ]
n. 迷宫

Chapter 10
潮流风尚：做个有格调的文化新鲜人

01 What Is Unique about a Korean Soap Opera
欲罢不能的韩国肥皂剧

肥皂剧有一个很形象的名字，叫做 soap opera，它是指"以家庭问题为题材的广播或电视连续剧"，以家庭妇女为主要观众，以家庭日用品商家为赞助商，以普通家庭生活环境为舞台。这些电视剧是专门给这些妇女看的，由于这些妇女往往一边做家务一边看，就是混合肥皂泡看的；也由于这些妇女是洗涤用品的消费者，往往这些剧当中插播的广告也是洗涤用品广告，所以就叫肥皂剧。

近些年也有观众把那些看起来节奏慢，篇幅长，看起来波折比较少的剧叫肥皂剧，认为情节像肥皂泡一样很多又容易破，破了也没什么感想。比如，韩国的《搞笑一家人》等就属于肥皂剧。起初，韩国的肥皂剧是针对韩国的民众，内容以历史题材和现代家庭生活为主。如今韩国的肥皂剧已经成为"韩流"的重要推力，整个产业也从国内扩展到整个国际市场，在世界上拥有数目巨大的粉丝群体，特别是在亚洲的中国、日本等地广受追捧。

The Korean television industry's unique approach to daytime drama has won it an **international** fan base. Korean soap operas are often romantic dramas or comedies with attractive stars, highly competent writing, and a definite plot that usually ends within a **maximum** of 200 **episodes**. This stands in contrast to the soap operas of Mexico or the US, which extend story lines over months or years and are not noted for the high quality of their acting or writing. The unique qualities of the Korean soap opera have impressed viewers throughout Asia, the Americas, and the world, via subtitled releases on **DVD** or the Internet.

In many countries, entertainment product is translated fare imported from other nations, especially from the United States. This does not always serve the importing country well, as the highly sexual and **violent** content of US programming does not suit nations with different cultural standards. South Korea's television industry responded by creating its own dramas, with content designed to **appeal to** its citizens. Historical, cultural, and language components were **crafted** to give them a broad appeal across the

♦ **international** [ˌɪntə(ː)ˈnæʃənəl]
adj. 国际的，世界性的
The United Nations has appealed for help from the international community. 联合国已经呼吁国际社会提供援助。

♦ **maximum** [ˈmæksɪməm]
n. 最大，最高值
The law provides for a maximum of two years in prison. 法律规定最高可处以两年监禁。

♦ **episode** [ˈepɪsəʊd]
n.（电视剧等的）一集
The next episode of this television movie will be shown on Friday. 这部电视剧的下一集将于星期五播映。

♦ **violent** [ˈvaɪələnt]
adj. 暴力的
The crowds became violent and threw petrol bombs at the police. 人群变得狂暴起来，并向警察投掷汽油弹。

♦ **appeal to**
vi. 吸引
If anything, swimming will appeal to her most strongly. 如果说有什么能强烈地吸引她，那就是游泳了。

Korean populace.

The Korean soap opera **turned out** to be quite popular in neighboring countries such as Japan and China. Surprisingly, it was also popular in countries that did not share a culture and history with Korea, such as Egypt, India, and Mexico. These Korean dramas, called k-dramas by fans, were soon imported to the United States, particularly to cities that had large Korean-American populations. The high production values of the k-dramas soon won fans who had no connections to the **Pacific Rim**. This universal appeal is itself one of the most unique things about the Korean soap opera.

Historical dramas, known in Korean as sa geuk, are among the most popular of the k-drama genre, even though the history they deal with is almost exclusively Korean. Lavish costumes and elaborate martial-arts sequences define this kind of Korean soap opera. It often conforms to the traditional values of Korea, such as Confucianism. Other k-dramas involve modern characters and situations, but maintain a distinctly Korean take on the proceedings.

The rising popularity of the Korean soap opera around the world has been **dubbed** the Korean wave. Fan clubs and websites are devoted to individual k-dramas or the art form as a whole. Fans trade information on subtitled DVDs and **await** the latest news on new series coming from Korea. Performers and production **crews** often use the genre's popularity to further their careers on an international scale. Korean-American actress Yunjin Kim, for example, got her start in Korean soap operas before landing a starring role on the hit American television series Lost.

♦ **craft** [krɑːft]
vt.（精心）构思，策划

♦ **turn out** 结果是
The result will definitely turn out to be just the opposite of their wish. 结果必然不会像他们所一厢情愿的那样，而只能适得其反。

♦ **Pacific Rim** 环太平洋地区（国家）

♦ **dub** [dʌb]
vt. 把……称为

♦ **await** [əˈweɪt]
vt. 等候，等待
I shall await your answer to my letter with eagerness. 急盼复信。

♦ **crew** [kruː]
n. 全体员工，工作人员
The crew of the ship gave them nothing but bread to eat. 船上的工作人员除了面包什么也不给他们吃。

02 Fashion Trend Leading by Jeon Ji-hyun
全智贤引领时装潮流

随着喜欢韩国电视剧和音乐的海外粉丝的增多，对韩国文化的关注也呈现着激增趋势。超人气的韩国电视剧《来自星星的你》剧终了，此部电视剧可以说是引起多种文化潮流的代表作。演员全智贤在剧中吃的炸鸡和啤酒在中国国内引起了"炸鸡加啤酒"的热潮，带给韩国式炸鸡饭店从未有过的销售额记录。他们在剧中约会的加平郡小法兰西餐馆和首尔N塔等场所也引来了络绎不绝的游客。这种关注不只局限在饮食和观光地上，就连对剧中主角们穿的服装和佩戴的首饰等时装元素方面的关注也在不断扩大。

从第一集开始，演员全智贤的登场就非常华丽。古典风格的长外套配上深色宽皮带，在凸显优美身材的同时还搭配了齐膝中长裙以及高筒靴。充分展现女性美的同时隐藏着神秘感，这就是她的魅力。

接下来，与端庄又古典的风格相反，穿着休闲的喇叭裙出场的全智贤用朝气蓬勃的魅力吸引了观众们的目光。膝上喇叭裙用它的超短长度更加突出体现了可爱的一面，此外氯丁橡胶的衣料也用它独有的卷曲加强了褶边的丰盛感，演绎出裙子的立体感。

与此同时，全智贤每集都佩戴不同的特别发饰也成为了运动风格的核心。最特别的是色彩亮丽的彩色发夹，既独特又完美的符合了"家居"风格。用彩色发夹固定的刘海看起来似乎很随意，但是却增添了亮丽又明快简练的感觉。

There are a **growing** number of people today who watch Korea-made soap operas and listen to Korean **hip hop** and dance music. This recent **uptick** in media consumption has brought increased attention to elements of the nation's mass media and content industry.

One of this year's most-watched soap operas, SBS's "My Love from the Star," is the **prime** example of this, having launched various "cultural fads" across a variety of industries. For example, the combination of fried chicken and beer that actress Jeon Ji-hyun, in the role of the main heroine, was shown eating in the show has aroused what's now called a "Chimaek Fever" in some parts of China, named for the Korean words for "fried chicken" and "beer." Also, **filming** locations across Korea that were visited by the main characters during the show,–the Petite France theme park in Gapyeong, the N Seoul Tower in central Seoul, and more– are still seeing an endless flow of tourists. Visitors' interest, however, is not limited to food and travel. The clothing and accessories worn by the characters on screen has **taken** fans **by storm**, too.

Starting with the very first episode, Jeon Ji-hyun has been **putting on** a splendid show. Her balanced style, with a modern, **tailored** jacket and a wide belt, gave her a **slender** look. She matched it with a knee-length skirt and thigh-high boots, perfectly mixing both the feminine and

♦ **growing** [ˈgrəʊɪŋ]
adj. 越来越多的；生长的，成长中的
Behind the mocking laughter lurks a growing sense of unease. 嘲笑声的背后潜伏着一种越来越强烈的不安。

♦ **hip hop**
嘻哈音乐，嘻哈即"Hip-Hop"。Hip-Hop 意为"摇摆的屁股"，源自美国黑人社区，其渊源可上溯至20世纪70年代。Hip-Hop 是一种由多种元素构成的街头文化的总称，它包括音乐、舞蹈、说唱、DJ技术、服饰、涂鸦等。Hip-Hop 是街头的文化，是一种生活态度。

♦ **uptick** [ˈʌptɪk]
n. 上升（的趋势）

♦ **prime** [praɪm]
adj. 最好的；首要的
Prime candidate to take over his job is Margaret Ramsay. 接替他工作的首要人选是玛格丽特·拉姆齐。

♦ **filming** [ˈfɪlmɪŋ]
n. 拍摄电影

♦ **take somebody by storm**
席卷，使大为轰动
Kenya's long distance runners have taken the athletics world by storm. 肯尼亚的长跑运动员在田径界获得了巨大成功。

♦ **put on** 上演
You really put on a wonderful performance tonight. 你们今晚的演出太精彩了。

♦ **tailored** [ˈteɪləd]

the chic.

Following both modern and classic cues, Jeon Ji-hyun achieved a casual look with her **flared** skirts. The short flared skirt, cut above the knee, adds to the look. The neoprene material creates more wrinkles, helping it look more **voluminous**.

For those who would want to try this style, it looks better with a sweat shirt that comes below the waist line. It **goes well with sneakers** rather than high heels. It's recommended to match the shoes with the socks, and to use laces and a cute design. Finally, complete the style with sunglasses in pop colors or else a small **tote** bag.

Along with clothing, the different hair accessories that Jeon Ji-hyun wore in each episode have also come under the limelight. A thick hair band was key to her simple, straight hair style, while a leather ribbon matched her baggy T-shirts, completing her **tom boy** look. In another episode, she showed a stylish **hairdo**, worn up with a sliver band, highlighting her femininity.

Finally, colorful hairpins created a natural, yet unique, look. With her bangs pinned back with a hair clip, she gave off an effortless air, but it still gave her a vibe that was bright and stylish.

---

adj.（衣服）剪裁讲究的，合身的
♦ **slender** [ˈslendə]
adj. 苗条的
The dark jeans with that belt display your slender figure. 深色牛仔裤配上那条腰带展现出你苗条的身材。
♦ **flared** [fleəd]
adj. 向外展开的（裙、裤）
flared skirts 喇叭裙
♦ **voluminous** [vəˈljuːmɪnəs]
adj. 大的，宽松的
I sank down into a voluminous armchair. 我一下子坐在了宽大的扶手椅里。
♦ **go well with** 相搭配
Does this color go well with that color? 这种颜色与那种颜色相配吗？
♦ **sneaker** [ˈsniːkə(r)]
n. 运动鞋
♦ **tote** [təʊt]
n. 手提
♦ **tom boy**
顽皮的女孩，男孩性格的女孩
♦ **hairdo** [ˈheədu:]
n.（尤指女子的）发式，发型

---

03 K-Pop Collaboration: A Newest Trend in Pop World
世界流行音乐新趋势：K-POP 合作

在韩国，获得人气的大众音乐被统称为"K-pop"。K-pop 这一概念是在上世纪 90 年代后期出现的。在那之前，韩国人普遍将美国与日本音乐视为"流行音乐"。以西欧音乐为基础，K-pop 这种新的音乐类型在韩国出现。现在，K-pop 冲出了韩国与亚洲，正在大力进军美国、欧洲与中南美等西欧市场。

K-pop 也受到了世界演唱会界的关注。有越来越多的世界流行歌手邀请 K-pop 歌手出演自己的演唱会，"联袂演出"相继出现。据说，一直关注亚洲明星与 K-pop 音乐并正在寻找合适嘉宾的 Lady Gaga 在观看完 Crayon Pop 的 MV 之后，被她们独特的形象所深深吸引，因此发出了邀请。

K-pop 歌手与海外明星的合作方式已不再局限于参演演唱会，而扩大到了参与专辑制作、出演 MV 等多样的形式。2NE1 组合的 CL 与 Bigbang 组合的权志龙（G-Dragon）也参与了在全世界引发 Dubstep 热潮的 DJ Skrillex 的新曲制作。不久前公开的这张专辑《Recess》在美国 Billboard 专辑排行榜 "Billboard 200" 与 iTunes 排行榜上分别获得了第四位与第二位，人气非常高。

超越国境、正在全世界大受欢迎的 K-pop 是韩国的，但又不只属于韩国。西欧音乐也一样，虽然充满西欧色彩，但也不只属于西欧。音乐是一种文化不断交流与沟通的产物。

All music that originates in Korea and that gains popularity overseas is broadly defined as "K-Pop". This umbrella **term** was first introduced only in the late 1990s. Up until that time, "popular music" was associated with any music that came from the US or Japan. Largely influenced by Western music, Korea has since that time created a new **genre**, K-Pop, which is now making its way back across Asia and even further **afield**, to the US, Europe and Central and South America.

In recent years, a new trend has **emerged** in the pop world centered on K-Pop and its singers. As K-pop stars become increasingly popular on the international stage, they are receiving a **flurry** of calls for collaboration concerts from pop stars overseas. A range of musical cooperative projects between K-pop singers and other pop stars is now **underway**.

Lady Gaga, in search of an opening act, **came across** the music video and made up her mind. Crayon Pop is set to open for at least 13 Lady Gaga concerts during the **upcoming** US and Canada tour.

When discussing the popularity of K-Pop on the international stage, you can't not mention the role of PSY. As his music video for Gangnam Style on **YouTube** hit an all-time high in 2012, becoming the most-watched video in the shortest amount of time, his horse-riding **choreography** grabbed an enormous amount of attention, both **at home**

♦ **term** [tə:m]
n. 概念，涵盖性术语

♦ **genre** [ʒɑ:ŋr]
n. 类型，种类；体裁

♦ **afield** [əˈfi:ld]
adv. 更远处，在远处
Many of those arrested came from far afield.
那些被捕者有许多来自很远的地方。

♦ **emerge** [ɪˈmə:dʒ] vi. 出现
At the same time some new problems emerge in the development. 同时在发展过程中，也出现了一些新的问题。

♦ **flurry** [ˈflʌrɪ]
n.（活动等的）一系列，（雨雪、兴奋心情等的）一阵。
a flurry of diplomatic activity
一系列外交活动

♦ **underway** [ˌʌndəˈweɪ]
adj. 在进行中的
Road and bridge construction is underway.
公路和桥梁正在建设中。

♦ **come across** 偶遇；偶然发现
I came across a group of children playing.
我碰到一群正在玩耍的小孩。

♦ **upcoming** [ˈʌpˌkʌmɪŋ]
adj. 即将来到的，即将出现的
We shall be attending the upcoming concert. 我们要去听即将上演的音乐会。

♦ **YouTube**
一个可供网民上载观看及分享短片的网站

♦ **choreography** [ˌkɒ(:)rɪˈɒgrəfɪ]
n. 编舞艺术，舞蹈编排

and abroad. The Gangnam Style video at his official YouTube channel has just over 1.9 billion views. In the wave of this newfound popularity, his dance move has been shared with a number of overseas pop stars.

Collaboration with K-Pop stars is not limited to concerts. As mentioned earlier, collaborative projects have gradually expanded in scope and now include jointly recording albums and featuring in music videos. Previously, G-Dragon and CL were featured on electronic dance musician Skrillex's new album, Recess, released last week. The album is now in second place on iTune's Chart, and fourth place in the Billboard 200.

There is still more to come from G-Dragon. He recently announced that he has a soon-to-be-released track with pop star Justin Bieber. Also, recently via twitter, G-dragon exchanged messages with **rapper** and producer Pharrell Williams that implied the possibility of collaboration, raising hopes among his fans.

Hip hop and pop from Korea now attract attention from across the world. It is Korean in origin, but its fan base and influences are not limited to Asia. Likewise, Western music comes from Western countries, but it does not completely belong to Westerners. Similarly, good music is the **fruitful** outcome of the endless back-and-forth of cultural communication and exchange.

♦ **at home and abroad** 在国内外
She gives frequent performances of her work, both at home and abroad. 她经常在国内外演出自己的作品。
♦ **collaboration** [kəˌlæbəˈreɪʃən]
n. 合作，协作
She wrote the book in collaboration with one of her students. 她和她的一个学生合写了这本书。
♦ **rapper** [ˈræpə]
n. 说唱歌手
♦ **fruitful** [ˈfruːtful]
adj. 果实累累的，富有成效的
It was a fruitful meeting; we made a lot of important decisions. 这是一次很有成效的会议，我们做出了许多重大决定。

04 PSY, the Man of *Gangnam Style*
鸟叔的华丽转身

PSY 原名朴载相，1977 年 12 月 31 日出生在首尔的一个富足家庭。他在首尔的江南区度过了自己从小学到高中的生涯，是韩国人口中典型的江南孩子。高中时他就喜欢在别人面前表现自己，他在学校里面分别担任娱乐部长、声援团团长、学校庆典的主持人和广播班的主持人。他看到棒球场或广场上聚集的人群就会情不自禁的兴奋，出入夜店就像回家一样频繁。他每次看到 MC Hammer 和皇后乐队的弗雷迪·墨丘利都会想"音乐原来可以这么酷"。

为了继承父亲的半导体企业，他进入了美国波士顿大学的商学院。但是在他完成学业之前他开始了自己的歌手生涯。

2001 年 1 月，他发表了处女专辑《PSY... From the Psycho World》。PSY 以自己夸张的表现，挑战传统的歌曲《鸟》出现在大众面前。就像他的歌词"我完全成了鸟"一样，他也成为坊间话题。当时大众文化的主要沟通窗口是电脑，他的风格正好符合当时追求搞笑的文化界潮流,因此他也被称为是"搞笑歌手"。他以稍显粗糙又非常直接的歌词痛戳了当时的社会权威、严肃和拥有两面性的社会面貌。他的第 5 张专辑《PSY Five》的主打曲是《Right Now》。他那庞大的身躯身着啤酒广告中使用的肌肉马甲,用破格的舞蹈让粉丝为之疯狂。他的气势一直延续到《江南 Style》。

"With people of all ages singing aloud day and night, the music continues without end." Third-century Chinese historian Chen Shou wrote this **account** of the Korean people in his **seminal** text Records of the Three Kingdoms. Chen also recorded that men and women alike gathered together to sing and dance, jumping in place and moving their hands and feet in **rhythm**.

"All of you who know how to have a good time are this country's true champions!

　　Everyone's party
　　No in or out, no taking sides, that's how we'll play
　　Just scream aloud or you'll be 'it,' today's 'sullae'
　　Together, round and round, Ganggangsuwollae! "

So goes the beginning of the song "Champion," written and performed ten years ago by PSY, the Korean pop singer whose latest hit "Gangnam Style" has taken the world by storm. The "Ganggangsuwollae" that appears in the **lyrics** to "Champion" is the name of a traditional Korean folk dance, also known as "Ganggangsullae," that brings people together in a large circle to dance and play. True to the earlier message of "Champion" –that the true champions are the ones who know how to have fun–PSY's "Gangnam Style" is continuing to **delight** fans across the world.

PSY, whose real name is Park Jae-sang, was born in Seoul on the last day of 1977. Coming from a **well-to-do** family, Park grew up in **Gangnam,** spending all of his school years in the affluent neighborhood in the **mold** of the typical "Gangnam kid". In high school, he enjoyed being in the **limelight** as the leader for all kinds of activi-

♦ **account** [əˈkaʊnt]
n. 记录,描述
♦ **seminal** [ˈsiːmɪnl]
adj. (书、作品等在某一领域)有重大影响的,影响深远的
Her theories were seminal for educational reform. 她的理论对教育改革影响很大。
♦ **rhythm** [ˈrɪθəm]
n. 节奏
♦ **lyric** [ˈlɪrɪk]
n. 歌词
♦ **delight** [dɪˈlaɪt]
vt. 使高兴,使欣喜
I am delighted you are able to come. 你能来,我很高兴。
♦ **well-to-do**
adj. 富有的,富裕的
Only the well-to-do can afford these houses. 只有富人能买得起这些房子。
♦ **Gangnam**
江南,即江南区,是韩国首都首尔的一个行政区,位于汉江以南。
♦ **mold** [məʊld] n. 类型,塑造
♦ **limelight** [ˈlaɪmˌlaɪt]
n. 众人注目的中心
I hated the limelight and found it unbearable. 我讨厌惹人注目,觉得实在令人难以忍受。
♦ **emcee** [ˈemˈsiː]
vt. 担任……的主持人,主持
♦ **entrepreneur** [ˌɒntrəprəˈnɜː]
n. 企业家
An entrepreneur is more than just a risk taker. He is a visionary. 企业家不仅要能承担风险,还应富于远见。
♦ **semiconductor** [ˌsemɪkənˈdʌktə]
n. 半导体

ties, including **emceeing** his school's annual festival and cheerleading. The sight of the huge crowds that would gather at baseball stadiums or at rallies brought him to life, he once shared. Outings to the local nightclub were a daily ritual for the young Park. Introduced to artists like rapper MC Hammer and Queen lead vocalist Freddie Mercury, the future star began to gain a deeper appreciation of music as something "rather grand".

In preparation for learning the family business from his father, an **entrepreneur** in Korea's **semiconductor** industry, PSY enrolled in the undergraduate business administration and management program at Boston University; but he soon dropped out to pursue his career as a singer.

Park **debuted** in January 2001 with the album PSY... from the Psycho World. With a stage name like PSY, short for psycho, and a main track entitled "Bird" that featured a **provocative** chorus, Park became a hot issue from his very arrival onto the music scene. At the time, the Internet was fast becoming a major vehicle for the discovery and spread of new trends. These increases in online connectivity, together with a growing taste in Korean pop culture for all things **bizarre**, helped give PSY enough exposure and appeal to endear him to the Korean public. His outspoken and uninhibited lyrics took sharp, witty jabs at the seeming incongruity between appearances and reality in Korean society while also lampooning the exaggerated solemnity of authoritarian-leaning cultural norms.

PSY's fifth album didn't fail to deliver for his expectant fans. The first song off of the album, "Right Now," gave PSY the chance to showcase his trademark high-energy dance moves with a fake six-pack affixed to his **stocky torso**.

♦ **debut** [ˈdebjʊ]
vi. 首次露面，首次推出
♦ **provocative** [prəˈvɒkətɪv]
adj. 煽动性的，刺激性的
His provocative words only fueled the argument further. 他的挑衅性讲话只能使争论进一步激化。
♦ **bizarre** [bɪˈzɑː]
adj. 奇特的，离奇的
They saw a bizarre animal in the lake. 他们在湖中看见一个奇怪的动物。
♦ **stocky** [ˈstɒkɪ]
adj. 矮壮的，健壮结实的
He always feels ashamed for his short, stocky figure. 他矮壮的体形总是让他觉得羞愧。
♦ **torso** [ˈtɔːsəʊ]
n. 身躯

05 Webtoons: Digital Comics in South Korea
韩国的网页漫画

上学路上，抓着智能手机的学生们忙着按动他们的手指。因为看了即时连载的 Webtoon（网页和卡通的合成语，是用各种网络多媒体工具制作而成的网络漫画），到学校才能和朋友们聊得上来。

"未生"、"Gaus 电子公司"等描写公司职员们的苦衷和生活悲欢的网络漫画（Webtoon）

大受欢迎，成为上下班路上必看的 Webtoon，同时成为公司职员们的"文化快餐"（用很少时间就可以便捷享受文化生活的新型文化潮流）。

大韩民国刮起了网络漫画热。点击率最高的 Naver Webtoon 每天有 620 万名，一个月有 1 700 万名用户。Naver Webtoon 从 2004 年 6 月 23 日问世以来已经发展了 10 年的时间了。通过实行在每周固定日期更新作品的制度"每周固定时间更新系统"以及试登载（Webtoon Audition）的"业余爱好者升级制度"而连载的作品足有 520 篇。

在韩国 Webtoon 在 10 年间能够一直保持高人气的秘诀是丰富的故事素材和庞大的作品数量。也就是特快的工作速度和独特的形式。以此为武器，韩国门户网站公司向世界市场发出了挑战书。

此外，政府也发布了"培养漫画产业的中长期计划（2014—2018）"，以此来共同扶持网络漫画市场的培养。网络漫画不只是收费资讯而已，它是能够创造更多价值的项目。除去稿酬之外，卡通形象商品和衍生产品，以及网络漫画的电影、电视化等多种收益都是"一源多用"。韩国网络漫画如今跨越了名为 Ktoon 的文化热，风靡整个文化产业。

These days, most students encountered during the morning **commute** are seen busy with their **smartphones**. They are reading online **comic strips**, or "webtoons," comics **updated** online in real time. They have to finish today's strip before they meet their friends because it is one of the major topics of daily conversation.

The same **applies to** adults, too. Recently, a number of online comic strips have won popularity among office workers, such as "Misaeng" and "Gauss Electric". The cartoons touched a **chord** in their readers by portraying the **agony** and difficulties of white-collar office workers. With its explosive popularity, reading online comic strips on the way to and from work has become a new **fad** among the city's millions. A number of online comic strips including Misaeng and Gauss Electric gain popularity among office workers.

Today, society is wild with its love for webtoons. Naver, Korea's largest search engine, attracts the largest number of webtoon fans, **clocking in** at 6.2 million readers daily and 17 million readers per month. Naver Webtoon has provided online comic strips for over a decade, since

♦ **commute** [kəˈmjuːt]
n. 乘车往返
♦ **smartphone** [ˈsmɑːtfəʊn]
n. 智能手机
♦ **comic strip** 连环漫画，连环图画
♦ **update** [ʌpˈdeɪt]
vt. 更新
They decided to update the computer systems. 他们决定更新计算机设备。
♦ **apply to** 适用于
This model does not apply to small firms. 这种模式不适用于小型企业。
♦ **chord** [kɔːd]
n. 心弦，弦
strike/touch a chord with 触动心弦，引起共鸣
Mr. Jenkins' arguments for stability struck a chord with Europe's two most powerful politicians. 詹金斯先生关于稳定的论点引起了欧洲两位最有影响的政治家的共鸣。
♦ **agony** [ˈægənɪ] n. 痛苦，苦恼
♦ **fad** [fæd]
n. 风尚，风靡一时之物
♦ **clock in**
打卡上班，此处指粉丝们阅读网上按时更新的漫画

June 2004. Over the years, it has **tightened** its publishing **prerequisites**, too, for instance making it a rule that the content be updated on specific dates of every week. Another tweak to the software allows readers to post their own creations. Today, there are nearly 520 separate online comic strips posted in the search engine's webtoon section.

Behind the decade-long popularity of webtoons is more than just the large number of postings and constructive **storylines**. The publishing speed and the combination of traditional art and technology in producing the comics have also played a key role in their recognition and **acclaim**. Domestic portal companies are now challenging themselves to **make inroads into** global markets with these popular comics.

The Korean government, too, works to promote the webtoon industry. It recently announced a long-term plan to help develop and promote such creative industries, scheduled to **roll out** from 2014 to 2018.

In sum, webtoons are something that can create higher commercial value. In addition to the storyline and dialogue of the cartoon, other business lines such as model **figurines**, movies and soap operas can also be developed. Such "One Source Multi-Use" creative properties are the life-blood for many comic strip artists and designers. With a strong foundation of ten years and growing, we can now see the influence of webtoons spreading across the rest of the creative industries.

♦ **tighten** [ˈtaɪtən]
vt. （对……）严加控制，使（规定、政策、制度）更加严格

♦ **prerequisite** [ˌpriːˈrekwɪzɪt]
n. 先决条件，前提
Correct decision-making is an important prerequisite for success in all work. 正确决策是各项工作成功的重要前提。

♦ **storyline** [ˈstɔːrɪlaɪn]
n. 故事情节

♦ **acclaim** [əˈkleɪm]
n. 称赞，赞扬
The novel received great acclaim. 这本小说备受赞扬。

♦ **make inroads into**
进军，进入（新的领域）
The company is starting to make inroads into the lucrative soft-drinks market. 公司开始开拓利润丰厚的无酒精饮料市场。

♦ **roll out** 陆续展开／进行

♦ **figurine** [ˈfɪɡjuriːn]
n. 小雕像，小塑像
She bought an exquisite china figurine. 她买了一尊小巧而精致的瓷塑像。

06　Is Japanese Animation Only for Fun?
日本动漫不可一笑而过

日本的动漫产业高度发达，这是不置可否的事实。作为动漫大国，2002 年日本替代美国成为世界最大的动漫出口国，以至有人这样问，"所有的连环漫画都是日本的吧？"答案显然是否定的，然而从 19 世纪 80 年代至今，日本动漫产业全球化的进程着实令世人惊叹。动漫给日本带来庞大的经济利益：日本外贸组织数据显示，2003 年日本向美国出口动漫游戏约 43.5 亿美元，是对美钢铁出口额的四倍；日本独占全球动漫市场 60% 的份额；在日本，动漫产业估计占到国内生产总值的 10%，成为仅次于工业和农业的第三大产业。

除了促进日本经济的繁荣，日本动漫还有另外三方面的作用：第一种很容易明白，动画中人物夸张的动作或者风趣的故事让大多数观众大笑不已；第二种也不难理解，它会让我们感动。美国动漫大多是关于超人拯救世界的，而日本动漫不同于此，动画师们以日本传统文化和普通民众的真实生活为基础制作动漫。远在12世纪，人们就通过漫画嘲讽政府腐败，从这可以看出，动漫的本质便是在虚拟世界里描绘现实生活。有时人们会明显感到——"动漫里说的就是我的生活，就是我！"

然而，人们很少提到动漫的第三种角色——传播知识。在观赏动漫时，里面有很明显的知识"信息"。这是因为许多日本动漫受到动画师们的影响，包括他们丰富的阅历，以及各自的世界观和人生观。以宫崎骏为例，他的母亲读书甚多，对社会准则常有质疑，后来他坦言自己继承了母亲质疑和好问的思维方式；因而他的作品中富有洞察深邃的主题，比如善恶、环境保护、反对战争和摆脱地球引力自由飞行。

Nobody can deny that Japan has a highly advanced **animation industry**. As animation **superpower**, Japan has replaced the United States as the world's largest exporter of animation in 2002. Someone even asked a question like, "Are all the comics from Japan?" Although the answer is absolutely not, the **globalization** of Japanese animation has been amazing the whole world from 1980s until the present. Japanese animation has created tremendous economic benefits: According to the Japan External Trade Organization (2003), the Japan exported approximately 4.35 billion dollars of **ACG** (Animation-Comic-Game) to US, which is four times of steel export to US; Japan also occupies more than sixty percent of the global animation **market share**; it is estimated that Japanese animation industry **accounts for** ten percent of Japan's GDP, and has become Japan's third largest business, only after industry and agriculture.

Apart from enhancing Japan's economic **prosperity**, animation in Japan has three other roles to play. It is very easy for us to understand the first role of Japanese animation. I believe that most people will laugh when they watch Japanese animation, either for the **exaggerated** actions of characters or the funny stories. The second part

◆ **animation industry**
动画产业，动漫产业
◆ **superpower** [sjuːpəˈpaʊə]
n. 超级大国
◆ **globalization** [ˌɡləʊbəlaɪˈzeɪʃən]
n. 全球化，全球性
◆ **ACG**
abbr. 动漫游戏（Animation—Comic—Game）的简称
◆ **market share** 市场份额
◆ **account for** （在数量、比例上）占
◆ **prosperity** [prɒsˈperɪtɪ]
n. 繁荣，兴旺
◆ **exaggerated** [ɪɡˈzædʒəreɪtɪd]
adj. 夸大的，言过其实的，夸张的
◆ **animator** [ˈænɪmeɪtə(r)]
n. 鼓舞者，漫画家
◆ **manga** [ˈmæŋɡə]
n. 日本漫画（由于日本词语没有复数形式，故而单复数同形）
◆ **make fun of** 取笑，嘲笑；戏弄，捉弄
Do not make fun of anyone for any reason.
不要因为任何原因去取笑别人。
◆ **Hayao Miyazaki**
宫崎骏，日本最著名的动画导演、动画师以及漫画家，1941年生于东京，是日本乃至世界动漫行业的领军性人物，作品包括电视动漫《幽灵公主》、《风之谷》等，

is also easy to understand, which is animation will make us moved. Unlike American animation, most of which are about superheroes saving the world, Japanese **animators** are based on Japanese tradition and depiction of real life of ordinary people. If we go back to the 12th century, in which people used **manga** to **make fun of** the corrupted government, we can easily find that, it is the nature of animation that it describes a really life in a virtue world. Sometimes, people have a strong feeling, "That's my life, and that's me!"

However, people rarely mention the knowledge part, which is animation contains a "message" and this message is usually knowledge. When we watch animation, we usually find "there is actually such a message." Many Japanese animations are influenced by animators' rich personal experiences, their values of life and their perspectives of the world. **Hayao Miyazaki**, for example, his mother was a **voracious** reader who often questioned socially accepted norms. Miyazaki later said that he inherited his questioning and skeptical mind from her. Many insightful themes are easily found in his works, like good and evil, **environmentalism** and antiwar, flying and liberation from gravity.

收山之作电视动漫《起风了》。2013 年 9 月 6 日宣布引退。

♦ **voracious** [vəˈreɪʃəs]
adj. 狼吞虎咽的，贪婪的

♦ **environmentalism**
[ɪn͵vaɪərənˈmentlɪzm]
n. 环境保护论，环境论

07 Uniforms: The Student Fashion in Japan
日本学生的制服热

日本的中学生大都穿着学校统一选定的校服，形成了日本独特的校服文化，就连小学生也偏爱校服。当然也会有一些例外，比如说私立中学中允许学生穿街头服装。日本的校服颜色一般是黑色或者藏青色，夏装价格在两万到三万日元之间，冬季校服要比夏装贵两万日元。此外，日本的校服属于正式服装，在葬礼等严肃、正式的场合都可以穿。

其实，日本的校服文化可以回溯到十九世纪末，到了六十年代也有学生进行过抵制，但是不久，随着款式时髦的校服产生，校服再次流行起来。如今，即便当初允许学生穿街头服装的私立学校也再次引入校服。

Most middle and high school students in Japan wear "uniforms" their schools have chosen. Some **exceptions** to that rule include private middle and high schools that allow street wear, and elementary schools that also prefer uniforms. The most common colors for school uniforms are black or **navy**, with summer uniforms costing

♦ **exception** [ɪkˈsepʃən]
n. 例外
without exception 毫无例外
Each candidate must answer all the questions without exception. 每个考生都必须回答全部问题，没有例外。

♦ **navy** [ˈneɪvɪ] adj. 深蓝色的，海军蓝的

between 20,000 to 30,000 yen, and winter uniforms between 40,000 to 50,000 yen. Additionally, Japanese school uniforms are considered formal **attire**, so students can wear them to attend funerals and other similar formal events.

School uniforms were first introduced in Japan during the late 19th century. This was because a more comfortable western alternative was needed to replace Japan's more formal attire, kimono. Thus the uniforms took on a military design, with **hard-collared** shirts for boys and **sailor-style** uniforms for girls. Additionally, since there was also a wide economic gap between the rich and poor back then, uniforms helped everyone seem equal to **one another**.

In the 1960s, students demonstrated their opposition to **obligatory** uniforms declaring that "uniforms were mere tools to control the students." As a result of this **movement**, some schools decided to abolish them. But after a while, the students' **crusade** faded as more fashionable uniforms, including suits and jackets, became popular. Today, even some private schools that initially **permitted** students to wear street clothes have reintroduced the uniform, while other schools have **enticed prospective** students just because of their attractive clothing.

However, sometimes students get a bad reputation for the way they wear their uniform, such as when girls "wear their skirt hems too short". There are even schools that impose strict guidelines on such "dressing down" alterations. Some teachers may **measure** with a ruler the length of a skirt while others stand watch outside school grounds.

♦ **attire** [əˈtaɪə]
n. 服装，衣服
Her attention was attracted by his peculiar attire. 他那奇特的着装引起了她的注意。

♦ **hard-collared** [ˈhɑːdˈkɒləd]
adj. 硬领的

♦ **sailor-style** [ˈseɪləstaɪl]
adj. 水手风格的

♦ **one another**
互相，同义词语：each other
The two countries do little trade with one another. 两国之间很少有贸易往来。

♦ **obligatory** [ɒˈblɪɡətərɪ]
adj. 必须的，强制性的

♦ **movement** [ˈmuːvmənt]
n. 运动
The press feels the need to associate itself with the green movement. 媒体感到有必要支持绿色运动。

♦ **crusade** [kruːˈseɪd]
n. 讨伐，声讨

♦ **permit** [pə(ː)ˈmɪt]
vt. 许可，准许
The state does not permit write-in votes. 该州不允许投票给非推荐候选人。

♦ **entice** [ɪnˈtaɪs]
vt. 吸引，诱惑
The bargain prices are expected to entice customers away from other stores. 低廉的价格意在把顾客从其他商店吸引过来。

♦ **prospective** [prəsˈpektɪv]
adj. 潜在的，想要成为一员的

♦ **measure** [ˈmeʒə]
vt. 测量
Measure the full width of the window. 测量一下窗户的全宽。

Chapter 11
异国风情:许你一个别样的日韩

01 A Usual Drama in Japan: Duty vs. Emotion
日本人的义理与人情

在日本，无论是人在现实生活中，还是虚构的剧情里，常常含有人们对于义理与人情之间抉择的冲突。

义理是日本人心目中的责任感，最典型的例子是日本武士要对将军誓死效忠的责任。将军可以要求武士做任何事情，甚至包括取其性命，而武士出于义理而必须服从。如今，在日本的家庭、工作和人际交往中，义理也是无处不在。

而人情是日本人对人类情感的表述，在现实生活中常常与义理发生冲突。比如，武士爱上了将军的女儿。出于义理，武士应该跟她保持距离；而出于人情，他会为了爱情不顾一切。

In Japan, both real life and **fictional** dramas usually involve the conflict between duty (giri) and human emotion (ninjo).

Giri（义理）is the Japanese sense of duty–the unwritten **social contracts** that ensure social harmony. The classic example of giri is the responsibility that Samurai had to their **masters**. A Shogun could ask anything of a Samurai–even that a Samurai is taken his own life. Samurai were **bound** by giri to obey.

More modern giri **relate to** work, family and interpersonal relationships. For example, if you work at a coffee shop it's your duty to **provide** good service for customers. If your customer happens to be a **jerk**–your duty remains. Japanese society finds it **distasteful** when staff assert themselves with customers.

However, ninjo（人情）is the Japanese word for human emotion. In life (and fiction) ninjo often comes into **conflict** with giri. The classic example is the Samurai who

♦ **fictional** [ˈfɪkʃənəl]
adj. 虚构的，小说的
Almost all fictional detectives are unreal. 几乎所有小说中的侦探都是虚构的。
♦ **social contract** 社会契约
♦ **master** [ˈmɑːstə]
n. 主人（尤指男性）
♦ **bind** [baɪnd]
vt. 约束；捆绑
We have no official business to bind us. 我们没有公务的约束。
♦ **relate to** 涉及，同……有关
Many entries relate to the two world wars. 很多条目与两次世界大战有关。
♦ **provide** [prəˈvaɪd]
vt. 提供
New technology should provide a secure firewall against hackers. 新技术应该能提供安全可靠的防火墙抵御黑客袭击。
♦ **jerk** [dʒɜːk]
n. 混蛋，傻瓜，笨蛋
♦ **distasteful** [dɪsˈteɪstfʊl]
adj. 使人不愉快的，令人厌恶的
I find his attitude highly distasteful. 我觉得他的态度很令人厌恶。
♦ **conflict** [ˈkɒnflɪkt]
n. 冲突，矛盾
come into conflict with 与……发生冲突
They have come into conflict, sometimes violently. 他们产生了矛盾，有时矛盾还非常激烈。
♦ **quit** [kwɪt]
vi. 辞职
If I don't get more money I'll quit. 不给我加薪我就辞职。
♦ **musician** [mjuːˈzɪʃən]
n. 音乐家
He feels that he was destined to become a

falls in love with the Shogun's daughter. He is bound by duty to stay away from her. However, he's in love–his ninjo is running wild.

A more modern example could be a salary man who hates his job. He wants to **quit** and follow his dream of becoming a professional **musician** (ninjo). However, he has a family to support (giri). A less dramatic example could be a waitress who has an **obnoxious** customer. Her giri tells to treat the customer with respect while her ninjo tells her to **spill** a drink on him.

Nowadays in Japan, **old timers** complain that young people have forgotten about giri and are driven by ninjo. When giri declines and ninjo **escalates**–social harmony is threatened (according to conventional Japanese thought).

A typical example comes up on Valentine's Day. That women in Japan buy chocolates for their boss, father and brothers is known as giri; but when a woman buys chocolate for her boyfriend it's not considered giri. Instead, this gift is driven by her ninjo.

musician. 他觉得自己注定会成为一名音乐家。

♦ **obnoxious** [əbˈnɒkʃəs]
adj. 令人讨厌的；使人反感的
My brother-in-law is an obnoxious know-it-all. 我的姐夫是个讨人厌的自以为是万事通的家伙。

♦ **spill** [spɪl]
vt. 洒出，泼出，溢出
Utmost care must be taken not to spill any of the contents. 千万注意里面的东西一点都不能洒出来。

♦ **old timer**
老前辈，老资格

♦ **escalate** [ˈeskəleɪt]
vi. 逐步上升
Ground rents are likely to escalate over time. 地租以后可能会逐渐上涨。

02 A Sight into Japanese Character
日本人是什么性格

日本作为太平洋西北部的岛国，四面环海，在很长一段历史中，与世隔绝；而且各个封建政权也采取闭关锁国的政策。这些因素造就了日本独特的社会文化，也塑造了日本人与众不同的民族性格。

2013年，有杂志从澳籍日本问题专家格雷戈里·克拉克之前提出的论点出发，发表文章分析了日本人的民族精神与心理。比较典型的日本民族性格有团队精神、诚实待人、具有强烈的荣辱感、尽量避免诉讼之扰等。

For most of its history, Japan was separated from the rest of the world by the surrounding seas and an **isolationist** policy strictly **enforced** by its feudal period government. These centuries of isolation led to a unique culture and Japanese character.

In 2013, a list of characteristics of the Japanese psyche was published according to the ideas **put forth** by an Australian, Gregory Clark, whose educational and professional career dealing with Japanese sociology, education, and economics has spanned more than five decades. Here are some of the points in the list.

1. Group mentality–First on Clark's list is Japan's well-known propensity for putting the group before the self, and by extension following orders from one's superiors. In ordinary circumstances, this tends to **manifest** itself most noticeably in the workplace. Part of the reason workers in Japan do so much overtime is that it's traditionally seen as bad form to leave the office before your coworkers, and especially before your boss. Even if you're done with your individual tasks, it's considered polite to remain in the workplace, either to lend a hand to your **fellow** employees or, as is sometimes the case, to busy yourself until everyone is ready to go home.

2. Honesty in dealing with others–In Japan, one of the major functions of the police boxes that dot the country is to serve as local **lost-and-found** centers, which are frequently utilized by honest citizens who find someone else's **unattended** property.

3. Preference for doing things by hand–In Japan, job hunters often buy blank **resume sheets** and painstakingly enter their **pertinent** information in neat, handwritten characters, as a show of sincerity in their respect for and interest in the **position** they are applying for. It probably also serves to show that you're one of the few who can still correctly recall and write kanji characters without relying on a computer to auto-convert it for you!

4. Importance of shame in **morality**–In Japan, one of the heaviest condemnations of character you can **lob at** someone is "haji shirazu", or "you have no concept of shame." People in Japan are usually concerned about the way in which their actions affect others, and so when a mistake is made, it's something to be taken seriously. It's no wonder that Japanese has no less than four commonly used ways to say "I'm sorry."

5. Dislike of **lawsuits**–Japan is far from a **litigious** so-

♦ **isolationist** [ˌaɪsəˈleɪʃnɪst]
adj. 孤立主义的
♦ **enforce** [ɪnˈfɔːs]
vt. 实施，执行
It's the job of the police to enforce the law.
警察的工作就是执法。
♦ **put forth** 提出，发表
The scientist put forth the new theory of evolution. 这位科学家提出了进化论的新理论。
♦ **manifest** [ˈmænɪfest]
vt. 显示，表明；证明
Her actions manifested a complete disregard for personal safety. 她的行动表明她全然不顾个人安危。
♦ **fellow** [ˈfeləʊ]
adj. 同伴的，共事的
Her independence of spirit marked her out from her male fellow officers. 她的独立精神使她有别于共事的男性军官。
♦ **lost-and-found** 失物招领
♦ **unattended** [ˈʌnəˈtendɪd]
adj. 无主的，未被注意的
An unattended bag was spotted near the bus station. 有人在汽车站附近发现了一个无主背包。
♦ **resume sheet** 履历表
♦ **pertinent** [ˈpɜːtɪnənt]
adj. 有关的，相干的
He raised several pertinent questions. 他提了几个有关的问题。
♦ **position** [pəˈzɪʃən]
n. 职位
I learnt of the position through a newspaper advertisement. 我是从报纸广告上得悉有此职位的。
♦ **morality** [mɒˈrælɪti]
n. 道德，道德准则
♦ **lob at** 攻击
He smashed the lob straight at his opponent's body. 他把高球冲着对手叩杀过去。
♦ **lawsuit** [ˈlɔːsuːt] n. 诉讼，诉讼案件
♦ **litigious** [lɪˈtɪdʒəs]
adj. 好诉讼的，好打官司的

ciety. Part of this can be attributed to a desire not to cause trouble for others, which often leads people in Japan to put up with situations they're not really happy with. Even when problems that must be rectified **crop up**, though, the preferred method is to meet as individuals and try to talk things out without getting extensive legal teams involved.

The nation is now made up of over 120,000,000 individuals, and, as the word implies, each has their own, unique mindset. These points above make a nice **primer**, but the best way, by far, to understand the "Japanese character" is to spend time in the country, interacting with its people.

♦ **crop up**
突然出现，发生
It had never occurred to her that a new possibility would crop up abruptly. 她万万没有想到会突然出现一种新的可能性。

♦ **primer** ['praɪmə]
n. 入门

03 Origin of a Peace Sign in Japan
日本 V 字形和平手势的由来

V 字手势的做法是除食指及中指竖起外其他手指向手心弯曲。通常，手心向内或外并无区别，但手心向内的手势在某些西方国家有侮辱含义。英国首相丘吉尔于第二次世界大战带起 V 字手势的风潮。他以 V 字手势代表胜利 (Victory) 的第一个字母 "V"，所以又名胜利手势。V 字手势在美国 1960 年代的反越战时期，"要爱，不要战争" 游行中亦被用作表达和平，所以 V 字手势亦可以有和平的意思，故又称和平手势。

尽管在二战结束后盟军占领日本的期间，日本人就已知道 V 字手势，但一些日本人认为琳恩是导致 V 字手势自 1970 年代起在日本开始流行的原因。1972 年冬季奥林匹克运动会时美国花式溜冰选手珍妮特·琳恩 (Janet Lynn) 在进行自由滑冰的阶段时曾一度滑倒，但即便她坐在冰块上，她依旧继续保持着微笑。虽然最后珍妮特·琳恩得到第三名，但她开朗的努力行径，却引起了许多日本人的共鸣，琳恩在一夜之间成了日本的外国偶像。作为和平主义运动者，琳恩在接受日本媒体采访时经常比出 V 字手势。手掌朝外的 V 字手势在日本经常用于非正式场合的拍照中，尤其年轻人间更是如此。在日本，人们常常会提出这一手势以至于身处其中的游客照相时也会忍不住举起 V 字手势。

It's one of the best known aspects of Japanese culture—many Japanese people like to give a two fingered V-sign in photos. Japan's **fondness** for this **pose** is well known around the world—or at least any spot that attracts Japanese tourists.

♦ **fondness** ['fɒndnɪs]
n. 喜爱，钟爱
I've always had a fondness for jewels. 我一直很喜欢珠宝。

♦ **pose** [pəʊz]
n. 手势，姿势

The **peace sign** began to appear in Japanese photographs in the late 1960s. At the time, the peace sign was part of the **hippie movement** in the United States. It was a symbol of opposition to the **Vietnam War**. Japan also had a hippie community in the late 1960s who were known to **frequent** the Shinjuku area. The use of the peace sign in Japan began within this hippie subculture.

How the peace sign made the jump from the hippie subculture to **mainstream** Japanese society isn't known. Urban legends link it to a popular American figure **skater** (Janet Lynn) or a 1972 Japanese Konika commercial. Whatever the spark–beginning in 1972 it was popular amongst Japanese youth to pose for photos with a peace sign.

The peace sign photo pose is often compared to the tradition of saying "cheese" before a photo (in the English speaking world). Saying "cheese" for a photo tends to make people smile. In Japan, the peace sign has become a visual "cheese"–a cue to the photographer that you're ready for the photo. Like saying cheese–it seems to make you more **photogenic** somehow.

These days, the V-sign is made at various angles of the hand (e.g. palm in or out). Such gestures aren't meant to have a meaning–it's just a photo pose.

If you visit Japan you may find yourself giving the peace sign in photos. Virtually every tourist to Japan does it. It's often done **mockingly** at first–but it's addictive. The V-sign pose is also common amongst fans of Japanese pop culture, such as the cosplayers.

She was sitting in a highly provocative pose. 她坐在那里姿势非常撩人。

♦ **peace sign**
和平手势，掌心向外，伸食指和中指表示的 V 字形和平手势。

♦ **hippie movement**
嬉皮士运动，在 20 世纪 60 年代的西方，有相当一部分蔑视传统、远离主流社会的年轻人所进行的，以文化的反叛和生活的反叛为主要内容的反叛运动。

♦ **Vietnam War** 越南战争

♦ **frequent** ['friːkwənt]
vt. 常到，常去，常出入于
I hear he frequents the Cajun restaurant in Hampstead. 我听说他经常光顾汉普斯特德的卡津餐厅。

♦ **mainstream** ['meɪnstriːm]
n. （思想或行为的）主流，主要趋势
Their views lie outside the mainstream of current medical opinion. 他们的观点不属于当今医学界观点的主流。

♦ **skater** ['skeɪtə(r)]
n. 滑冰者，溜冰选手

♦ **photogenic** [ˌfəʊtəʊ'dʒenɪk]
adj. 上相的，上镜的
I'm not very photogenic. 我不大上相。

♦ **mockingly** ['mɒkɪŋlɪ]
adv. 嘲弄地，取笑地，愚弄地
The rich peasants answered mockingly. 富农带着讥笑的声调回答。

04 Flower Symbolism in Japanese Culture
日本花语解析

生活在大千世界的人对鲜花有着全方位的接触，不同的角度，产生不同的着眼点，于是也就产生不同的感受，也就会对鲜花有所寄情。赏花要懂花语，花语是构成花卉文化的核心，在花卉交流中，花虽无声，但可谓"此时无声胜有声"，其中的含义和情感表达甚于言语。不能因为想表达自己的一番心意而在未了解花语时就乱送别人鲜花，这是会引来别人的误会。

日语中花语是 hanakotoba。常见的一些花语，如水仙花——你是一个冷酷的人；葵白丁香——彼此相爱吧；钱花——天真烂漫；冬青——喜悦快乐；凌霄花——慈母之爱；僧鞋菊——保护、爱护；樱草——青春长存。

Even those with little knowledge of Japan **can't help but** notice the prominence of flower **symbolism** in Japanese culture. From cherry blossom, found everywhere from **haiku verse** to **manga** comics, to chrysanthemum, appearing on everything from **crockery** to coins, flower symbolism plays a vital role in Japanese art, literature and everyday life.

Being a spiritual, nature-loving nation influenced by Buddhist ideology, it is fitting that flower symbolism should form such a big part of the Japanese way of life. This article examines some of the most important flower symbols in Japan, **unpicking** their meanings and giving examples of their uses.

Hanakotoba is the Japanese "language of flowers". Essentially, each flower has its own meaning, often based on its physical **attributes** and/or well known appearances in historical art and literature. Each flower symbol can therefore be used to convey a specific emotion or **sentiment** without the need to use words. Here are some popular examples of flower symbolism in Japanese culture.

Cherry blossom: This is the most popular flower symbol in Japan, so much so that there's even a festival to celebrate its arrival in the spring (hanami). Cherry blossom is a symbol of wabi-sabi, an important world view in Japan relating to the acceptance of **transience** and imperfection, as well as gentleness and kindness.

Chrysanthemum: The chrysanthemum is the symbol of the Emperor and the Imperial family, and as such appears on the Imperial Seal, Japanese passports and the 50

♦ **can't help but**
不禁，不得不
A writer can't help but reveal himself. 一个作家在作品中，总不免要显露出一些自身的影子。

♦ **symbolism** ['sɪmbəlɪzəm]
n. 象征意义，象征

♦ **haiku verse**
俳句诗，日本的一种古典短诗，由十七字音组成，要求严格，受"季语"的限制。所谓季语是指用以表示春、夏、秋、冬及新年的季节用语。在季语中除"夏季的骤雨"、"雪"等表现气候的用语外，还有像"樱花"、"蝉"等动物、植物名称。另外，如"压岁钱"、"阳春面"这样的风俗习惯也多有应用。这些"季语"通常带着现代日本人民对于幼小时代或故乡的一种怀念眷恋之情。

♦ **manga** n. （日本）漫画

♦ **crockery** ['krɒkərɪ]
n. 陶器，瓦罐
All the crockery had been smashed to bits. 所有的陶器都摔成了碎片。

♦ **unpick** ['ʌn'pɪk]
vt. 发现，找出

♦ **attribute** [ə'trɪbjʊ(:)t]
n. （人或物的）属性，特征

♦ **sentiment** ['sentɪmənt]
n. 感情，情操
He has illustrated this sentiment thoroughly in a drama. 他在一出戏剧里充分地表现了这种感情。

♦ **transience** ['trænzɪəns]
n. 短暂，转瞬即逝，无常
There is a sense of transience about her, a feeling that she has only stopped off here

yen coin. It is also said to represent **longevity** and **rejuvenation**.

Peony: Also known as the "King of Flowers", the peony is a symbol of good fortune, bravery and honor, and is often used in tattoos to signify a **devil-may-care** attitude.

Besides, lotus represents purity of the body, speech, and mind; derived from Buddhist symbolism; carnation symbolizes fascination, distinction and love, which are often given on Mother's Day.

The clearest practical example of the use of flower symbolism in Japanese culture can be seen in ikebana, the Japanese art of flower arrangement. This involves a **minimalist** approach, with well defined structures often based around a **scalene triangle**. Like other arts, ikebana is highly expressive and the finished arrangement should reveal the emotion or sentiments that go into its creation—and this is where the symbolism of each flower comes in.

Other than that, flower symbolism features across many different areas of traditional and contemporary Japanese culture, and can be seen in art prints, literature, poetry, films and songs. You can also find it on a vast array of consumer goods, including (amongst many other things): kimono, tableware, stationery, origami paper, **parasols**, fans and accessories.

en route to another place. 她给人一种转瞬即逝的感觉，仿佛她只是在前往他处的途中在此略作停留。

♦ **longevity** [lɒnˈdʒevɪtɪ] n. 长寿
We wish you both health and longevity. 我们祝愿您二位健康长寿。

♦ **rejuvenation** [rɪˌdʒuːvəˈneɪʃn]
n. 复兴；恢复活力
All this signs rejuvenation of agriculture. 所有这些都预示着农业将复苏。

♦ **peony** [ˈpɪənɪ] n. 牡丹，芍药

♦ **devil-may-care**
adj. 漫不经心的，满不在乎的；逍遥自在的
His devil-may-care sense of humor made him a famous comedian. 那漫不经心的幽默感，使他成为一著名的喜剧演员。

♦ **minimalist** [ˈmɪnɪməlɪst]
adj. 简约的
Some of the most respected designers in the world are best known for their minimalist styles. 世上一些最受人尊敬的设计师往往因其简约风格而声名远扬。

♦ **scalene triangle** 不等边三角形

♦ **parasol** [ˌpærəˈsɒl]
n. 太阳伞，遮阳伞
Many girls walk around with parasols in the summer. 夏天，许多女孩子出门都打阳伞。

05 Itadakimasu: Respect for Food in Japan
尊重食物的日本人

说"我要开始吃了"、"我准备吃了"、"我要动了"，表示告知对方要用餐了，并提醒大家开始一起用餐吧。对于日本人来说，吃饭（我要开动了）、出门前（我准备出门了），回家（我回来了）等日常事件，会很礼貌地告诉别人自己将要进行的动作，表示礼貌，尊重对方的存在，以及大家的共鸣和分享。

♦ **say grace** 做饭前祷告

♦ **in unison**
齐声，一齐
They ran together, their legs moving in unison. 他们步调一致地一起跑。

♦ **clasp** [klɑːsp]
vt. 扣住，紧握
Clasp the chain like so. 像这样扣上链子。

这种饮食文化可能与日本的佛教文化有一定的关系。日本的佛教信仰中，有尊重生命的原则，比如要感谢奉献了自己生命的动物和植物。当然也要感谢渔夫、农民和厨师等，没有他们，也就不会有桌上的食物。因此日本人十分尊重食物，自己盘子里的食物如果吃不完，在日本人看来，是十分浪费的。

In Japan, it's common to say itadakimasu before eating a meal. Itadakimasu can be translated "I humbly receive". It's often compared to the Christian tradition of **saying grace** before a meal.

Itadakimasu should be said before you eat. Ideally, everyone is seated at the table and ready to eat when you say it. It's common for a group to say itadakimasu **in unison**. However, it's just as common for just one person to say it. You should **clasp** your hands together and bow your head **slightly** when you say itadakimasu.

Japan is a Buddhist culture. Itadakimasu is related to Buddhist principles of respecting all living things. Itadakimasu **is meant to** thank the animals and plants that gave up their life for the meal. It's also meant to thank all those who played a part in bring the meal to the table–including fisherman, farmers and the **chef**.

In Japan, it's considered **wasteful** not to finish your plate. This is related to the Buddhist philosophy that all life is **sacred**. In other words, since something gave up its life for your meal–it's a shame to waste it. Besides, Japanese dishes are generally small and few people **have problems** finishing their plate. If you don't like something you've ordered and can't finish it–you'll be forgiven. Offer it to your dining **companions** to see if they'll eat it.

In Japan, it's rude to leave food behind on your plate. This applies equally whether you're in someone's home or in a restaurant. Japan is an island nation with a high population. Throughout history resources have been **slim**. De-

---

♦ **slightly** [ˈslaɪtlɪ]
adv. 轻微地，轻轻地
On first acquaintance she is cool and slightly distant. 初次相见时她表现冷淡并有点待搭不理。

♦ **be meant to**
用来做……的，表示……的意思
What are these regulations to come on stage meant to protecting citizen individual information? 这些规定的出台对于保护公民个人信息意味着什么？

♦ **chef** [ʃef]
n. 厨师
James works as assistant chef at a fast food restaurant. 詹姆斯在一家快餐店当助理厨师。

♦ **wasteful** [ˈweɪstful]
adj. 浪费的；挥霍的
It is wasteful to throw way glass, paper and metal. 把玻璃、纸张以及金属扔掉是很浪费的。

♦ **sacred** [ˈseɪkrɪd]
adj. 神圣的，值得崇敬的
The owl is sacred for many Californian Indian people. 对于很多加利福尼亚的印第安人而言，猫头鹰是圣物。

♦ **have problems**
有困难（做某事）

♦ **to have problems (in) doing sth.**
Many people have problems getting to sleep at night. 很多人晚上难以入睡。

♦ **companion** [kəmˈpænjən]
n. 同伴；伴同
You come over as a capable and amusing companion. 你给人的感觉是一个能干、风趣的同伴。

♦ **slim** [slɪm]
adj. 极少的，微小的
There's still a slim chance that he may become Prime Minister. 他仍然有一丝希望当上首相。

♦ **regret** [rɪˈgret]
n. 后悔，悔恨
They are burdened by guilt and regret. 他

spite modern Japan's obvious wealth–it still has few natural resources of its own. This also explains one of the fundamental concepts in Japanese culture–mottainai. Mottainai is the sense of **regret** after having wasted something. It could be **loosely** translated as "what a waste!". Japanese tend to go out of their way to avoid wasting things. This is why it's rude to waste food in Japan.

们内心充满内疚和悔恨。

♦ **loosely** ['luːslɪ]
adv. 大致，粗略地
We can loosely think of the solar surface as a rapidly thinning atmosphere. 我们可以粗略地认为太阳表面是一层快速变薄的大气。

06 Diet of Health in Japan
日本食谱：吃出健康

日本是全世界肥胖率最低的国家之一，而且平均寿命也在全世界名列前茅，心血管疾病患病率更是尤其低。这些都与日本人的饮食分不了关系，其中隐藏着日本人饮食健康的秘密。

日本人用餐是根据身体所需摄取必需的营养和能量，而不会随心所欲，没有节制。因此，在日本料理中，食物的分量都很小。日本人喜欢用很小的碗碟做容器，他们有句俗语，大意是每餐都只能吃到八分饱。尽管你还能吃下一些东西，也不要再吃了。

传统日本料理中，每顿饭都含有极高比例的碳水化合物，能帮助人体降低热量摄入，更是极好的解毒剂。高质量的碳水化合物仍保留着接近自然的形态，较少被加工，这样才营养丰富，并且含有较高的膳食纤维，能在提供身体所需能量的同时促进肠胃蠕动，还容易让人产生饱足感。而且，一日三餐都有固定的饮食计划，是很好的健康食谱。

Japanese diet is known to make you healthy without having to **put on weight**. It is also used to **lose weight**. This article **elaborates on** Japanese diet plan and recipes.

It is known all over the world that the Japanese are some of the healthiest people and have a long life expectancy. But not everyone knows that Japanese women are the least **obese** women in the world, and they **owe it to** their diet. The **essence** of Japanese diet is losing weight by eating fresh and seasonal foods in limit, and eating for the body and not for the mind. They include every kind of

♦ **put on weight** 发福，体重增加
Men tend to put on weight in middle age. 男人到了中年往往会发福。

♦ **lose weight** 减肥，体重减轻
You must cut down on sugar to lose weight. 你必须少吃糖以减轻体重。

♦ **elaborate** [ɪˈlæbərət]
vi. 详尽阐述，详细说明
to elaborate on sth. 详细说明某事
The minister did not elaborate on his plan. 部长没有详细说明他的计划。

♦ **obese** [əʊˈbiːs]
adj. 过分肥胖的，虚胖的
The tendency to become obese is at least in part hereditary. 发胖至少有一部分是源于遗传。

♦ **owe to** 把……归因于
I owe the restoration of my hearing to this remarkable new technique. 我之所以能恢复听觉完全是因为采用了这项非凡的新技术。

food that has specific nutrients in the proper amount. They include fresh vegetables, fish, meat, rice, pulses, cereals, and legumes to **go with** the entire diet, to make it filling as well as delicious.

It is perfect for health as it involves the right amount of fat as well as carbohydrates in every meal so as to **balance** the amounts of nutrient consumption. Rice and fish being the staple food of Japan, it has to be included in the diet, but **vegetarians** can ignore fish. They can eat any other food which is rich in iodine, e.g. Misco soup is a fermented soy product which is easy to **digest** and simple to consume.

Upon following this diet strictly without any **alterations**, a person will not only lose a few pounds but also stay healthy. It is low in cholesterol and fats, so there is no chance of putting on extra pounds. While rice and vegetables provide starch and necessary nutrients, chicken and meat is rich in **proteins** and vitamins. The diet plan given below provides all the information about foods one could eat as a part of various meals of the day.

Here're the ingredients for three meals of the traditional Japanese diet–Breakfast: Miso Soup, 1 cup white rice, 1 egg, Nori seaweed strips, green tea; lunch: teriyaki fish, rice, Asian greens, green tea; dinner: chicken, rice, **Miso soup**, sea vegetables with tofu. These recipes are healthy and easy to cook. They have all the essential vegetables with nutrients, and are the tastiest for a filling lunch or dinner.

♦ **essence** ['esns]
n. 本质，实质
We must try to get to the essence of things. 我们必须想法抓住事物的本质。

♦ **go with** 跟……相配
Does this skirt go with my jumper? 这条裙子和我的套头毛衫相配吗？

♦ **balance** ['bæləns]
vt. 使平衡，使均衡

♦ **vegetarian** [,vedʒɪ'teərɪən]
n. 素食者，素食主义者
She became a strict vegetarian two years ago. 两年前她成为严格的素食主义者。

♦ **digest** [dɪ'dʒest]
vt. 消化，吸收（食物）
The function of the stomach is to digest food sufficiently to enable it to pass into the intestine. 胃的功能是充分消化食物，以便让其进入肠道。

♦ **alteration** [,ɔːltə'reɪʃn]
n. 变化，变更；（行为上的）折扣
Prices may be subject to alteration. 价格可能会有所变动。

♦ **protein** ['prəʊtiːn]
n. 蛋白质

♦ **Miso soup**
味噌汤，一种很道地的日式汤品，日本的每个家庭主妇一定都会煮。味噌是一种调味料，由发酵过的黄豆制成，为糊状，主要用来作汤底。在日本街头，无论多晚，街旁的日式餐馆都会提供一碗暖心的味噌汤：看似清汤寡水，用勺子轻轻一舀，"内里乾坤"婉转浮现。据说，日本人的长寿与经常食用味噌有关，这也侧面说明味噌营养丰富。

07 Korea's Traditional Tea Culture
在韩国喝茶

夏日的炎热让人身心疲惫，为了给身体"充电"，同时为了补充换季时严重日温差而造成的气虚，韩国人认为用一杯热茶暖身有助于健康。首尔市第 27 号非物质文化财官中茶礼仪式持有者金宜正表示，对于韩国人来说，茶并不是一种单纯的嗜好，而是一种拥有悠久历史，并配有高级仪式与礼节的高品质饮品。

　　韩国的传统茶文化中,利用植物的各种营养成分和拥有治疗能力的功能性物质来制作成茶品。韩国的传统茶有很多种类,有用谷物做成的薏米茶和玉米茶,用各种植物叶片做成的杜仲茶和柿子树叶茶,用植物果实做成的柚子茶和木瓜茶,用花瓣、根茎等做成的菊花茶和人参茶,还有用药材做成的金银花茶。此外还有甘草茶、桂皮茶等数十种不同种类的茶。每种茶具备的功能都不止一项,所以很久以前当人们感到身体不适的时候,都将韩国的传统茶当作药来食用。

　　一般来说,茶是需要用五感来品尝的。先聆听倒第一杯茶的声音,之后用眼睛来看斟满的茶杯,将茶杯拿到近前闻茶香之后,再细细品味茶的味道。品茶是要动员全身的所有感觉来进行的。在节奏变得快速的现代社会中,茶文化成了另一个极端。而"缓慢的美学"也作为一个新的文化重新走向现代人。

With temperatures continuing to drop and trees beginning to show the richer, redder **hues** of autumn, few things are more **inviting** than a steaming cup of tea. Whether needing a quick defense on unexpectedly chilly mornings or still low on energy after a draining summer, a hot drink with nutritional benefits to **boot** is an ideal fall staple.

In Korea, where the culture of tea consumption and **cultivation** as both lifestyle and ritual can be **traced** back to the 7th century A.D., regard for the multifold **merits** of tea is particularly high. Even as consumers' enthusiasm for coffee continues to grow, efforts to preserve Korea's rich tea heritage also continue.

"More than a **luxury** or a hobby, our tea culture boasts a long history and is significant in terms of royal rituals as well as social etiquette," said Kim Eui-jung, the title holder for Seoul's Intangible Cultural Property No. 27, Gungjung Darye (royal tea ceremony).

One aspect of Korean culture **highlighted** in the practice of drinking various teas is the traditional belief, standardized by traditional medicine, that food and medicine are **homologous**–good food can be, in and of itself, good medicine for the body. Moreover, ingredients that

♦ **hue** [hjuː]
n. 色彩,色调
♦ **inviting** [ɪnˈvaɪtɪŋ]
adj. 吸引人的,诱人的
The kitchen smelled warm and inviting and blessedly familiar. 这间厨房的味道温暖诱人,使人感到亲切温馨。
♦ **boot** [buːt]
vi. 而且,另外;加之
He is making money and receiving free advertising to boot! 他既挣了钱,又做了免费的广告!
♦ **cultivation** [ˌkʌltɪˈveɪʃən]
n. 种植,栽培
These high yields have been achieved largely through better methods of cultivation. 这样高的产量主要是通过改良耕作方法取得的。
♦ **trace** [treɪs]
vt. 追溯,追踪
Her family can trace its history back to the 15th century. 她的家史可追溯到15世纪。
♦ **merit** [ˈmerɪt]
n. 价值,优点
For him, box-office success mattered more than artistic merit. 对他来说,票房上的成功比艺术价值更重要。
♦ **luxury** [ˈlʌkʃərɪ]

make good medicine can also become a welcome part of good food.

Among the kinds of tea, or cha, traditionally enjoyed in Korea are those made from grains, mixtures of various plant leaves, fruits, flower blossoms, and medicinal **extracts**. Teas made from grain include the creamy yulmu tea made from powdered job's tears, and **cornsilk** tea, **lauded** for being rich in **antioxidants**. Popular leaf teas include duchung tea, which uses eucommia bark, a favorite ingredient in herbal medicine, as well as persimmon leaf tea. Sweeter options like yuja (citron) and mogwa (quince) are also popular. Chrysanthemum tea and insam (ginseng) tea, made from the plant buds and roots, show the wide range of Korean teas.

From preparation to drinking, tea was traditionally regarded in Korea less as a beverage and more as an experience. The sound of the hot water as it is carefully poured, the sight of varyingly clear and colored liquids filling empty cups, the unique aromas that are created by different mixtures of ingredients, the hands that extend with **poise** to bring the tea to the taster's lips, and the first appreciative and slow sip–the experience is described as one that appeals to all five senses.

n. 奢侈品，不常有的乐趣（或享受）
Hot baths are my favourite luxury. 泡个热水澡是我的最大乐事。

♦ **highlighted** ['haɪlaɪtɪd]
adj. 突出的，强调的

♦ **homologous** [hɒ'mɒləɡəs]
adj. 类似的，一致的
The seal's flipper is homologous with the human arm. 海豹的鳍肢与人类的手臂同源。

♦ **extract** [ɪks'trækt]
n. 提炼物

♦ **cornsilk** ['kɔːn'sɪlk]
n. 玉米穗

♦ **laud** [lɔːd]
vt. 称赞，赞美
Dickens was lauded for his social and moral sensitivity. 狄更斯以其敏锐的社会和道德触觉为人称道。

♦ **antioxidant** [ˌæntɪ'ɒksɪdənt]
n. 抗氧化剂

♦ **poise** [pɒɪz]
n. 风度，自信
I think it must just be because I look as if I'm full of poise. 我想那一定是因为我看上去样子非常沉着自信吧。

08 Fun Facts in South Korea
你不知道的韩国趣闻

韩国，全称大韩民国，又称南韩、南朝鲜，位于东北亚朝鲜半岛南部。在韩国的神话传说里，桓雄创造了熊女，然后与之结婚生下来檀君，也就是韩国之父，他在公元前 2333 年创造了朝鲜王朝。

除了关于起源的传说，还有许多有趣的故事可以帮助我们进一步了解韩国。比如，每年新年的第一个夜晚，韩国人都会把自己的鞋子藏起来。传说有鬼怪会试穿人们的鞋子，并把喜欢的带走，这样，鞋子被带走的人在接下来的一年会经常倒霉。

Officially known as the Republic of Korea, South Korea is one of the most advanced countries in the world. It is located in East Asia on the southern part of the Korean Peninsula. In Korean

mythology there is a story about how the Korean nation was born. The story is that a god named Hwanung came from heaven and **transformed** a bear into a woman. He married her and she **gave birth to** a son, **Tangun**, the founder of Korea. Tangun created the first capital of the Korean nation in 2333 B.C. and called it Joseon–"Land of the Morning Calm".

Apart from the interesting tale of its origin, some other fun facts would offer you a better understanding of South Korean.

When the first night of the New Year comes everybody hides their shoes. This is because there is a belief that a ghost will come down and **try on** everyone's shoes. If the ghost finds a pair it likes it will take it. It is thought that the owner of the shoes will then have bad luck for the whole year.

Korean taxis are color **coded** and each color is an **indicator** of the type of services you can **avail**. For example, gray and white taxis offer basic comfort, whereas a black colored **cab** is a luxurious car and a **veteran** driver. The Korean drivers are **notorious** for watching TV in the cab while driving passengers around.

South Korea **boasts of** some of the biggest shopping malls in the world, in fact, some of the malls are bigger than a European town. For instance, in one mall for the connoisseurs of alcohol, you can buy a pint of beer and instead of heading home; you can start gulping it at any place you feel you are comfortable in! Yes! Public drinking is permissible as per South Korean lawns, so, don't be surprised if you find someone drinking in the park, don't **sneer**, probably nobody would understand the reason for your **contempt**!

As like most of the people of the world, South

♦ **mythology** [mɪˈθɒlədʒɪ]
n. 神话（传说）
In Greek mythology, Zeus was the ruler of Gods and men. 在希腊神话中，宙斯是众神和人类的统治者。

♦ **transform** [trænsˈfɔ:m] vt. 改变，变形
It will transform a poverty-stricken part of Brazil's backlands. 巴西腹地的贫穷面貌将会得到彻底的改变。

♦ **give birth to** 生（孩子），生育
The tiger gave birth to three cubs this time. 那只母老虎这次生育了三只可爱的小虎仔。

♦ **Tangun** 檀君

♦ **try on** 试穿
Try on clothing and shoes to make sure they fit. 试穿一下衣服和鞋子，看看是否合适。

♦ **code** [kəʊd] vt. 把……编码

♦ **indicator** [ˈɪndɪkeɪtə] n. 指示

♦ **avail** [əˈveɪl] vt. 利用，使用
She was availed upon for gain. 她被人用作捞钱的工具。

♦ **cab** [kæb]
n. 出租车

♦ **veteran** [ˈvetərən]
adj. 老练的，资深的，经验丰富的
The baseball veteran loved to coach young players. 这位棒球老手喜欢指导年轻选手。

♦ **notorious** [nəʊˈtɔ:rɪəs]
adj. 臭名昭著的，臭名远扬的；声名狼藉的
He was notorious as a gambler. 他是臭名昭著的赌徒。

♦ **boast of** 夸耀，吹嘘
A modest man will never boast of his merits. 谦虚的人决不夸自己的功劳。

♦ **sneer** [snɪə]
vi. 讥笑，冷笑
sneer at sth./sb. 嘲笑某事或某人
Some city consumers may sneer at that statement. 这种说法也许会引起某些城里人的冷嘲热讽。

♦ **contempt** [kənˈtempt]
n. 轻蔑，轻视
Mack felt a pitiless contempt for her. 麦克对她没有同情，只有鄙夷。

Koreans too have their set of superstitions, and one of its **manifestations** is the absence of 4th floor in most of the South Korean buildings. And have you heard about Snuppy? Yes, the first cloned dog in the world was "manufactured" at the Seoul National University.

♦ **manifestation** [ˌmænɪfesˈteɪʃən]
n. 表现（形式）
The riots are a clear manifestation of the people's discontent. 骚乱清楚地表明了人们的不满情绪。

09 Fan Death in South Korea
韩国怪谈：电扇致死论

在一个密闭的空间里，使用电风扇的时间过长，会最终致人死亡吗？你或许不相信，但是在科技发达的韩国，很多人对此坚信不疑。因此，你会注意到，韩国的电扇上都安装有用于电扇自动关停的定时器。

这最初来自于一些传言，比如有人发现一些离奇死亡案件中，死者房子里有电风扇。甚至不乏医学或者物理理论的支持；加之，电视、报纸等媒体的推波助澜，风扇致死论在韩国大行其道。在众多有关在密室使用电风扇致死医学研究中，失温与窒息是主要两个曾经在医学上假设探讨的致命原因。比如，根据医学上的研究，由于人体在晚上阶段的新陈代谢减慢，对温度变化更加敏感，而电风扇直接吹向人体上，会把身体上附近范围的空气温度降低，或会把因炎热产生的汗水在瞬间被蒸发，使身体出失温的情况。另一个关于密室电风扇杀人的医学可能，是因为电风扇直接吹向面部导致氧气供应不足而死亡。

如今，一些韩国政府部门和社会健康机构仍然不时地发布关于在密闭空间慎用电扇的警告。

Anyone who purchases an electric fan in South Korea may notice something unusual: an **automatic** shut-off **timer**. This is one popular method for preventing what a number of South Koreans refer as fan death. Fan death **allegedly** occurs whenever an electric fan is used for many hours in a **sealed** room.

It's not the fan itself which causes fan death through physical injury or electrical **shock**, but rather the **cumulative** effect of the circulating air. Some believe the fan's rotating **blades** create a partial **vacuum** near a sleeper's face, causing a disruption in normal breathing and ultimately fatal **suffocation**. Others suggest the fan some-

♦ **automatic** [ˌɔːtəˈmætɪk]
adj. 自动的
And did you want an automatic or a manual transmission? 还有你是要自动的还是用手操作的传动系统？
♦ **timer** [ˈtaɪmə] n. 定时器，计时器
♦ **allegedly** [əˈledʒɪdlɪ]
adv. 据称，据说
The traffic accident was allegedly due to negligence. 这次车祸据说是由于疏忽造成的。
♦ **sealed** [siːld]
adj. 密封的；封锁的；未知的
♦ **shock** [ʃɒk] n. 休克
They escaped the blaze but were rushed to

how uses up the available oxygen, allowing the room to fill up with deadly carbon dioxide. A third theory **blames** fan death on a gradual hypothermia as the circulating air lowers the sleeper's body temperature. **Paradoxically**, others believe fan death is caused by hyperthermia as the hot circulating air raises a sleeper's body temperature during a heat wave.

The urban legend of fan death seems to be limited to South Korea. Stories have circulated in that country for decades concerning victims being discovered in small, **enclosed** rooms with no obvious contributing factors except the presence of an electric fan. Depending on the circumstances, a victim of fan death may have frozen to death, suffered **heatstroke** or suffocated for no apparent reason. These accounts tend to be attributed to a very small newspaper or a "friend of a friend" who heard about such an incident of fan death years earlier. **Skeptics** of the fan death phenomenon suggest that the real cause of death in these cases may have been carbon monoxide poisoning, an existing physical condition or **electrocution** from an improperly wired appliance. The fact that an appliance as common as an electric fan happened to be in the room could very well be **coincidental**.

While many other countries consider fan death to be little more than a South Korean urban legend, the South Korean government and many health officials still issue warnings on the use of electric fans in small rooms with limited **ventilation**. The timer units on South Korean electric fans are supposed to prevent fan death by stopping the circulation of air after a number of hours. This would allow the heavier carbon dioxide gases to remain separate from the breathable oxygen in the room. A sleeper would also not risk dehydration after hours of exposure to a constant stream of air, and his or her body temperature would not be raised or lowered to dangerous levels **overnight**.

hospital suffering from shock. 他们虽然逃离了火海，却因休克而被迅速送往医院。

♦ **cumulative** [ˈkjuːmjʊlətɪv]
adj. 累积的，渐增的
It is simple pleasures, such as a walk on a sunny day, which have a cumulative effect on our mood. 一些简单的娱乐，譬如在一个阳光明媚的日子散步，就能使我们的心情更愉快。

♦ **blade** [bleɪd]
n. （机器上旋转的）叶片

♦ **vacuum** [ˈvækjʊəm]
n. 真空 常用习语：feel a vacuum in the lower regions 觉得肚子空空的，觉得饿

♦ **suffocation** [ˌsʌfəˈkeɪʃn] n. 窒息

♦ **blame** [bleɪm]
vt. 把责任推给，指责，谴责
He blamed the crisis on poor planning. 他把危机归咎于计划不周。

♦ **paradoxically** [ˌpærəˈdɒksɪkəlɪ]
adv. 荒谬的是，自相矛盾地

♦ **enclosed** [ɪnˈkləʊzd]
adj. 封闭的，与外界隔绝的，不透气的
Do not use this substance in an enclosed space. 切勿在不透气的地方使用此物质。

♦ **heatstroke** [ˈhiːtstrəʊk] n. 中暑

♦ **skeptic** [ˈskeptɪk]
n. 怀疑者；怀疑论者

♦ **electrocution** [ɪˌlektrəˈkjuːʃn]
n. 电死

♦ **coincidental** [kəʊˌɪnsɪˈdentl]
adj. 巧合的，同时发生的
Any resemblance to actual persons, places or events is purely coincidental. 如与真人、真实地点或真实事件有雷同之处，纯属巧合。

♦ **ventilation** [ˌventɪˈleɪʃn]
n. 通风，空气流通

♦ **overnight** [ˈəʊvəˈnaɪt]
adv. 一夜之间
There were two bomb explosions in the city overnight. 一夜之间城里发生了两起炸弹爆炸事件。

Chapter 12
尚礼之道：非礼莫属生活志

01 Seken No Me: Neighborhood Eyes in Japan
爱面子的日本邻居

虽然人类不乏独居生活的，但群居生活才是人类共同的特点。源于远古时代人类出于共同抵御自然灾害等而团结在一起群居生活，邻居生活是今天的人们不可摆脱的情感圈子。在日本，人们对脸面很重视，尤其是街坊邻里之间的眼光和看法，会极大地影响日本人的生活态度和方式。

同一个社区的居民会修建和祭拜共同的寺庙和神社；有人生病了，邻居们会热情地赠送一些小礼物作为慰问；当邻居有人去世的时候，人们一般都会出席葬礼，表示对死者家人的精神支持。但随着城市化进程的推进，对很多人来讲邻居的看法变得越来越无所谓。

Many Japanese neighborhoods are close knit communities. Neighbors support the local shrine and temple. They **participate in** local festivals. If someone falls seriously ill– the neighbors bring over small gifts(omimai). When someone dies neighbors all **show up** to the funeral to show their support for the family.

As nice as all this sounds–close knit communities do have their **drawbacks**. In Japan, neighbors tend to **gossip**. This isn't exactly a uniquely Japanese phenomenon. However, in Japan the desire to be a respected member of the community can be extremely strong. Many people live **in fear of** seken no me (neighborhood eyes).

Let's say a married woman return to her home town without her husband to visit her parents. A visit of a few days is fine. However, if she stays a week she might worry the neighborhoods will wonder if she's had a **spat** with her husband. Maybe the case is her husband is **on a** long **business trip**; therefore, she'd like to visit her parents for a week. But she'd **prefer** to avoid any potential gossip.

Japan has a fairly low divorce rate (27%). A little more than 1 in 4 marriages ends in divorce. In the US, more than half of married couples **eventually** divorce. This doesn't necessarily mean that Japanese couples are happier. Within

---

♦ **participate in** 参加，参与
She didn't participate in the discussion. 她没有参加讨论。

♦ **show up** 到场，现身
We waited until five o'clock, but he did not show up. 我们一直等到了 5:00，但是他始终没有露面。

♦ **drawback** ['drɔːbæk]
n. 缺点，缺陷
He felt the apartment's only drawback was that it was too small. 他觉得这个公寓唯一的缺点就是太小了。

♦ **gossip** ['gɒsɪp]
vi. 说闲话，八卦；传播流言，说三道四
She can spend a whole day gossiping with her neighbors. 她能一整天都跟邻居们一起说长道短。

♦ **in fear of**
害怕……，为……提心吊胆
The thief passed the day in fear of discovery. 那小偷整天提心吊胆怕被发现。

♦ **spat** [spæt]
n. 口角，小争吵

♦ **on a business trip**
出公差，因公出差

♦ **prefer** [prɪ'fəː] vi. 宁愿，更喜欢
prefer to do sth. rather than do sth. 宁愿……也不……

Japan, fear of neighborhood gossip is considered a major factor in the low divorce rate. Many couples are willing to stay in a bad marriage to **keep up** appearances.

The truth is that neighborhood eyes are on the decline. In 1962, more than 40% of Japanese people were farmers who lived in small communities. Today, only 2.5% of Japanese people are farmers. Japan has **urbanized** more quickly than any other country in history. Japanese cities such as Tokyo are spread urban environments. Many Tokyoites live in houses and have close relationships with neighbors. However, in recent years mansions (condominiums) are increasingly common. People who live in mansions often don't maintain close relationships with neighbors.

Highly urbanized people **contribute to** major shrines that have countless **patrons** (such as Meiji shrine in Tokyo). They attend massive festivals where they'd be unlikely to see anyone they know. When a neighbor in your building dies–they might not even be informed (or notice). So many urban **dwellers** in Japan are **free of** neighborhood eyes.

◆ **eventually** [ɪˈventjʊəlɪ]
adv. 最后，终究
He was eventually diagnosed as suffering from terminal cancer. 他最终被诊断出患了晚期癌症。

◆ **keep up** 保持，跟上
A successful company must keep up with the pace of technological change. 一家成功的公司必须得跟上技术变革的步伐。

◆ **urbanize** [ˈɔːbənaɪz]
vi. 城市化，都市化
For China to modernize its economy, it must further industrialize, and urbanize. 为了使经济现代化，中国必须扩大工业化和城市化。

◆ **contribute to**
捐献；贡献；促进 如，How much did you contribute to the relief fund? 你为那笔救济金捐了多少？

◆ **patron** [ˈpeɪtrən] n. 守护神

◆ **dweller** [ˈdwelə(r)] n. 居民，居住者

◆ **free of** 不受……的干扰
She retains her slim figure and is free of wrinkles. 她保持着苗条的身材，脸上也没有皱纹。

02 Driving a Car in Japan
在日本，谨慎驾驶

东京、大阪等日本大都会有便利密集的公共交通网络，没有汽车，不会驾车也可以很快捷地去往任何一个地方。然而在几个大城市之外，公共交通不很发达的地方，汽车还是很重要的交通工具。当然，驾驶车辆首先要注意遵守交通规则。比如，在日本，车辆是靠左侧行驶，方向盘和驾驶席在车内的右侧。最小法定驾驶年龄是18岁。酒后驾驶是被严格禁止的。

在日本，除高速公路或者和一些风景路线以外，多数道路是不收费的。公路状况基本良好，城市边缘、古老街道可能相当狭窄。节假日、主要交通干线附近的交通堵塞问题比较严重。

外国人在进入这个国家一年以后可以以一份被认可的国际驾照在日本开车。被认可的国际驾照必须是在动身去日本之前在本国获得，通常由全国性汽车协会颁发。对于所有在日本停留超过一年的司机，日本驾照执照是必需的。只是当离开日本超过连续三个月，才再次准许使用一份国际驾驶执照在日本开车一年。

Japan's large metropolitan areas around Tokyo, Osaka and Nagoya are served by highly efficient public transportation systems. Consequently, many residents do not own a car or do not even possess a **driver's license**. Outside the big cities, however, public transportation tends to be inconvenient or **infrequent**, and most people rely on cars to get around.

Firstly, let's see some general rules when driving on roads.

Cars drive on the left side of the road and have the driver's seat and **steering wheel** on their right side. The legal **minimum** age for driving is 18 years. Road signs and rules follow international standards, and most signs on major roads are in Japanese and English. Drinking and driving is strictly prohibited.

The typical speed limits are 80 to 100 km/h on **expressways**, 40 km/h in urban areas, 30 km/h in **side streets** and 50 to 60 km/h elsewhere; however, drivers tend to go a little over the posted speed limits.

Most roads in Japan are **toll** free with the exception of expressways and some **scenic** driving routes. Road conditions tend to be good, although side streets in the cities can be rather narrow or even **impassable** to larger vehicles. Traffic congestion is a frequent problem in and around urban centers.

Drivers generally tend to be well **mannered** and considerate, however some common dangers on Japanese roads include drivers **speeding** over **intersections** even well after the traffic light has turned red, people stopping their vehicles at the edge of the road in a way in which they block traffic, and careless cyclists, especially those who ride on the wrong side of the road.

As for foreigners, they can drive in Japan with an International Driving Permit (IDP) for a maximum of one year, even if the IDP is valid for a longer period. It is not possible

♦ **driver's license** 驾驶执照
♦ **infrequent** [ɪnˈfriːkwənt]
adj. 稀少的，罕见的
This is an infrequent stamp. 这是一张罕见的邮票。
♦ **steering wheel**
n. 方向盘，驾驶盘
♦ **minimum** [ˈmɪnɪməm]
adj. 最低的，最小的
The Companies Act lays down a set of minimum requirements.《公司法》规定了一系列最低标准。
♦ **expressway** [ɪkˈspresweɪ]
n. 高速公路
♦ **side street** 小街，小巷
♦ **toll** [təʊl]
n. 通行费
You have to pay a toll to drive on a turnpike. 在收费公路上开车要缴通行费。
♦ **scenic** [ˈsiːnɪk]
adj. （路线）景色优美的，观光的
The scenic beauty of the place entranced the visitors. 这里的美丽风光把游客们迷住了。
♦ **impassable** [ɪmˈpɑːsəbl]
adj. 不能通行的，无法通过的
The mud made the roads impassable. 道路因为泥泞而无法通行。
♦ **mannered** [ˈmænəd]
adj. 有礼貌的，彬彬有礼的
They are always perfectly polite and beautifully mannered. 他们总是很懂礼貌，彬彬有礼。
♦ **speed** [spiːd] vi. 加速
speed up 加速
Catalysts are materials which greatly speed up chemical reactions. 催化剂是可以大大加速化学反应的物质。
♦ **intersection** [ˌɪntə(ː)ˈsekʃən]
n. 交叉口
The policeman regulated traffic at the intersection. 警察在交叉路口指挥交通。
♦ **consecutive** [kənˈsekjʊtɪv]
adj. 连续的，不间断的

to drive on an International Driving Permit again unless you return to your home country for at least three **consecutive** months in between.

International driving permits are not issued in Japan and should be obtained in your home country in advance. They are usually issued through your country's national **automobile** association for a small fee. Japan only recognizes international driving permits based on the 1949 Geneva Convention, which are issued by a large number of countries.

People from other countries whose international driving permits are not recognized by Japan and people who stay in Japan for more than one year must obtain a Japanese driver's license.

The numbers 7, 8, 9 are consecutive. 7、8、9 这三个数字是连续的。

♦ **automobile** [ˈɔːtəməubiːl]
n. 汽车
The automobile slowed down to go around the curves in the road. 汽车在路上转弯时放慢了速度。

03 Never Shake Your Legs in Japan
不要在日本抖腿

大家在生活中肯定都遇到过爱抖腿的人，他们只要一坐下来，腿就开始不停地上下抖动。提醒他一句会让他停几分钟，可不一会，他准会又抖起来了。关于抖腿有很多说法，比如有人认为爱抖腿的人神经质，甚至还有不少人认为抖腿相当于做运动，能消耗热量，是个减肥的好方法。但在日本，抖腿是个很大的忌讳。

日语中 bimbo yusuri 表示在坐着时抖动两腿或者膝盖，就字面上的意思，还指"穷人的抖动"。其实，坐着抖腿是一种无意识的行为，尤其发生在广大男性中。在日本人眼里，抖腿的人性格急躁或紧张，或者缺乏自信。但是，由于日本文化中，人们尽可能地考虑对方的脸面和感受，因此一般不会有人直接要求对方停下来，而是采取忽略的态度。

Bimbo yusuri is the Japanese term for shaking of the legs or knees while seated. The term can be **literally** translated as "poor person shake".

Shaking the leg while seated is often an **unconscious** habit. It's far more common amongst men. There are several theories why people do it. These include that it improves one's blood circulation when seated, **burns calories** or releases nervous energy.

♦ **literally** [ˈlɪtərəli]
adv. 照字面地
He translated the passage literally. 他逐字逐句地翻译这段文字。

♦ **unconscious** [ʌnˈkɒnʃəs]
adj. 无意的，不自觉的，无意识的
Mr Battersby was apparently quite unconscious of their presence. 巴特斯比先生显然没有注意到他们在场。

♦ **burn calories** 消耗热量

♦ **avoid** [əˈvɔɪd]
vt. 避开，避免
avoid doing sth. 避免做某事
I avoid working in places which are too public. 我避免在过于抛头露面的地方工作。

♦ **indicate** [ˈɪndɪkeɪt]
vt. 表明，暗示
Dreams can help indicate your true feelings. 梦可以反映你的真实感情。

However, it's highly recommended to **avoid** shaking your legs in Japan. According to Japanese manners, leg shaking is extremely rude. It **indicates** that you're **impatient** or nervous about something and lack self control.

A habit of shaking your legs may seem innocent enough. However, in Japan it can seriously damage your professional and social life. Shaking your legs in front of a customer or a date indicates that you're an impatient person of low **manners** (according to local customs).

When you do bimbo yusuri, Japanese people are unlikely to ask you to stop. This is because Japanese culture avoids conflict (such as directly **embarrassing** someone). In other words, telling you to stop would cause you to **lose face**. People will try to ignore your bad behavior.

If you're in the habit of shaking your legs unconsciously it's recommended not to cross your legs a lot when in Japan. Nobody knows exactly where the term bimbo yusuri originated. One theory is that it's an **idiom** based on poor people shaking due to the cold.

♦ **impatient** [ɪmˈpeɪʃənt]
adj. 不耐烦的，急躁的
He was so impatient that I could hardly hold him back. 他是那样急躁，我简直拉不住他。

♦ **manner** [ˈmænə]
n. 礼貌，规矩
They commended him upon his good manner. 他们称赞他有礼貌。

♦ **embarrass** [ɪmˈbærəs]
vt. 使窘迫，使难堪
He didn't mean to embarrass you. 他不是成心让你难堪。

♦ **lose face** 丢脸，面上无光
His careless work made him lose face with his teacher. 他工作疏忽使他在老师面前丢脸。

♦ **idiom** [ˈɪdɪəm]
n. 习语，成语
Each idiom in our dictionary is illustrated with a sentence. 我们词典中的每一个习语都有一个例句说明。

04 Common Lip Service in Japan
日本人的应酬之辞

在人们的日常交往中，并非所有的言语都"名副其实"，有时，人们出于寒暄或者恭维原因,会使用应酬的话。这种现象在日本文化中也十分常见，日语 shakou jirei 说的就是一种空口的应酬或者顺耳的恭维。

对于 shakou jirei 这种应酬之辞，并无实意，切不可当真对待，你可以一笑了之，也可以直接指出对方"言过其实"。这种文化很利于保持谈话的友好氛围，要学会区分这种话语的真实性。比如说，"有时间一块吃午饭吧"是一种假意寒暄，而"下周有时间一块吃午饭吧"才是真诚的约请。

♦ **compliment** [ˈkɒmplɪmənt]
n. 赞美，恭维（话）
He addressed her with high compliment. 他以非常恭维的话向她献殷勤。

♦ **lip service**
说得好听的话，空口的应酬话
All the parties pay lip service to environmental issues. 对环境问题，各方都是口惠而实不至。

♦ **flattery** [ˈflætərɪ]
n. 奉承（话）
John found himself surrounded by insincere flattery. 约翰发现自己为虚情假意的

In Japan, it's somewhat common for people to give **compliments** that they don't mean. This is referred to as shakou jirei. It can be loosely translated as **lip service** or **flattery**.

Shakou jirei isn't usually intended to be cruel. However, if you let it go to your head you end up looking **foolish**. It's important to recognize shakou jirei for what it is– meaningless social noise. The best way to deal with Shakou jirei is to show that it doesn't **work** on you. **Laugh** it **off**. If you feel that someone is laying on the shakou jirei too thick – you can call their bluff. Say home sugi (too much praise!).

Flattery is fairly common in many cultures. However, it's very common in Japan. This is because Japanese people tend to go out of their way to keep conversations positive and friendly. So it happens when the person wants to be nice but can't think of something **authentically** nice to say – so they come up with something **superficially** nice (flattery).

Sometimes Shakou jirei takes the form of **insincere** invitations. If you run into an old friend and they say "we should have lunch sometime". If the invitation isn't sincere– it's shakou jirei. Insincere invitations are common in many cultures. The way that you can tell it's insincere is that no specific time is given. "Let's have lunch next week" might be sincere "Let's have lunch sometime" usually isn't.

These **subtleties** are more difficult to **detect** when you're speaking a second language. Gaijin are more likely to become victims of shakou jirei. If you take shakou jirei seriously you risk looking foolish.

奉承阿谀所包围。

♦ **foolish** [ˈfuːlɪʃ]
adj. 可笑的，愚蠢的
His foolish act has brought a storm about his ears. 他的愚蠢行动招致了人们的强烈不满。

♦ **work** [wəːk] vi. 有效果，起作用
I think your suggestion will work. 我看你的建议行得通。

♦ **laugh off**
对……一笑置之；笑言以对
An actor has to learn to laugh off bad reviews. 演员需学会能对贬斥性评论一笑置之的本事。

♦ **authentically** [ɔːˈθentɪkəlɪ]
adv. 确实地，真正地
Consumers are increasingly interested in the authentically exotic tastes. 消费者对于真正的异国风味越来越情有独钟。

♦ **superficially** [sjuːpəˈfɪʃəlɪ]
adv. 表面上，乍看起来地
Their experiences are superficially similar. 他们的经历从表面看很相似。

♦ **insincere** [ˌɪnsɪnˈsɪə]
adj. 不诚恳的，不真诚的
Kennedy thought the Canadian insincere and did not like or trust him. 肯尼迪觉得这个加拿大人不够诚恳，也就不喜欢他，也不信任他。

♦ **subtlety** [ˈsʌtltɪ]
n. 微妙之处，细微差别
In time you'll appreciate the beauty and subtlety of this language. 总有一天你会体会到这门语言的优美和微妙之处。

♦ **detect** [dɪˈtekt] vt. 查明，发现
He was detected stealing something. 有人发现他在偷东西。

05 Never Pick a Sakura Petal in Japan
毋摘樱花

花见是日本的风俗，意思即赏花，多在春天进行，欣赏的主要是樱花，也会欣赏梅花。每年3至4月间，日本人尤其各企业单位，经常在樱花树下举行露天赏花大会。日本各地樱花开放的时间不一，也会受气候影响，所以每年樱花开花期间，日本的网站都会详列各地的开花情况，有些还有照片显示开花度，方便公众参考。

日本人赏有有许多礼节和规则，其中最需要谨记的事情是，不要摘樱花甚至折花枝。这其中有许多原因，比如，如果大家都去摘樱花，那么每年成千上万的赏花人会很快把樱花摘光，就没有风景可言了；再比如，日本人认为樱花是武士的象征，凋零的花瓣如同牺牲的武士一样悲壮，因此，摘樱花会让日本人很不舒服。

Hanami parties have a relaxed and fun filled atmosphere. There aren't many rules of **etiquette** associated with hanami. However, the one thing that one should never do is pick sakura petals or branches. There are several reasons for this.

The **common sense** comes first. Popular hanami spots are filled with thousands of people night after night. If everyone picked the flowers they'd be gone quickly. Everyone hopes that hanami will last as long as possible.

The cultural and religious significance of sakura is more of the reason. Sakura are deeply **engrained** in Japanese culture. According to Japanese Buddhist traditions, falling sakura petals represent the **impermanence** of life. Sakura petals only live a week. They bloom brilliantly and fall with the wind. The beauty of falling sakura has been the topic of countless Japanese poems and songs.

For hundreds of years, sakura petals have also symbolized warriors. Samurai ideals stated that a warrior should live passionately and die young. This was symbolized by sakura petals. According to Japanese cultural traditions,

♦ **etiquette** [etɪˈket]
n. 礼节，规矩
♦ **common sense** 常识，直觉判断力
For goodness' sake, just use your common sense! 我的老天，你也凭常识想想！
♦ **engrained** [ɪnˈɡreɪnd]
adj. 根深蒂固的
The bad phenomenon is engrained, and will be hard to eradicate. 现在这种坏现象已经是蔓草难除了。
♦ **impermanence** [ɪmˈpɜːmənəns]
n. 无常；短暂，暂时
Change, impermanence is characteristic of life. 变化和无常是生命的特征。
♦ **reincarnated** [riːˈɪnkɑːneɪtɪd]
adj. 转世的
If you be reincarnated as a plant, what's your choice then? 如果你的来生只能投胎成为一种植物，但你可以选择，你会选哪种植物？
♦ **probably** [ˈprɒbəb(ə)lɪ]
adv. 大概，很可能
It is probably the most polluted body of water in the world. 这很可能是世界上受污染最严重的一片水域。

falling sakura petals represent the **reincarnated** souls of warriors who fell in battle.

If you pick a sakura petal in Japan people will likely feel uncomfortable but **probably** won't say anything. If you pick a branch (even a small one) people will likely **speak up**. In the Edo-era people did pick Sakura as part of hanami celebrations. This died out some time in the Meiji-era (1868–1912).

♦ **speak up**
（尤指为某人辩护或抗议某事物）大胆地说，公开表态
I am not suggesting that individuals never speak up about wrong-doing. 我并不是在暗示说，个人永远不要去谴责那些恶行。

06 Jishuku: The Way Japanese Mourn
日本人的哀悼方式

2011年，日本3·11大地震引发的福岛核电站泄漏事故，不仅让方圆30公里居民的生活发生了巨变。他们在避难中心吃不饱穿不暖，更没有个人隐私可言，越来越多人冒险回到撤离区的家中，只为寻找食物和洗个热水澡。核辐射污染和政府的禁售令，使得福岛农民不得不倾倒几百万公斤的牛奶，烧毁数吨发烂的蔬菜。甚至是远在东京的人们取消赏樱派对、拒绝唱卡拉OK……他们似乎很有默契地集体放弃娱乐活动，用自我约束为灾民打气。天灾人祸面前，日本的普通人都是这样过日子的。这是日本人特有的"自肃"现象。

日语中的"自肃"，意为"自我约束"。在日本民众眼中，在他人遭受天灾人祸等各种悲惨经历后，自己应当约束各种庆祝活动，以表达内心的同情、哀悼，表示精神上的支持。日本的"自肃"，不只是群体行为，也可能是个人举动。

Jishiku（自肃）is a type of **mourning** that's common in Japan. It's often translated "self restraint". It means that when you're in mourning you shouldn't celebrate.

After the **tragic** March 11, 2011 Tohoku Earthquake and **Tsunami** the entire nation fell into a long period of jishiku. Spring cherry blossom parties and graduation ceremonies all over the country were cancelled. Even summer festivals were cancelled that year. For example, approximately half of Tokyo's big summer festivals were cancelled **in the name of** jishiku.

Jishiku isn't just about cancelling celebrations. It's

♦ **mourning** [ˈmɔːnɪŋ] n. 哀悼，悲痛
The government announced a day of national mourning for the victims. 政府宣布全国为受害者哀悼一日。

♦ **tragic** [ˈtrædʒɪk] adj. 悲剧的，悲惨的
These tragic incidents have had an immediate effect. 这些悲剧性事件造成的后果即刻显现。

♦ **tsunami** [tsjuːˈnɑːmɪ] n. 海啸
Many countries provided Indonesia with aid after the tsunami. 在海啸过后，许多国家对印度尼西亚提供援助。

♦ **in the name of** 以……的名义
Wholesale slaughter was carried out in the name of progress. 大规模的屠杀在维护进步的名义下进行。

♦ **engage in** 参加，进行，从事
Think hard and engage in conversation. 深入思考问题并且要与人交谈。

also considered bad form to **engage in** self promotion while in mourning. This **encompasses** things like publicity **stunts** and aggressive sales tactics. In fact, it's generally better to **tone down** money making activities altogether while in mourning.

Walking down the shopping streets of Shibuya in the weeks after the 2011 Tohoku disaster you'd immediately notice that shops had softened their sales tactics. The shop staff with **megaphones** were gone. The normally lively sales girls at women's department stores looked **somber**. Sure, lights were turned off to save **electricity** (after the nuclear crisis at Fukushima had created a regional electricity shortage)–but it was also jishiku **at work**.

Some foreign observers have criticized jishiku as **irrational**. After all, the economy needs stimulation after a national tragedy. It should be the time to get out and spend, spend, spend; but the Japanese would consider this to be **in bad taste**.

Jishiku is sometimes misunderstood as being a group activity. For example, if a company executive dies a company may cancel all parties for a month for jishiku. However, jishiku can also be a personal thing.

Ask a friend out for drinks in Japan and they might say they can't because their grandmother died last month. There's no social pressure to engage in jishiku. It's a personal choice. That's why it's usually translated "self restraint".

♦ **encompass** [ɪnˈkʌmpəs]
vt. 包括，包含
The course will encompass physics, chemistry and biology. 课程将包括物理、化学和生物学。

♦ **stunt** [stʌnt] n. 引人注意的花招，噱头
It was all a publicity stunt. 这完全是个宣传噱头。

♦ **tone down**
收敛（行为）；使（调子）缓和
You'd better tone down the more offensive remarks in your article. 你最好把你文章里的攻击性词句写得含蓄些。

♦ **megaphone** [ˈmeɡəfəʊn] n. 扩音器
He often speaks in public with a megaphone. 他常用扩音器当众演说。

♦ **somber** [ˈsɒmbə(r)]
adj. 忧郁的
He had a somber expression on his face. 他面容忧郁。

♦ **electricity** [ɪlekˈtrɪsɪti]
n. 电力
It will produce electricity more cheaply than a nuclear plant. 它的发电成本要比核电站低。

♦ **at work** 起作用
The report suggested that the same trend was at work in politics. 这份报告表明，同一趋势也在影响着政治。

♦ **irrational** [ɪˈræʃənəl]
adj. 不理智的，缺乏理性的
His behaviour was becoming increasingly irrational. 他的行为变得越来越不理智了。

♦ **in bad taste** 粗俗的，品位低的
She dresses in bad taste. 她穿得很俗气。

07 What to Wear with Seasons in South Korea
在韩国，随季而"衣"

韩国的气候四季分明：3—5月是春季，6—8月是夏季，9—11月是秋季，12—2月是冬季。季节更替，人们的衣着也随之而变，这是生活必备的常识。

在衣着上，韩国人的季节意识很强。比如，春天的气温在 **7.1—17.8℃**，由于受到寒流的影响，一直到三月韩国天气通常还是有些寒冷；尽管从三月底开始，气候开始回暖，到了四五月份，日落以后，气温下降也比较明显。因此，韩国的春装以薄外套为主，比较流行的打扮还包括开襟羊毛衫配上丝巾、鸭舌帽，再佩戴一副墨镜，甚是潇洒。

Korea has four **distinct** seasons: spring (March–May), summer (June–August), fall (September–November), and winter (December–February). The changing of seasons also means changing of **attires**. With temperatures varying greatly by season, it is important to dress for the weather. Here are the essential items for each season.

Spring is the **transition** period between winter and summer. Average temperatures in spring **range** between 7.1℃ and 17.8℃. The weather remains chilly in March due to the last **cold snaps**, but begins **warming up** at the end of the month. Still, even in April and May, temperatures may drop after **sunset**. Therefore, a light outerwear is essential in spring. Popular spring fashion items include **cardigans**, scarves, hats and sunglasses.

Summer is the hottest season. Receiving the majority of annual rainfall, it is also the wettest season. In fact, summer begins with the rainy season called "jangma", which generally lasts from mid-June until the end of July. During jangma, umbrellas and **raincoats** are essential.

After jangma, the weather begins heating up, with temperatures rising up to anywhere between 35℃ and 40℃ during daytime. Light clothing, often made with "cooling" fabric, becomes essential for preventing overheating. Popular summer fashion items include light and/or short pants, short-sleeved or **sleeveless** shirts, hats and sunglasses. Applying **sunscreen** is also highly recommended.

Fall, referred to as the season of "cheongomabi", is the transition period between summer and winter. Hu-

♦ **distinct** [dɪsˈtɪŋkt]
adj. 明显的，清楚的
There is a distinct improvement in your spoken English. 你的英语口语有明显的进步。
♦ **attire** [əˈtaɪə]
n. 服装，衣服
♦ **transition** [trænˈzɪʒən]
n. 过渡，转变
Adolescence is the period of transition between childhood and adulthood. 青春期是童年与成年之间的过渡时期。
♦ **range** [reɪndʒ]
vi. 变化
The temperature of this city ranges from 0℃ to 30℃. 这个城市的气温在0℃到30℃之间。
♦ **cold snap** 寒流
♦ **warm up** 变热，变暖和
How long should the engine warm up before we start? 引擎需要预热多久我们才能出发？
♦ **sunset** [ˈsʌnset]
n. 日落（时），薄暮，黄昏
Every evening at sunset the flag was lowered. 每天傍晚日落时都要降旗。
♦ **cardigan** [ˈkɑːdɪɡən]
n. 毛衣，羊毛衫
♦ **raincoat** [ˈreɪnkəʊt]
n. 雨衣
♦ **sleeveless** [ˈsliːvlɪs]
adj. 无袖的
This is the season for sleeveless dresses. 现在是穿无袖连衣裙的时候了。
♦ **sunscreen** [ˈsʌnskriːn]
n. 防晒霜
If you don't wear sunscreen, you are apt to get a sunburn. 如果不擦防晒霜，你很可能会晒黑。

midity **subside** and cold snaps return. As in late-May, the weather in early September is warm. Then, it turns colder and drier starting late-September, **contributing to** the changing of colors of leaves throughout October. An outerwear is essential in fall. Popular fall fashion items include **trench coats** in early to mid-fall, and jackets in mid- to late-fall.

Winter is the coldest season. The northern region, **largely** comprised of Gangwon-do and Gyeonggi-do Provinces as well as Seoul and Incheon Metropolitan Cities, is generally colder than the southern region including Busan Metropolitan City and Jeju Island. After a cold wave passes through the Korean Peninsula, the "sam-han-sa-on", the unique climate pattern of three cold days and four warmer days, repeats. Warm clothing is essential in winter. Popular winter fashion items include winter coats, sweaters, scarves, **shawls**, beanies, gloves, and boots. Naebok or thermal underwear produced with lighter fabric and in trendy design is also worn a lot.

♦ **subside** [səb'saɪd]
vi.（热度/痛苦等）消退，减弱
The pain had subsided during the night. 晚间疼痛已经减轻了。
♦ **contribute to** 导致
Smoking is a major factor contributing to cancer. 吸烟是致癌的一个重要因素。
♦ **trench coat** 风衣
♦ **largely** ['lɑːdʒlɪ]
adv. 主要地，在很大程度上
Social status is largely determined by the occupation of the main breadwinner. 社会地位很大程度上是由家里经济支柱的职业决定的。
♦ **shawl** [ʃɔːl]
n. 围巾，披肩

08 The Value of the Korean Family
重视家庭的韩国人

韩国与中国隔海相望，深受中华文明的影响，儒家思想在韩国根深蒂固。以孔子为代表的儒家思想认为从家庭到社会，直至整个宇宙，人与人之间以及人与社会之间，都有着同样的从属和依赖联系；只有"家和"，方有"邦兴"。即便在今天的韩国社会，家庭的观念和影响依然很大。

不同于西方国家，韩国的家庭关系紧密，成员相互依赖。西方人眼中的独立，在韩国人看来则是孤立和冷漠。孩子们生来就对父母欠下了债，子女们有孝敬和赡养父母的义务，而且如果不能为家族生儿育女，延续香火，也被视为是不孝行为。

In most western countries, individuals should **think of** themselves as separate from their parents and families. The close family ties and dependencies valued so highly in Korea might seem unhealthy to a westerner; a westerner may think a child's sense of **autonomy** necessary to mental health. To Koreans such autonomy is not a virtue. A life in which egos are all autonomous, separate, **discrete** and self-sufficient is too cold, **impersonal**, lonely and inhuman.

Children **incur** a debt to their parents who gave birth to them and raised them. This debt lies behind the idea of filial duty: treating parents respectfully at all times, taking care of them in their old age, mourning them well at proper funerals, and performing ceremonies for them after their deaths. Even fulfilling these duties, however, is not enough to **repay** the debt to one's parents. The full repayment also **entails** having children and maintaining the continuity of the family line. The continuity of the family is thus a biological fact which human society, **in accordance with** natural law, should reflect.

Man's existence does not begin with a **cut-off point** called birth. Nor does it end with death as a **terminus**. A part of him has been in continuous biological existence from his very first **progenitor**. A part of him has been living, in existence, with every one of the **intervening** ancestors. Now he exists as part of that **continuum**. After his death, a part of him continues to exist as long as his biological descendants continue to live.

Koreans incorporate the fact of biological continuity into their family life according to ancient ideas of birth and conception. Mothers traditionally were thought to produce the flesh of their children, and fathers to provide the bones. As bone endures longer than flesh, **kinship** through males was thought more binding than through females. Even today men pass on membership in their clan to their children, while women do not. Thus, although **maternal** second cousins may marry, no one with any degree of kinship through males, no matter how remote, can.

More than Japanese and Chinese, Koreans adhere to traditional Confucian principles of family organization. Confucius (6th century B.C.) and his followers

♦ **think of** 考虑，认为
I like to think of myself as a free spirit. 我愿意把自己看成是个无拘无束的人。

♦ **autonomy** [ɔːˈtɒnəmi]
n. 自治，人身自由

♦ **discrete** [dɪsˈkriːt]
adj. 分离的，不相关联的
Social structures are not discrete objects; they overlap and interweave. 社会结构之间不是离散的，他们相互重叠交织。

♦ **impersonal** [ɪmˈpɜːsənl]
adj. 没有人情味的

♦ **incur** [ɪnˈkɜː]
vt. 承受，承担
Needless to say, we shall refund any expenses you may incur. 不用说，我们将会偿还你所担负的任何费用。

♦ **repay** [rɪ(ː)ˈpeɪ]
vt. 偿还，付还
I feel bound to repay the money I borrowed. 我觉得有责任归还我借的钱。

♦ **entail** [ɪnˈteɪl]
vt. 牵涉，导致；需要
Such a decision would entail a huge political risk. 这样的决定势必带来巨大的政治风险。

♦ **in accordance with** 符合，根据
He acted in accordance with his beliefs. 他按照自己的信念行事。

♦ **cut-off point** 分界点

♦ **terminus** [ˈtɜːmɪnəs]
n. 终点
What time does the train reach the terminus? 火车什么时间到达终点站？

♦ **progenitor** [prəˈdʒenɪtə]
n. 祖先

♦ **intervening** [ˌɪntəˈviːnɪŋ]
adj. 介于中间的，发生于其间的
Little had changed in the intervening years. 这些年间没有发生什么变化。

♦ **continuum** [kənˈtɪnjuəm]
n. 连续体，统一体
The fact is that language varieties exist along a continuum. 实际上语言的变化是连续的。

taught that only a country where family life was harmonious could be peaceful and prosperous. The state, indeed the universe, was the family writ large–with the Chinese emperor, the patriarchal link to **cosmic** forces (through rituals he performed), and the Korean king his younger brother. This conception of the universe ties the warm feelings of attachment and dependence generated within the family to all human relationships. Confucians celebrated this link with a symbol of smaller circles within larger, the ever widening sphere of human relationships from the self, to the family, to society, to the universe.

♦ **kinship** [ˈkɪnʃɪp]
n. 亲属（关系），血缘关系
There is no kinship between them, but they two are very close. 他们两个人没有血缘关系，却非常亲近。

♦ **maternal** [məˈtɔːnl]
adj. 母系的，母亲方面的
Her maternal grandfather was Mayor of Karachi. 她的外公是卡拉奇市的市长。

♦ **cosmic** [ˈkɒzmɪk]
adj. 宇宙的

Chapter 13
节庆趣谈：恋上缤纷节日没商量

01 Lunar New Year in South Korea
韩国的春节

虽然 1 月 1 日是新年的开始，但对于韩国人来说，农历春节的意义更为重大。春节意味着农历正月的第一天，作为除旧迎新的日子，人们在这一天祈愿新的一年幸福平安。春节时，全家人会团聚一堂，共度佳节。

在春节假期开始的前一天和春节假期的第一天，人们为了回家过春节，开始了"民族大移动"。为了能在春节假期期间回老家过年，很多人在很早就提前预订好了火车票或长途汽车票。回故乡过春节的人们可以和全家人团聚一堂，在行完茶礼以后，一家人一起玩尤茨游戏、踢毽子、跳跳板、放风筝、打陀螺等各种传统游戏。

正月初一那天，人们带着新年新气象，在摆着年糕汤、野菜、水果等贡品的祭祀桌前行茶礼。茶礼结束之后，人们会把贡品分着吃掉，此举被称为"饮福"，意指"吃祖先吃过的食物，会得到祖先的福气"。在行完茶礼之后要进行岁拜，这是春节的另一大代表传统。进行完岁拜以后，全家人会在一起分着吃祭祀桌上的贡品。

在分享完美食之后，全家人会在一起玩各种传统游戏。尤茨游戏就是传统民俗游戏中的一种，在投掷完四个半月形的尤茨后，根据结果走步，直到到达终点。该游戏的玩法是，首先将尤茨高高抛起，然后根据平面朝上的尤茨数来走步。三扑一翻为"豚"，两扑两翻为"犬"，一扑三翻为"羊"，全翻为"牛"，全扑为"马"，这些名称都来自于家畜的名字。

Seollal, or Lunar New Year's Day, is **drawing** near. Although January 1 is, in fact, the first day of the year, Seollal, the first day of the lunar calendar, is more meaningful for Koreans. Celebration of the Lunar New Year is believed to have started to **let in** good luck and **ward off** bad spirits all throughout the year. With the old year out and a new one in, people gather at home and sit around with their families and relatives, catching up on what they have been doing.

There is usually a mass **exodus** from major cities the day before the holiday and on the beginning of the Lunar New Year holiday. People usually buy bus or train tickets for their hometowns a month **ahead of** Seollal before tickets **sell out**. On Seollal, traditional folk games **abound**, including yutnori, a traditional board game played with yut sticks,

♦ **draw** [drɔː]
vi.（事件或时间）接近，临近
The next spring's elections are drawing closer. 明年春天的选举即将来临。

♦ **let in** 让……进入
The public are usually let in half an hour before the performance begins. 通常在演出前半小时让观众入场。

♦ **ward off** 避开，挡住
Such a thin padded coat cannot ward off the cold mountain wind. 这么薄的棉衣挡不住山上的寒风。

♦ **exodus** ['eksədəs]
n. 大批离去，成群撤离
The medical system is facing collapse because of an exodus of doctors. 由于医生大批离去，医疗系统面临崩溃。

♦ **ahead of** 提前，在……之前
Mark was out of earshot, walking ahead of

jegichagi (shuttlecock kicking), neolttwigi (seesawing), kite flying, and paengi chigi (top-spinning).

On the very day of Seollal, Korean families perform an **ancestral ritual** called charye, where a table full of various foods, such as tteokguk (rice-cake soup), vegetables, and fruits, is prepared. The ancestral rite is an important part of Seollal to pay respect to ancestors, based on Confucianism. After the ancestral ritual, they share the food on the table, which is called eumbok. They hope that the virtues of their ancestors will be **passed on t**o themselves by doing eumbok.

After charye, people also perform sebae to their elders by going down on both knees and bowing deep toward the floor, and wishing them blessings for the New Year. Then, the elders reward the bows with **fresh** banknotes, called sebaedon, and word of wishes, in hopes that their young loved ones will make lots of money and achieve their goals in the coming year. After performing sebae, they share the food placed on the table, followed by many games.

Among a variety of traditional games enjoyed on Seollal, yutnori is played with four half moon-shaped yut sticks being cast to determine how far a token (yut mal) can **advance**. The rule of this traditional game is that yut mals are moved according to the counting of the yut sticks whose flat sides face **upwards** and those whose round sides are up. Each combination has a name. One stick over (with its flat side up) and three sticks up (with their round sides up) are called do. Two sticks up and two sticks over are called gae. One stick up and three sticks over are called geol. All sticks over is called yut, while all sticks up is called mo. The names of "do, gae, geol, yut, and mo" are actually named after animals; do refers to pig, gae to dog, geol to sheep, yut to cow, and mo to horse.

---

them. 马克走在前面，听不见他们的声音。

♦ **sell out** 卖光，脱销
Football games often sell out well in advance. 足球比赛经常在开赛前很久票就已经售光了。

♦ **abound** [ə'baʊnd]
vi. 非常多，大量存在
Examples abound in modern texts. 在现代的文章中这类例子不胜枚举。

♦ **ancestral ritual** 祭祖仪式

♦ **pass on** 传递
The late Earl passed on much of his fortune to his daughter. 已故伯爵将他的大部分财产传给了女儿。

♦ **fresh** [freʃ]
adj. 崭新的

♦ **advance** [əd'vɑːns]
vi. 前进
The deep mud negatived all the efforts to advance. 这路太泥泞使所有前进的努力都白费劲。

♦ **upwards** ['ʌpwədz]
adv. 向上地
Hunter nodded again and gazed upwards in fear. 亨特又点了点头，满眼恐惧地朝上望去。

---

02 Dano: a Festival of Health
韩国端午节：为健康祈福

同中国一样，韩国的端午节也在每年农历的五月初五。韩国人将"端午"称为"上日"，意为神的日子。过去韩国人家家户户都会在端午节当天摆上白白的散发着艾草和糯米香味的

艾子糕，用菖蒲汤洗头求吉利，喝菖蒲水以辟邪。人们还会穿着传统服装参加祭祀、演出和运动会，观看荡秋千和摔跤比赛。

2005年11月，韩国"江陵端午祭"被联合国教科文组织宣布为"人类口头和非物质遗产代表作"。这是目前韩国保存比较完整的传统节日习俗之一，通常于农历4月初开始，持续一个月之久。每年都有百万游客从四面八方前往江陵，参加"江陵端午祭"活动，感受端午文化。

In Korea, there are two methods to determine the date, by using the **solar** calendar or the lunar **calendar**; thus, the dates on the solar calendar are different from the dates on the lunar calendar. Most of the traditional Korean holidays are dated on the lunar calendar, and an odd numbered day in the same odd numbered month has been thought to be a lucky day. Therefore, the 1st of January, the 3rd of March, the 5th of May, the 7th of July, the 9th of September, etc. on the lunar calendar have been chosen to be traditional holidays.

Particularly, the 5th day of May on the lunar calendar is believed to be the most **auspicious** day because the **celestial** body of the universe converges on this date so that all the energies of nature are one. It is also believed that it is easy for young people to fall in love **passionately** on the day of Dano, the 5th day of May on the lunar calendar. As a result, young women have enjoyed swinging beautifully in traditional Korean dresses to attract young men's attention. **Likewise**, men have participated in Ssireum (traditional Korean wrestling) to show their **robustness** and **prowess**.

In addition, the 5th month on the lunar calendar, the month of Dano, is around the time of the rainy season in Korea when bad diseases were easily spread in the olden days. Therefore, traditional customs to prevent various **misfortunes** have been passed down. Following **superstitious** customs of Dano for preventing evil spirits and misfortunes, women wash their hair in water **infused** with

♦ **solar** [ˈsəulə]
adj. 太阳的，根据太阳决定或测定的
♦ **calendar** [ˈkælɪndə] n. 日历
♦ **auspicious** [ɔːsˈpɪʃəs]
adj. 吉利的，吉祥的
His career as a playwright had an auspicious start. 他的剧作家生涯有了一个好的开头。
♦ **celestial** [sɪˈlestjəl]
adj. 天的，天空的
celestial body 天体
♦ **passionately** [ˈpæʃənɪtlɪ]
adv. 热情地，激昂地
She could hate as passionately as she could love. 她能恨得咬牙切齿，也能爱得一往情深。
♦ **likewise** [ˈlaɪkˌwaɪz]
adv. 同样地
These requests are ignored; his requests for rent are likewise sometimes ignored. 这些要求被置之不理，他关于支付租金的要求有时也同样未被理睬。
♦ **robustness** [rəˈbʌstnɪs] n. 健壮
♦ **prowess** [ˈpraʊɪs]
n. 英勇，高超技艺
He was famous for his prowess as an athlete. 他作为一名运动员以技艺高超而著称。
♦ **misfortune** [mɪsˈfɔːtʃən]
n. 厄运，不幸
She seemed to enjoy the misfortunes of others. 她似乎喜欢幸灾乐祸。
♦ **superstitious** [ˌsjuːpəˈstɪʃəs]
adj. 迷信的
Jean was extremely superstitious and believed the colour green brought bad luck.

irises as well as wear red or blue dresses. For men, they put the roots of irises into the waist of their trousers.

In the olden times, children took baths and adults **splashed** water on their backs to avoid the summer heat on the day of Dano. Noblemen were satisfied only when they put their feet into a water **jar** to maintain their dignity. Dano was a day to promote health and well-being right before **summertime**; as a result, on this day, there is a traditional custom of giving a folding fan to close **acquaintances** as a present, which means hoping for a healthy, cool summer.

Furthermore, ancestors' main entertainments on the day of Dano were swinging which was designated for women and wrestling which was designated for men. They also enjoyed a mask dance, a dance with a lion's mask, and a mask drama. Because Dano is a representative traditional holiday just like Korean New Year's Day, ancestors used to wear hanboks and pray for a good harvest on the day of Dano.

琼非常迷信，认为绿色会带来厄运。

♦ **infuse** [ɪnˈfjuːz]
vi. 浸泡，充满
Add the tea leaves and leave to infuse for five minutes. 放进茶叶，浸泡5分钟。

♦ **iris** [ˈaɪərɪs]
n. 鸢尾（花）

♦ **splash** [splæʃ]
vt. 泼洒（水等），使（液体）溅起
He closed his eyes tight, and splashed the water on his face. 他紧闭双眼，将水泼在自己脸上。

♦ **jar** [dʒɑː] n. 罐子，缸

♦ **summertime** [ˈsʌmətaɪm]
n. 夏季，夏天
Even in the summertime we might be struck by blizzards. 甚至在夏天，我们也可能受到暴风雪的袭击。

♦ **acquaintance** [əˈkweɪntəns]
n. 相识的人，熟人
I have a large circle of friends and acquaintances engaged in photography. 我在摄影界交游甚广。

03 Korean Thanksgiving Day
秋夕节：韩国的感恩节

正如美国人庆祝感恩节，韩国人则庆祝秋夕节，这一天，家人团聚，满怀感恩，向祖先表达敬意。这是个喜庆的节日，伴有传统戏剧演出，舞蹈表演，还有各种游戏和丰盛的食物。

时间：秋夕节持续三天，包括秋夕日和前后各一天，最早可追溯到古代，每当阴历八月十五，正是月亮又圆又亮的时候。按照我们所熟知的格雷戈里历，有时在9月或10月份。

饮食：庆祝节日最重要的食物之一便是松糕，即在米糕里包上芝麻，大豆和其他传统佐料。糕点染成粉红，黄色，葱绿，或者保持白色，在下面铺上一层松针后蒸熟，有了松针，松糕独具风味。

羌羌水月来：一种传统朝鲜族舞蹈，孩子或妇女们身着传统丝质韩服，围成一圈跳舞。先由一人唱歌，然后舞者手拉手转动，逐渐变换队形。移动时，两人用手搭桥，其中一人从下面钻过。最终，一圈人缠绕得弯弯曲曲，或者分成一些小圈。

游戏：游戏大多跟秋夕节相关，如韩式摔跤——相扑，选出最强壮的男人，还有射箭和

拔河比赛。有时也会有武术和走钢丝表演。荡秋千，看谁荡得最高。再有，用跷跷板把人弹射起来，在空中表演翻筋斗或者其他特技。

Often compared to the American Thanksgiving, the **Chuseok Festival** in Korea brings families together to celebrate and be thankful and to express respect for their ancestors. The festival is a time of happiness, with traditional plays, dancing, games and an **abundance** of food. It is celebrated in South Korea with enthusiasm and great **fanfare**. In North Korea, the celebration is low key due to governmental restrictions on travel and economic hardship.

Timing

The Chuseok Festival lasts for three days, on Chuseok Day and the days before and after. Originally called Hangawi, the celebration **dates back to** ancient times and takes place on the 15th day of the eighth lunar month when the moon is full and bright. This falls sometime in September or October on our more familiar **Gregorian calendar**.

Festival Foods

One of the most important foods in the Chuseok celebration is **songpyeon**, a rice cake formed to hold sesame seeds, beans and other traditional ingredients. The small cakes are **tinted** pink, yellow or pale green, or are left white and steamed while sitting on a layer of pine needles. This gives the songpyeon a distinctive flavor.

Ganggangsullae

The traditional Korean dance, the **Ganggangsullae**, is performed by children or by women in traditional silk clothing called **Hanbok**. The dance begins in a circle to singing by a specially appointed singer. The dancers move in a circle while holding hands and slowly form other shapes as the dance progresses. One movement involves

♦ **Chuseok Festival**
（韩国）秋夕节或秋祭节，每年阴历八月十五日。

♦ **abundance** [əˈbʌndəns]
n. 丰富，充裕，大量
in abundance
Oil is found in abundance here. 这里发现大量石油。

♦ **fanfare** [ˈfænfeə]
n. 热闹
The company was privatised with a fanfare of publicity. 公司的私有化搞得沸沸扬扬。

♦ **date back to**
从……时就有，回溯到，远在……（年代）
The marathon can date back to the 5th century B.C. 马拉松可以追溯到公元前5世纪。

♦ **Gregorian calendar**
格里历，是现行国际通行的历法，属于阳历的一种，通称阳历，其前身是奥古斯都历。

♦ **Songpyeon**
松糕，韩国传统的节庆点心，是一种半月形的糯米糕点。

♦ **tint** [tɪnt]
vt. 染，给……着色

♦ **Ganggangsullae**
羌羌水月来，韩国中秋游戏，数十名妇女手拉手围成圈，一边唱着羌羌水月来歌谣，一边绕圈转的游戏。

♦ **Hanbok**
n. 韩服，韩国传统服饰，特色是设计简单、颜色艳丽和无口袋

♦ **file** [faɪl]
vi. 列队行进

♦ **Ssireum** 相扑，韩式摔跤

♦ **see-saw**
n. 跷跷板

♦ **catapult** [ˈkætəpʌlt]
vt. 弹起，射出，猛投，使……快速移动

two dancers who make a bridge with their hands while the dancers **file** through underneath. The circle of dancers sometimes becomes serpentine or separates into several smaller circles.

She was catapult to stardom by the success of her first record. 她因为第一张唱片的成功一举成名。

Games

Many games are associated with the Chuseok celebration. Wrestling matches called **Ssireum** are held to determine the strongest man. Participants take part in archery contests and tug-of-war games. Martial arts displays and tightrope walking are a part of some celebrations. A swinging game involves competition to see who swings the highest. Another game uses a special **see-saw** to **catapult** a jumper who then turns somersaults or performs other tricks while in the air.

04 Korea's Traditional Rituals on Chuseok
秋夕节，韩国人还做什么

月光美丽的夜晚，秋夕临近。秋夕是指阴历的八月十五，也指中秋的月亮。韩国人之所以重视月亮的大小与模样，是因为在农耕社会，满月象征着丰收与富饶。农事与一年的生计息息相关，五谷成熟的秋夕的到来，对农耕人来说是最大的喜悦与幸福。人们恳切地希望一整年都可以像秋夕一样富足地生活。

进入产业化社会以后，工业成为了生计的中心，过去与农事相关的岁时风俗逐渐弱化，传统色彩也有所褪色。然而，制作松饼、为祖上准备节日茶礼，为祖上扫墓，在秋夕到来之前前往祖上的墓地进行"伐草"，将一夏天生长的茂盛的杂菜拔掉，为祖上祭祀的传统已经深入到了社会深处。

韩国每个地区和家庭的祭祀方式与在祭祀时供奉的食物都不太相同。但祭祀基本上都在大厅或里屋进行，正月初一的时候人们向祖上供奉年糕汤，秋夕的时候供奉松饼，此外还会准备水果、脯、汤、酒酿、烤鱼串、烤肉串、野菜与饼等。

整理墓地周围的杂草，进行"伐草"的目的是为了保持古老墓地的相对洁净。韩国有一句古话叫做，"秋夕前不焚烧杂草的话，祖上会在过节时带着杂草来捣乱"，可见韩国人对秋夕前进行伐草的重视。

Chuseok is just around the corner and Koreans are waiting for the brightest daytime full moon of the year. Chuseok, one of the two biggest holidays in Korea, falls on August 15 on the lunar calendar and the very middle day of fall. The reason behind Koreans' strong attention to the Moon came from the old traditional **lifecycle** that relied heavily on the size and shape of the Moon in planning when to start and end **agricultural** work each year. Koreans especially welcomed Chuseok's full moon, which comes up in the harvest season bringing **bountiful** ripe fruit and grains.

The traditional seasonal customs have faded away into history since the **industrialization** of the nation, but the major duties, including making songpyeon, performing ancestral rites, and visiting ancestors' graves before Chuseok, still remain.

The ritual ceremony varies **depending on** region and family. However, the general rule is that the main food–rice cake soup for Seollal (the first day of the lunar calendar) and songpyeon for Chuseok–is prepared with some side dishes such as freshly harvested fruit, soup, beef jerky, sikhye (sweet rice drink), seasoned vegetables, and **pancakes**. Early in the morning of Chuseok, the oldest son makes a deep bow at the food arranged on a table and offers a glass of alcoholic **beverage** and then a bowl of rice to ancestors is presented on the table. After the ritual performer marks the cross on the rice and leaves a spoon **embedded** in the rice at a 45-degree angle, everybody else behind bows together. After a while, the soup will be replaced with nureungji (scorched-rice water) which is mixed with three spoons of rice. The second and third sons, one by one, take a step forward to bow, and everyone else bows at once to finish the ritual.

After the morning ritual ceremony, Koreans visit family graves to pay their respects to their ancestors. The ceremonial custom named Seungmyo seemed to have formed based on traditional Confucian ideas of worshipping and honoring one's ancestors.

Another important **customs** is Beolcho, an action of clearing weeds and **tidying up** around the gravesites one or two weeks ahead of Chuseok. Modern Koreans lost many of the traditional ritual steps and perform both Seungmyo

◆ **lifecycle** [ˌæɡrɪˈkʌltʃərəl]
n. 生命周期
Some insects as bee and butterfly have 4 periods in their lifecycle. 有些昆虫，像蜜蜂、蝴蝶，一生中有4个阶段。

◆ **agricultural** [ˌæɡrɪˈkʌltʃərəl]
adj. 农业的，耕种的
The drought has severely disrupted agricultural production. 旱灾已严重影响了农业生产。

◆ **bountiful** [ˈbaʊntɪfʊl]
adj. 丰富的，大量的
The land is bountiful and no one starves. 这片土地物产丰富，没有人挨饿。

◆ **industrialization**
[ɪnˌdʌstrɪəlaɪˈzeɪʃn]
n. 工业化
We can't hold out against industrialization any longer. 我们不能再拒绝工业化了。

◆ **depend on** 依据，根据
Those risk models are regularly updated depending on the economic environment. 这些风险模型会根据经济环境定期更新。

◆ **pancake** [ˈpænkeɪk]
n. 烙饼，薄煎饼
Spread some of the filling over each pancake. 在每个薄煎饼上摊上一些馅。

◆ **beverage** [ˈbevərɪdʒ]
n. 饮料
Coffee is a fragrant beverage. 咖啡是一种香味浓郁的饮料。

◆ **embed** [ɪmˈbed]
vt. 把……嵌入，插在
They used to kind of embed it in the glass. 他们往往把它嵌在玻璃里。

◆ **custom** [ˈkʌstəm]
n. 风俗，习俗
This custom was still current in the late 1960s. 这种习俗在20世纪60年代末仍然很普遍。

◆ **tidy up** 整理，收拾
We should tidy up the place before we move in.

and Beolcho on Chuseok day, but there is an old saying that "Ancestors will come covered with **messy** bushes to eat the food offerings unless descendents cleared the gravesites in advance," reflecting Korean's devotion to ancestors.

在我们搬进去之前应该先把那地方收拾一下。

♦ **messy** ['mesɪ]
adj. 凌乱的，肮脏的
The house was always messy. 这房子总是乱糟糟的。

---

05 Christmas in Korea
圣诞节在韩国

以中国儒学与大乘佛教为其主要传统文化与宗教的韩国，天主教传入的历史有两百年，而新教传入只有一百年。尽管如此，韩国传统文化却在很大程度上受到了基督教的影响。可以说，韩国的圣诞节是比起欧美国家而言更具有宗教意味的圣诞节。

在圣诞夜，韩国的年青教徒们会举行盛装游行庆祝节日。根据传统，屋子的主人必须开门聆听他们的歌唱，并且邀请他们进屋去喝点酒吃点东西。传统的圣诞餐是在教堂里享用的。但是，没有火鸡，也没有烤火腿，有的只是米饭、一种类似于卷心菜的蔬菜，还有蜜柑和甜饼。

然而，圣诞节早已不是宗教的独宠，普通韩国民众也会进行各种方式庆祝圣诞节。比如，商店会悬挂节日装饰，一般家庭里也装饰圣诞树，人们会交换礼物等等。此外，圣诞老人也非常受孩子们的欢迎。

Christianity is relatively new to Asia, but today about 30% of the South Korean population is Christian. Christmas (Sung Tan Jul) is celebrated by Christian families and is also a public holiday (even though Korea is officially Buddhist). Korea is the only East Asian country to **recognize** Christmas as a national holiday.

Korean Christians celebrate Christmas similar to the way it's celebrated in the West, but since it's **primarily** a religious holiday in Korea, there is **considerably** less **fanfare** and presents. Some families do put up Christmas trees, people exchange presents, and stores do put up holiday decorations, but the **festivities** start much closer to Christ-

♦ **Christianity** [ˌkrɪstɪˈænɪtɪ]
n. 基督教

♦ **recognize** ['rekəgnaɪz]
vt. (正式) 承认，认可
Most doctors appear to recognize homeopathy as a legitimate form of medicine. 大多数医生似乎都接受顺势疗法是一种合理的医疗手段。

♦ **primarily** ['praɪmərɪlɪ]
adv. 首先；首要地，主要地
Public order is primarily an urban problem. 社会治安主要是城市的问题。

♦ **considerably** [kənˈsɪdərəbəlɪ]
adv. 相当，非常，颇
The river widens considerably as it begins to turn east. 河流转向东流时河道大幅度变宽。

♦ **fanfare** [ˈfænfeə]
n. 热闹的庆祝或大张旗鼓的宣传，炫耀
The company was privatised with a fanfare of publicity. 公司的私有化搞得沸沸扬扬。

♦ **festivity** [fesˈtɪvɪtɪ]
n. 欢庆，庆祝活动，庆典
He entered the village almost unobserved amid the general festivity. 在一片喜庆的

mas day. Families may attend mass or a church service on Christmas Eve or Christmas day (or both), and **caroling** parties are popular for young Christians on Christmas Eve.

Grandpa Santa is popular with kids in Korea (Santa Harabujee) and he wears either a red or blue santa suit. Kids know him as a happy grandfather figure who gives out presents, and stores employ Santas to greet shoppers and **hand out** chocolate and candies. People in Korea usually exchange presents on Christmas Eve and instead of piles of presents, one present (or a gift of money) is **customary**.

Some families celebrate Christmas with meals and gatherings at homes, but Koreans also celebrate Christmas by going out. Restaurants are busy on Christmas, as it is considered a romantic holiday for couples, and theme parks and shows have special Christmas events. Many younger people celebrate and **party** on Christmas with friends and spend New Year's Day with their families (the **reverse** to Christmas/New Year's in the West). For non-Christian Koreans, Christmas is a popular shopping day.

气氛中，他进村时几乎没有人注意到。

♦ **carol** [ˈkærəl]
vi. 欢乐地唱；唱圣诞颂歌
The children went carolling during the week before Christmas. 在圣诞节前的一周，孩子们去唱圣诞颂歌。

♦ **Grandpa Santa** 圣诞老人

♦ **hand out** 分发，拿出
One of my jobs was to hand out the prizes. 我的职责之一是分发奖品。

♦ **customary** [ˈkʌstəməri]
adj. 习惯的，通常的，照惯例的
The king carried himself with his customary elegance. 国王保持着一贯的温文尔雅。

♦ **party** [ˈpɑːti]
vi. 举行或参加社交聚会

♦ **reverse** [rɪˈvɜːs]
n. 相反，反向
Amis tells the story in reverse, from the moment the man passes away. 埃米斯以倒叙的方式讲述了这个故事，从这个男人逝世的时候开始讲起。

06 Celebrations of the Japanese New Year
日本人过新年

日本新年指的是公历1月1日至1月3日，相当于其他东亚地区的春节，是一年当中最重要的节日。明治维新之前日本也使用夏历修改而来的阴阳历计年，但1873年日本改采用格里历之后，除冲绳县、鹿儿岛县的奄美诸岛等地外，大多数地方不庆祝旧正月。普通的企业在新年期间一般都休息。

过年之前除了要打扫房内，房子外面也会装饰有松、竹、梅等季节性植物。为了过一个"干干净净"的新年，无论是公司还是普通民众，都会在新年到来之前结清各种账目，还会举办忘年会忘掉一年中的不快。有意思的是，在除夕之夜，日本人大都在观看一档年度综艺节目——"红白歌会"。新年这一天，孩子们会收到长辈的红包。当然，新年也是日本人亲朋相聚的日子，又是一个崭新的开始。

Unlike most other Asian countries which mark the Lunar New Year, Japan celebrates the New Year on January 1, western-style. But the Japanese have different traditions to usher in each year. The start of the New Year in Japan is a time of cleaning the home and spirit, and reconnecting with family and friends.

Until the late 1800s, Japan marked the start of each year on the Chinese lunar calendar, like most other Asian countries. But in 1873, the country **adopted** the **Gregorian calendar**, making January 1 "Oshogatsu", or New Year's Day.

In the days **leading up to** New Year's Day, people have lots of things to do. Because the New Year is considered a clean start for everyone, Japanese try to **settle** all accounts, pay their **debts** and complete any unfinished projects, then **throw parties** leading up to the holiday to forget the year that's ending. Besides, homes are cleaned **in preparation for** the fresh year. The outside of homes are decorated with seasonal ornaments of bamboo, pine, and **plum**. And it's also **customary** for Japanese to send special New Year's postcards to each other, the way Americans send Christmas cards.

The day before New Year's Day is called "Omisoka", and going from party to party and toasting a **countdown** at midnight isn't the main event. Instead, much of the country sits in front of TV sets, watching one of the country's most popular annual shows.

In 1951, a few years after World War II, Japan's public broadcasting company NHK began **airing** an annual New Year's Eve music show called "Kohaku Uta Gassen" ("Red and White Battle of Songs"), a singing contest between the country's most popular men and women singers. Men are the white team and women are the red team, and they take turns singing pop songs. The audience and celebrity **judges** decide which team won the year's competition,

♦ **adopt** [əˈdɒpt]
vt. 采用，采取
The factories have adopted the newest modern technology. 那几家工厂采用了现代的最新技术。

♦ **Gregorian calendar**
格里历，阳历，公历

♦ **lead up to**
（时间）临近，紧挨在……之前

♦ **settle** [ˈsetl]
vt. 付清（欠款），结算（账单）
We have to settle the gas bill. 我们得付煤气费。

♦ **debt** [det] n. 债务
be in someone's debt 欠某人人情债；受某人的恩惠
We were poor but we never got into debt. 我们穷是穷，但从不负债。

♦ **throw parties** 举办派对

♦ **in preparation for**
为……准备，作为……的准备
They are collecting information in preparation for the day when the two sides sit down and talk. 他们正在收集情报，为双方坐下来谈判的那一天做准备。

♦ **plum** [plʌm]
n. 李子

♦ **customary** [ˈkʌstəməri]
adj. 习惯的，惯常的
He makes his customary visit every week. 他每星期都按照惯例造访一次。

♦ **countdown** [ˈkaʊntˌdaʊn]
n. 倒数读秒，倒计时；大事临近的时期
The director began the countdown ten seconds before the broadcast. 距离开播还有十秒，导播开始倒读数。

♦ **air** [eə]
vt. 播送，广播
Tonight this channel will air a documentary called Democracy in Action. 今晚该频道将播放一部名为《民主进行时》的纪录片。

♦ **judge** [dʒʌdʒ]

which ends just before midnight.

The show began on radio, but is now broadcast on TV. For years, the show was the most popular program in the country. "Kohaku", as it's called, is not as popular today, but it's still a **highlight** of the year, and the biggest music program on Japanese television.

New Year's Day is called "Oshogatsu", and lasts three days from January 1 through 3. Instead of spending January 1 eating pizza and watching college football, Japanese enjoy the company of family and friends, host a New Year's feast and over the period of three days, visit other family and friends and make their Hatsumode, first visit to a shrine or temple, if they weren't there for the midnight bell ringing. Japanese children traditionally receive money (sometimes as much as $100 or more) in a custom called "Otoshidama", in small ceremonial **envelopes**. Children also play traditional New Year's games with toys including tops and kites.

New Year in Japan is a time for celebration as it is worldwide, but it's also a time for reflection and appreciation for one's close circle of family and friends. It's also a time for a fresh start and a time to put the past year behind and look ahead.

n. 评判员，评审
♦ **highlight** ['haɪlaɪt]
n. 最重要的事情，最精彩的部分
Recorded highlights of today's big football game will be shown after the news. 今天足球大赛最精彩场面的录像镜头将在新闻之后播出。
♦ **envelope** ['envɪləup]
n. 信封，封皮
Write the address on the envelope. 请将地址写在信封上。

07 Hatsumode: First Visit to a Shrine of the Year
新年"初诣"：神社首拜

日语中"初诣"是指日本人在新年第一天到神社参拜的习俗。其中，"初"表示第一次，"诣"表示"参加"或者"拜访神社"。

每当除夕结束，迎来新年，人们纷纷踏着午夜的钟声前往神社参拜。其实"初诣"并没有除夕严肃，反而更显轻快。年轻人可以借此溜出去玩耍，直到深夜；许多日本民众，尤其是妇女儿童，穿着色彩斑斓的和服，甚是赏心悦目。当然也有人选择新年前三天之外的其他时间拜访神社，还有捐钱、撞钟等等活动，以祈求一年的顺利和兴旺。

Hatsumode（初诣）is the first shrine visit of the New Year. The first character 初 means "first", and the second character 诣 means "attend" or "visit a shrine".

Most of Japanese are **off work** from December 29 until January 3rd, but people often visit shrines right after midnight when the New Year's Eve turns the New Year's Day. Visiting shrine at midnight is also a good excuse for young people who live with their parents to go out by themselves so late in the evening.

In contrast to New Year's Eve, the atmosphere of hatsumode is light and **festive**. For the visitor, hatsumode is a chance to see many Japanese, especially women and children, fully **decked out** in colorful kimono.

Many visit on the first, second, or third day of the year. Visitors offer some change (or bills) and ring the bell at the main shrine building, then pray and wish for a peaceful and **prosperous** new year. There are often long lines at major shrines throughout Japan. Until the 19th century, it was normal to visit the local Shinto Shrine which protected the family, called Ujigami (氏神), but nowadays it is normal to visit a famous, powerful Shinto Shrine. Most people visit the Meiji Jingu Shrine (have millions of visitors over the three days) during this time with the next largest showing at the kawasaki Haishi Temple in Kanagawa Prefecture.

Generally, whishes for the New Year are made, new omamori (**charms**) are bought, and the old ones are returned to the shrine so they can be burned. There are various kinds of them, which gives you good luck in studying, health, love, etc.

A common custom during hatsumode is to buy a written omikuji (means **oracle**). If your omikuji predicts bad luck you can tie it onto a tree on the shrine grounds, in the hope that its prediction will not **come true**. The omikuji goes into detail, and tells you how you will do in various areas in your life, such and business and love, for that year. Often a good-luck charm comes with the omikuji when you buy it, that is believed to **summon** good luck and money your way.

♦ **off work** 休班，停工
She's been off work since Tuesday. 星期二以来她一直没上班。

♦ **in contrast to** 比之下，与……相比
In contrast to his usual manner, Jackson began quietly, in an almost benevolent voice. 杰克逊一反他往常的作风，平和地、用一种几乎是与人为善的声音开始讲话。

♦ **festive** ['festɪv]
dj. 喜庆的，欢乐的
The whole town is in festive mood. 全城喜气洋洋。

♦ **deck out** 扮，妆饰
Lots of pubs like to deck themselves out with flowers in summer.
夏日里有许多酒吧喜欢用鲜花来装饰店面。

♦ **prosperous** ['prɒspərəs]
adj. 荣的，富裕的
It used to be a very prosperous town. 这个城镇过去很繁荣。

♦ **charm** [tʃɑːm]
n. 护身符，符咒

♦ **oracle** ['ɒrəkl]
n. 神谕，神的指示
They sought the woods, and revolved the oracle in their minds. 他们躲进树林，苦苦思索着神谕的含义。

♦ **come true** 应验，成真；实现
His wish to visit China has at last come true. 他要访华的愿望终于实现了。

♦ **summon** ['sʌmən]
vt. 召唤；传唤，传讯
The oddest events will summon up memories. 那些非常稀奇古怪的事情会唤起人们的记忆。

08 Coming-of-Age-Day in Japan
在日本过成人礼

每年，日本都会庆祝公共假日——成人节。从这天起，年轻人获得权投票，可以吸烟、

买酒等，得到成年人所有的权利和义务；政府在这天还专门举行成人仪式。

对于日本人，20岁是人生的一大转折点，举办仪式是为了鼓励刚刚成年的年轻人学会独立自主的生活。2000年之前，成人节在1月15日举行；从2000年起，改在每年1月的第二个星期一。

20岁的成人大多会参加典礼，通常包括演讲等活动；由于存在代沟，最近几年的仪式上时有骚乱，比如在演讲进行时打电话、燃放烟火，甚至质问市长或致辞嘉宾。对此，一些地方政府缩短演讲时间，让仪式更有趣味，千叶县还直接把仪式搬到了迪尼斯乐园。实际上，过去几年关于成人节的报道越来越关注发生的骚乱事件。当然，媒体每年都会一贯地关注逐年减少的参加典礼的人数；随着出生率持续下降，日本人口预计在接下来的三到五年达到最多，随后开始减少。

日本成人节已有数世纪的历史。在江户时代（1603—1868），男子15岁成年，剪掉额发，女子则在13岁左右，将牙齿染黑。直到1876年，日本政府才把法定成年年龄定在20岁。

成人节也是摄影的好机会。男子一般穿着西装（当然会有例外）；女子大都穿上传统振袖和服（这种和服，设计精致，袖子加长），这差不多是未婚女子穿的最正式的服装了，他们在节日里穿上振袖，开启成人生活。

On Sunday 14th of January, Japan celebrated a public holiday called "Seiji-no-hi" (Coming-of-Age Day). Although young adults reach the legal age on their 20th birthday and from there on **are entitled to** vote, allowed to smoke **tobacco**, purchase **alcohol** etc, and have all of the rights and responsibilities of adulthood, local governments hold special ceremonies on "Seiji-no-hi" to mark the **rite** of passage.

The age of 20 is a big **turning point** for Japanese people. The ceremonies are supposed to encourage those who have newly entered adulthood to become **self-reliant** members of society. (The holiday used to be on January 15, but in 2000 it was moved to the second Monday of the month.)

Most 20 year olds **attend the ceremonies**, which usually include speeches etc, however in recent years the generation gap has been creating some **disturbances**. These have ranged from talking on cellphones to letting off fireworks during the speeches, and **heckling** the mayor or

♦ **be entitled to**
被赋予……的权利或资格；获得……的题名或称号
You will be entitled to your pension when you reach 65. 你到65岁就有资格享受养老金了。

♦ **tobacco** [tə'bækəʊ]
n. 烟草（制品）；抽烟
I gave up tobacco. 我戒烟了。

♦ **alcohol** ['ælkəhɒl]
n. 酒，酒精

♦ **rite** [raɪt]
n. 典礼，仪式
the funeral/burial rite 丧礼/葬礼 the rite of baptism 洗礼仪式

♦ **turning point**
转折点，转机，关键时刻
Life is one long curve, full of turning points. 人生犹如一条长长的曲线充满转折。

♦ **self-reliant** [selfrɪ'laɪənt]
adj. 独立的，自力更生的，自食其力的
self-reliant innovation 自主创新

guest speaker. Some local governments have responded by shortening the speeches and making the ceremony more fun (in some cases including entertainment and even bingo games and karaoke). A city in Chiba **prefecture** moved the ceremony to Disneyland. In fact the evening news coverage of the holiday during the past few years has tended to **concentrate more and more upon** the disturbances.

The only other thing consistently **highlighted** in the news each year is the steadily falling number of participants each year. Japan's birthrate is continuing to fall and the population is expected to peak during the next 3-5 years before beginning its decline.

Coming of Age ceremonies have been held in Japan for centuries. During the Edo period (1603-1868) boys became adults at around the age of 15 (and **had their forelocks cropped off**), girls became adults when they turned 13 or so (and had their teeth dyed black). It wasn't until 1876 that the government of Japan decided to set the legal age of adulthood to 20 years.

Seijin-no-hi is a good photo opportunity. The young men generally wear suits (some exceptions of course), but the majority of young women choose to wear traditional **furisode**. The furisode is a special type of kimono with extended sleeves and elaborate designs. For unmarried women, this is probably the most formal **attire** they can wear before marriage, and so many of them wear it to the event to mark the start of their adult life.

♦ **attend the ceremonies**
参加典礼

♦ **disturbance** [dɪsˈtɔːbəns]
n. 骚乱，打扰
quiet a disturbance 平息骚乱 without disturbance 不受干扰地

♦ **heckle** [ˈhekl]
vt. 诘问，责问，激烈质问，集中质问

♦ **prefecture** [ˈpriːfektjʊə]
n. 辖区，（法国）省，（日本）县

♦ **concentrate upon**
集中在，专心于，全神贯注于
I can't concentrate on my work when I'm tired. 我累了就无法集中精力工作。

♦ **highlight** [ˈhaɪlaɪt]
vt. 加亮，使显著，使突出，强调

♦ **have one's forelocks cropped off**
将额发剪掉 基本结构：to have sth. done 已经做完某事；让事情发生，使某人做某事

♦ **furisode**
振袖和服（也称宽袖），日本女子婚前穿着的传统和服。

♦ **attire** [əˈtaɪə]
n. 服装

---

09 A New Holiday for Overworked Japanese
日本登山节：放下工作，亲近自然

日本参院全体会议 5 月 23 日通过《假日法》修正案，将每年的 8 月 11 日定为法定假日"山之日"，将自 2016 年起实施。在日本，法定假日由《假日法》规定。上一次修改《假日法》是在 2005 年，当时分别设定 4 月 29 日和 5 月 4 日为"昭和日"和"绿之日"。加上山之日，日本每年的法定假日总天数将增至 16 天。据了解，此次制定修正案的目的是"得到亲近大山的机会，感谢大山带来的恩惠"，并且还蕴含着将富饶的大自然完整地传承给子孙后代的美好期冀。

日本政府对于国民的过渡工作很是担心，希望民众能够平衡找工作和生活。然而公司职员们似乎总是会忽视带薪休假的权利。虽然假日设定的初衷是好的，但是由于日本国民通常只在公共假日才会休班，也会造成交通阻塞、宾馆和航班价格飞涨等一系列社会问题。对此，日本政府也在寻找其他解决方法。

On May 23, 2014, the Diet of Japan passed a new law establishing Mountain Day as August 11, although it won't officially start until 2016. Japan already has several other holidays based on nature, including those celebrating the spring and fall **equinox**. Adding one more that **enshrines** and celebrates Japan's long mountain chains, which stretch along almost the **entirety** of the four home islands, doesn't seem unusual.

Despite Japan's **penchant** for honoring its national identity through **symbolic** festivals and holidays, Mountain Day is likely being introduced for another reason altogether. This will become the country's sixteenth national holiday, a high number compared to 10 in the US. Combined with an average of 10 to 20 vacation days, Japan would seem to have a very progressive **approach** to the balance between work and life.

Actual numbers, however, show that this is often not the case, at least not within the structure of most Japanese businesses. A Japanese government survey **quoted** in the Wall Street Journal shows that the average Japanese worker only takes 8.6 days of personal vacation a year. Japanese politicians and **bureaucrats** are worried. In Japan, there is of course paid vacation, but people don't take it.

The hope that by giving people an extra national holiday, they will be more inclined to take their personal holidays seems slightly **illogical**. It doesn't address the **core** issue of Japanese people not taking the time that they are legally allowed to have. "Many Japanese people don't understand," says a senior researcher at the Japan

♦ **equinox** [ˈiːkwɪnɒks]
n. 昼夜平分点，春分或秋分
The Autumnal Equinox is the best time for wheat-sowing. 秋分种麦最相宜。

♦ **enshrine** [ɪnˈʃraɪn]
vt. 铭记，把⋯⋯奉为神圣

♦ **entirety** [ɪnˈtaɪrətɪ]
n. 整体，全部，全面
We must view the problem in its entirety. 我们必须全面地看这个问题。

♦ **penchant** [ˈpɒnʃəːŋ]
n. （强烈的）倾向，偏好；嗜好
She has a penchant for champagne. 她酷爱香槟酒。

♦ **symbolic** [sɪmˈbɒlɪk]
adj. 象征的，象征性的
The dove is symbolic of peace. 鸽子是和平的象征。

♦ **approach** [əˈprəʊtʃ] n. 方法，途径
The only way to come out on top is to adopt a different approach. 脱颖而出的唯一途径就是采用一种不同的方法。

♦ **quote** [kwəʊt] vt. 引述，引述
The actor, striking an attitude, began to quote Shakespeare. 这位演员装腔作势地开始引用莎士比亚的原文。

♦ **bureaucrat** [ˈbjʊərəʊkræt]
n. （政府）官员，官僚
He was just another faceless bureaucrat. 他只不过是一个典型呆板的官员。

♦ **illogical** [ɪˈlɒdʒɪkəl]
adj. 不合逻辑的，无意义的
It is clearly illogical to maintain such a proposition. 坚持这种主张显然是没有道理的。

♦ **core** [kɔː] adj. 核心的

♦ **leave** [liːv] n. 假期，准假
Employees are entitled to an annual paid

Institute for Labor Policy and Training, "that paid annual **leave** is their right."

The increase in holidays also comes with its own set of problems. As Japanese workers tend to only take off work on national holidays, it causes **congestion** on roads and trains and drives up the prices of **flights** and hotels, which is especially felt in Japan's top tourist destinations.

The government is beginning to suggest other ways to address the issue of worker fatigue and poor life-work balance by recommending **naps**. In March, a **guidance** issued by the Ministry of Health, Labor and Welfare suggests workers take a nap for up to half an hour. Originally staff take short 10–20 minute naps to improve attention and mood.

leave of fifteen days. 职员一年可享受 15 天带薪的假期。

♦ **congestion** [kən'dʒestʃən]
n. 拥挤，堵车，阻塞
♦ **flight** [flaɪt] n. 航班
I arrived just in time for my flight to London. 我及时赶上了飞往伦敦的航班。
♦ **nap** [næp]
n.（尤指在白天）打盹，小睡
Use your lunch hour to have a nap in your chair. 利用午饭时间坐在椅子上打个盹吧。
♦ **guidance** ['gaɪdəns] n. 指导；指引
She received very little careers guidance when young. 她年轻时基本没有接受过就业指导。

10 Hanami in Japan
日本赏花节

日语中的"花见"，意思是赏花，是日本的传统习俗。通常日本的赏花指的是樱花，当然了，实际上，除了樱花还有其他品种在内。

日本人把赏花作为一个重大节日来庆祝。其中会有各种活动，比如在樱花林中聚会畅聊，也少不了边吃边观赏美景，甚至会有人播放音乐，场面很是热闹。由于日本的赏花是种全民性质的活动，在东京这样的大城市，赏花的场地则会比较紧张，有些同事甚至会一早翘班，带着毯子，在公园占位。

最惹眼的花当是日本樱花了，粉红色的花瓣远远看去有些泛白，开满樱花的树连在一块，仿佛一片云海。赏花过后，代表着假期该结束了，人们开始相互拜别，回到工作或者学校。人们相信樱花开得好还预示着新的一年会取得大的成功。

Hanami（花见）meaning flower viewing, is a traditional Japanese custom of appreciating flowers. Hanami usually refers to the viewing of the Cherry blossoms, commonly known by the Japanese name **Sakura**. However the term is referred to all kinds of flowers.

Hanami involves having an **outdoor** party usually beneath or near a blossoming Sakura tree. People usually pack large amounts of food and drink for a hanami, sake is a very popular drink to be taken and consumed at a hanami along with **bento**, dumplings and **yakitori** to eat. Many hanami involve playing and listening to music on portable devices and being involved with lots of noise and celebration.

Large groups of people attend hanami and every year thousands of people gather in parks around Japan to celebrate the short annual event. There is great **demand** for good hanami spots in popular parks, particularly in the cities, such as Tokyo, and sometimes a person will sit on a large mat to reserve the groups' spot all day while others are at work or preparing festivities.

Hanami is a centuries old tradition which is first documented in the eleventh century. Emperor Saga from the Heian period used to hold hanami parties with sake and feasts at the Imperial Court in Tokyo, at the time it was only held for **elite** part of society, but the hanami tradition began to spread to Samurai society finally becoming a common place event during the Edo period. Originally Sakura was used to predict the quality of rice harvesting and to indicate it was time to plant rice seeds for the new season, and the drinking of sake at a hanami is a tradition that has stayed through the centuries.

Sakura tree is the most popular flower for hanami, there are many sakura trees in Japan lining the streets and parks. Around May there are lots of falling sakura flowers on the streets and filling park **lawns**. There is a list of top 100 spots for sakura hanami, and there is at least one spot from every prefecture in Japan. So no matter where you are staying in Japan, you can enjoy the beauty of the blossoming Sakura tree.

The sakura tree has small **pale pink** petals they are so small that from a distance the petals appear white, the trees filled with the small flowers and often referred to as looking like trees of clouds. The sakura tree is originally a fruit tree producing small cherries, though there are now smaller plants that are made to flower without fruit. The beauty of the flowers is **likened** to the transience of human life and the short period that they bloom.

♦ **Sakura**
n. (日本)樱花，每年的三、四月间盛开，樱花品种很多，有红、白两色，花开时绚丽无比，但花期短暂，给人展示了自己的所有美丽之后很快便凋谢了，日本人很欣赏樱花这种壮烈的性格。

♦ **outdoor** [ˈaʊtdɔː]
adj. 户外的，露天的
Breathable, waterproof clothing is essential for most outdoor sports. 大多数户外运动衣服必须透气且防水。

♦ **bento** [ˈbentəʊ]
n. 便当，盒饭

♦ **yakitori** [ˌjɑːkɪˈtɔːrɪ]
n. 日式烤鸡，烤鸡串烧

♦ **demand** [dɪˈmɑːnd]
n. 需求，需要
in demand 很需要的
All these skills are much in demand. 所有这些技术都十分需要。

♦ **elite** [eɪˈliːt]
adj. 上层的，精英的

♦ **lawn** [lɔːn]
n. 草地，草坪
He continued to mow the lawn and do other routine chores. 他继续剪草坪，并做些其他日常杂务。

♦ **pale pink** 淡粉色，浅桃红

♦ **liken** [ˈlaɪkən]
vt. 比拟，把……比作
liken…to… 把……比作……
We often liken the heart to a pump. 我们常把心脏比拟为水泵。

♦ **farewell** [ˌfeəˈwel]
n. 告别，欢送
I bade farewell to all the friends I had made in Paris. 我告别了我在巴黎结交的所有朋友。

♦ **fiscal year** 财政年度
The increase of taxation is an important fiscal policy. 增税是一项重要的财政政策。

Blooming of Sakura indicates the end of holidays and people go back to work or school, and graduating college. Sometimes a hanami is held as a type of **farewell** or goodbye event for those who may be going away to study at university or a new job. It is also the beginning of the new **fiscal year** in Japan, and the quality of the blossom is used to predict the success of the New Year.

11 Sea Day in Japan
日本海洋节

日本是一个四面环海的岛国，由古至今不管是国外文化的传入，还是人员往来，物品的运输，以至于涉及到生产生活的各个方面，日本都与大海有着密不可分的关系。正因为对于日本来讲，大海是如此的重要，在日本曾掀起了提倡设定一个法定节假日——"海洋日"的大规模的国民运动。于是，从 1996 年开始将 7 月 20 日定为"海洋日"——即"感谢大海的恩惠，期盼海洋国家日本的繁荣的日子。"

日本的海洋节不只是为了感恩大海的惠赠，也是庆夏季的到来。值此机会，海滩开始向民众开放，人们成群结地涌向海边，享受夏季的畅快。各种与海洋相关的环保活动也同时展开，比如全国上下都会举行的活动——扔泥球，每年此时，成年上万的泥球被投到海里。传统习俗与缤纷的活动让人眼花缭乱，兴奋不已。

In Japan, there is a holiday that is meant for the celebration of the ocean's **bounty**. Since centuries past, the sea is important to the lives of the Japanese people. This is quite **understandable** since Japan is an island nation. Sea Day is also known as "Marine Day" or "Ocean Day" and is called Umi no Hi in Japanese. Originally, it was celebrated on July 20, back in 1995, but since the introduction of the Happy Monday System (**whereby** some holidays are moved to Monday to allow for long weekends), it has been celebrated on the third Monday of July beginning in the year 2000.

Despite being a relatively modern holiday in Japan, Sea Day **traces** its roots back to the Meiji Era when, in 1876, the Meiji Emperor took a **voyage** on a ship called Meiji Maru through the Tohoku Region. The emperor ended the voyage in Yokohama on the 20th of July.

♦ **bounty** [ˈbaʊnti]
n. 慷慨的赠予，大量提供的东西
He is famous for his bounty to the poor. 他因对穷人慷慨相助而出名。

♦ **understandable** [ˌʌndəˈstændəb(ə)l]
adj. 可理解的
Their attitude is perfectly understandable. 他们的态度是完全可以理解的。

♦ **whereby** [(h)weəˈbaɪ]
adv. 通过……，借以
We need to devise some sort of system whereby people can liaise with each other. 我们须想出一套方法，凭此大家能够互相联络。

♦ **trace** [treɪs] vt. 追溯
I first went there to trace my roots, visiting my mum's home island of Jamaica. 我最初到那里是为了寻根，探访我妈妈的故乡牙买加岛。

♦ **voyage** [ˈvɔɪɪdʒ] n. 航海旅行
The explorer accomplished the voyage in

Subsequently, in 1941, July 20 was named Marine Memorial Day **in commemoration of** that trip but it was only in 1995 when it was **declared** a national holiday. The ocean has been a source of the country's income before Japan opened its doors to foreign trade, so it's no wonder why the Japanese would designate a day to offer **gratitude** for the sea, which has supported their economy for hundreds of years during the Edo period.

This holiday is not only a celebration for the gifts that the ocean brings to **maritime** Japan, but also has been associated with the official beginning of summer. At this time, beaches begin to open with people flocking to the seaside to enjoy the season, while all across the country, many events take place. On this occasion, museums, swimming pools and **aquariums** begin offering discounts to its customers during this busy season.

Just as well, environmental activities are held to help keep Japan's oceans healthy and **pristine**. All over the country, a mud ball-throwing event is held **simultaneously**, but these are no ordinary mud balls. Called EM mud balls, these balls of dried mud are **kneaded** with safe **chemicals**. Yearly, thousands of these mud balls are thrown out into the water. Celebrating the Sea Day is an event that mixes tradition with an array of magnificent and visually pleasing activities that is uniquely Japanese.

three weeks. 探险家在三周内完成了这次航行。

♦ **subsequently** [ˈsʌbsɪkwəntlɪ]
adv. 其后，随后
He was born in Hong Kong where he subsequently practised as a lawyer until his retirement. 他出生在香港，后来在那里从事律师工作，直到退休。

♦ **in commemoration of** 为了纪念

♦ **declare** [dɪˈkleə] vt. 宣布，宣告
When will the results of the election be declared? 选举的结果什么时候宣布？

♦ **gratitude** [ˈgrætɪtjuːd] n. 感激，感谢

♦ **maritime** [ˈmærɪtaɪm]
adj. 海的，海洋的
That country was a great maritime power. 那个国家曾是海上强国。

♦ **aquarium** [əˈkweərɪəm] n. 水族馆

♦ **pristine** [ˈprɪstaɪn]
adj. 原始状态的，纯朴的，未受腐蚀的
No man ever looks at the world with pristine eyes. 没有一个人以纯净而无偏见的眼光来看待世界。

♦ **simultaneously** [ˌsɪməlˈteɪnɪəslɪ]
adv. 同时地，一齐
The radar beam can track a number of targets almost simultaneously. 雷达波几乎可以同时追踪多个目标。

♦ **knead** [niːd] vt. 捏（面团、湿粘土等）

♦ **chemical** [ˈkemɪkəl]
n. 化学药品，化学制品